# FOCUS ON PSYCHOLOGY

**Second Edition**

# FOCUS ON PSYCHOLOGY

A Guide to Mastering

PETER GRAY'S **PSYCHOLOGY**

**Mary Trahan**

Randolph-Macon College

Worth Publishers

**Focus on Psychology**  A Guide to Mastering Peter Gray's **Psychology**, Second Edition
by Mary Trahan

Copyright © 1994, 1991 by Worth Publishers, Inc.

Printed in the United States of America

ISBN 0-87901-695-7

Printing:     2   3   4   5      Year: 98   97   96   95

Cover: Johannes Vermeer, *Head of a Young Girl* (detail), 17th century. Oil on canvas.
Mauritshuis, The Hague. Photo: © The Granger Collection, New York City

**Worth Publishers**
33 Irving Place
New York, New York  10003

# CONTENTS

# To the Student

## Why This Guide Is Written As It Is

I have written this guide to help you master Peter Gray's *Psychology*. The guide is interactive—like a tutorial or the classes I teach. I write something, and you write something back; often our back-and-forth writing amounts to a brief conversation about the ideas presented in Peter Gray's textbook. Like my classes, and like Gray's textbook, the guide is intended to do more than develop a knowledge base in your mind. It is my hope that you will not only only come to understand psychology better but will gain a deeper understanding of what it *means* to understand, and will see better how to achieve understanding in your other studies. Additionally, I hope you will develop an increased confidence in your own ability to think and to learn.

This study guide puts into practice some of the principles psychologists have discovered through investigations of learning and memory, namely, the importance of organization and elaboration. Organization repeatedly has been shown to facilitate the learning, retention, and use of information. It is not only the organization of the information on the page, but the organization of the information in the mind that matters. The former merely facilitates the latter. I have tried to produce a study guide that helps you to organize what you are putting into your memory. Elaboration involves *doing* something active and meaningful with the material you read, not just transferring it passively from the textbook page to your mind to the study guide page. We are engaging in elaboration when we draw parallels, summarize, produce examples, criticize, compare, ponder analogies, and apply general concepts to specific cases. Elaboration, in short, involves thinking. And thinking is not only the most effective way to learn, it is also the most interesting!

## How to Use This Guide

This guide is not intended to be a supplement to your study of the textbook; nor is it simply a means of checking your understanding after you have finished studying. It is designed to be your guide in studying the text. Each chapter of the study guide has the following features:

1.  An **introductory summary** gives you an overview or "map" of the chapter in the textbook and an initial acquaintance with some of its major ideas before you begin to read the chapter.

2.  **Italicized instructions** advise you on how to proceed at each step in the study process—letting you know, for example, when to read the chapter thoroughly and when to skim it, when to go on to the next section and when to review first.

3. The **Integrated Study Workout** is the heart of the study guide. Divided into sections according to the major topics of the text chapter, the Workout contains a variety of questions as well as brief passages that help to put the questions in context. Often hints are provided that direct you to examine a relevant table or graph. The questions help you to identify what is most important in the textbook, to break sections down into manageable parts, and to probe the material for critical ideas.

   Preceding the Workout is a table that shows which study guide questions are related to each of the Focus Questions in the text. The Focus Questions are designed to help you concentrate on the purpose of each segment of the text. If your instructor has recommended that your exam preparation include or center on specified Focus Questions, the corresponding study guide material would make a particularly effective review.

4. Two **Self-Tests** will help you to assess your understanding. Each Self-Test contains fifteen multiple-choice questions and two essay questions.

5. **Answers** are provided for selected items from The Integrated Study Workout, generally those items that are objective or have very short answers. Answers for all multiple-choice questions, many accompanied by explanatory comments, and model answers to essay questions are also included, along with textbook page references.

Because of the organization of each study guide chapter and the instructions that guide you through them, I need say little more about how to use this study guide. However, I do wish to make two recommendations: One is that you read and implement the following section by the psychologist Richard O. Straub on organizing your time and studying more effectively. The second is that you avoid an all-or-none attitude in your studying. I hope you will make the time to complete each chapter of this guide, because doing so will maximize your learning. But please do not feel that you must answer every single question to make its use worthwhile. Doing three-fourths of the questions is better than doing none. Further, do not feel that you must write out all of your answers in complete sentences. The correct few words will usually help you most. Make sure your answers are clear, organized, and complete enough to be valuable to *you*. After all, this is your guide—only you will read it.

I wish you success in your studies and encourage you to write to me if you have any comments or suggestions.

## Acknowledgments

I have so many people to thank, yet I know just where to begin. That is with Peter Gray, who in this second edition has produced a textbook even better than his first. It is a textbook that is truly worth studying, an exceptional accomplishment. I feel fortunate indeed that my chance to "teach on paper" came with Peter Gray's book. Peter, along with Phyllis Fisher at Worth, worked with me to shape the original version of this guide, to translate shared pedagogical goals into effective methods for achieving them.

I owe a great deal to Barbara Curialle Gerr, whose organizational skill, availability, sound judgment, and calm assurance helped me to produce the first edition of this guide. Betty Probert, who edited the bulk of both editions of the guide, won my trust and gratitude for her keen editorial sense and careful attention to detail. It has been a pleasure to work with them. Worth is a remarkable publisher, with an uncommon commitment to excellence and innovation, and there are so many others there I would like to thank—among them Tom Gay, Anne Vinnicombe, Vicki Frankel, and Susan Seuling.

To my colleagues and students over the years, who have taught me about psychology and about teaching, thanks. I am indebted to my teachers at Loyola University in New Orleans, where I began my study of psychology; to faculty and students at the University of Michigan, where, as a graduate student, I developed a love for psychology and a devotion to teaching; and especially to many students and colleagues here at Randolph-Macon College for their friendship, support, and for the inspiration of their example. Two Randolph-Macon students who deserve special mention for their thoughtful reviews of study guide chapters are Deborah Gosser and Sara Absher.

Thanks seem too little to offer to my friends here in Virginia, who gave such solid support and encouragement. My greatest thanks are to my ultimate friend and teacher, to whom I owe all.

# How to Manage Your Time Efficiently and Study More Effectively

## by Richard O. Straub

How effectively do you study? Good study habits make the job of being a college student much easier. Many students, who *could* succeed in college, fail or drop out because they have never learned to manage their time efficiently. Even the best students can usually benefit from an in-depth evaluation of their current study habits.

There are many ways to achieve academic success, of course, but your approach may not be the most effective or efficient. Are you sacrificing your social life or your physical or mental health in order to get A's on your exams? Good study habits result in better grades *and* more time for other activities.

## Evaluate Your Current Study Habits

To improve your study habits, you must first have an accurate picture of how you currently spend your time. Begin by putting together a profile of your present living and studying habits. Answer the following questions by writing *yes* or *no* on each line.

_____ 1. Do you usually set up a schedule to budget your time for studying, recreation, and other activities?

_____ 2. Do you often put off studying until time pressures force you to cram?

_____ 3. Do other students seem to study less than you do, but get better grades?

_____ 4. Do you usually spend hours at a time studying one subject, rather than dividing that time between several subjects?

_____ 5. Do you often have trouble remembering what you have just read in a textbook?

_____ 6. Before reading a chapter in a textbook, do you skim through it and read the section headings?

_____ 7. Do you try to predict exam questions from your lecture notes and reading?

_____ 8. Do you usually attempt to paraphrase or summarize what you have just finished reading?

_____ 9. Do you find it difficult to concentrate very long when you study?

_____10. Do you often feel that you studied the wrong material for an exam?

Thousands of college students have participated in similar surveys. Students who are fully realizing their academic potential usually respond as follows: (1) yes, (2) no, (3) no, (4) no, (5) no, (6) yes, (7) yes, (8) yes, (9) no, (10) no.

Compare your responses to those of successful students. The greater the discrepancy, the more you could benefit from a program to improve your study habits. The questions are designed to identify areas of weakness. Once you have identified your weaknesses, you will be able to set specific goals for improvement and implement a program for reaching them.

## Manage Your Time

Do you often feel frustrated because there isn't enough time to do all the things you must and want to do? Take heart. Even the most productive and successful people feel this way at times. But they establish priorities for their activities and they learn to budget their time. There's much in the saying "If you want something done, ask a busy person to do it." A busy person knows how to get things done.

If you don't now have a system for budgeting your time, develop one. Not only will your academic accomplishments increase, but you will actually find more time in your schedule for other activities. And you won't have to feel guilty about "taking time off," because all your obligations will be covered.

### Establish a Baseline

As a first step in preparing to budget your time, keep a diary for a few days to establish a summary, or baseline, of the time you spend in studying, socializing, working, and so on. If you are like many students, much of your "study" time is nonproductive; you may sit at your desk and leaf through a book, but the time is actually wasted. Or you may procrastinate. You are always getting ready to study, but you rarely do.

Besides revealing where you waste time, your diary will give you a realistic picture of how much time you need to allot for meals, commuting, and other fixed activities. In addition, careful records should indicate the times of the day when you are consistently most productive. A sample time-management diary is shown in Table 1.

### Plan the Term

Having established and evaluated your baseline, you are ready to devise a more efficient schedule. Buy a calendar that covers the entire school term and has ample space for each day. Using the course outlines provided by your instructors, enter the dates of all exams, term paper deadlines, and other important academic obligations. If you have any long-range personal plans (concerts, weekend trips, etc.), enter the dates on the calendar as well. Keep your calendar up to date and refer to it often. I recommend carrying it with you at all times.

### Develop a Weekly Calendar

Now that you have a general picture of the school term, develop a weekly schedule that includes all of your activities. Aim for a schedule that you can live with for the entire school term. A sample weekly schedule, incorporating the following guidelines, is shown in Table 2.

Table 1    Sample Time-Management Diary

### Monday

| Behavior | Time Completed | Duration Hours: Minutes |
|---|---|---|
| Sleep | 7:00 | 7:30 |
| Dressing | 7:25 | :25 |
| Breakfast | 7:45 | :20 |
| Commute | 8:20 | :35 |
| Coffee | 9:00 | :40 |
| French | 10:00 | 1:00 |
| Socialize | 10:15 | :15 |
| Videogame | 10:35 | :20 |
| Coffee | 11:00 | :25 |
| Psychology | 12:00 | 1:00 |
| Lunch | 12:25 | :25 |
| Study Lab | 1:00 | :35 |
| Psych. Lab | 4:00 | 3:00 |
| Work | 5:30 | 1:30 |
| Commute | 6:10 | :40 |
| Dinner | 6:45 | :35 |
| TV | 7:30 | :45 |
| Study Psych. | 10:00 | 2:30 |
| Socialize | 11:30 | 1:30 |
| Sleep | | |

Prepare a similar chart for each day of the week. When you finish an activity, note it on the chart and write down the time it was completed. Then determine its duration by subtracting the time the previous activity was finished from the newly entered time.

**1.** Enter your class times, work hours, and any other fixed obligations first. *Be thorough.* Using information from your time-management diary, allow plenty of time for such things as commuting, meals, laundry, and the like.

**2.** Set up a study schedule for each of your courses. The study habits survey and your time-management diary will direct you. The following guidelines should also be useful.

**(a)** Establish regular study times for each course. The 4 hours needed to study one subject, for example, are most profitable when divided into shorter periods spaced over several days. If you cram your studying into one 4-hour block, what you attempt to learn in the third or fourth hour will interfere with what you studied in the first 2 hours. Newly acquired knowledge is like wet cement. It needs some time to "harden" to become memory.

**(b)** Alternate subjects. The type of interference just mentioned is greatest between similar topics. Set up a schedule in which you spend time on several *different* courses during each study session. Besides reducing the potential for interference, alternating subjects will help to prevent mental fatigue with one topic.

Table 2    Sample Weekly Schedule

| Time | Mon. | Tues. | Wed. | Thurs. | Fri. | Sat. |
|---|---|---|---|---|---|---|
| 7–8 | Dress Eat | Dress Eat | Dress Eat | Dress Eat | Dress Eat | |
| 8–9 | Psych. | Study Psych. | Psych. | Study Psych. | Psych. | Dress Eat |
| 9–10 | Eng. | Study Eng. | Eng. | Study Eng. | Eng. | Study Eng. |
| 10–11 | Study French | Free | Study French | Open Study | Study French | Study Stats. |
| 11–12 | French | Study Psych. Lab | French | Open Study | French | Study Stats. |
| 12–1 | Lunch | Lunch | Lunch | Lunch | Lunch | Lunch |
| 1–2 | Stats. | Psych. Lab | Stats. | Study or Free | Stats. | Free |
| 2–3 | Bio. | Psych. Lab | Bio. | Free | Bio. | Free |
| 3–4 | Free | Psych. | Free | Free | Free | Free |
| 4–5 | Job | Job | Job | Job | Job | Free |
| 5–6 | Job | Job | Job | Job | Job | Free |
| 6–7 | Dinner | Dinner | Dinner | Dinner | Dinner | Dinner |
| 7–8 | Study Bio. | Study Bio. | Study Bio. | Study Bio. | Free | Free |
| 8–9 | Study Eng. | Study Stats. | Study Psych. | Open Study | Open Study | Free |
| 9–10 | Open Study | Open Study | Open Study | Open Study | Free | Free |

This is a sample schedule for a student with a 16-credit load and a 10-hour-per-week part-time job. Using this chart as an illustration, make up a weekly schedule, following the guidelines outlined here.

(c) Set weekly goals to determine the amount of study time you need to do well in each course. This will depend on, among other things, the difficulty of your courses and the effectiveness of your methods. Many professors recommend studying at least 1 to 2 hours for each hour in class. If your time-management diary indicates that you presently study less time than that, do not plan to jump immediately to a much higher level. Increase study time from your baseline by setting weekly goals [see (4)] that will gradually bring you up to the desired level. As an initial schedule, for example, you might set aside an amount of study time for each course that matches class time.

(d) Schedule for maximum effectiveness. Tailor your schedule to meet the demands of each course. For the course that emphasizes lecture notes, schedule time for a daily review soon after the class. This will give you a chance to revise your notes and clean up any hard-to-decipher shorthand while the material is still fresh in your mind. If you are evaluated for class participation (for example, in a language course), allow time for a review just before the class meets. Schedule study time for your most difficult (or least motivating) courses during hours when you are the most alert and distractions are fewest.

(e) Schedule open study time. Emergencies, additional obligations, and the like could throw off your schedule. And you may simply need some extra time periodically for a project or for review in one of your courses. Schedule several hours each week for such purposes.

3. After you have budgeted time for studying, fill in slots for recreation, hobbies, relaxation, household errands, and the like.

4. Set specific goals. Before each study session, make a list of specific goals. The simple note "7–8 PM: study psychology" is too broad to ensure the most effective use of the time. Formulate your daily goals according to what you know you must accomplish during the term. If you have course outlines with advance assignments, set systematic daily goals that will allow you, for example, to cover fifteen chapters before the exam. And be realistic: Can you actually expect to cover a 78-page chapter in one session? Divide large tasks into smaller units; stop at the most logical resting points. When you complete a specific goal, take a 5- or 10-minute break before tackling the next goal.

5. Evaluate how successful or unsuccessful your studying has been on a daily or weekly basis. Did you reach most of your goals? If so, reward yourself immediately. You might even make a list of five to ten rewards to choose from. If you have trouble studying regularly, you may be able to motivate yourself by making such rewards contingent on completing specific goals.

6. Finally, until you have lived with your schedule for several weeks, don't hesitate to revise it. You may need to allow more time for chemistry, for example, and less for some other course. If you are trying to study regularly for the first time and are feeling burned out, you probably have set your initial goals too high. Don't let failure cause you to despair and abandon the program. Accept your limitations and revise your schedule so that you are studying only 15 to 20 minutes more each evening than you are used to. The point is to identify a regular schedule with which you can achieve some success. Time management, like any skill, must be practiced to become effective.

## Taking Lecture Notes

Are your class notes as useful as they might be? One way to determine their worth is to compare them with those taken by other good students. Are yours as thorough? Do they provide you with a comprehensible outline of each lecture? If not, then the following suggestions might increase the value of your note-taking.

1. Keep a separate notebook for each course. Use $8\frac{1}{2} \times 11$-inch pages. Consider using a ring binder, which would allow you to revise and insert notes while still preserving lecture order.

2. Take notes in the format of a lecture outline. Use roman numerals for major points, letters for supporting arguments, and so on. Some instructors will make this easy by delivering organized lectures and, in some cases, by outlining their lectures on the board. If a lecture is disorganized, you will probably want to reorganize your notes soon after the class.

3. As you take notes in class, leave a wide margin on one side of each page. After the lecture, expand or clarify any shorthand notes while the material is fresh in your mind. Use this time to write important questions in the margin next to notes that answer them. This will facilitate later review and will allow you to anticipate similar exam questions.

# Evaluate Your Exam Performance

How often have you received a grade on an exam that did not do justice to the effort you spent preparing for the exam? This is a common experience that can leave one feeling bewildered and abused. "What do I have to do to get an A?" "The test was unfair!" "I studied the wrong material!"

The chances of this happening are greatly reduced if you have an effective time-management schedule and use the study techniques described here. But it can happen to the best-prepared student and is most likely to occur on your first exam with a new professor.

Remember that there are two main reasons for studying. One is to learn for your own general academic development. Many people believe that such knowledge is all that really matters. Of course, it is possible, though unlikely, to be an expert on a topic without achieving commensurate grades, just as one can, occasionally, earn an excellent grade without truly mastering the course material. During a job interview or in the workplace, however, your A in COBOL won't mean much if you can't actually program a computer.

In order to keep career options open after you graduate, you must know the material and maintain competitive grades. In the short run, this means performing well on exams, which is the second main objective in studying.

Probably the single best piece of advice to keep in mind when studying for exams is to *try to predict exam questions*. This means ignoring the trivia and focusing on the important questions and their answers (with your instructor's emphasis in mind).

A second point is obvious. How well you do on exams is determined by your mastery of both lecture and textbook material. Many students (partly because of poor time management) concentrate too much on one at the expense of the other.

To evaluate how well you are learning lecture and textbook material, analyze the questions you missed on the first exam. If your instructor does not review exams during class, you can easily do it yourself. Divide the questions into two categories: those drawn primarily from lectures and those drawn primarily from the textbook. Determine the percentage of questions you missed in each category. If your errors are evenly distributed and you are satisfied with your grade, you have no problem. If you are weaker in one area, you will need to set future goals for increasing and/or improving your study of that area.

Similarly, note the percentage of test questions drawn from each category. Although exams in most courses cover both lecture notes and the textbook, the relative emphasis of each may vary from instructor to instructor. While your instructors may not be entirely consistent in making up future exams, you may be able to tailor your studying for each course by placing additional emphasis on the appropriate area.

Exam evaluation will also point out the types of questions your instructor prefers. Does the exam consist primarily of multiple-choice, true–false, or essay questions? You may also discover that an instructor is fond of wording questions in certain ways. For example, an instructor may rely heavily on questions that require you to draw an analogy between a theory or concept and a real-world example. Evaluate both your instructor's style and how well you do with each format. Use this information to guide your future exam preparation.

Important aids, not only in studying for exams but also in determining how well prepared you are, are the Self-Tests provided in this study guide. If these tests don't include all of the types of questions your instructor typically writes, make up your own practice exam questions. Spend extra time testing yourself with question formats that are most difficult for you. There is no better way to evaluate your preparation for an upcoming exam than by testing yourself under the conditions most likely to be in effect during the actual test.

## A Few Practical Tips

Even the best intentions for studying sometimes fail. Some of these failures occur because students attempt to work under conditions that are simply not conducive to concentrated study. To help ensure the success of your time-management program, here are a few suggestions that should assist you in reducing the possibility of procrastination or distraction.

1. If you have set up a schedule for studying, make your roommate, family, and friends aware of this commitment, and ask them to honor your quiet study time. Close your door and post a "Do Not Disturb" sign.

2. Set up a place to study that minimizes potential distractions. Use a desk or table, not your bed or an extremely comfortable chair. Keep your desk and the walls around it free from clutter. If you need a place other than your room, find one that meets as many of the above requirements as possible—for example, in the library stacks.

3. Do nothing but study in this place. It should become associated with studying so that it "triggers" this activity, just as a mouth-watering aroma elicits an appetite.

4. Never study with the television on or with other distracting noises present. If you must have music in the background in order to mask outside noise, for example, play soft instrumental music. Don't pick vocal selections; your mind will be drawn to the lyrics.

5. Study by yourself. Other students can be distracting or can break the pace at which your learning is most efficient. In addition, there is always the possibility that group studying will become a social gathering. Reserve that for its own place in your schedule.

If you continue to have difficulty concentrating for very long, try the following suggestions.

6. Study your most difficult or most challenging subjects first, when you are most alert.

7. Start with relatively short periods of concentrated study, with breaks in between. If your attention starts to wander, get up immediately and take a break. It is better to study effectively for 15 minutes and then take a break than to fritter away 45 minutes out of an hour. Gradually increase the length of study periods, using your attention span as an indicator of successful pacing.

## Some Closing Thoughts

I hope that these suggestions help make you more successful academically, and that they enhance the quality of your college life in general. Having the necessary skills makes any job a lot easier and more pleasant. Let me repeat my warning not to attempt to make too drastic a change in your life-style immediately. Good habits require time and self-discipline to develop. Once established they can last a lifetime.

# CHAPTER 1 THE HISTORY AND SCOPE OF PSYCHOLOGY

*Read the introduction below before you read the chapter in the text.*

Psychology is defined as the science of behavior and the mind. Even before the official beginnings of psychology in the nineteenth century, developments in philosophy and science prepared the way for it. For example, the work of the British empiricists in philosophy and the work of Charles Darwin in science helped to lay the groundwork for a science of psychology.

Once psychology was established as an area of scientific inquiry, it was shaped by the influences of several different perspectives. Each perspective has been based on a different notion of what psychology's focus should be, and each has made a unique contribution. For example, structuralism, an approach associated with Wilhelm Wundt and Edward Titchener, had the goal of identifying the basic elements, or structures, of the mind. William James focused instead on the purposes and functions of the mind, which led to his approach being called functionalism. Gestalt psychology proposed that the mind cannot be understood as a collection of elements but must be seen in terms of organized wholes. Behaviorism, founded by the zoological psychologist John B. Watson, excluded the mind from study altogether because, unlike behavior, the mind cannot be observed directly. Ethology, like behaviorism, focused on animal behavior but emphasized the study of animals in their natural habitats. Physiological psychologists sought to understand the physiological mechanisms underlying all behavior. Sigmund Freud's psychoanalysis developed around the concept of the unconscious mind and its influence on conscious thought and behavior. Humanistic psychology was based on an optimistic view of human nature and promoted positive self-concepts and self-actualization. In different ways, both cultural and social psychology take account of the importance of the social context in which thought and behavior occur. Cognitive psychology, the dominant approach for more than 20 years now, explores the acquisition, organization, retrieval, and use of knowledge to guide behavior.

Psychology is both an academic discipline and a profession. Professional psychologists may work to add to our knowledge of mind and behavior or to apply that knowledge for practical ends. They are employed in settings that include colleges and universities, elementary and secondary schools, mental health clinics, hospitals, and businesses, among others.

*LOOK over the table of contents for this chapter in your textbook before you continue with your study.*

*Notice that there are focus questions in the margins of the text for your use in studying the material. The following chart lists which study guide questions relate to which focus questions.*

| Focus Questions | Study Guide Questions |
| --- | --- |
| Psychology: Preparing the Intellectual Ground | |
| 2–4 | 1–6 |
| 5–6 | 7 |
| 7 | 8 |
| The Evolution of Psychology: A History of Alternative Perspectives | |
| 8–23 | 1 |
| 8–12 | 2–5 |
| 13–16 | 6–9 |
| 17–18 | 10 |
| 19–20 | 11 |
| 21–23 | 12–13 |
| Psychology as a Discipline and a Profession | |
| 24 | 1 |

# The Integrated Study Workout

*Complete one section at a time.*

## Before Psychology: Preparing the Intellectual Ground   (pages 4–7)

*CONSIDER these questions before you go on. They are designed to help you start thinking about this subject, not to test your knowledge.*

Is it really possible for us to study behavior and the mind scientifically?

Is psychology related to other academic areas, such as philosophy or biology, or is it an isolated field of study?

*READ this section of your text lightly. Then go back and read thoroughly, completing the Workout as you proceed.*

Psychology, the science of behavior and the mind, emerged in the second half of the nineteenth century. The very idea of this new science would have been unimaginable without earlier developments in philosophy. René Descartes was a key figure in these developments.

1.  Explain the following two terms as they apply to Descartes's theory of mind and behavior.

    a.  dualism

    b.  interactionism

2.  Explain Descartes's view of the relationship between behavior and the soul.

3.  How does Descartes's theory limit psychology?

Another, very different philosophy that prepared the way for psychology was British empiricism. This philosophical approach was advanced by John Locke, David Hume, and James Mill. British empiricism also owed a debt to Thomas Hobbes, whose ideas helped to inspire this school of thought.

4.  What ideas central to Thomas Hobbes's materialism influenced British empiricism?

5.  According to the empiricists, what is the original basis of all knowledge and thought?

6.  From the perspective of the empiricists, is a scientific psychology possible? Why or why not?

Progress in science during the nineteenth century also helped to create an intellectual climate in which psychology could develop.

7.  Physiology was one field of science in which knowledge was growing.

    a.  How did physiology's new understanding of reflexes help to lay the foundation for a scientific psychology?

    b.  What about increased understanding of localization of function?

8. What contribution did Darwin's theory of evolution make to the new science of psychology?

b. Describe his procedure.

## The Evolution of Psychology: A History of Alternative Perspectives (pages 7–22)

CONSIDER these questions before you go on. They are designed to help you start thinking about this subject, not to test your knowledge.

Where and when did psychology get its start?

How much has psychology changed over the years?

Every discipline has its heroes—for example, Shakespeare in English literature and Einstein in physics. Name some of the great figures of psychology's past.

READ this section of your text lightly. Then go back and read thoroughly, completing the Workout as you proceed.

Although German scientists had already been doing psychological research for about 20 years, 1879 is usually cited as the date of psychology's birth. In that year Wilhelm Wundt started a laboratory at the University of Leipzig. Since psychology's founding, several competing schools of thought have developed. Each has perceived psychology's goals, possibilities, and methods differently.

1. Fill in the chart on pages 4 and 5 to get an overview of the most important approaches in psychology. ("Major figures" should include those individuals who were most directly responsible for developing a given school of thought. "Significant influences or related approaches" may refer to persons, concepts, or schools of thought to the extent that each applies.)

Now that you have a firm foundation in the most important approaches to psychology, answer the following more specific questions.

2. An approach central to Wundt's work involved measuring the speed of mental processes.

a. Why did Wundt want to do this?

3. Why did Titchener's method of introspection fail scientifically?

4. How did James's use of introspection differ from that of Titchener?

5. How does the *phi phenomenon* illustrate the Gestalt psychologists' major point?

6. Why is *zoological psychology* generally a more accurate term than the more accustomed *comparative psychology*?

7. What were four principles of Watson's behaviorism?

8. What was Skinner's contribution to behaviorism ?

| Approaches to psychology | Major figure(s) | Significant influence(s) or related approaches | Major goal(s) or concept(s) | Primary method(s) | Impact on psychology | Limitations |
|---|---|---|---|---|---|---|
| Structuralism | | | | | | |
| Functionalism | | | | | | |
| Gestalt psychology | | | | | | |
| Behaviorism | | | | | | |
| Ethology | | | | | | |
| Physiological psychology | | | | | | |

| Approaches to psychology | Major figure(s) | Significant influence(s) or related approaches | Major goal(s) or concept(s) | Primary method(s) | Impact on psychology | Limitations |
|---|---|---|---|---|---|---|
| Psychoanalysis | | | | | | |
| Humanistic psychology | | | | | | |
| Cultural psychology | | | | | | |
| Social psychology | | | | | | |
| Cognitive psychology | | | | | | |

9. How and why did behaviorism and ethology eventually interact?

What kind of work do psychologists do and where do they do it?

> *READ this section of your text lightly. Then go back and read thoroughly, completing the Workout as you proceed.*

Colleges and universities are generally made up of departments representing specific academic disciplines. Often, we speak of disciplines as falling into one of three divisions—natural sciences, social sciences, and humanities.

10. What observations led Freud to his psychoanalytic approach?

   1. How does psychology fit into this way of categorizing the disciplines? Explain your answer.

11. How do cultural and social psychology differ?

12. Analogies have often been important in helping psychologists understand and communicate about mind, brain, and behavior. What is the primary analogy for the mind used in cognitive psychology? (Be specific.)

The many influences in psychology's past have helped to make psychology a very diverse field today. That diversity is evident not only in the content of academic psychology, but also in the many professional endeavors of psychologists.

   2. List five types of settings in which psychologists work and indicate the kind of activity they might carry out there.

     a.

     b.

13. How did Jean Piaget and Noam Chomsky contribute to the emergence of cognitive psychology?

     c.

     d.

     e.

## *Psychology as a Discipline and a Profession* (pages 22–24)

> *CONSIDER these questions before you go on. They are designed to help you start thinking about this subject, not to test your knowledge.*

Is psychology considered a natural science? a social science? or one of the humanities?

> *Be sure to READ the Concluding Thoughts at the end of the chapter. Note important points in your Workout. Then consolidate your learning by answering the focus questions in the margins of the text.*

> *After you have studied the chapter thoroughly, CHECK your understanding with the self-test that follows.*

# Self-Test 1

*Multiple-Choice Questions*

1. As defined in the chapter, psychology is the scientific study of:
   a. behavior.
   b. the brain.
   c. the mind.
   d. behavior and the mind.

2. Descartes's theory of human action was called dualism because it included both:
   a. mind and behavior.
   b. mind and spirit.
   c. body and soul.
   d. philosophy and science.

3. The British empiricists believed that thought derives from:
   a. logical analysis.
   b. the brain's innately determined physiology.
   c. free will.
   d. sensory experience.

4. Which important advance in nineteenth-century physiology helped to prepare the way for scientific psychology?
   a. new understanding of the neurological basis of reflexes
   b. rejection of the idea that specific parts of the brain have specific functions
   c. discovery of the basic arrangement of the nervous system
   d. work in psychophysics

5. Darwin felt that natural selection:
   a. could not help us to explain evolution.
   b. could help us to understand anatomy but not behavior.
   c. could be applied to plants and nonhuman animals, but not to humans.
   d. gradually formed the anatomy and behavior of living things.

6. The person usually credited with the founding of scientific psychology is:
   a. Hermann Ebbinghaus.
   b. Ernst Weber.
   c. Wilhelm Wundt.
   d. Edward Titchener.

7. What were the "structures" that structuralists wanted to understand?
   a. structures of the brain
   b. structures of the sensory systems
   c. structures of overt, physical behavior
   d. structures of the mind

8. The consensus today concerning the method of introspection is that:
   a. it was successful because it was systematic and objective.
   b. it was successful because it forced subjects to break down conscious experience into basic elements.
   c. it was unsuccessful because it depended on the private conscious experience of the person introspecting.
   d. it was unsuccessful because it was performed by untrained individuals.

9. The functionalists believed that, in order to understand the human mind, one must first understand its:
   a. elementary parts and processes.
   b. purposes.
   c. physiology.
   d. counterpart in lower species.

10. A contemporary psychologist says, "A square cannot simply be reduced to a set of four lines." What historical influence on this person's thinking is evident?
    a. functionalism
    b. structuralism
    c. psychoanalysis
    d. Gestalt psychology

11. The person usually credited with the founding of behaviorism is:
    a. Konrad Lorenz.
    b. Clark Hull.
    c. John B. Watson.
    d. Jean Piaget.

12. Behaviorism's name stems from the central belief that:
    a. studying the mind is useful only as a way of explaining behavior.
    b. studying behavior is the only way to unlock the secrets of the mind.
    c. behavior is psychology's only proper object of study because it alone is observable.
    d. behavior can be understood only in its pure state, isolated from environmental influences.

13. A psychologist is studying the defensive behavior of ground-nesting birds by observing them in their natural environment. What school of thought does this person most likely represent?
    a. ethology
    b. behaviorism
    c. physiological psychology
    d. structuralism

14. In Freud's psychoanalytic theory, which of the following is true of the conscious mind?
    a. It represents only a small portion of the mind.
    b. It has complete and direct access to the unconscious mind.
    c. It is unaffected by the unconscious mind.
    d. It must never become aware of disturbing memories if the patient is to recover.

15. Which person(s) among the following would be considered (a) theoretical "ancestor(s)" of today's cognitive psychology?
    a. B. F. Skinner
    b. Wilhelm Wundt
    c. Konrad Lorenz
    d. both B. F. Skinner and Konrad Lorenz

*Essay Questions*

16. Discuss the commonalities, differences, and interrelations of behaviorism and ethology.

17. Explain and contrast the basic theoretical tenets of structuralism and Gestalt psychology. Be sure to make clear why followers of these two schools of thought would tend to disagree, even about the very questions to be asked by psychology.

*After you have assessed your understanding on the basis of Self-Test 1 and have tried to strengthen your preparation in any areas of weakness, GO ON to Self-Test 2.*

# Self-Test 2

*Multiple-Choice Questions*

1. According to Descartes's dualism:
    a. a great deal of behavior occurs without any involvement of the soul.
    b. the body has exclusive control over behavior, while the soul has exclusive control over thought.
    c. all behavior involves interaction with the soul.
    d. the body fully controls both behavior and thought.

2. Which of the following philosophical approaches sets the strictest limits on a science of psychology?
    a. Cartesian dualism
    b. Hobbes's materialism
    c. British empiricism
    d. Dualism, materialism, and empiricism are all equally hospitable to the notion of a scientific psychology.

3. Reflexology, the notion that all behavior involves reflex action, was a predecessor of:
    a. psychoanalysis.          c. behaviorism.
    b. structuralism.           d. functionalism.

4. Darwin's emphasis on the survival value of behavior was a major influence on:
    a. psychoanalysis.
    b. social psychology.
    c. cognitive psychology.
    d. functionalism.

5. For psychologists 1879 has historical significance because it was the year that the:
    a. first psychological research was done.
    b. first laboratory of psychology was opened at a university.
    c. first book on structuralism was published.
    d. field of psychophysics was founded.

6. Wundt used the results of reaction-time tasks to break down complex mental processes into their component parts. In which of the following approaches would this method fit?
    a. cognitive
    b. psychoanalytic
    c. physiological
    d. none of the above

7. One of the founders of structuralism was:
   a. Kurt Lewin.
   b. William James.
   c. Edward Titchener.
   d. Jean Piaget.

8. Which early psychological approach focused on the special nature of organized wholes?
   a. structuralism
   b. Gestalt psychology
   c. cognitive psychology
   d. psychoanalysis

9. Which of the following is true of the early behaviorists?
   a. They believed that there is no basic difference between the principles of animal and human behavior and often studied animals.
   b. They believed that there is little basic difference between the principles of animal and human behavior but restricted their study to humans.
   c. They believed that there are fundamental differences between the principles of animal behavior and the principles of human behavior and so restricted themselves to studying humans.
   d. They believed that there are fundamental differences between the principles of animal behavior and the principles of human behavior and were more interested in studying animal behavior.

10. The behaviorists were primarily influenced by _____ , whereas the ethologists were primarily influenced by _____ .
    a. the British empiricists; Darwin
    b. Darwin; the British empiricists
    c. the British empiricists; Descartes
    d. Darwin; the structuralists

11. The person sitting next to you on the plane tells you that her work involves injecting chemicals into a small area of a cat's brain to learn if there are any effects on motor behavior. You could correctly say, "Oh, you're a(n) _____ ."
    a. behaviorist
    b. physiological psychologist
    c. ethologist
    d. cognitive psychologist

12. The term *psychoanalysis* refers to:
    a. Freud's method of treating individuals with psychological problems.
    b. Freud's theory of the mind.
    c. an approach to psychology that emphasizes the mind's use of rational analysis.
    d. both a. and b.

13. Arthur is a graduate student who has studied the history and customs of Japan and the United States in order to understand differences in the people of these nations. He is most likely studying _____ psychology.
    a. humanistic
    b. cultural
    c. social
    d. psychoanalytic

14. Cognitive psychology often uses a _____ analogy, likening the mind to _____ .
    a. computer; a program
    b. computer; computer hardware
    c. mechanical; a hydraulics system
    d. communications; a switchboard

15. Which method of investigation does cognitive psychology generally employ?
    a. observing and describing actual behavior in natural settings
    b. introspection
    c. inferences about mental processes based on observable behavior in controlled situations
    d. interviews

## Essay Questions

16. What is the proper subject matter of psychology according to the behaviorist? according to the cognitive psychologist? Be sure your answer specifies the role of behavior in each approach.

17. Discuss the ways that Descartes and the British empiricists helped to prepare the way for a scientific psychology. Also point out the limits that each set on such a science.

# Answers

*Self-Test 1*

1. **d.** (p. 3)
2. **c.** (p. 4)
3. **d.** (p. 6)
4. **a.** (p. 6)
5. **d.** (p. 7)
6. **c.** Psychological research had been conducted in Germany prior to the founding of Wundt's laboratory at the University of Leipzig. But the founding of that laboratory represented an official acceptance of psychology by the academic establishment and provided a firm basis for the growth of the field. (p. 8)
7. **d.** (p. 9)
8. **c.** Introspection is inherently unsuitable as a form of scientific evidence because it is private. What one person experiences cannot be directly experienced by another person and thus cannot be verified. (p. 9)
9. **b.** This emphasis on purposes was related to Darwinian influences on the functionalists. (p. 9)
10. **d.** Gestalt views on the special status of organized wholes are directly implied by the statement. (pp. 10–11)
11. **c.** (p. 12)
12. **c.** (p. 13)
13. **a.** (pp. 14–15)
14. **a.** In Freud's thinking, the conscious mind represented only the proverbial "tip of the iceberg."

According to Freud, the unconscious mind is purposely hidden from direct inspection by the conscious mind. Freud believed that the conscious mind could be powerfully affected by the forces of the unconscious and by the mind's attempts to modify those forces. He used various methods to bring the disturbing thoughts into consciousness so that patients could deal with them. (pp. 16–17)

15. **b.** There is a certain similarity not only in the aims of cognitive psychologists and those of Wundt, but also in their approach to the study of the mind. Wundt and cognitive psychologists would agree that the mind must be understood in terms of basic structures and processes. The method of using reaction time as a way of uncovering these elementary structures and processes is a major tool of cognitive psychologists. (p. 20)

16. Both behaviorists and ethologists concentrated on animal behavior and insisted on careful observation, but their methods, motivations, and points of view were quite different. Behaviorists were interested in learning, while ethologists were interested in complex behaviors that animals did not need to learn. The behaviorists were influenced by the British empiricists, who claimed that all knowledge comes through sensory experience, and is thus learned. The ethologists, on the other hand, were most influenced by Darwin; they believed that adaptive behavior was powerfully shaped by evolutionary forces. The behaviorists were generally interested in animals because they provided a scientifically controllable way of studying learning, which, they thought, involved the same principles in both animals and humans. In contrast, the ethologists were interested in animal behavior for its own sake. The two schools began to interact more cooperatively after each learned lessons consistent with the other viewpoint. For example, by the 1960s, it was becoming clear to behaviorists that animal species differed in the types of responses they could learn. This forced them to acknowledge that learning must be examined in the context of a particular species' evolutionary history and survival needs. Ethologists, as they branched out to study mammals, were forced to acknowledge that these animals were much more affected by learning than the animals, such as birds and fish, that they had previously studied. (pp. 12–15)

17. The structuralist approach had as its goal the identification of the basic elements of the mind. Structuralists saw the mind as being made up of basic structures combined to form more complex structures combined to form still more complex

structures. They believed that the complex could be understood by separating the whole into its parts and seeing how the parts were put together. The Gestalt psychologists had a very different viewpoint about the nature of parts and wholes. They believed that a whole, whether a whole perception or a whole problem solution, had a special status. It could not be completely understood in terms of its parts. Some characteristics or qualities of the whole only emerge at the level of the whole, as in the *phi phenomenon*. The fundamental question for structuralists is: What are the parts that make up the complex whole? But the Gestalt psychologists would see this question as quite incomplete and potentially misleading. (pp. 8–11)

*Self-Test 2*

1. **a.** (p. 4)
2. **a.** The soul that is a major part of Descartes's theory of human action is a spiritual entity and is not subject to natural laws. This soul is responsible for thought and for the initiation of voluntary, nonreflexive action. Since science is designed to uncover natural laws, the limits on scientific psychology should be clear. (pp. 4–5)
3. **c.** (p. 6)
4. **d.** (p. 7)
5. **b.** (p. 8)
6. **a.** (pp. 8, 20)
7. **c.** Titchener was a student of Wundt's and his approach was heavily influenced by that of his mentor. (pp. 8–9)
8. **b.** (pp. 10–12)
9. **a.** (pp. 12–13)
10. **a.** (pp. 14–15)
11. **b.** (p. 16)
12. **d.** (p. 16)
13. **b.** (p. 18)
14. **a.** Using the computer analogy, the brain would be comparable to the hardware of the machine, and the mind to a computer program. (p. 20)
15. **c.** (pp. 19–20)

16. Behavior was the very thing that behaviorists wanted to understand. The mind, with all its perceptions and judgments and desires, had been the traditional object of study in psychology. The behaviorists felt that this traditional work had come to nothing because it was hopelessly tangled in unscientific speculation. The mind could not be seen or touched or measured. It was, in the behaviorist view, an elusive abstraction. Behaviorists demanded an objective, observable science of psychology and believed it could only be had if behavior—observable and even quantifiable— were the object of study. (Although the radical behaviorists refused even to consider mental constructs, some later *S-O-R* behaviorists such as Tolman admitted into their theories some mentalistic kinds of ideas.) For the cognitive psychologist, the mind is still the proper object of study. Its abstract and hidden nature does not exclude it from scientific study, just as the abstract and hidden nature of the atom does not prevent physicists from studying it. However, because the mind is not directly observable, as the behaviorists pointed out, the structures and processes of the mind must be inferred from observable behavior. (pp. 12–14, 19–20)

17. Descartes's dualism suggested the existence of a body and a soul, both of which affect behavior. According to the theory, the body can control some behavior directly, without any involvement of the soul. Descartes offered a new view of the body as a mechanism that follows natural laws and can thus be understood through science. However, the nonmaterial soul was believed by Descartes to be responsible for all thought. Unlike the body itself, the soul was not subject to natural law. Rather, it was thought to have free will. Because it was not operating under natural law, the soul, and the behaviors it willed the body to perform, could not be studied by science. The British empiricists believed that nothing existed beyond the material world. They contended that all behavior was based on physical mechanisms and that all knowledge, thought, and action could be traced back to the world of sensory experience and thus could be studied scientifically. (pp. 4–6)

# CHAPTER 2  METHODS OF PSYCHOLOGY

*Read the introduction below before you read the chapter in the text.*

Psychologists use scientific procedures in their effort to be objective and logical, and they value a skeptical attitude and careful observation. To answer the questions psychology poses in a scientific way, researchers employ various strategies. These strategies are categorized along three dimensions. One dimension is research design. Some studies involve controlled experimentation; others search for correlations between variables; and others simply describe behavior systematically. Another dimension is the data-collection method. In some cases, the data may consist of information reported by the individuals being studied. Alternatively, the data may come from direct observations and measurements made by the researchers. The final dimension is the setting. Some research is conducted in laboratories, but other studies are carried out in natural environments—in classrooms, public parks, city streets, or sports arenas, for example.

Statistical analysis is used to help psychologists understand the meaning of the data collected through research. Descriptive statistics summarize the data in useful ways; inferential statistics indicate whether patterns in the data are reliable or repeatable, given that data are always somewhat affected by random fluctuations.

Because psychological researchers—and often research subjects themselves—are human, research must be designed with various precautions in place. Some measures must be taken to keep the researchers' expectations from affecting the data. Other measures must be taken because the expectations of research subjects can produce misleading data. Finally, a number of research guidelines exist for ethical reasons, to protect the rights and welfare of research subjects.

*Look over the table of contents for this chapter in your textbook before you continue with your study.*

*Notice that there are focus questions in the margins of the text for your use in studying the material. The following chart lists which study guide questions relate to which focus questions.*

| Focus Questions | Study Guide Questions |
| --- | --- |
| Lessons from Clever Hans | |
| 1–2 | 1–56 |
| A Taxonomy of Research Strategies | |
| 3–6 | 6–10 |
| 7 | 11–14 |
| 8 | 15 |
| Statistical Methods in Psychology | |
| 9–10 | 1–8 |
| 11–12 | 9–11 |
| Sources of Error and Bias in Psychological Research | |
| 13–15 | 1–5 |
| 16–17 | 6–8 |
| 18 | 9–10 |
| Ethical Issues in Psychological Research | |
| 19 | 1–5 |

## The Integrated Study Workout

*Complete one section at a time.*

### Lessons from Clever Hans  (pages 27–29)

*CONSIDER these questions before you go on. They are designed to help you start thinking about this subject, not to test your knowledge.*

What makes a scientific approach to knowledge different from other approaches?

Is skepticism important only for combatting deliberate attempts to deceive?

*READ this section of your text lightly. Then go back and read thoroughly, completing the Workout as you proceed.*

Psychology has been considered a science since its beginnings. Therefore, as scientists, psychologists must approach their research with appropriate attitudes and methods. The story of Clever Hans helps to teach us some important lessons about the scientific approach.

1. What was claimed for Clever Hans? Who made the claim?

2. Was the case of Clever Hans a deliberate hoax? Explain.

3. How did Oskar Pfungst uncover the truth about Clever Hans? What was his final conclusion about the basis for Hans's amazing performance?

4. Why do you think Pfungst succeeded in learning the truth when other scientists were convinced of the authenticity of Hans's performance?

5. What is the major lesson to be learned from the case?

*A Taxonomy of Research Strategies*
(pages 30–34)

*CONSIDER these questions before you go on. They are designed to help you start thinking about this subject, not to test your knowledge.*

What makes an experiment an experiment?

What other methods besides experiments do psychologists use to study behavior and the mind?

How can psychologists study behavior in a natural setting?

*READ this section of your text lightly. Then go back and read thoroughly, completing the Workout as you proceed.*

One useful way to organize information is in a taxonomy. A taxonomy systematically groups items into categories and subcategories according to similarities and differences. A taxonomy of living things did much to advance the science of biology. A much smaller-scale taxonomy can help us to understand the variety of research strategies in psychology. (See Figure 2.2 on text page 30.)

Below are listed three dimensions of research strategies—the research design, the method of data collection, and the research setting. Identify each strategy described.

1. The research design:

   a. _____ A procedure in which a researcher systematically varies one or more independent variables to determine their effect on one or more dependent variables

   b. _____ A study in which a researcher observes or measures two or more variables to find a relationship among them but does not manipulate the variables of interest

   c. _____ A study in which the goal is not the systematic investigation of relationships between variables but rather the description of behavior

2. Data-collection methods:

   a. _____ The people being studied rate or describe their own mental state in some way

   b. _____ The researcher observes and describes the behavior of interest

3. Research settings:

   a. _____ Subjects are studied in a specially designated area that allows better control of environmental conditions or facilitates data collection

   b. _____ Subjects are studied in an environment not specially set up for purposes of research, such as a park, a restaurant, a kindergarten, or a living room

4. Categorize each of the following situations along the three dimensions of the taxonomy.

   a. A developmental psychologist has randomly divided elderly residents of a nursing home into three groups, each of which receives a different type of treatment intended to enhance life satisfaction. At the end of the study, the psychologist asks the residents to rate their life satisfaction using a series of questions.

      Type of design? _____

      Type of data collection? _____

      Type of setting? _____

   b. A psychologist is interested in spatial skills as they relate to aviation safety. Subjects who are licensed pilots are brought in and tested on a special apparatus that simulates various emergencies. The apparatus records how quickly and appropriately the subjects maneuver the "aircraft" to avoid imminent danger. The psychologist wants to see whether performance on this apparatus is related to the number of flight hours each pilot has logged.

      Type of design? _____

      Type of data collection? _____

      Type of setting? _____

   c. A clinical psychologist wants to understand better the means by which social support systems help terminally ill patients. The psychologist sits in on group support sessions and family visits of selected patients, carefully recording what happens. Subjects have consented to the presence of the psychologist but are kept unaware of the true nature of the psychologist's interests.

      Type of design? _____

Type of data collection? _____

Type of setting? _____

Experiments allow researchers the greatest degree of control and permit strong conclusions about cause and effect.

5. How do the terms *independent variable* and *dependent variable* relate to the terms *cause* and *effect*?

6. In the following examples, indicate which are variables by writing *V* in the blank provided.

   _____ a. intelligence

   _____ b. height of adult males

   _____ c. number of days in a week

   _____ d. major in college

7. In the following situations, indicate independent variables with *IV* and dependent variables with *DV*.

   a. A researcher randomly assigns subjects to groups that differ in size (_____). All subjects are then asked to perform the same task. The researcher measures the average amount of work each person does (_____).

   b. Subjects report childhood memories that come to mind (_____) after being exposed to verbal, visual, or smell cues (_____) associated with common childhood experiences.

   c. Researchers observe how long subjects work on a word puzzle (_____) after being told that they are good or poor puzzle solvers (_____).

   d. Subjects are injected with varying amounts of a drug (_____) designed to reduce symptoms of depression. They are then rated by themselves, by family members, and by counselors on various dimensions related to depression (_____).

**e.** Researchers calculate the average academic grades of children (_____) at 3 months, 6 months, 1 year, and 2 years after the death of a parent (_____).

**8.** What is the difference between a within-subject and a between-groups experiment?

**a.** self-report

**b.** observation

Correlational studies can provide useful and interesting information when it is not possible to manipulate a variable directly.

**9.** Correlational studies do not permit us to draw cause-effect conclusions as experiments do.

  **a.** Why is this so?

**14.** Compare the advantages and disadvantages of self-report methods, naturalistic observation, and tests.

  **b.** Consider Diana Baumrind's work on parenting styles, as described in the chapter. Why would cause-effect conclusions be inappropriate in this study?

Research can be conducted in a laboratory setting or in a field setting. Each has certain advantages and drawbacks.

**15.** What are the special merits and limitations of laboratory research? of field research?

Researchers often use several different approaches to try to answer the same basic questions.

**10.** Why is it best to use different research strategies to study a given research issue?

*Statistical Methods in Psychology*
(pages 35–38)

> *CONSIDER these questions before you go on. They are designed to help you start thinking about this subject, not to test your knowledge.*

What does it really mean when someone says two things are correlated?

Science has the reputation of being quantitative. How does psychology make use of math?

Psychologists can collect data in a number of different ways within two broad categories.

**11.** Two major ways of collecting self-report data are _____ and _____ .

**12.** Two major ways of collecting observational data are _____ and _____ .

**13.** Provide two concrete examples of each data-collection method mentioned in the right-hand column. (Use examples from the text or, better still, make up your own examples.)

> *READ this section of your text lightly. Then go back and read thoroughly, completing the Workout as you proceed.*

Data are useful only to the extent that they can be interpreted. Statistical procedures are critical to that step in the research process.

1. What can descriptive statistics do for us?

The mean and median are measures of central tendency. They help to summarize the data by giving us one "typical" number that serves to represent the whole data set. (Hint: Look at Table 2.1, text p. 35.)

2. The mean of the numbers 4 6 9 8 3 is

    _____ .

3. The median of the numbers 6 12 10 8 5 is

    _____ .

The standard deviation is a common measure of variability. In a sense, the measure of variability tells us how well the measure of central tendency represents the data set. For example, if all the scores in the set are fairly similar, the mean might represent them well. If there are many different scores, the mean would represent them less well.

4. Which set below has the higher variability? (Circle a. or b.)

    a.   3 6 7 6 8 5

    b.   1 5 2 9 4 11

A correlation coefficient is a statistic that describes the strength and direction of the relationship between two variables. (Hint: Look at Figure 2.4, text p. 36, for the items below.)

5. A correlation coefficient can vary between

    _____ and _____ .

6. The sign + or – indicates whether the relationship is positive or negative—in other words, the

    _____ of the relationship.

7. The absolute value of the coefficient indicates the

    _____ of the relationship.

    Lower numbers indicate _____

    relationships, while higher numbers indicate

    _____ relationships. Numbers

    at or near zero indicate _____ cor-

    relation.

8. In the following graph, what kind of correlation is indicated—negative or positive? low, moderate, or high?

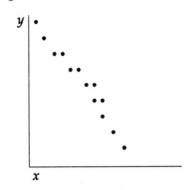

Data are always subject to a certain amount of random or chance variation. These random influences can deep us from seeing real, systematic patterns in the data, somewhat the way noise on a telephone line prevents us from hearing the speaker's voice clearly. They can also make it appear as if certain patterns exist when in reality they do not. Inferential statistics help us to decide when the patterns we see are real and repeatable, not just a product of chance.

9. Define the term *research hypothesis*.

10. Explain what it means to say that a given set of results are significant at the 5 percent level.

11. What factors are taken into account in determining statistical significance in an experiment? in a correlational study?

*Sources of Error and Bias in Psychological Research*  (pages 38–42)

CONSIDER *these questions before you go on. They are designed to help you start thinking about this subject, not to test your knowledge.*

What things should you look for in evaluating the believability of a psychological study?

Are scientists as objective as they ideally would like to be or are they sometimes swayed by their own biases, like nonscientists?

READ *this section of your text lightly. Then go back and read thoroughly, completing the Workout as you proceed.*

Considerable care is involved in designing sound research studies. There are several known sources of bias and error in research, and researchers must constantly guard against them.

1. Explain the difference between error and bias. Why is bias a more serious problem?

The measurement procedure used by the researcher is an important factor in minimizing error and bias.

2. What does it mean to say a measure is reliable? What problem results from low reliability?

3. What does it mean to say a measure is sensitive? What problem results from low sensitivity?

4. Define validity. What problem results from low validity?

5. A measurement procedure has _____ validity if it seems to make sense on the surface. A measurement procedure has _____ validity to the extent that it correlates well with another, more direct measure of the same characteristic.

Bias can result from the expectations brought into the research situation by either observers or subjects.

6. How can an observer's expectations bias results? How can we best prevent such observer-expectancy effects?

7. Explain the concept of a subject-expectancy effect. What is the best solution for this problem?

8. An experiment that guards against both observer- and subject-expectancy effects is called a _____ .

Research is almost invariably carried out on a sample, a subset of the larger population of interest to the researcher.

9. What is a biased sample?

10. In which of the following cases would a biased sample be more troublesome? Why?

   a. A researcher studies color vision in college students and generalizes to all adults.

   b. A researcher studies achievement motivation in college students and generalizes to all adults.

*Ethical Issues in Psychological Research*
(pages 42–44)

CONSIDER *these questions before you go on. They are designed to help you start thinking about this subject, not to test your knowledge.*

What are the most serious ethical concerns in psychological research?

Do psychologists give serious attention to ethical issues involved in using animals as research subjects?

What kinds of ethical principles do psychologists observe?

READ *this section of your text lightly. Then go back and read thoroughly, completing the Workout as you proceed.*

Those who conduct psychological research are obliged to observe ethical as well as scientific principles.

1. List the three major issues in research with human subjects.

   a. _____

   b. _____

   c. _____

2. How are these issues handled?

3. How can the use of deception in some psychological research be justified?

4. What are the obligations of researchers who use animal subjects?

5. What steps has the profession as a whole taken to oversee ethical practices in psychological research?

Be sure to READ *the Concluding Thoughts at the end of the chapter. Note important points in your Workout. Then consolidate your learning by answering the focus questions in the margins of the text.*

After *you have studied the chapter thoroughly,* CHECK *your understanding with the self-test that follows.*

# Self-Test 1

*Multiple-Choice Questions*

1. What lesson should be learned from the case of Clever Hans?
   a. We must not be misled by science's claims of objectivity.
   b. Unless we take a skeptical approach to any situation, we may be led to believe what is simply not true.
   c. When an unusual and interesting claim is made, we should suspend our skepticism and look for evidence to support it.
   d. The intelligence of nonhuman species should not be underestimated out of human arrogance.

2. Research strategies are categorized in terms of:
   a. research design, description, and data analysis.
   b. data collection, type of experiment, and statistical analysis.
   c. research design, data-collection method, and setting.
   d. observation, correlation, and setting.

3. A procedure in which the researcher systematically varies one variable, holding all others constant, to see if another variable is affected, is called a(n):
   a. correlational study.
   b. observational study.
   c. experiment.
   d. blind study.

4. An experimenter wants to see whether caffeine has any effect on the ability to concentrate on a visual task. In this study, the caffeine would be the:
   a. independent variable.
   b. between-groups variable.
   c. dependent variable.
   d. within-subject variable.

5. Cause is to effect as _____ is to _____ .
   a. constant; variable
   b. dependent variable; independent variable
   c. independent variable; dependent variable
   d. experiment; correlational study

6. A psychologist tries to find out whether there is any relationship between the number of older siblings a child has and the child's vocabulary size at age 3. This is an example of a(n):
   a. experiment.
   b. correlational study.
   c. descriptive study.
   d. within-subject experiment.

7. A psychologist explores the behavior of children in their first competitive sports experience, recording the variety and frequency of their social behaviors. What type of research strategy is involved here?
   a. experimental
   b. correlational
   c. descriptive
   d. within-subject

8. The purpose of descriptive statistics is to:
   a. help us decide whether research conclusions based on the data are warranted.
   b. help us collect data more efficiently.
   c. help us summarize data in a meaningful way.
   d. do none of the above.

9. Which of the following is the mean of the numbers 2, 4, 4, 6, 9?
   a. 2            c. 5
   b. 4            d. 25

10. Which of the following is the median of the numbers 5, 15, 20, 25, 30?
    a. 5           c. 19
    b. 15          d. 20

11. The value of a correlation coefficient varies between:
    a. 1.00 and 100.00.
    b. −10.00 and +10.00.

    c. 0.00 and 1.00.
    d. −1.00 and +1.00.

12. A result is termed "statistically significant" if it:
    a. is probably due to chance.
    b. cannot possibly be due to chance.
    c. has less than a 5 percent probability of being due to chance.
    d. is large enough to be practically important.

13. A psychologist uses test X to measure a person's creativity. The test is administered several times with widely varying results. Test X apparently lacks:
    a. observer expectancy.
    b. face validity.
    c. a double blind.
    d. reliability.

14. A measurement procedure that is able to detect small differences between individuals or conditions is said to be:
    a. biased.
    b. sensitive.
    c. high in criterion validity.
    d. reliable.

15. Clever Hans's abilities were apparently due to:
    a. placebo effects.
    b. low reliability.
    c. observer expectancy.
    d. a double blind procedure.

### Essay Questions

16. On what grounds should psychology be considered a science?

17. What are the three major ethical issues that must be considered in psychological research with human subjects? How do psychologists deal with these issues?

---

*After you have assessed your understanding on the basis of Self-Test 1 and have tried to strengthen your preparation in any areas of weakness, GO ON to Self-Test 2.*

## Self-Test 2

*Multiple-Choice Questions*

1. Which of the following describes an independent variable?
   a. a variable not correlated with other variables
   b. the variable the researcher observes and measures in an experiment
   c. the variable the researcher deliberately varies in an experiment
   d. a variable that is not affected by an experimenter's manipulation

2. A study examines the effect of different incentives ($2 and $10) on people's willingness to perform a mildly embarrassing task. In this study, _____ would be the independent variable and _____ would be the dependent variable.
   a. incentive; willingness to perform the task
   b. willingness to perform the task; incentive
   c. incentive; whether subjects receive $2 or $10
   d. willingness to perform the task; the number of people tested

3. A within-subject experiment is one in which:
   a. there is only a single subject.
   b. a given subject experiences all the different conditions of the experiment.

c. the data are collected by self-report.
d. the experimenter is interested only in the subjective experiences of the subject.

4. A psychologist varies the amount of practice time provided for different groups of subjects in a target-shooting task. The question is whether accuracy will be affected. The psychologist is conducting a:
   a. correlational study.
   b. between-groups experiment.
   c. within-subject experiment.
   d. descriptive study.

5. A psychologist asks people to complete a confidential questionnaire to determine whether physical fitness is related to self-esteem. The psychologist is conducting a(n) _____ study.
   a. experimental
   b. correlational
   c. double-blind
   d. descriptive

6. A psychologist visits a chemical plant to interview people engaged in a labor strike there. This would be:
   a. an experiment in which data collection is by self-report.
   b. a correlational study in which data collection is observational.
   c. a descriptive study in which data collection is observational.
   d. a field study in which data collection is by self-report.

7. Which type(s) of research design permit(s) direct cause-and-effect conclusions?
   a. experiments
   b. correlational studies
   c. descriptive studies
   d. both experiments and correlational studies

8. We often use _____ as an indicator of the central tendency in a data set.
   a. the standard deviation
   b. inferential statistics
   c. a correlation coefficient
   d. the mean

9. Which of the following is the mean of the numbers 10, 20, 30, 40, 100?
   a. 10
   b. 30
   c. 40
   d. 55

10. Which of the following correlation coefficients would indicate the strongest correlation between two variables?
    a. −0.80
    b. 0.00
    c. +0.50
    d. +0.75

11. Suppose a research result shows a difference between the two groups studied. Suppose further that inferential statistics show that the likelihood of the difference being due to chance is 50 percent. Is the result statistically significant by the usual standards?
    a. yes
    b. no
    c. well, yes and no—it's 50 percent significant
    d. It's impossible to say based on the information provided.

12. In an experiment, which of the following factors is *not* taken into account in a test of statistical significance?
    a. the size of the observed difference between means
    b. the number of times the study has been repeated
    c. the number of subjects
    d. the variability of the data in each group

13. The more consistent the result of a measurement procedure when used on the same subject under the same circumstances, the more _____ the measure is.
    a. reliable
    b. unbiased
    c. sensitive
    d. valid

14. A procedure that succeeds in measuring what it is intended to measure is said to be:
    a. unbiased.
    b. reliable.
    c. valid.
    d. sensitive.

15. If the results of an experiment are actually due to the beliefs of the subjects and not to a real effect of the independent variable, we say:
    a. subjects are blind.
    b. the study involves a double blind.
    c. there is a placebo effect.
    d. that an observer-expectancy effect is causing the results.

*Essay Questions*

16. Briefly describe the case of Clever Hans and explain the lessons we should learn from it.

17. Explain the phenomena of observer-expectancy and subject-expectancy effects in research. What measures can be taken to guard against them?

# Answers

*A Taxonomy of Research Strategies*

1. a. experiment
   b. correlational study
   c. descriptive study
2. a. self-report
   b. observational
3. a. laboratory
   b. field
4. a. experiment; self-report; field
   b. correlational; observational; laboratory
   c. descriptive; observational; field
6. Items a., b., and d. are variables, whereas c. is a constant.

7.  a.  IV, DV
    b.  DV, IV
    c.  DV, IV
    d.  IV, DV
    e.  DV, IV
11. questionnaire; interview
12. naturalistic observation; test

### Statistical Methods in Psychology

2.  6
3.  8
4.  Set b. has higher variability
5.  −1.00 and +1.00
6.  direction
7.  strength or magnitude; weaker; stronger; no
8.  This would appear to be a fairly high negative correlation.

### Sources of Error and Bias in Psychological Research

5.  face; criterion
8.  double blind experiment
10. Situation b. would be more troublesome.

### Ethical Issues in Psychological Research

1.  a.  right to privacy
    b.  possible discomfort or harm
    c.  use of deception

### Self-Test 1

1.  b.  (p. 29)
2.  c.  (pp. 30–34)
3.  c.  Only the experiment involves this much control. It is the control that allows conclusions about cause-and-effect relationships from experimental data. (pp. 30–31)
4.  a.  (pp. 30–31)
5.  c.  (pp. 30–31)
6.  b.  (pp. 31–32)
7.  c.  (pp. 32–33)
8.  c.  (p. 35)
9.  c.  (p. 35)
10. d.  Remember, the median is the middle number when numbers are ranked from lowest to highest.

The mean, on the other hand, is the arithmetic average. (p. 35)

11. d.  (p. 36)
12. c.  Scientists have established 5 percent as an arbitrary cutoff point. The rationale is that a 5 percent chance that a result could be due to random factors is a small enough chance to take a gamble on. (p. 37)
13. d.  (p. 39)
14. b.  (p. 39)
15. c.  (p. 40)
16. Psychology is considered a science for two major reasons. One is that the subjects of psychology—behavior and the mind—operate according to natural laws. It is psychology's job to discover the laws that govern behavior and the mind. The other reason concerns the method used for uncovering the laws of behavior and the mind. Science is in part a method for answering questions. That method involves the systematic, objective, and logical collection and interpretation of observations. Some approaches that represent important parts of psychology, such as psychoanalysis, are considered unscientific to the extent that they fail to meet these standards of science. (p. 27)
17. The three major ethical issues involved in psychological research are the right to privacy, the possibility of discomfort or harm to subjects, and deception. The first issue demands that information obtained from or about subjects be dealt with in a way that safeguards the individual's anonymity. Both the issues of privacy and harm or discomfort can be handled largely by obtaining informed consent from subjects and by letting them know they can quit the study at any point. Psychologists must also compare the potential risks to subjects with the potential scientific benefits for humankind before entering into the research. If risks can be avoided or minimized, there is an obligation to do that. Deception is probably the most controversial issue. Opponents say deception is never acceptable, but others counter that it is comparatively rare, generally benign, and often scientifically necessary. (pp. 42–44)

### Self-Test 2

1.  c.  (p. 30)
2.  a.  (pp. 30–31)
3.  b.  (p. 31)

4. **b.** (p. 31)

5. **b.** (pp. 31–32)

6. **d.** (pp. 33–34)

7. **a.** (p. 30)

8. **d.** (p. 35)

9. **c.** (p. 35)

10. **a.** To assess the strength of the relationship, look only at the absolute value of the coefficient, not the sign. The second strongest correlation coefficient among the alternatives would be d. Alternative b. indicates the absence of any relationship between the two variables. (p. 36)

11. **b.** The arbitrary cutoff point to establish statistical significance is often 5 percent. Below the cutoff, the results are considered significant; above the cutoff, the results are considered not significant. In other words, if the results had only a 5 percent or lower probability of occurring by chance, then we are essentially "betting" that they *aren't* due only to chance. There is no such thing as a partially significant result. Further, if there really were a 50:50 chance that our results were due to random factors, it would be a very risky bet to proclaim that they really weren't. (p. 37)

12. **b.** (pp. 37–38)

13. **a.** (p. 39)

14. **c.** (p. 39)

15. **c.** (p. 41)

16. Clever Hans was a horse owned by a German schoolteacher named von Osten. At about the turn of the century, von Osten tried to prove his hypothesis that horses were as smart as people and simply needed to be educated to show that they were. After several years of training, Hans could apparently answer questions about math, geography, history, and so on, by nodding his head or tapping his hoof. Von Osten's claims were widely accepted, even by many scientists. However, a psychologist by the name of Pfungst discredited poor Hans in a series of careful experiments. When Hans was prevented from receiving subtle unintentional cues from his "teacher" or others in his admiring audiences, he was unable to answer the questions put to him. This case is a classic lesson in the value of skepticism in science. We must not accept something as true just because we would like it to be true. We must test a claim and see whether it can be explained in some other fashion than the one we favor. It is also a lesson about the importance of making observations under carefully controlled and systematically varied conditions. Further, the case of Clever Hans can serve as an illustration of observer-expectancy effects, a problem that results when a researcher inadvertently cues a subject as to what is expected from him or her. (pp. 27–29)

17. One difficulty that psychological researchers often face comes from the very fact that they and their subjects are intelligent, thinking creatures. The researcher on the one hand and the subject on the other may both be affected by expectations. The researcher may unwittingly pass on expectations to the subject, who may just as unwittingly comply with those expectations. If that happens, the results of the study are not a reflection of nature as the researcher hoped they would be. Instead, they are just a reflection of the researcher's own scientific imagination. Likewise, the researcher's observations and judgments may be influenced by expectations. For example, if the researcher expects the subject to behave nonaggressively in a particular situation, behavior that is ambiguous or even slightly aggressive may be perceived as nonaggressive. These kinds of effects are referred to as observer-expectancy effects. Subjects, too, may develop their own expectations. For example, a subject who knows she is receiving a drug intended to suppress appetite may experience appetite suppression for reasons due to the expectation, not to the drug. Blind and double-blind studies can be very useful in preventing expectancy effects. In blind studies, the observers are not given access to information that could fuel such effects. In double blind studies, both the observer *and* the subject are unaware of what treatment the subject is receiving. Thus double blind studies protect against both observer- and subject-expectancy effects. (pp. 40–41)

# CHAPTER 3   GENETICS OF BEHAVIOR

*Read the introduction below before you read the chapter in the text.*

Chapter 3 deals with the issue of genetic effects on behavior. The relative influence of nature (genetics) and nurture (environment) on behavior have been discussed for centuries. The issue first came under scientific scrutiny with the work of Francis Galton in the nineteenth century. Since then, as the text explains, the debate has continued, illuminated by new understanding of genetic transmission and action.

The first section of the chapter describes the genetic materials and the process by which genetic information is transmitted from one generation to the next. Genes, which are segments of DNA molecules, affect our anatomy and physiology and, through these, behavioral characteristics such as intelligence. They exert their influences by one, and only one, means—by governing the manufacture of many different protein molecules. However, at all levels of analysis, from biochemical to behavioral, the effects of genes are entwined with the effects of environment.

In some cases, a single gene can affect a particular aspect of behavior or cause genetic disorders that have behavioral consequences. For example, a study of two dog breeds—one quiet and timid, the other noisy and confident—revealed that the differences between the two breeds in each of these traits are independently controlled by a single gene. In humans, Huntington's disease, a rare but fatal disorder, is caused by a single dominant gene. Phenylketonuria (PKU), a disorder that can result in severe mental retardation, is caused by a recessive gene. However, the right diet—an environmental influence—can drastically reduce the damage done by this disease, which underscores the point that genes and environment work together. Other human disorders caused by a single gene are sex-linked disorders, such as red-green color blindness, and fragile X syndrome, which causes mental retardation as a result of a specific defect on the X chromosome. Some disorders, such as Down syndrome, result from abnormalities not of individual genes but of chromosomes.

Most differences among individuals stem from the combined effects of many genes in interaction with the environment. With such complex patterns of genetic influence, scientists cannot be as precise as they can with single-gene or chromosomal disorders. They must generally settle for statistical models. Heritability, a major concept in this approach, is the degree to which variation among individuals on a particular trait, in a particular population, can be attributed to genetic differences among those individuals.

Considerable research effort has focused on the heritability of IQ. By comparing correlation coefficients for various categories of relatives (such as identical twins, fraternal twins, and nontwin siblings, some raised in the same home, some raised apart), scientists have discovered that there is a strong genetic influence on variation in IQ. There is also evidence that environmental differences explain a substantial portion of the variation. A highly politicized scientific debate has centered on average IQ differences between various cultural and racial groups. It is important to realize that, despite high heritability *within* groups, differences *between* groups may be entirely environmental in origin.

Heritability has also been estimated for schizophrenia, a serious mental disorder. As with IQ, studies reveal that both genetic and environmental factors help to determine who does and who does not develop the disorder. Several current research efforts are investigating environmental conditions that bring out this disorder in individuals who have a genetic predisposition to it.

*Look over the table of contents for this chapter in your textbook before you continue with your study.*

*Notice that there are focus questions in the margins of the text for your use in studying the material. The following chart lists which study guide questions relate to which focus questions.*

| Focus Questions | Study Guide Questions |
|---|---|
| Principles of Gene Action and Heredity | |
| 1–2 | 1–5 |
| 3–7 | 6–21 |
| Single-Gene and Chromosomal Effects on Behavior | |
| 8–9 | 1–5 |
| 10–14 | 6–17 |
| 15–16 | 18–23 |
| Polygenic Effects on Behavior | |
| 17 | 1–2 |
| 18–19 | 3–7 |
| 20–21 | 8–10 |
| 22–30 | 11–22 |
| 31–36 | 23–29 |

## The Integrated Study Workout

*Complete one section at a time.*

### Principles of Gene Action and Heredity
(pages 50–55)

*CONSIDER these questions before you go on. They are designed to help you start thinking about this subject, not to test your knowledge.*

What is a gene? What is a chromosome?

How can a microscopic physical thing like a gene affect something psychological such as verbal ability?

How are genes passed from parents to children?

What factors determine the genes a child will receive?

How genetically similar are people who are biologically related?

*READ this section of your text lightly. Then go back and read thoroughly, completing the Workout as you proceed.*

The nature-nurture issue is an old one. It still commands much attention in psychology. To understand the issue scientifically, we must understand the basic biology of genes and their hereditary transmission.

1. Behavioral genetics is the study of the _____ _____ .

2. Genes direct the synthesis of _____ molecules by controlling the sequence of _____ in them. A gene is itself a portion of a long molecule called _____ .

3. How do genes affect behavior?

It is very important to understand that the effects of genes are always interwoven with the effects of the environment. Neither one alone can affect the biology or the behavior of an individual.

4. In the context of this chapter, what does environment mean? List two ways in which the environment could affect physical development and behavior.

5. Distinguish between genotype and phenotype.

Genes are the basic units of heredity. The genes within each individual are received from the biological parents.

6. The text introduces several terms related to the genetic material. For each item below, fill in the appropriate term.

   _____ a. a photographic representation of the chromosomes in a single cell

   _____ b. structures that contain the long strands of DNA that exist in each cell

_____ **c.** all chromosomes except the sex chromosomes

_____ **d.** different sequences of these molecules can make up a tremendous variety of protein molecules

_____ **e.** a pair of chromosomes consisting of two large *X* chromosomes for females and a large *X* and small *Y* chromosome for males

7. A single human cell (except an egg or sperm cell) contains _____ chromosomes.

Cells can divide in two ways: through *mitosis* and *meiosis.* An understanding of meiosis is important for understanding the hereditary transmission of genetic information.

8. What is the purpose of mitosis? How is the genetic material in one resulting cell related to the genetic material in the other resulting cell?

9. (To answer this question about meiosis, see text and Figure 3.3 on text page 52.) Meiosis occurs in _____ cells and produces _____ cells. One precursor cell produces _____ egg or sperm cells. The egg or sperm cells each contain _____ chromosomes.

10. Each egg or sperm cell resulting from meiosis looks alike in terms of its chromosomes (except for the *X* in some sperm and the *Y* in others). However, each cell contains different genes. The process during meiosis that results in the "individuality" of each egg or sperm cell is called _____ . (See Figure 3.4 on text page 53.)

In human sexual reproduction, the egg and sperm cells unite, combining their genetic information.

11. The type of cell that results from the union of the egg and sperm is called a(n) _____ .

It contains _____ chromosomes.

12. Explain the evolutionary advantage of reproducing sexually as opposed to asexually.

13. What is the difference between identical and fraternal twins?

We often talk about chromosomes in terms of pairs. In the case of humans, we usually say there are 23 pairs of chromosomes, not 46 chromosomes, although both are true. The pairing is emphasized because it has important consequences. It is not only the chromosomes that are paired but also the genes they carry. (See Figure 3.5 on text page 54.)

14. Define *allele.*

15. What does it mean to say someone is heterozygous at a particular locus? to say someone is homozygous at a particular locus?

16. What does it mean to say an allele is dominant? to say an allele is recessive?

17. In each of the following cases, assume that there is an allele *M* which is dominant and an allele *m* which is recessive. Indicate which allele (*M* or *m*) will be expressed in the phenotype for each case.

_____ **a.** The individual is heterozygous.

_____ **b.** The individual is homozygous for *M.*

_____ **c.** The individual is homozygous for *m.*

**18.** Explain the concept of percent relatedness.

What causes a genetic problem such as Down syndrome?

Is it possible to counteract a genetic problem by environmental means?

Why are males more likely than females to get certain genetic disorders?

---

*READ this section of your text lightly. Then go back and read thoroughly, completing the Workout as you proceed.*

Gregor Mendel is famous for his elegant studies of genetics in peas. Though Mendel's work was done in the nineteenth century, it still offers a clear picture of certain hereditary patterns.

**19.** In one experiment, Mendel studied wrinkled-seed peas and round-seed peas. Explain Mendel's breeding procedures.

**20.** Why did all of the $F_1$ generation have round seeds?

**21.** Why did three-fourths of the $F_2$ generation have round seeds (the dominant trait) and the other one-fourth, wrinkled seeds (the recessive trait)? (See Figure 3.6 on text page 55.)

Behavioral genetics has advanced in part by looking for cases in which there is a pattern of inheritance like the one Mendel uncovered. Scott and Fuller revealed just such a pattern in the behavior of two dog breeds—cocker spaniels and basenjis. (See Figure 3.7 on text page 56 and Figure 3.8 on page 57.)

**1.** How did pure-bred cocker and basenji puppies react when approached by a human who was a stranger to them?

**2.** When dogs of the two breeds were cross-bred, how did the resulting ($F_1$) offspring behave in the same fear test?

**3.** State Scott and Fuller's conclusion about the genetic basis of this type of behavior in cockers and basenjis.

*Single-Gene and Chromosomal Effects on Behavior* (pages 55–61)

---

*CONSIDER these questions before you go on. They are designed to help you start thinking about this subject, not to test your knowledge.*

Are patterns of hereditary transmission in humans always complex, or are some as simple as those in Mendel's peas?

**4.** How did Scott and Fuller further test this hypothesis?

5. Why would it be wrong to conclude that environment is irrelevant to the matter of fear in cockers and basenjis?

Certain disorders in humans, called Mendelian disorders, are also inherited in this basic single-gene fashion. One example is Huntington's disease, in which brain cells atrophy, leading to progressive deterioration and eventually to death.

6. The chance that a child of a Huntington's victim

will also have the disease is _____

percent because there is a _____

percent chance of inheriting the

_____ gene that causes the disorder.

7. The symptoms of Huntington's disease don't begin to appear until the affected person is 35–45 years old. Why is that fact critical in the continued genetic transmission of this dominant disorder? How does this situation compare to recessive disorders?

8. Geneticists now know the location of the Huntington's gene—near one end of chromosome 4. What important possibilities are opened up by knowing the location of a critical gene?

Most single-gene disorders are produced not by a dominant but by a recessive allele. Phenylketonuria (PKU) is an example of such a recessive disorder.

9. What are the results of PKU if it is left untreated?

10. What is the cause of PKU at the biochemical level? at the genetic level?

11. How can the effects of PKU be minimized?

12. What is the genotype of a person with a full-blown case of PKU? How do you know?

Sex chromosomes provide an important exception to the general pattern of inheriting genes in pairs.

13. What do we mean when we say a trait is sex-linked?

14. Why do males have more genetic disorders than females do? Explain in terms of red-green color blindness.

Not all single-gene disorders can be neatly classified as dominant, recessive, or sex-linked. Some involve more complicated and unusual patterns of gene replication and expression. Fragile X, now thought to be the most common inherited type of mental retardation, is such a disorder. The faulty gene produces a protein molecule which apparently interferes with brain processes.

15. Briefly describe the behavioral problems characteristically associated with fragile X syndrome.

16. How is the pattern of inheritance for fragile X different from that for a typical sex-linked disorder, such as red-green color blindness?

17. What is the most unusual genetic feature of fragile X?

Some disorders are due not to single genes, but to abnormalities involving entire chromosomes or large pieces of chromosomes. Though egg and sperm cells with chromosomal abnormalities generally cannot result in a living infant, about 1 out of 200 live newborns has a detectable chromosomal abnormality. One type of chromosomal abnormality involves the presence of too many or too few sex chromosomes in an individual's genetic makeup.

18. What chromosomal abnormality is involved in Turner's syndrome and what does it lead to?

19. What chromosomal abnormality is involved in Klinefelter's syndrome and what does it lead to?

Down syndrome is the most common disorder caused by a chromosomal abnormality that does not involve a sex chromosome.

20. Down syndrome is also called _____ because it results from an _____

    _____ .

21. Describe the characteristics of children with Down syndrome.

22. Discuss recent evidence suggesting that Down syndrome and Alzheimer's disease have something in common.

23. Down syndrome occurs in about 1 out of _____ live births. The incidence of the disorder _____ (increases/decreases) with the age of the parents.

## Polygenic Effects on Behavior  (pages 62–77)

*CONSIDER these questions before you go on. They are designed to help you start thinking about this subject, not to test your knowledge.*

Could individual differences in something as complex as intelligence be due to a single gene?

What clues lead scientists to believe that differences between individuals on some specific trait are due to a single gene or to many genes?

What types of evidence help to uncover the relative contributions of genes and environment in determining the variability in a particular trait?

What is the scientifically reasonable response to claims that certain racial or social-class groups differ in IQ for genetic reasons?

*READ this section of your text lightly. Then go back and read thoroughly, completing the Workout as you proceed.*

Some people have more friends than others, and some people learn skills more easily than others. Most of the differences between individuals involve the combined influences of many genes (in interaction with the environment, of course), not the effects of single genes or abnormal numbers of chromosomes.

1. With a polygenic characteristic, measured differences are _____ , whereas they are _____ for a single-gene trait. Most often, the set of scores obtained for polygenic traits approximates a _____ distribution. (See Figure 3.10 on text page 62.)

2. What is the goal of quantitative genetics?

The concept of heritability is crucial to an understanding of polygenic effects. Misunderstandings have led to faulty scientific thinking and biased political arguments.

3. Define heritability.

4. Heritability is a quantitative concept. Answer the following questions about the heritability coefficient.

   a. The formula for computing a heritability coefficient is _____ .

   b. What does a coefficient of 0.25 mean? a coefficient of 0.00? a coefficient of 1.00?

   c. How accurate a measure is heritability?

5. Does it make sense to talk about heritability in reference to an individual person? Explain. (See Figure 3.11 on text page 63.)

6. a. What happens to heritability as genetic diversity increases? Why?

   b. What happens to heritability as environmental diversity increases? Why?

7. What concept is the complement of heritability? Suppose you know from an estimate of heritability that genetic variation accounts for 30 percent of observed variability in some trait; do you then know anything about the remaining 70 percent of observed variability? Explain.

Selective breeding has been practiced for thousands of years to produce more desirable strains of plants and animals. Scientists find selective breeding useful for studying polygenic effects on behavior in animals.

8. How can selective breeding help to reveal the heritability of a trait?

Robert Tryon's work with "maze bright" and "maze dull" rats clearly pointed out that even complex abilities, such as a rat's ability to learn a maze, can be genetically influenced.

9. What method did Tryon use and what did he find? (See Figure 3.13 on text page 66.)

10. One must be careful not to interpret Tryon's results simplistically, however.

    a. Why is it important to note that Tryon tested his subjects only on their ability to learn a particular task?

    b. Briefly describe an experiment that shows that the differential performance of "maze bright" and "maze dull" rats depends in part on environment.

Since selective breeding cannot be used to study polygenic effects in humans, another approach must be taken. The primary method involves studying individuals with different degrees of genetic relatedness. Intelligence is the characteristic that has received the most attention in such heritability studies. Serious scientific attention was given to this issue in the nineteenth century, with Francis Galton and John Stuart Mill being two of the major figures in the debate.

11. Galton developed what are now called the adoptive method and the twin method for studying heritability. Describe the rationale behind these methods. How was Galton's use of the adoptive method flawed in the case of papal adoptees?

12. Answer the following questions on Galton's thinking about the nature-nurture issue.

    a. What was Galton's most careful scientific conclusion about the nature-nurture issue?

    b. What change in his position occurred when his thinking was less closely tied to the data he produced?

    c. Define *eugenics* and briefly describe Galton's views on this subject.

13. Briefly discuss John Stuart Mill's position on the issue of heritability.

Modern studies of the heritability of intelligence have depended on standardized IQ scores as measures of intelligence.

14. What scientific patterns in the data reviewed by Bouchard and McGue suggested a genetic contribution to variation in IQ? What specific pattern in the data suggest a substantial environmental contribution? (See Table 3.2 on text page 70.)

Heritability coefficients can be calculated from correlations such as those in text Table 3.2 (page 70).

15. There are various ways of estimating heritability mathematically. One approach is to use the correlation for identical twins reared

    _____ as a direct estimate of heritability. If that correlation were 1.00, it would mean that IQ variation is due entirely to

_____ . If the correlation were

instead 0.00, it would mean that IQ variation is

due entirely to _____ .

16. Actually, this correlation is about

_____ , which suggests both

genetic and environmental contributions to variability. Estimates using other methods and/or other cases have varied somewhat. Overall, estimates of the heritability of IQ fall in the range

_____ to _____ .

17. The assumptions one brings to bear in calculating heritability are important.

 a.   What is the selective-placement argument?

 b.   Does the argument suggest that heritability estimates have therefore been too high or too low?

 c.   What light does the Minnesota Twin study shed on this issue?

 d.   Does the fact that the subjects in the Minnesota study were adults matter? Explain.

Studies of IQ frequently show that there are average differences among various racial and cultural groups. Considerable debate has centered on black-white differences in the United States and on social-class differences in Europe. The central issue has been

whether the observed differences are due partly to genetic differences between the groups or are entirely due to environmental differences.

18. What argument did Jensen make in this debate?

19. How did Jensen's critics challenge his argument?

20. Explain how it is possible to have high heritability within groups and no heritability across groups.

21. Studies can be designed to separate out genetic and environmental factors in group IQ differences. Briefly describe two such studies and summarize their results.

 a.

 b.

22. In what sense is the scientific debate embedded in a political debate?

Another major area of research on heritability in humans concerns schizophrenia, a serious mental disorder. Symptoms often associated with the disorder are hallucinations, delusions, and absent or inappropriate emotional responses. Schizophrenia tends to run in families, but that fact in itself does not settle the heritability issue; the tendency could be due to shared genes or to shared environments.

23. How did Kety and Rosenthal use the adoptive method to learn about the heritability of schizophrenia? What did they find? (See Figure 3.15 on text page 75.)

24. Why did Kety and Rosenthal include relatives of nonschizophrenic adoptees in their study?

Twin studies have also been used to shed light on the heritability of schizophrenia. (See Table 3.3 on text page 76.)

25. In twin studies, a group of individuals diagnosed as having schizophrenia is identified. These individuals are called _____ cases. Relatives of these individuals are then examined. The percentage of relatives of a particular class (for example, identical twin, nontwin sibling, and so on) who develop the disorder is called the _____ .

26. Table 3.3 shows that over many studies, the average concordance for identical twins is _____ percent, while that for fraternal twins is _____ percent, only a little higher than the concordance for _____ . Since the concordance for identical twins is not _____ percent, these results suggest that there is a strong _____ component as well as a strong genetic component.

27. From concordances, behavioral geneticists have estimated the heritability for the _____ for schizophrenia to be about 0.70. This figure does not apply to the chances of being diagnosed as having schizophrenia, but of being _____ to it.

Even though genetic differences among people are influential in determining who gets schizophrenia, it is important to consider environmental factors as well.

28. Tuberculosis (TB) offers a good analogy for understanding just how much environment matters. Answer the following questions.

   a. In the 1930s and 1940s, when TB was more common, the evidence indicated that genes played the major role in who got the disease. Explain.

   b. How have scientists used environmental control to combat the disease successfully?

29. How are researchers today studying environment as a way of helping people with a predisposition to schizophrenia?

*Be sure to READ the Concluding Thoughts at the end of the chapter. Note important points in your Workout. Then consolidate your learning by answering the focus questions in the margins of the text.*

*After you have studied the chapter thoroughly, CHECK your understanding with the self-test that follows.*

# Self-Test 1

*Multiple-Choice Questions*

1. Whose research into differences in intellectual achievement initiated the so-called nature-nurture debate?
   a. Gregor Mendel
   b. Francis Galton
   c. Richard Mulcaster
   d. Robert Tryon

2. Genes affect both physical development and behavior by directing the synthesis of:
   a. structural proteins.
   b. enzymes.
   c. cells.
   d. proteins, including structural proteins and enzymes.

3. Suppose a person well-informed in the area of genetics refers to "genes for spatial ability." A correct interpretation of this phrase would be:
   a. "genes that directly control a person's ability to process spatial information and have no other function."
   b. "genes that produce a particular anatomy and physiology, which in turn affect a person's spatial ability."
   c. "genes that directly control cognitive ability in general and spatial ability in particular."
   d. that it's a joke since genes have no effect (direct or indirect) on psychological functioning.

4. The photographic representation of chromosomes in a single cell is called a(n):
   a. phenotype.
   b. autosome.
   c. genotype.
   d. karyotype.

5. Meiosis results in egg and sperm cells containing _____ the number of chromosomes contained in each of the body's other cells.
   a. exactly
   b. half
   c. twice
   d. three times

6. The purpose of sexual—as opposed to asexual—reproduction is to produce offspring that are:
   a. genetically diverse.
   b. genetically uniform.
   c. genetically similar to their parents.
   d. numerous.

7. Genes that can occupy the same locus—and can thus pair with one another—are called:
   a. homozygous.      c. alleles.
   b. dizygotic.        d. dominant genes.

8. The very effective dietary treatment of phenylketonuria (PKU) is evidence that:
   a. the disease is not hereditary as was once believed.
   b. nutrition can change genetic makeup.
   c. environmental and genetic factors interact to determine physical and behavioral outcomes.
   d. the disease does not involve a dominant gene.

9. Which abnormalities involving sex chromosomes lead to sexual underdevelopment and infertility?
   a. *XO, XXX, XXY,* and *XYY*
   b. *XO* and *XXY*
   c. *XXY* and *XYY*
   d. only *XO*

10. Any characteristic that varies in a continuous fashion in a population should be presumed:
    a. to be polygenic.
    b. to be based on a single gene.
    c. to involve whole chromosomes.
    d. not to be genetically influenced.

11. Which of the following statements concerning heritability is *not* true?
    a. Heritability applies to groups rather than to individuals.
    b. Heritability can be exactly and accurately calculated through the use of a standard formula.
    c. Heritability increases as genetic diversity increases.
    d. Heritability and environmentality have a complementary relationship.

12. Tryon's attempt to selectively breed "maze bright" and "maze dull" rats:
    a. resulted in failure.
    b. showed that only very small differences could be produced, even over 20 generations.
    c. showed that large differences could be produced over several generations.
    d. proved that genes are more important than environment in determining intelligence.

13. In measuring characteristic *X* in siblings reared together, we find a 0.39 correlation for adopted siblings, compared with 0.48 for fraternal twins and 0.63 for identical twins. This suggests that:
    a. there is no environmental contribution to variation in *X*.

b. there is no genetic contribution to variation in X.

c. there is an environmental contribution to variation in X, but only for twins.

d. there are both genetic and environmental contributions to variation in X.

14. Overall, recent studies of biologically related individuals suggest that the heritability of IQ lies in the range:
   a. 0.00–0.25.
   b. 0.25–0.50.
   c. 0.50–0.75.
   d. 0.75–1.00.

15. On IQ tests, black children raised by white, middle- and upper-class adoptive parents:
   a. do better than other black children, which suggests that racial differences in IQ are due to environment.
   b. do better than other black children, which suggests that racial differences in IQ are due to genetics.
   c. do no better than other black children, which suggests that racial differences in IQ are due to environment.
   d. do no better than other black children, which suggests that racial differences in IQ are due to genetics.

*Essay Questions*

16. What is heritability? Does it depend on the genetic diversity of the group being studied? on the environmental diversity of the group being studied? How can heritability be high within two groups and yet not account for differences between the groups?

17. What evidence suggests that genes play a role in determining who develops schizophrenia? Is it useless to take an environmental approach in trying to control the disorder? Explain.

---

*After you have assessed your understanding on the basis of Self-Test 1 and have tried to strengthen your preparation in any areas of weakness, GO ON to Self-Test 2.*

# Self-Test 2

*Multiple-Choice Questions*

1. The study of the effects of genes on behavior is called:
   a. genetic engineering.
   b. quantitative genetics.
   c. environmental genetics.
   d. behavioral genetics.

2. The primary job of genes is to direct the sequence of _____ that make up each type of protein molecule.
   a. DNA
   b. amino acids
   c. RNA
   d. enzymes

3. The normal human cell (other than egg or sperm cells) contains _____ pairs of chromosomes.
   a. 12          c. 23
   b. 22          d. 46

4. The process by which cells divide for the purpose of normal body growth is:
   a. mitois.
   b. meiosis.
   c. crossing over.
   d. protein synthesis.

5. We can assume that _____ are genetically identical.
   a. identical twins
   b. fraternal twins
   c. both identical and fraternal twins
   d. no two people

6. A friend of yours has brown eyes and her mother has blue eyes. Assuming that blue is recessive and brown is dominant, you can conclude that your friend:
   a. is heterozygous for eye color.
   b. is homozygous for eye color.
   c. is monozygotic for eye color.
   d. is brown-eyed as far as phenotype is concerned, but you can infer nothing about her genotype.

7. Percent relatedness is a measure of the _____ two people (say, father and child) will probably share.
   a. chromosomes
   b. genes
   c. rare genes
   d. phenotype

8. When Mendel crossed purebred wrinkled-seed peas with purebred round-seed peas, he found that all of the $F_1$ generation had round seeds. When he bred the $F_1$ peas with one another, he found that:
   a. the $F_2$ peas all had round seeds.
   b. the $F_2$ peas all had wrinkled seeds.
   c. half the $F_2$ peas had round seeds and the other half had wrinkled seeds.
   d. three-fourths of the $F_2$ peas had round seeds and the other one-fourth had wrinkled seeds.

9. Which of the following is true of Huntington's disease?
   a. It is caused by a rare but dominant allele.
   b. The child of a Huntington's victim will inevitably manifest the disease.
   c. The presence of the gene for Huntington's cannot as yet be determined through genetic testing.
   d. The disease has persisted in the population because its debilitating effects begin in early childhood.

10. Because of the nature of sex-linked disorders:
    a. men are more often affected by these disorders than women are.
    b. women are more often affected by these disorders than men are.
    c. men are the only victims of these disorders.
    d. women are the only victims of these disorders.

11. Which of the following is true of polygenic effects?
    a. Most measurable differences between people can be explained in terms of single genes; that is, they are not polygenic.
    b. Without examining the genetic material itself, there is no way to determine whether a characteristic is polygenic in origin.
    c. Eye color is a classic example of a polygenic effect.
    d. The distribution of scores for a polygenic trait often approximates a normal distribution.

12. Down syndrome is a disorder that:
    a. results from a single gene.
    b. results from an extra chromosome 21.
    c. inevitably produces individuals who cannot benefit from education.
    d. is most common when the mother is under 18.

13. The heritability coefficient measures the proportion of:
    a. variance in a particular trait in a particular individual that is due to genetic influence.
    b. the variability in some characteristic in a group of individuals that is due to genetic differences among those individuals.
    c. genes that two particular individuals have in common.
    d. genes that a parent will pass on to his or her offspring.

14. Francis Galton studied the heritability of intelligence. From twin studies and a study of eminent men and their relatives, he concluded that:
    a. nature predominates greatly over nurture within a given social class and country.
    b. nurture predominates greatly over nature within a given social class and country.
    c. nature and nurture are equally powerful influences.
    d. environment prevails within a social class but genetics produces the differences between social classes.

15. If there is high heritability for a trait within groups, heritability across groups:
    a. must be high.
    b. can still be zero.
    c. cannot be zero.
    d. must be at least moderate.

## Essay Questions

16. What are genes and how do they affect behavior?

17. What is PKU? What causes the disorder? How does the example of PKU illustrate the importance of considering genetics and environment together?

# Answers

## Principles of Gene Action and Heredity

1. effects of genes on behavior

2. protein; amino acids; DNA

6. a. karyotype

   b. chromosomes

   c. autosomes

   d. amino acids

   e. sex chromosomes

7. 46 (or 23 pairs of)

9. precursor; egg or sperm; four; 23 (not 23 pairs of)

10. crossing over

11. zygote; 46 (or 23 pairs of)

17. a. *M*                c. *m*

    b. *M*

## Single-Gene and Chromosomal Effects on Behavior

6. 50; 50; dominant

20. trisomy-21; extra (or part of one extra) chromosome 21

23. 700; increases

## Polygenic Effects on Behavior

1. continuous; step-like; normal

4. a.  $h^2 = \dfrac{\text{variance due to genes}}{\text{total variance}}$

15. apart; genes; environment

16. 0.70 (e.g., 0.69 in one study and 0.72 in another); 0.50; 0.75

25. index; concordance

26. 48; 17; nontwin siblings; 100; environmental

27. liability; susceptible

## Self-Test 1

1. **b.** (p. 49)

2. **d.** (p. 50)

3. **b.** Genes have their effect only by controlling the manufacture of proteins. In that way, they affect an individual's anatomy and physiology. Their effects on behavior are due to the particular anatomy and physiology they create and are thus indirect. (p. 50)

4. **d.** (p. 51)

5. **b.** There are 23 pairs of chromosomes in most of the body's cells, but only 23 chromosomes in an egg or sperm cell. When the egg and sperm combine to form the zygote, the full complement of 23 pairs of chromosomes is restored. (p. 52)

6. **a.** Sexual reproduction essentially "shuffles the genetic deck" to produce great diversity in offspring. Diversity offers an evolutionary advantage in that some of the many different types of individuals may be capable of adapting to changing environmental conditions. (p. 53)

7. **c.** (p. 54)

8. **c.** (p. 58)

9. **b.** The individual with the *XO* karyotype is said to have Turner's syndrome, while the individual with the *XXY* karyotype is said to have Klinefelter's syndrome. (p. 60)

10. **a.** A polygenic characteristic can often be described in terms of a normal distribution. A

single-gene kind of pattern is indicated by step-wise variation. (p. 62)

11. **b.** There is disagreement about how to estimate heritability. (pp. 62–65)

12. **c.** (p. 65)

13. **d.** (pp. 69–70)

14. **c.** (p. 70)

15. **a.** (pp. 72–73)

16. Heritability refers to the extent to which genetic differences in a group of individuals can account for observed differences in some characteristic. Heritability is a product of the group's environmental as well as its genetic diversity. This can be seen by carrying both types of variability to extremes. Suppose there were no genetic differences among individuals in a given group. Any differences observed would have to be due to environment and heritability would be 0.00. On the other hand, if the members of the group were exposed to identical environments and still differed in some trait, we would have to assume that the differences were due to genetic variation and thus heritability would be 1.00, the highest possible coefficient. Heritability can be high within groups and low or nonexistent between them if the individuals within a group have very similar environments and the two groups have different environments. (pp. 62–64)

17. Both adoptive and twin studies seem to indicate that heritability for schizophrenia is substantial. One study looked at adoptees who were diagnosed as having schizophrenia and control adoptees who did not have the disorder but were similar in other regards. For both groups, the researchers found the individuals' biological relatives and checked through a series of blind interviews to see whether any of them had schizophrenia. They found that the biological relatives of adoptees with schizophrenia were much more likely than the others studied to have symptoms of schizophrenia.

A twin study carried out at Maudsley Hospital in England computed concordance rates for fraternal and identical twins after one twin in each set had been diagnosed as having schizophrenia. The rate was about 50 percent for identical twins but was no higher for fraternal twins than for ordinary sisters and brothers. The fact that concordance for identical twins was not 100 percent indicates that there is also an important environmental contribution to the matter of who develops schizophrenia.

As with TB in earlier decades, it may be possible to attack the disease environmentally. If we learn more about the environmental characteristics that bring out genetic susceptibility, we may be able to control environment to lessen risk. (pp. 73–77)

*Self-Test 2*

1. **d.** (p. 49)

2. **b.** (p. 50)

3. **c.** (p. 51)

4. **a.** (p. 52)

5. **a.** (p. 53)

6. **a.** Since your friend's mother has blue eyes and blue is recessive, you know her genotype; she has two blue-eye alleles. Since your friend received one of her genes for eye color from her mother, she must have one blue-eye allele. Since she's brown-eyed, the other allele must be a dominant brown-eye allele from her father. (p. 54)

7. **c.** (p. 54)

8. **d.** The original purebred round-seed peas had only round-seed alleles to contribute to offspring, whereas purebred wrinkled-seed peas had only wrinkled-seed alleles. In the $F_1$ generation, all peas have one round-seed allele and one wrinkled-seed allele. Because the $F_1$ generation all had round seeds, we know that round-seed alleles are dominant. When $F_1$ peas are bred with one another, one-fourth of the peas will have two wrinkled-seed alleles, one-fourth will have two round-seed alleles, and the remaining peas will have one of each type of allele. But because round-seed alleles are dominant, all but the one-fourth with two wrinkled-seed alleles will be round-seeded. (p. 55)

9. **a.** (p. 57)

10. **a.** Sex-linked disorders are more common in men because a recessive disease-producing gene on the X chromosome cannot be counteracted by a corresponding gene (the man does not have a second X chromosome to carry such a gene). However, the disease can occur in women if they receive the recessive gene from both parents. It is statistically much less likely that a female will get two such genes than that a male will get just one. (p. 59)

11. **d.** (p. 62)

12. **b.** (pp. 60–61)

13. **b.** It is critical to remember that heritability is about the variability of some characteristic in a group, not the characteristics that a particular individual possesses. (p. 62)

14. **a.** (pp. 67–68)

15. **b.** (p. 72)

16. Genes are specific portions of a DNA molecule. Each gene controls the making of a specific type of protein. Different types of proteins result from different sequences of amino acids and that order is dictated by the gene. An individual's particular anatomy and physiology are determined by the proteins that the genes dictate. It is only through the characteristics of the person's anatomy and physiology that behavior can be affected. For example, a person with a particular anatomy and physiology may consequently have sharper vision, poorer hand-eye coordination, or a greater need for sleep. (p. 50)

17. PKU stands for phenylketonuria, a genetic disorder produced by a single recessive gene. A person with PKU lacks an enzyme for handling phenylalanine, an amino acid found in milk and other protein foods. Without the enzyme, phenylalanine is turned into a toxic acid that severely damages the brain. But the disease can be treated environmentally—specifically, through diet. If the person does not take in phenylalanine, the acid is not produced and the brain is not damaged. Keeping phenylalanine out of the diet is especially important in infancy since brain development is critical then. It is also important when a woman with PKU is pregnant. (p. 58)

# CHAPTER 4 THE ADAPTIVENESS OF BEHAVIOR I: EVOLUTION

*Read the introduction below before you read the chapter in the text.*

Chapter 4, which focuses on evolutionary adaptation and examines behavior in the light of evolutionary principles, is the first of a two-chapter sequence on adaptation, or accommodation to changed life circumstances. Evolution is just one level on which adaptation occurs, but it undelies all other forms of adaptation because it determines the biological machinery enabling such adaptation. Learning, another form of adaptation that psychologists study, will be considered in Chapter 5.

The mechanism by which evolutionary adaptation takes place is natural selection, the label Charles Darwin gave to selective breeding in nature. Current evolutionary thinking combines Darwin's critical insights with a modern understanding of genetics, and recognizes that both environmental change and genetic variability contribute to evolution. It is important to remember that evolution does *not* involve foresight, since many common misconceptions about evolution stem from this erroneous assumption.

Because the mechanisms of behavior evolve in the context of natural environments, ethologists prefer to examine behavior in its natural context and attempt to understand it from an evolutionary perspective. Ethology is the study of species-specific behaviors, behaviors so characteristic of a species that they can help to identify it. Ethologists have found that, in some species, relatively fixed patterns of behavior occur in response to particular stimuli. In other species, especially humans and other mammals, behaviors are much more flexible and less controlled by specific stimuli. Ethologists have used deprivation experiments to uncover the environmental conditions necessary for the development of certain behavior patterns in individual animals. To understand the evolutionary development and functions of behaviors, they utilize two types of comparisons—homology and analogy. Research into emotional expressions illustrates the evolutionary analysis of species-specific behaviors.

Sociobiologists attempt to explain the social behaviors of humans and other animals in evolutionary terms, focusing on the ultimate functions of such behaviors. One major focus of sociobiologists has been sexual behavior. Robert Trivers, for example, has suggested that the relative parental investments made by males and females of a given species will strongly affect the mating patterns of that species. Another focus of sociobiology has been aggression, both that involved in territorial defense and that involved in establishing social status within a living group. Sociobiologists have also offered hypotheses to explain helping behavior in animals. The most controversial ideas in sociobiology concern human behavior. Because of past abuses of evolutionary thinking, many people are skeptical or actively critical of work in this area. Sociobiologists have nevertheless identified certain tendencies in human behavior that may have arisen due to evolutionary factors. The chapter describes several fallacies in evolutionary thinking that we must avoid.

*LOOK over the table of contents for this chapter in your textbook before you continue with your study.*

*Notice that there are focus questions in the margins of the text for your use in studying the material. The following chart lists which study guide questions relate to which focus questions.*

| Focus Questions | Study Guide Questions |
| --- | --- |
| Basic Concepts: Natural Selection and Evolutionary Adaptation | |
| 1–5 | 1–11 |
| 6–8 | 12–14 |
| 9–11 | 15–17 |
| Ethology: The Study of Species-Specific Behavior Patterns | |
| 12–14 | 1–4 |
| 15–16 | 5–6 |
| 17–19 | 7–11 |
| 20–24 | 12–20 |

| Focus Questions | Study Guide Questions |
|---|---|
| Sociobiology: The Comparative Study of Animals' Social Systems | |
| 25–31 | 1–12 |
| 32–34 | 13–17 |
| 35 | 18–21 |
| 36 | 22–23 |
| 37–39 | 24 |

# The Integrated Study Workout

*Complete one section at a time.*

## Basic Concepts: Natural Selection and Evolutionary Adaptation (pages 81–88)

*CONSIDER these questions before you go on. They are designed to help you start thinking about this subject, not to test your knowledge.*

Did Darwin know about genes when he developed his theory of evolution?

Since evolution is supposed to involve adaptation, how does nature "know" what traits will be adaptive in future generations?

Can individuals inherit traits that their parents have acquired through experience?

How do different groups of people come to have different genetic profiles?

How fast does evolution take place?

*READ this section of your text lightly. Then go back and read thoroughly, completing the Workout as you proceed.*

The publication of Charles Darwin's *The Origin of Species* in 1859 was a landmark event. It has had a tremendous impact on the way we understand both biological and psychological issues. The subject of the book—evolution—determines the biological apparatus and processes on which all *psychological* processes are based.

1. What were two reasons for the book's strong impact?

2. Darwin described two kinds of selection that could shape the genetic future: artificial selection and natural selection. Define both.

   a. artificial selection

   b. natural selection

Darwin developed his theory without knowing anything about genes. Mendel's work was not yet known in the scientific world.

3. What is the modern synthesis?

4. From the perspective of the modern synthesis, first state what it is that changes over generations in evolution and then rephrase the principle of natural selection.

Genetic variability and environmental change are both essential ingredients in evolutionary change.

5. What are the two primary sources of genetic variability?

6. What is a mutation? Is it likely to be helpful or harmful? How important are mutations as a source of genetic variation?

7. Can acquired characteristics provide a basis for evolution? Explain.

8. How does the case of London's peppered moths demonstrate the effect of environmental change on evolution?

9. Does the rate of evolutionary change depend at all on the degree to which genetic variability already exists? Explain.

People sometimes fall into intellectual traps in thinking about evolution. Several related misconceptions stem from the mistaken assumption that evolution involves foresight.

10. State three specific manifestations of this fundamental misunderstanding.

   a.

   b.

   c.

Psychologists are of course interested in the effects of evolution on behavior.

11. Briefly explain how the process of natural selection can affect behavior.

Evolution is one form of adaptation, but it is not the only form of adaptation that psychologists must consider in trying to understand behavior.

12. The term _____ means changing to suit new conditions.

13. Psychologists often consider three levels at which adaptation occurs: _____ , _____ , and _____ .

   a. Are the three levels independent of one another? Explain.

   b. Identify the function of adaptation at each level.

Psychologists and biologists who take an evolutionary perspective distinguish between two complementary kinds of explanations of behavior.

14. A(n) _____ explanation concerns the survival or reproductive value of the behavior. A(n) _____ explanation concerns the stimuli and physiological mechanisms involved in the behavior.

An explanation may be plausible, even elegant, and yet be incorrect. We must be careful to insist on scientific evidence in evaluating an explanation. We must also be careful to realize that not every characteristic requires an adaptational explanation.

15. Populations of a particular species living in different locations may differ genetically. These differences could be due to different selection criteria in the two locations, but could also be due to _____ factors. When the groups differ because of chance events, we say the differences are due to _____ . An important example is the _____ effect, in which one population was established by a group that just happened to carry with them some unusual genes. (Hint: To see how a given population difference can be explained in adaptational or nonadaptational terms, consider the case of schizophrenia in northern Sweden.)

16. A specific characteristic may evolve not for its own adaptational benefits, but as a mere _____ of an adaptive change. Darwin labeled such nonadaptive changes _____ . Gould explained the enlarged clitoris of the female hyena in this way.

17. Your brain is a product of evolution. Does everything you do with your brain have a direct adaptational explanation? Support your answer.

## Ethology: The Study of Species-Specific Behavior Patterns  (pages 89–103)

CONSIDER these questions before you go on. They are designed to help you start thinking about this subject, not to test your knowledge.

Are there certain behaviors that seem to mark a dog as "doggy" or a salmon as "salmony" or a person as "human"?

Since the evolution of behavior couldn't be videotaped or even recorded in writing, what data do scientists use to figure out how or why a particular behavior evolved?

Do facial expressions mean the same thing across different cultures or does each culture develop its own code?

Can we effectively hide what we are feeling or do our expressions automatically give us away?

READ this section of your text lightly. Then go back and read thoroughly, completing the Workout as you proceed.

Ethology originated in Europe in the 1930s. Ethologists observe animal behavior as it occurs in natural settings, and attempt to understand that behavior in its evolutionary context.

1. Behavior patterns so characteristic of a species that they help to identify the species, such as dam-building in beavers or language in humans, are called _____ behaviors. In the case of the insects, fish, and birds studied by early ethologists, specific environmental stimuli may reliably produce the same response in all members of the species. The stimulus that can elicit such a response is called a _____ and the response is called a _____ . Such responses are governed by mechanisms provided through _____ and are essentially unchanged by learning.

2. Tinbergen uncovered several specific sign stimuli in studying the stickleback.

   a. What is the sign stimulus for attack in the male stickleback? How did Tinbergen discover the sign stimulus?

   b. What is the sign stimulus for the zigzag dance? How did Tinbergen discover the sign stimulus?

3. In what way did the ethologists' perspective on species-specific behavior change as they began to study mammals, especially humans and other primates?

4. The text points out that species-specific behavior must be treated as a relative concept, not an absolute one. Explain.

A major interest of ethologists has been the environmental conditions necessary for the development of species-specific behavior in a given individual's lifetime. The deprivation experiment has often been used to investigate this issue.

5. Answer the following questions about deprivation experiments.

   a. Explain the logic behind this type of experiment.

   b. What did Irenäus Eibl-Eibesfeldt find in the case of fighting in rats?

   c. What did Peter Marler find in the case of the white-crowned sparrow's song?

Stephen Emlen performed a series of ingenious and systematic experiments to learn about the navigation of the indigo bunting, a species that, like most songbirds, migrates at night. As is often true in fruitful scientific research, each stage of Emlen's detective work uncovered new knowledge and also provided a new question.

6. Trace the path of questions and answers that Emlen followed to his ultimate conclusion. Be sure you are clear about the question being investigated, the method, the answer, and the new question generated at each stage in the process. (See Figure 4.5 on text page 93.)

Ethologists cannot uncover the evolutionary course of behavior the way other scientists can uncover the evolutionary course of anatomy. Behavior leaves no fossil record, after all. An approach that is available to the ethologist is to systematically compare behaviors in living species.

7. Ethologists distinguish two classes of similarities between species. (See Figures 4.6 and 4.7 on text page 94.)

   a. A(n) _____ is any similarity between species that exists because of convergent evolution.

   b. A(n) _____ is any similarity between species that exists because of their common ancestry.

   c. _____ has taken place when different species independently evolve a common characteristic because they have similar habitats or lifestyles.

8. In practice, how can ethologists distinguish between similarities based on homology and those based on analogy?

9. What kinds of questions can each type of similarity help us to answer?

   a. analogies

b. homologies

10. How did Darwin use comparison by homology to infer the evolution of hive-building in bees?

11. What is a vestigial characteristic? How can homology help us to understand a vestigial characteristic such as the human infant's grasp reflex? Can motivations be vestigial in nature?

Verbal communication is specific to humans, but nonverbal communication takes place in many species. Darwin gave considerable attention to an evolutionary analysis of nonverbal communication.

12. Try to think of some specific examples of animal or human behaviors that could be considered nonverbal communication.

13. Still valued today are Darwin's three principles regarding the evolutionary development of nonverbal signals.

a. According to the principle of
_____ , some signals originally served a noncommunicative purpose.

b. The principle of _____
applies when a species adopts an opposite posture or movement to communicate the opposite meaning of the original posture or movement.

c. The principle of _____
refers to signals that arise from involuntary autonomic responses that accompany physiological arousal.

Good science rests on thorough and accurate observation. Such observation has paid substantial rewards in the study of facial expressions.

14. What kind of atlas did Paul Ekman and Wallace Friesen produce and how did they do it? (See Figure 4.12 on text page 99.)

15. Why do we often express emotions in terms of blends? How is a blend most often expressed? (See Figures 4.13 and 4.14 on text page 100.)

One area of enduring interest in the study of facial expressions has been their universality.

16. State Darwin's conclusions regarding facial expressions. What was wrong with his evidence on this issue?

17. How have modern researchers nevertheless confirmed Darwin's conclusions?

18. Can a universal expression such as the eyebrow flash be modified by learning? Support your answer.

Homologies have been useful in understanding the evolution of smiling and laughing.

19. Humans produce two kinds of smiles:
_____ and
_____ .

20. How do primate homologies suggest that the two kinds of smiles have separate evolutionary origins?

### Sociobiology: The Comparative Study of Animals' Social Systems   (pages 104–117)

> CONSIDER these questions before you go on. They are designed to help you start thinking about this subject, not to test your knowledge.

Why do some species have long-term male-female sexual relationships, whereas others do not?

Do nonhuman animals avoid incest?

Why do songbirds sing?

Does fighting between animals of the same species make sense in evolutionary terms? Wouldn't it be costly to the species?

Can human behavior be reasonably explained in evolutionary terms?

Are there some identifiable errors to watch out for in evolutionary arguments?

> READ this section of your text lightly. Then go back and read thoroughly, completing the Workout as you proceed.

In most species, especially very social species like ants, chimpanzees, and humans, a comprehensive understanding of behavior requires us to consider behavior in its social context.

1. Sociobiology is the study of _____ in animals.

2. An approach often used in sociobiology is comparison by analogy. Briefly describe this approach.

3. Patterns of mating have been a major area of study in sociobiology. One way species differ is in the number of mating partners an individual has over a given period, such as a breeding season. In _____ , one male mates with more than one female. In _____ , one female mates with more than one male. In _____ , a male and female mate only with one another. And in _____ , a group of males and females mate with one another.

Robert Trivers has proposed the concept of parental investment, which he has related to various patterns of courtship and mating behavior.

4. Define parental investment.

5. What general principle relates parental investment to courtship and mating patterns in Trivers's theory?

6. Answer the following questions about polygyny, the most common mating system in mammals.

   According to Trivers, why does high female parental investment lead to:

   a. polygyny?

   b. the large size of males?

   c. high selectivity in the female's choice of a mate?

7. Answer the following questions regarding polyandry, the most common mating system in nonmammalian species.

   a. Why does polyandry make sense for egg-laying species?

   b. How do sex differences in pipefish illustrate Trivers's notion that polyandry is related to high male and low female parental investment?

8. Answer the following questions regarding monogamy.

   a. What conditions should lead to equal parental investment and thus monogamy?

   b. In what kinds of species is monogamy common?

   c. Sarah Hrdy argues that in some species females force a shift from polygyny to monogamy. How and why is this shift accomplished?

   d. How might a certain amount of promiscuity be to the evolutionary advantage of a basically monogamous male? a basically monogamous female?

9. Answer the following questions regarding polygynandry.

   a. How might polygynandry help to promote group living in chimpanzees?

   b. What is a consortship?

Incest, mating between close genetic relatives (such as parent-child or brother-sister), is avoided in most species.

10. Why and how would evolution tend to favor incest avoidance?

11. Identify the two general classes of incest-avoidance mechanisms that are common in various animal species.

    a.

    b.

12. What is the strange female effect?

Sociobiologists have also given a great deal of attention to the subject of aggression.

13. How do ethologists and sociobiologists define aggression?

An important form of aggression is territorial aggression.

14. Why do animals engage in territorial aggression?

15. Note two means by which animal species may accomplish territorial defenses without actual physical battle.

    a.

    b.

Another significant use of aggression is the establishment and maintenance of social status within a colony.

16. How and why are submissive signals used to limit aggression?

17. Another important means of avoiding or limiting physical fighting involves ranking individuals in a group from highest to lowest; this is called a

    _____ .

    a. How does this system limit physical aggression?

    b. Using chimpanzees as an example, explain how the female dominance hierarchy can affect the male hierarchy.

Animals of a species may fight with one another even to the point of injury or death. But they may also help one another. Help sometimes takes the form of cooperation; at other times it appears to be altruistic.

18. Correctly identify each of the following patterns.

    a. _____ occurs when an individual helps another at the expense of its own survival or reproductive capacity.

    b. _____ is any behavior that increases the survival or reproductive capacity of another individual.

    c. _____ involves an individual helping another while at the same time helping itself.

19. How does kin selection theory explain the occurrence of altruistic behavior?

20. How does reciprocity theory explain the occurrence of altruistic behavior?

21. In what sense are both theories attempting to redefine altruistic behavior as not really altruistic?

The most provocative and controversial area for sociobiological thinking has been human social behavior.

22. What historical distortions of evolutionary thinking have prompted many people to be especially cautious about human sociobiology?

23. In considering human sociobiology, we must be aware of certain fallacies that can lead to distorted thinking.

    a. The _____ involves the view that genes control behavior in a way that cannot be modified by an individual's environment.

    b. The _____ is the position that whatever is "natural" is morally right.

    c. The _____ involves picking and choosing from among many species only those that support a particular viewpoint.

Cautions aside, sociobiologists have produced quite interesting hypotheses regarding human behavior. In general, the aim of sociobiology as applied to humans is to explain hereditary biases or tendencies in behavior. Of course, we must keep in mind that individual differences exist and that human behavior is highly modifiable through learning.

24. State five sociobiological hypotheses about human behavior. For each, briefly note any empirical support for the hypothesis and the possible evolutionary reasons for the tendency described.

    a.

    b.

    c.

    d.

    e.

> Be sure to READ the Concluding Thoughts at the end of the chapter. Note important points in your Workout. Then consolidate your learning by answering the focus questions in the margins of the text.

> After you have studied the chapter thoroughly, CHECK your understanding with the self-test that follows.

# Self-Test 1

*Multiple-Choice Questions*

1. In the process called *natural selection*:
   a. the breeding of certain domestic animals is controlled in order to produce desirable traits in future generations.
   b. inherited traits helpful in overcoming barriers to reproduction are more likely to be passed down to offspring.
   c. genes that will be helpful in suiting offspring to future environments are selected for.
   d. nature "selects" the traits of the next generation by way of a random shuffle of genes.

2. Is behavior affected by evolution?
   a. No, behavior cannot be affected by evolution because there are no genes for behavior.
   b. No, evolution cannot affect behavior, because behavior is totally a product of learning and culture.
   c. Yes, genes directly control behavior and evolution directly affects the genes that control behavior.
   d. Yes, behavior is affected by evolution because evolution shapes the biological mechanisms that produce behavior.

3. Biological evolution, learning, and cultural evolution are all forms of:
   a. goal-directed progress.
   b. adaptation.
   c. random change over time.
   d. natural selection.

4. If chance factors cause the gene pools in two populations of a species to differ, we refer to the situation as:
   a. genetic drift.    c. artificial selection.
   b. genetic deviance.    d. proximate change.

5. What are *correlates of structure*?
   a. two or more adaptive changes that occur together
   b. behaviors that are directly related to anatomical structures
   c. nonadaptive side effects of adaptive changes
   d. homologies

6. Suppose members of a particular species of geese exhibit an unlearned and very reliable series of movements to retrieve an egg that has rolled out of the nest. This behavior would be an example of a(n):
   a. sign stimulus.
   b. vestigial behavior.
   c. altruistic behavior.
   d. fixed action pattern.

7. Deprivation experiments are designed to answer ethological questions about:
   a. whether a particular behavior is species-specific.
   b. the sign stimulus for a particular behavior.
   c. the evolutionary course of a particular behavior.
   d. the environmental conditions needed for an individual to develop a species-specific behavior.

8. Stephen Emlen found that if caged indigo buntings are exposed to natural seasonal changes and have a view of the night sky, they will:
   a. make random movements to escape.
   b. direct their escape movements north in spring and south in the fall.
   c. make no attempt to escape their cages.
   d. memorize the entire pattern visible to them.

9. Similarities between species that are due to convergent evolution are called:
   a. analogies.
   b. homologies.
   c. analogies in mammals and homologies in nonmammalian species.
   d. blends.

10. The ability of premature human infants to support their weight with the grasp reflex is probably an example of:
    a. the inheritance of acquired characteristics.
    b. a vestigial behavior.
    c. a correlate of structure.
    d. ritualization.

11. Darwin suggested that many nonverbal communicative signals (e.g., threat displays) evolved from behaviors that served noncommunicative functions (e.g., fighting). This is called the principle of:
    a. antithesis.
    b. autonomic responses.
    c. ritualization.
    d. reduction.

12. Which of the following statements is true of research into the universality of certain human facial expressions?
    a. Darwin's early evidence in favor of universality has been contradicted by more recent evidence.
    b. Darwin's early study was criticized on methodological grounds, but his conclusion that certain facial expressions are universal was later supported by strong research evidence.
    c. Darwin's belief that there are no universal facial expressions has received widespread support from more recent cross-cultural studies.
    d. The evidence on this subject is so contradictory that the question is still considered unanswered.

13. The silent bared-teeth display in primates is:
    a. related to human laughter and smiles of happiness.
    b. a signal of threatened aggression.
    c. a kind of greeting between a more dominant and a more submissive animal.
    d. used only by the most dominant animals in a colony.

14. According to Robert Trivers, polygyny is related to _____ parental investment.
    a. high female/low male
    b. low female/high male
    c. equal male and female
    d. no particular pattern of

15. Kin selection theory suggests that an animal risking itself for others:
    a. is truly altruistic because the animal has nothing to gain for its act of unselfishness.
    b. may lose its own life but save close relatives that carry the gene promoting this "altruistic" behavior.
    c. is simply engaging in cooperative behavior that will tend to be repaid by its kin.
    d. is not meaningful in evolutionary terms because such risk-taking behavior is merely a random occurrence.

## Essay Questions

16. Sociobiologists contend that certain behavioral tendencies in humans arise from our evolutionary history. Discuss two of these tendencies.

17. Are humans and other primates biologically predisposed to avoid incest? Provide evidence to support your answer. Is there any evolutionary advantage to an incest-avoidance mechanism?

*After you have assessed your understanding on the basis of Self-Test 1 and have tried to strengthen your preparation in any areas of weakness, GO ON to Self-Test 2.*

# Self-Test 2

## Multiple-Choice Questions

1. The modern synthesis combines:
   a. Darwin's notion of natural selection with modern principles of artificial selection.
   b. Darwin's notion of natural selection with a modern understanding of genetics.
   c. a modern understanding of genetics with sociobiology.
   d. sociobiology with the idea of inheritance of acquired characteristics.

2. Which of the following is true of mutations?
   a. Mutations have little effect on the course of evolution because they are so rare.
   b. Mutations are errors in the replication process; as such, they inevitably lead to harmful changes in the structure of DNA.
   c. Although mutations usually have harmful consequences, they are sometimes helpful.
   d. Mutations are the new collections of genes that result from the normal reshuffling of genes in sexual reproduction.

3. The case of the peppered moths living in and around London illustrates that:
   a. environmental pressures can lead to rapid evolutionary change if a species already has sufficient genetic variability.
   b. modern problems such as pollution can prevent the normal process of evolution from taking place.
   c. when environmental change is rapid, evolutionary change cannot keep pace and species may die out.
   d. evolution can have foresight.

4. Which of the following represents a question posed from a functionalist perspective?
   a. At what rate does evolution take place?
   b. Which species are most closely related to one another?
   c. What are the possible uses of the human voice?
   d. Why do dogs have such a keen sense of smell?

5. An *ultimate explanation* of behavior is an explanation of:
   a. the mechanism that actually produces the behavior.
   b. the immediate environmental conditions that bring on the behavior.
   c. the form a behavior will ultimately take upon further evolution.
   d. why a particular evolutionary development offered an adaptive advantage.

6. If we decide that two geographically separated populations of the same species differ because of a founder effect, we are essentially saying that their differences are *not* due to:
   a. genetic drift.
   b. chance factors.
   c. natural selection.
   d. the unusual genes carried by one group's original members.

7. Web-building would be considered a _____ in spiders.
   a. correlate of structure
   b. species-specific behavior
   c. product of biological preparedness
   d. vestigial characteristic

8. Birds, some insects, and some mammals can fly. Similarities among these groups are not due to common ancestry and would thus represent:
   a. homologies.
   b. analogies.
   c. vestigial behaviors.
   d. fixed action patterns.

9. The human taste for sugar, which may have several negative health consequences, can be understood as a:
   a. vestigial characteristic.
   b. correlate of structure.
   c. species-specific behavior.
   d. result of nutritional deprivation.

10. In the terminology of Paul Ekman and Wallace Friesen, a blend is:
    a. any facial expression that involves both the upper and lower portions of the face.
    b. a combination of two or more facial expressions representing a combination of emotions.
    c. a facial expression that can be observed in related species.
    d. an insincere or artificial emotional expression in which the individual combines isolated movements of various facial regions.

11. A species in which an individual female bonds with several males would be classified as:
    a. polygynandrous.    c. polygynous.
    b. polyandrous.       d. monogamous.

12. According to Sarah Hrdy, a shift from polygyny to monogamy in primates is often:
    a. resisted by females because polygyny is to their genetic advantage.
    b. forced by females because monogamy is to their genetic advantage.
    c. encouraged by males because monogamy reduces the need for competition over mates.
    d. forced by males because monogamy is to their genetic advantage.

13. The tendency for female chimpanzees to move to another colony at sexual maturity is a mechanism for reducing the likelihood of:
    a. incest.
    b. the strange female effect.
    c. promiscuity.
    d. artificial selection.

14. Which of the following is *not* a means of limiting fights between members of the same species?
    a. the tendency for animals to keep out of territories marked by others

b. the establishment of dominance hierarchies
c. the tendency for an intruder in another animal's territory to become less aggressive
d. the adoption of a polygynous mating system

15. When we assume that human genetic biases toward certain behaviors cannot be countered by learning or culture, we are falling prey to the _____ fallacy.
    a. deterministic
    b. reciprocity
    c. naturalistic
    d. analogical

## Essay Questions

16. Why is it important for a psychologist to be able to view human behavior from an evolutionary perspective?

17. Describe two common errors made in thinking about evolutionary adaptation.

# Answers

*Basic Concepts: Natural Selection and Evolutionary Adaptation*

12. adaptation
13. evolutionary; individual; cultural

14. ultimate; proximate

15. random (or chance); genetic drift; founder

16. side effect; correlates of structure

### Ethology: The Study of Species-Specific Behavior Patterns

1. species-specific; sign stimulus; fixed action pattern; heredity

7. a. analogy

   b. homology

   c. convergent evolution

13. a. ritualization

    b. antithesis

    c. autonomic responses

19. happy; nonhappy

### Sociobiology: The Comparative Study of Animals' Social Systems

1. social systems

3. polygyny; polyandry; monogamy; polygynandry

17. dominance hierarchy

18. a. altruism

    b. helping

    c. cooperation

23. a. deterministic fallacy

    b. naturalistic fallacy

    c. misleading use of analogies

### Self-Test 1

1. **b.** Remember that natural selection acts to produce offspring better suited to the current environment, not some future environment. Natural selection is driven by success or failure in that current environment. It cannot be affected by an unforeseen future. (p. 82)

2. **d.** (p. 84)

3. **b.** All are forms of adaptation. Adaptation does not involve progress toward some particular goal. It is not oriented toward a specified end. (p. 85)

4. **a.** (p. 87)

5. **c.** As Darwin pointed out, not all changes that come about through the process of evolution are themselves adaptive. (pp. 87–88)

6. **d.** (p. 89)

7. **d.** (p. 91)

8. **b.** (p. 92)

9. **a.** Convergent evolution refers to a situation in which similarities of environment or lifestyle lead to similar but independent evolutionary developments. The root of the similarity is not genetic relatedness. In this case, we have an analogy, not a homology. (p. 93)

10. **b.** It may help to remember that a vestige is a leftover trace of something from the past. (p. 96)

11. **c.** (p. 97)

12. **b.** (pp. 100–101)

13. **c.** (p. 103)

14. **a.** (p. 105)

15. **b.** Both kin selection and reciprocity theory try to reframe behavior that is apparently selfless as behavior that is in some sense selfish. Kin selection theory suggests that the gene promoting the "altruistic" act in an individual may be destroyed, but other copies of the same gene in the individual's kin will be saved as a result; in this case, it is the gene that is "selfish." In reciprocity theory, there is an expectation of the favor being returned at some future time. (p. 112)

16. Sociobiologists seek to find biases in human behavior that are understandable from an evolutionary perspective. One such bias is the tendency to live in communities. Whether humans live in smaller towns or larger cities, they tend to group together, with smaller groups, such as families, forming within the larger ones. Humans suffer loneliness when apart from human companionship and regard those who deliberately avoid such companionship as deviant. The tendency may have come about because humans were better able to preserve their safety, acquire food, rear children, and do other things that aid in survival of self and species as part of a group than alone.

Another tendency is toward nepotism, in which individuals help kin more than nonkin. In a number of societies, related individuals are more likely to share goods and land with one another than with nonkin. Kin tend to come to one another's aid more than nonkin, for example, taking in orphaned children and caring for them. Also, violence may be lower among related individuals than among unrelated individuals in similar living arrangements. The evolutionary explanation for this tendency would be similar to that offered by the kin selection theory of altruism. Individuals helping kin or sharing with kin are helping to perpetuate genes they share with those individuals. (Note: Other tendencies identified by sociobiologists and discussed in the text would work equally well in answer to this question.) (pp. 115–117)

17. In general, animals tend to recognize close relatives and avoid mating with them. Another important mechanism for avoiding incest is the migration of animals from the colony of origin to another colony at the time they reach sexual maturity. In humans, incest is condemned or otherwise frowned upon in all cultures that have been examined. Studies show that males and females tend to reject as a dating or a marriage partner those with whom they were reared. So, it seems to be the social identity of "sibling" rather than the biological identity of "sibling" that individuals reject; of course, these are usually one and the same. The evolutionary reasons for avoiding incest are clear. Close kin produce offspring with higher chances of genetic disorders due to the greater likelihood of two recessive genes for such disorders being inherited. (pp. 108–109, 117)

*Self-Test 2*

1. **b.** (p. 82)

2. **c.**   As the text states, mutation is ultimately the basis of all genetic variation, because it alone introduces truly new genetic information. (p. 82)

3. **a.** (p. 83)

4. **d.** (p. 85)

5. **d.** (p. 86)

6. **c.** (p. 87)

7. **b.** (p. 89)

8. **b.** (pp. 93–94)

9. **a.** (p. 96)

10. **b.** (p. 99)

11. **b.** (p. 104)

12. **b.**   Monogamy is to the advantage of the female to the extent that a male can help her to raise more, or more successful, offspring. (p. 107)

13. **a.** (p. 109)

14. **d.** (pp. 110–111)

15. **a.** (p. 113)

16. Psychologists need to examine the mind and behavior from any perspective that sheds light on them. Evolution has formed humans and animals in ways that allowed them to succeed in the environments they faced. What we see now in behavior, especially human behavior, is determined in part by learning and cultural factors, but is also greatly affected by the species' evolutionary history. Natural selection has exerted a tremendous influence on what we have become. Our tendencies toward monogamy and polygyny, for example, may be partially explained in sociocultural terms. But trying to understand how certain mating strategies might have conferred evolutionary benefits and thus have persisted in human behavior can help broaden our perspective. The virtually universal tendency to avoid incest, even in cultures where the biological reasons for doing so are unknown, can also be better understood from an evolutionary viewpoint. Finally, an evolutionary perspective gives a holistic quality to our thinking. People and animals are not considered in isolation but rather in relation to the natural environment and in relation to one another. (pp. 115–117)

17. One of the most common errors people make in thinking about evolutionary adaptation is to assume it involves foresight. Natural selection operates on the basis of the current environment, not on the basis of some future environment. Selection comes about only because individuals with genes helpful in overcoming obstacles to reproduction pass those genes on, whereas individuals with unhelpful or harmful genes will tend not to pass them on since they will have fewer or no offspring. Future environments can't sort individuals into these two categories—those who successfully reproduce and those who don't. Only the present environment can. This "foresight" error in thinking about evolution can take several forms.

A second common error is the assumption that every trait has evolved for its adaptive value. Random factors can affect the direction in which a particular population evolves, as in genetic drift. Also, some traits evolve as nonadaptive side effects of adaptive changes. Finally, some structures that evolved for particular adaptive reasons can then be used for other nonadaptive purposes. For example, there is nothing particularly adaptive about solving crossword puzzles. The human brain can be used for that purpose but it certainly did not evolve for that purpose. (pp. 84, 86–88)

# CHAPTER 5   THE ADAPTIVENESS OF BEHAVIOR II: LEARNING

*Read the introduction below before you read the chapter in the text.*

Learning involves adaptation to the environment that occurs within an individual's lifetime. It is a set of processes through which experience can have a relatively long-lasting effect on an individual's behavior. As a central topic in psychology with relevance to many different subfields, learning has been much studied and much debated over the course of psychology's history. Three primary perspectives—behavioral, cognitive, and ecological—combine to give us a fuller view of learning and deeper insights into what it is, how it takes place, and what factors affect it.

The behavioral perspective is noted for characterizing learning purely in terms of observable stimuli and responses. Early behaviorists such as John B. Watson and B. F. Skinner insisted that what takes place inside the learner is irrelevant to scientific psychology because it cannot be observed and thus cannot be investigated scientifically. One category of learning that has been intensively studied by behaviorists is classical conditioning, which involves the learning of reflexes. Ivan Pavlov discovered classical conditioning as a by-product of his research on digestive processes. He then switched his focus to this type of learning, analyzing the process through which it occurs and studying various phenomena of classical conditioning, such as extinction, spontaneous recovery, generalization, discrimination, and higher-order conditioning. The chapter discusses conditioned emotional reactions and drug reactions in illustrating the practical significance of classical conditioning.

Unlike classical conditioning, which focuses on reflexive behavior, operant conditioning involves taking certain actions to produce certain consequences: We study to get good grades, we buy food to alleviate hunger, we work for money, and so on. The most fundamental idea in operant conditioning is the law of effect, which essentially states that the probability of our performing a given behavior depends on the effects it has had in previous experience. B. F. Skinner was the best-known investigator in this area and in fact coined the term *operant conditioning*. The basic concepts in operant conditioning, as explained in the text, are reinforcers, discriminative stimuli, shaping, extinction, schedules of partial reinforcement, and punishment. Operant conditioning has important practical applications, including behavior therapy and biofeedback training.

Advocates of the cognitive perspective contend that the very thing behaviorists would leave out—those unseen and mysterious processes inside the learner—are the things one must study to really understand learning. The essential point of the cognitive theorist is that learning involves information that is meaningful to the learner. It causes the learner to expect or predict certain things to happen under certain circumstances. The chapter explains how classical and operant conditioning can be understood from this perspective and presents evidence to support the cognitive view. The cognitive perspective has also been applied to place learning, with the work of Edward Tolman being especially prominent. Tolman showed that animals learning their way around mazes are actually forming cognitive maps—mental representations of spatial layouts—an extremely radical view given the traditional behaviorism that prevailed at the time. Another kind of learning that fits well with the cognitive viewpoint is learning based on watching what others do. Both animals and people are capable of such observational learning.

The ecological perspective, which emphasizes that learning has been developed through evolution to better enable animals to survive in their natural environment, makes sense of certain findings that are otherwise puzzling from the behavioral or cognitive perspective. For example, the ecological perspective helps to explain special cases of learning involving food aversion and food preference. It also helps us to understand why some stimuli work better than others in experiments that attempt to condition fear, what happens when baby birds become imprinted, how salmon find their way to their breeding grounds, and more.

*Look over the table of contents for this chapter in your textbook before you continue with your study.*

*Notice that there are focus questions in the margins of the text for your use in studying the material. The following chart lists which study guide questions relate to which focus questions.*

| Focus Questions | Study Guide Questions |
|---|---|
| The Behavioral Perspective: Acquiring New Responses to and for Stimuli | |
| 1 | 1–4 |
| 2–4 | 5–20 |
| 5–11 | 21–31 |
| 12–15 | 1–10 |
| 16–23 | 11–30 |
| The Cognitive Perspective: Acquiring Information About the World | |
| 24–31 | 1–14 |
| 32 | 15–16 |
| 33–34 | 17–20 |
| The Ecological Perspective: Filling the Blanks in Species-Specific Behavior Patterns | |
| 35–40 | 1–7 |
| 41–43 | 8–10 |

# The Integrated Study Workout

*Complete one section at a time.*

## The Behavioral Perspective: Classical Conditioning   (pages 121–130)

*CONSIDER these questions before you go on. They are designed to help you start thinking about this subject, not to test your knowledge.*

Can an emotional response like fear be learned? Can it be unlearned?

What are some examples of classical conditioning in everyday life?

Does classical conditioning have any practical applications?

*READ this section of your text lightly. Then go back and read thoroughly, completing the Workout as you proceed.*

Learning lies at the heart of psychology. Behavioral psychology, cognitive psychology, and developmental psychology, for example, deal with it directly. But there is hardly an area that does not need to consider the matter of learning. The social psychologist, the personality theorist, and the clinical psychologist are all dealing with individuals who bring a history of learning to current situations.

1. Define learning.

2. Indicate, by circling yes or no, whether the individual's behavior in each case is due to learning.

   Is it due to learning?

   Yes No **a.** A new employee in the customer service department watches videotapes of employees handling difficult customers effectively, then handles her first grouch with aplomb by using the same techniques.

   Yes No **b.** A toddler touches a hot stove, then immediately withdraws his hand and starts crying.

   Yes No **c.** A student passes a bakery on the way to class one morning and finds that the sight of the fresh bread literally makes her mouth water.

   Yes No **d.** A child receives warm applause and praise after singing for dinner guests, then volunteers to sing again on a similar occasion.

Behaviorism is an approach within psychology that has been important in several ways. It has helped to establish psychology as an objective, scientific endeavor, and it has taught us a great deal about learning.

3. What are the major characteristics and goals of behaviorism?

4. The terms below label two forms of learning that have been intensively studied by behaviorists. Define each.

   a. classical conditioning

   b. operant conditioning

Behaviorists have spent decades studying classical conditioning—and with considerable success. They have discovered basic principles that underlie this type of learning and have developed some interesting and useful applications of those principles. In order to understand classical conditioning, you will need to learn some essential terminology—beginning with words such as *reflex*. Classical conditioning concerns the learning of reflexes.

5. Define reflex.

6. a. A _____ is a particular, well-defined event in the environment.

   b. A particular, well-defined bit of behavior is a

   _____ .

7. Give three examples of a stimulus and three examples of a response.

8. Why is it important to note that reflexes are mediated by the nervous system?

9. A decline in the magnitude of a reflexive response when the stimulus is repeated several times in succession is called _____ , which _____ (is/is not) a form of learning.

Ivan Pavlov, a Russian physiologist, is a key figure in classical conditioning. Even before he discovered classical conditioning, he was well-known for his staunch devotion to scientific rigor and for his research on digestive reflexes.

10. How did Pavlov come to discover classical conditioning?

The phenomenon that was at first only a nuisance soon attracted Pavlov's scientific eye. He began to analyze classical conditioning through a number of carefully controlled experiments. In his early experiments, he broke classical conditioning down into its elementary parts and gave them descriptive names. (See Figure 5.2 on text page 124 for help in answering the following questions.)

11. Explain the concept of a conditioned reflex. Why is the term *conditioned* used?

12. What is a conditioned stimulus? a conditioned response?

13. What is an unconditioned stimulus? an unconditioned response?

14. Identify the following aspects of Pavlov's classic experiment, in which a dog learned to salivate in response to a bell.

    a.  The conditioned reflex involved was

    _____ .

    b.  The unconditioned stimulus was

    _____ .

    c.  The unconditioned response was

    _____ .

    d.  The conditioned stimulus was the

    _____ .

    e.  The conditioned response was

    _____ .

15. Trace the course of classical conditioning by answering the following questions about the same experiment you described in item 14 above.

    a.  How did the dog respond to the food prior to its pairing with the bell?

    b.  How did the dog respond to the bell prior to its pairing with the food?

    c.  How did the dog respond to the bell after it was paired with the food?

16. The nature of the conditioned response is determined by the nature of the _____ .

17. What kinds of stimuli can serve as conditioned stimuli? What kinds of responses can be conditioned?

Classical conditioning is not just a phenomenon that psychologists study in laboratories. It is something you encounter in everyday life.

18. Give two simple examples of classically conditioned responses that a person or animal might make under appropriate circumstances. (See the examples on text page 125 and try to think of analogous situations.)

    a.

    b.

Long before Pavlov, philosophers had contemplated the nature of learning. Aristotle had proposed a law of learning called the law of association by contiguity. There is a certain similarity between this law and Pavlov's law of conditioning—but there are also important differences.

19. State Aristotle's law of association by contiguity.

20. How was Pavlov's law of conditioning similar to Aristotle's law? How was it critically different?

Pavlov and his colleagues did hundreds of experiments on classical conditioning. In the course of that work, they uncovered a number of phenomena that are still considered of major importance. One issue—the permanence of conditioned reflexes—was of particular interest to Pavlov.

21. Answer the following questions concerning extinction.

    a.  What is extinction and under what conditions does it occur?

b.  Does extinction mean that conditioning has been totally erased? Explain.

c.  Can all conditioned responses be extinguished with equal ease? (Note: Students often make a leap from the term "extinction" to saying that a response has become "extinct." However, the proper terminology is to say a response has been extinguished.)

Pavlov's team also studied the complementary phenomena of generalization and discrimination.

22.  What is generalization? How does an organism's response change as the test stimulus becomes less and less similar to the actual conditioned stimulus?

23.  Describe the procedure of discrimination training. How does it affect an organism's tendency to generalize?

24.  How can classical conditioning and discrimination training be used to study an animal's sensory capabilities?

In classical conditioning, a learned reflex is established "on the back" of an existing reflex. Once that learned reflex exists, it can serve as the basis for learning yet another reflex.

25.  How is higher-order conditioning produced?

26.  How far can we go in higher-order conditioning, that is, in "stacking" one conditioned reflex upon another? What happens to the strength of the reflex as we move from first-order to second-order to third-order conditioning?

John B. Watson was a pioneer in the area of behaviorism and in the application of classical conditioning to human behavior.

27.  Describe the work of John B. Watson and Rosalie Rayner on conditioned fear.

28.  Give some other examples of conditioned emotional responses from everyday life. (Don't restrict yourself to examples involving fear.)

Some of the most fascinating and practical work in classical conditioning has involved conditioned drug reactions.

29.  Describe the results of Pavlov's experiment on conditioned drug reactions.

30.  What is a conditioned counteractive drug effect?

31. How can conditioned counteractive drug effects in morphine or heroin use help to explain some drug overdose cases?

Edward Thorndike was studying learning at about the same time as Pavlov, but was approaching it from a very different angle.

2. Describe Thorndike's basic experimental procedure.

## *The Behavioral Perspective: Operant Conditioning* (pages 130–141)

> *CONSIDER these questions before you go on. They are designed to help you start thinking about this subject, not to test your knowledge.*

How do the consequences of a behavior affect the chances of that behavior occurring again?

How would a behaviorist explain the fact that some people study hard and others never open a book? that some people are compulsively neat and others are hopelessly messy? that some people save their money and others spend as if there were no tomorrow?

Can we learn to control internal bodily processes such as heart rate or blood pressure?

How can we develop desirable habits in ourselves and eradicate bad ones?

Is punishment always an effective way to handle a child's misbehavior? Are there preferable alternatives?

> *READ this section of your text lightly. Then go back and read thoroughly, completing the Workout as you proceed.*

Throughout each day, we engage in behaviors that have consequences. We turn a key in a lock and are thus able to open a door. We give money to a clerk and leave a store happily bearing some new treasure. We smile at someone and receive a smile in return. We try to carry too many books at once and watch them tumble into a heap at our feet.

1. Why are the terms *instrumental* and *operant* used to describe certain responses?

3. In what ways did Thorndike's research reveal a different picture of learning than Pavlov's?

4. State Thorndike's *law of effect.*

B. F. Skinner did not originate the law of effect. But he spent many years studying this simple but powerful idea, elaborating on it, and presenting it both to other psychologists and to the general public. In fact, he gave us some of the tools we use to study this type of learning and much of the language we use to talk about it.

5. Describe a Skinner box.

6. *Operant conditioning* is a term coined by Skinner. You have already defined operant conditioning in item 4b. on page 57, but it would be a good idea to look back at that definition now and write it below.

7. Define *reinforcer.*

Skinner argued that operant conditioning determines virtually all of our behavior. It may not seem to us that we are being controlled by relationships between our responses and their consequences, but that doesn't mean it isn't so.

8. Can people be operantly conditioned without even realizing it? Briefly describe the work of Ralph Hefferline in answering this question.

Psychologists have taken the principles of learning discovered through research on operant conditioning and applied them to real-life problems such as smoking and headaches.

9. Briefly describe the work of a behavior therapist.

10. Explain how biofeedback training works and describe some of its uses.

Like classical conditioning, operant conditioning is understood and discussed in terms of specific concepts and terminology. (Note: In several instances, the same term, such as *extinction*, is used in both classical and operant conditioning. Make sure you understand how the term applies in each case.)

11. Describe the technique of shaping. Why is it sometimes necessary? Give an example to illustrate how shaping might be carried out.

12. The absence of reinforcement for a response and the resulting decline in response rate are both called _____ .

13. Every occurrence of a particular response is reinforced in _____ reinforcement.

In contrast, a response is only reinforced sometimes in _____ reinforcement.

Partial reinforcement is more precisely described in terms of four types of schedules, which are related to specific rates and patterns of responding in the individual being reinforced. The behavior produced by two of these schedules of reinforcement is especially resistant to extinction. Schedules are either fixed or variable and either ratio- or interval-based.

14. Write the name of the schedule that applies in each of the cases below. The response alternatives are fixed-ratio (FR), variable-ratio (VR), fixed-interval (FI), and variable-interval (VI). (See Figure 5.10 on text page 136.)

_____ a. A response must be emitted a certain average number of times before a reinforcer is given.

_____ b. A specific period of time following a reinforced response must elapse before another response is reinforced.

_____ c. This schedule produces a burst of steady-rate responding until a reinforcer is given, then, after a pause, another burst of responding, and so on.

_____ d. This schedule underlies many gambling systems and helps to explain gambling behavior.

_____ e. A specific number of responses must be made before reinforcement will be given (for example, a specific number of sweaters must be knitted before a worker is paid).

_____ f. This schedule produces a scalloping effect in response rate; that is, there is a pause after reinforcement, followed by an accelerating rate until reinforcement is available again.

_____ g. This schedule produces a slow, steady rate of responding.

_____ h. Reinforcement becomes available only after some average amount of time has elapsed, but the exact amount of time at any given point is unpredictable.

15. In general, a _____ (ratio/interval) schedule produces faster responding. In general, a _____ (fixed/variable) schedule produces steadier response rate

16. What is the partial-reinforcement effect? Which schedules produce the greatest resistance to extinction? Why?

In classical conditioning, the stimuli that are of interest to us precede the response. In fact, in this reflexive kind of responding the stimuli actually elicit the response. In operant conditioning, reinforcers are stimuli that follow the response. But operant behavior is also influenced by stimuli that precede it.

17. What is a discriminative stimulus?

18. How does operant behavior come under the control of a discriminative stimulus?

By definition, reinforcers are capable of affecting behavior, but reinforcers differ in that some are "born" and others are "made."

19. Describe chaining and mention one practical use of it.

20. Label the following reinforcers.

  _____ **a.**  a stimulus that has acquired its reinforcing value through previous training

  _____ **b.**  a stimulus that is innately reinforcing

  _____ **c.**  a secondary reinforcer, such as money, that can be saved and turned in later for another reinforcer

Reinforcement, which increases the chances that a particular response will occur, can be either positive or negative. It is important that you clearly understand what the terms *positive* and *negative* refer to (and what they don't refer to).

21. Define positive reinforcement. What is a positive reinforcer? Give two examples of positive reinforcement.

22. Define negative reinforcement. What is a negative reinforcer? Give two examples of negative reinforcement.

23. What do the terms *positive* and *negative* refer to in these cases? What do they not refer to?

Psychologists have often used a two-compartment apparatus to study escape and avoidance learning in animals. (See Figure 5.11 on text page 140.)

24. What constitutes an escape response? Is escape learning a case of positive or negative reinforcement?

25. How must test conditions be modified before the animal can learn to make an avoidance response?

In any discussion of how consequences affect future behavior, we must consider the case of punishment.

26. What is punishment? What is positive punishment? negative punishment?

27. Reinforcement and punishment are distinguished by their different effect on the

_____ .

28. Recall from item 23 that the terms *positive* and *negative* refer to arrival and removal, respectively, not to the direction of change in behavior. A stimulus that serves as a positive reinforcer, such as money, can become a _____ punisher. A stimulus that acts as a negative reinforcer, such as a queasy feeling in the stomach, can become a _____ punisher.

Skinner and others have suggested that we might do better to use positive reinforcement rather than punishment in modifying the behavior of others, especially children.

29. Why might positive reinforcement be preferable to punishment in correcting a child's behavior?

30. Is punishment ever a good idea? Explain.

## The Cognitive Perspective: Acquiring Information About the World (pages 142–151)

> CONSIDER these questions before you go on. They are designed to help you start thinking about this subject, not to test your knowledge.

What actually happens in the learner's mind when classical or operant conditioning takes place?

What would happen to the rate of operant responding if the magnitude of the reinforcer were suddenly increased or decreased?

When is it—and when is it not—a good idea to deliberately reinforce someone's behavior? For example, is it a good idea to give a child money for reading or for practicing the piano?

How do animals find their way around the environment? Do they learn a sequence of simple responses, such as "turn left," "turn left," "go through the door," "turn right"? Or do they learn something more sophisticated?

Can we learn just by watching someone else?

> READ this section of your text lightly. Then go back and read thoroughly, completing the Workout as you proceed.

The cognitive approach is now the dominant approach in psychology. It has roots in behaviorism, in part through those behaviorists who called themselves *S-O-R*, as opposed to *S-R*, theorists. That little *O* in *S-O-R* represented a very significant departure from strict behaviorism, because it stood for the events occurring inside the organism, which mediate the relationship between stimulus and response. The cognitive approach focuses on mental events that take place inside the organism during learning.

1. How have cognitive psychologists and *S-O-R* theorists before them defended a scientific interest in mental constructs? How can they study such unseen processes?

Cognitive theorists differ from traditional behaviorists in how they interpret conditioning. One important difference lies in how they view the role of the stimulus.

2. According to cognitive theorists, behaviorists ignore a critical aspect of the stimulus, which is its _____ .

3. In an experiment involving human subjects and linguistic stimuli, Gregory Razran showed that meaning is critical in classical conditioning. Briefly describe this experiment.

4. How did Richard Herrnstein show that meaning is critical in classical conditioning, even when pigeons are the subjects and the stimuli are pictorial? What alternative explanation of the data did he rule out?

A major question in learning theory concerns the nature of the connection that is forged through classical conditioning. One camp has proposed an *S-R* interpretation, the other an *S-S* interpretation.

5. What is learned, according to the *S-R* view of classical conditioning?

6. What is learned, according to the *S-S* view of classical conditioning?

7. Considerable research has been done to settle the *S-R* versus *S-S* dispute. Robert Rescorla's work is illustrative. Describe Rescorla's research procedure. Which position did his data support?

The *S-S* view of classical conditioning is inherently more cognitive than the *S-R* view, because it assumes that the learner has a mental representation of the unconditioned stimulus.

8. How do cognitive theorists describe this mental representation?

9. How does expectancy theory help to explain why the conditioned response is often different from the unconditioned response?

10. List three types of evidence supporting the notion that the learner uses the conditioned stimulus to predict the arrival of the unconditioned stimulus.

   a.

   b.

   c.

The cognitive viewpoint also provides insight into findings on operant conditioning.

11. What kind of mental representation or knowledge do cognitive theorists believe is involved in operant conditioning?

12. What are reward contrast effects? How do they support the cognitive view of operant conditioning?

13. How has Bitterman explained the fact that fish and reptiles do not show reward contrast effects?

14. Explain the overjustification effect. How does it fit in with the cognitive emphasis on meaning and means-end relationships?

Edward Tolman provided considerable early support for the cognitive position through his work on place learning.

15. Contrast Tolman's view of maze learning with that of traditional behaviorists of his time. Briefly explain how Tolman supported his view.

16. Does place learning occur without rewards? What is the evidence?

Classical and operant conditioning are not the only categories of learning that have been extensively studied. Another important type of learning, especially in humans, is observational learning.

17. Describe observational learning. Is this type of learning restricted to humans?

18. Albert Bandura has suggested that observational learning can serve two functions, those of:

_____

_____ .

19. Describe the results of Bandura's experiment with the Bobo doll.

20. The four interacting mental processes that Bandura believed must be taken into account in order to understand observational learning are

_____ , _____ ,

_____ , and

_____ .

*The Ecological Perspective: Filling the Blanks in Species-Specific Behavior Patterns*
(pages 151–157)

*CONSIDER these questions before you go on. They are designed to help you start thinking about this subject, not to test your knowledge.*

If nature were to build in certain kinds of specialized learning abilities, what types of activities might they concern?

How do animals know which foods are safe to eat and which are not?

What would happen if a baby were allowed to choose its own food?

How do baby ducks know whom to follow around?

How do salmon find their way back "home" to breed?

Does the maze-learning situation really tell us about place-learning behavior as it occurs in nature?

*READ this section of your text lightly. Then go back and read thoroughly, completing the Workout as you proceed.*

Both the behavioral and cognitive perspectives have worked to develop general principles of learning that apply across species and across situations.

1. How does the ecological perspective (also called the specific-process perspective) differ from the general-process perspective of behaviorists and cognitivists?

Finding food that is safe to eat is a significant undertaking for many species, especially omnivorous creatures such as rats and humans. The ecological perspective has helped to reveal some specific types of learning associated with this survival need.

2. How has food-aversion learning been demonstrated experimentally?

3. What characteristics distinguish this type of learning from traditional examples of classical conditioning?

4. Why do the special characteristics of food-aversion learning make sense in the context of a natural environment?

Animals have to find foods that are not only safe, but also nutritious. Apparently, learning is involved in food preference as well as food aversion.

5. How did Paul Rozin and James Kalat show that rats will choose the food containing a vitamin they need? How can the rats' behavior be explained?

6. Describe Clara Davis's findings when she allowed babies to choose their own diets. Why should we be cautious in interpreting her results?

7. What evidence suggests that social learning plays a part in food selection?

Nature seems to have equipped animals with other special learning abilities in addition to those involved in food selection.

8. Present evidence shows that some stimuli can become conditioned fear stimuli more easily than others. Why is this the case?

9. Describe imprinting. What is meant by a critical period? Are all stimuli equally likely choices for young birds to be imprinted on?

10. What are some examples of special learning abilities in place learning?

> Be sure to READ the Concluding Thoughts at the end of the chapter. Note important points in your Workout. Then consolidate your learning by answering the focus questions in the margins of the text.

> After you have studied the chapter thoroughly, CHECK your understanding with the self-test that follows.

# Self-Test 1

*Multiple-Choice Questions*

1. What term is defined as "the process or set of processes through which experience at one time can affect an individual's behavior at a future time"?
   a. behaviorism
   b. learning
   c. responses
   d. higher-order conditioning

2. Identification of specific learning mechanisms that have evolved to meet particular survival needs is the focus of the _____ perspective.
   a. operant conditioning        c. behavioral
   b. cognitive                   d. ecological

3. A specific, well-defined event in the environment is called a(n):
   a. reflex.          c. operant.
   b. stimulus.        d. response.

4. In classical conditioning, a(n) _____ comes to elicit a response only as a result of training.
   a. conditioned stimulus
   b. unconditioned stimulus
   c. unconditioned response
   d. discriminative stimulus

5. Spontaneous recovery is defined as the:
   a. equivalent of extinction.
   b. restoration of an extinguished response after further pairing of the conditioned stimulus with the unconditioned stimulus.
   c. restoration of an extinguished response after the passage of time.
   d. restoration of the individual to the state that existed prior to conditioning.

6. Once a conditioned reflex has been learned, it can be used as the basis for yet another conditioned reflex. This phenomenon is referred to as:
   a. higher-order conditioning.
   b. extinction.
   c. generalization.
   d. discrimination training.

7. We could best explain why someone might feel sleepy on returning to a room where he or she had taken sedatives in terms of:
   a. a conditioned drug reaction.
   b. observational learning.
   c. spontaneous recovery.
   d. imprinting.

8. The law of effect lies at the heart of the form of learning called:
   a. classical conditioning.
   b. habituation.
   c. operant conditioning.
   d. observational learning.

9. If reinforcement is based on the average number of responses produced (e.g., 10), with a different number of responses required on each occasion (e.g., 7, 11, 12), the learner is on a:
   a. fixed-interval schedule.
   b. fixed-ratio schedule.
   c. variable-interval schedule.
   d. variable-ratio schedule.

10. When the same stimulus serves as a secondary reinforcer for one behavior and as a discriminative stimulus for a subsequent behavior, we have an instance of:
    a. shaping.
    b. habituation.
    c. partial reinforcement.
    d. chaining.

11. If the arrival of a stimulus following a response increases the likelihood of that response recurring, the stimulus is a:
    a. discriminative stimulus.
    b. secondary reinforcer.
    c. positive reinforcer.
    d. negative reinforcer.

12. Classical conditioning generally _____ occur if the conditioned and unconditioned stimuli are presented simultaneously, a fact supporting _____ views.
    a. does; *S-S*         c. does not; *S-S*
    b. does; *S-R*         d. does not; *S-R*

13. The overjustification effect involves a change in the:
    a. amount of work that will be rewarded.
    b. meaning of a behavior and thus the likelihood of engaging in it.
    c. conditions under which a particular behavior will be rewarded.
    d. schedule of partial reinforcement, which results in greater resistance to extinction.

14. Rats deprived of the vitamin thiamine will:
    a. tend to eat all foods unselectively despite their nutritional deficiency.
    b. lose their ability to differentiate foods on the basis of taste and will thus fail to avoid poison.

c. come to prefer foods containing thiamine after sampling various foods.

d. consequently become incapable of learning operant responses.

15. Animals can more easily learn to:

   a. fear certain types of stimuli as compared to other types.

   b. avoid harmful foods if they become sick after eating them.

   c. choose the right foods if they observe an adult model doing so.

   d. do all of the above.

### Essay Questions

16. What is generalization in classical conditioning? How can a learner be taught not to generalize? How might the phenomenon of generalization have important implications for conditioned emotional reactions in human life?

17. Explain the difference between reinforcement and punishment, between positive and negative reinforcement, and between positive and negative punishment.

*After you have assessed your understanding on the basis of Self-Test 1 and have tried to strengthen your preparation in any areas of weakness, GO ON to Self-Test 2.*

# Self-Test 2

### Multiple-Choice Questions

1. You may find yourself salivating in response to a television commercial that shows a luscious dessert. This behavior would be explained by:

   a. classical conditioning.

   b. operant conditioning.

   c. habituation.

   d. discrimination training.

2. What kind of conditioning involves the learning of reflexes?

   a. habituation

   b. classical conditioning

   c. operant conditioning

   d. both classical and operant conditioning

3. A noise may startle you enough to make you jump. If it occurs several times, you will jump less and less each time. This is an instance of:

   a. a conditioned reflex.

   b. habituation.

   c. extinction.

   d. spontaneous recovery.

4. Aristotle proposed that learning results when we experience two events close together in space and time. This idea is called the:

   a. law of effect.

   b. principle of habituation.

   c. law of association by contiguity.

   d. principle of reflex action.

5. Stimuli similar to the conditioned stimulus are able to elicit the conditioned response in the phenomenon called:

   a. higher-order conditioning.

   b. habituation.

   c. generalization.

   d. discrimination.

6. A young man suffering from headaches is hooked up to a machine that presents a pleasant tone whenever he keeps the muscles in his forehead sufficiently relaxed. The man is undergoing:

   a. classical conditioning.

   b. biofeedback training.

   c. discrimination training.

   d. observational learning.

7. The technique in which successive approximations to the desired response are reinforced is:

   a. habituation.

   b. discrimination training.

c.  higher-order conditioning.
d.  shaping.

8.  Which schedule of partial reinforcement underlies many gambling systems and may help to explain compulsive gambling?
   a.  fixed-interval
   b.  fixed-ratio
   c.  variable-interval
   d.  variable-ratio

9.  Which of the following is true of a discriminative stimulus?
   a.  It elicits an operant response from an animal.
   b.  It serves as a cue that reinforcement is available for a particular response.
   c.  It tells an animal how long it must continue to respond before the next reinforcer will be delivered.
   d.  It is used to develop new responses in animals.

10. Sam has a habit of launching into long political tirades by saying, "Well, here's how I see it." As soon as she hears this, Betsy excuses herself. Betsy has learned a(n):
   a.  escape response.
   b.  avoidance response.
   c.  observational response.
   d.  response chain.

11. A stimulus that can serve as a positive reinforcer can:
   a.  also serve as a positive punisher.
   b.  also serve as a negative punisher.
   c.  also serve as a negative reinforcer.
   d.  only serve as a positive reinforcer.

12. Gregory Razran performed an experiment in which lemon juice was squirted into the mouths of college students just before a printed word was presented to them. He found that:
   a.  the students could not be conditioned to verbal stimuli.
   b.  the actual conditioned stimuli that elicited salivation were not the word meanings, but the physical appearance of the words.
   c.  students later generalized, salivating to the words that meant the same thing as the original words but not to sound-alike words.
   d.  students could not learn to salivate in response to words, though they could learn other reflexive responses.

13. One group of rats receives several food pellets for each response, while another group receives only one pellet for each response. When the first group is then treated like the second, they:
   a.  stop responding altogether.
   b.  continue to respond at a higher rate than the second group.
   c.  drop to a response rate equal to that of the second group.
   d.  drop to a response rate below that of the second group.

14. In an experiment on place learning, rats were placed in a maze with three routes to the goal box containing the reward. After training, they preferred the shortest of the routes, but would take the best alternative path if the preferred one were blocked at some point. This suggested that:
   a.  their knowledge of the maze consisted of sequences of specific motor responses.
   b.  their knowledge of the maze consisted of a mental representation of the maze's layout.
   c.  they were operating at the level of trial and error, much like cats in a puzzle box.
   d.  rats have an instinctive, unlearned ability to find their way to food.

15. A child who learns how to behave at a birthday party by seeing how other children behave is exhibiting:
   a.  observational learning.
   b.  classical conditioning.
   c.  instrumental conditioning.
   d.  biofeedback.

## Essay Questions

16. Edward Tolman claimed that operant conditioning involves the learning of means-end relationships. Explain Tolman's view and present evidence for or against it.

17. Interpret and present an argument for the following statement: Learning mechanisms are products of natural selection and as such are suited to help a species deal with biologically important matters.

# Answers

## The Behavioral Perspective: Classical Conditioning

2. **a.** yes, **b.** no, **c.** yes, **d.** yes

6. **a.**   stimulus

    **b.**   response

9. habituation; is

14. **a.**   salivating in response to a bell

    **b.**   food

    **c.**   salivation

    **d.**   bell

    **e.**   salivation

16. unconditioned stimulus

## The Behavioral Perspective: Operant Conditioning

12. extinction

13. continuous; partial

14. **a.** VR, **b.** FI, **c.** FR, **d.** VR, **e.** FR, **f.** FI, **g.** VI, **h.** VI

15. ratio; variable

20. **a.**   secondary reinforcer

    **b.**   primary reinforcer

    **c.**   token

27. response rate

28. negative; positive

## The Cognitive Perspective: Acquiring Information About the World

2. meaning

18. acquiring specific actions and learning general styles of behavior

20. attention; memory; motor control; motivation

### Self-Test 1

1. **b.** (p. 121)

2. **d.** (p. 121)

3. **b.** (p. 122)

4. **a.** (p. 124)

5. **c.** The conditioned response will also reappear if the conditioned stimulus is once again paired with the unconditioned stimulus, but spontaneous recovery refers specifically to the case in which the mere passage of time is sufficient to restore the extinguished response. (p. 126)

6. **a.** (p. 128)

7. **a.** The physical surroundings in which the drug is taken may act as a conditioned stimulus. (p. 129)

8. **c.** (p. 132)

9. **d.** (p. 136)

10. **d.** (p. 138)

11. **c.** (pp. 139–140)

12. **c.** Simultaneous conditioning, in which the conditioned and unconditioned stimuli occur together in time, is not an effective means of producing classical conditioning. From the cognitive perspective, the S-S theory of classical conditioning, this makes sense. If the two are simultaneous, the conditioned stimulus cannot produce an expectancy that the unconditioned stimulus will occur. (p. 145)

13. **b.** (p. 148)

14. **c.** Food preferences of this sort seem to be accomplished by consuming foods singly in order to isolate which ones lead to feeling healthier and which ones lead to feeling worse. (p. 153)

15. **d.** (pp. 152–155)

16. Generalization in classical conditioning is demonstrated when the learner produces a conditioned response to a stimulus other than the original conditioned stimulus. The strength of the subject's response to a new stimulus depends on its similarity to the actual conditioned stimulus: The closer it is to the original, the more the response will be like the usual conditioned response.

    A learner can be taught not to generalize through discrimination training. This procedure involves: (1) pairing the conditioned stimulus with the unconditioned stimulus in further trials; and (2) presenting the stimulus to which the learner generalized *without* the unconditioned stimulus. The learner eventually continues to respond to the conditioned stimulus and no longer generalizes to the other stimulus.

The phenomenon of generalization could be important in real-life conditioned emotional reactions in several ways. In fear learning, for example, we may find ourselves reacting fearfully to someone or something that is similar to someone or something that once affected us negatively. This could be useful, as when a man avoids not just the dark alley in which he was mugged, but other similarly dark and isolated places. It could be a problem, though. For example, a child who has one teacher who humiliates her when she has given an incorrect answer may generalize to teachers or situations she perceives to be similar. (pp. 127–129)

17. Reinforcement and punishment differ in terms of their effects on the likelihood of a behavior recurring. They not only differ in this regard; they are opposites. Reinforcement occurs when the consequences of a response increase the chances that the response will occur again, while punishment occurs when the consequences of a response decrease the chances that the response will occur again.

Both positive and negative reinforcement involve increasing the likelihood of a response through the consequences of that response. But in positive reinforcement, the consequence involves the *arrival* of some stimulus, such as praise or money or food. In negative reinforcement, the consequence involves the *removal* of some stimulus, such as shock or a headache or forced confinement.

Positive and negative punishment also both involve the same behavioral result—a decrease in the likelihood of the behavior. Positive punishment involves the *arrival* of some stimulus, such as shock or a headache or forced confinement, contingent on a behavior. Negative punishment involves the *removal* of a stimulus such as praise or money or food. (pp. 139–141)

*Self-Test 2*

1. **a.** (p. 122)
2. **b.** (p. 122)
3. **b.** (p. 123)
4. **c.** (p. 125)
5. **c.** (p. 127)
6. **b.** (p. 134)
7. **d.** (p. 135)

8. **d.** The gambler is being influenced by the unpredictability of the reinforcement schedule. In the past, reinforcement sometimes occurred after the gambler played just once or twice, other times only after extended playing. One never knows, thinks the gambler, when the next win is due. (p. 136)

9. **b.** A discriminative stimulus never elicits an operant behavior. Operant behaviors are freely emitted. The discriminative stimulus simply sets the occasion, letting the learner know that a specific response emitted now could be reinforced. (p. 138)

10. **b.** (p. 140)

11. **b.** A positive reinforcer is one for which the learner is willing to work. It is also presumably a stimulus whose removal would be punishing—hence, it is negative punisher. Remember that the terms positive and negative refer to presentation and removal, respectively. Reinforcer and punisher refer to consequences that, respectively, increase and decrease the behaviors they follow. (pp. 140–141)

12. **c.** Razran's results support the cognitive viewpoint because they show that what matters about the stimulus is its meaning. (pp. 142–143)

13. **d.** (p. 147)

14. **b.** Such a mental representation of the spatial layout is called a cognitive map. (p. 149)

15. **a.** (pp. 150–151)

16. As a cognitively oriented theorist, Edward Tolman was comfortable interpreting behavioral phenomena in terms of mental entities. He was suggesting that what takes place through operant conditioning is the acquisition of knowledge by the learner, specifically knowledge about what action should lead to what result under what circumstances. The learner can then use that knowledge to fit current needs or desires and current conditions.

Tolman's view found substantial support. In one experiment, for example, rats learned to lever-press for either water or food, then were deprived of water. When tested with no reinforcement available, the thirsty rats that had learned to expect water from lever presses performed this action much more than rats that had learned to expect dry food from the same action. Reward contrast effects provide another example suggesting that Tolman was right. Animals that have received a big reinforcer for an operant and are then switched to a small reinforcer don't respond as much as animals that received a small reinforcer all along. This makes sense if we assume that the animal had a certain conception of what ought to happen, but it doesn't make sense in strict *S-R* terms. (Note: The overjustification effect in humans also fits well with Tolman's view.) (pp. 146–148)

17. Natural selection operates under the pressure of the survival and reproductive needs of a particular species in a particular environment. It produces in each species tools for dealing with those needs in that environment. Learning mechanisms are examples of such tools. They are an inborn means of modifying behavior to suit the demands an organism faces in its lifetime.

    A number of different findings in research on learning make sense if we view them in this ecological perspective. For example, there are apparently innate tendencies in learning that affect which stimuli can become conditioned fear stimuli and which responses can be learned as avoidance responses. In an attempt to repeat the Watson and Rayner experiment using little Albert, an experimenter tried to condition fear to blocks and pieces of fabric rather than to a rat. It didn't work. One explanation is that we are biologically predisposed to fear some things (like rats) but not other things (like blocks).

    Research on food aversion provides another line of support for the ecological view. Food-aversion learning seems to be special—different in important ways from classical or operant conditioning. For example, the events that need to be linked through learning—the food and the subsequent illness—can be separated in time by a whole day. In classical and operant conditioning, on the other hand, the two events must occur close together in time if learning is to take place. (pp. 151–157)

# CHAPTER 6   THE NERVOUS SYSTEM

*Read the introduction below before you read the chapter in the text.*

The nervous system is the basis of all that we refer to as psychological—thoughts, feelings, moods, behaviors. The most fundamental structure of the nervous system is a single cell called a neuron. Some neurons bring sensory information to the brain, others carry commands from the brain to muscles and glands, and still others serve communication functions entirely within the brain and spinal cord. Although neurons play different roles and come in a variety of sizes and shapes, all can be described in terms of the same functional parts, including dendrites, axons, and axon terminals. A neuron's dendrites receive incoming information; its axon carries the information to other cells through axon terminals, which send a chemical messenger to other cells.

The nerves that connect the brain and spinal cord (the central nervous system) to sensory organs, muscles, and glands form the peripheral nervous system. In the peripheral nervous system, the sympathetic division (of the autonomic portion) mediates responses to stress and the parasympathetic division serves regenerative and growth-promoting functions. A bundle of axons of sensory neurons (which carry information to the central nervous system) or motor neurons (which carry commands to muscles and glands) make up a nerve.

In the central nervous system, the spinal cord functions as a conduit between the brain and many of the nerves in the peripheral nervous system. It is also responsible for mediating spinal reflexes, behaviors that can be triggered and carried through to completion without the help of the brain.

The brain controls all other behaviors. Beginning just above the spinal cord are the subcortical structures of the brain, such as the brainstem, cerebellum, thalamus, hypothalamus, and limbic system, each with particular functions. The cerebral cortex, the outermost and most massive part of the brain, is divided into two symmetrical hemispheres. The cortex is critical to high-level processes, such as language and decision making, as well as certain sensory and motor functions.

In many cases, the functions of the nervous system are organized hierarchically, with the most primitive, reflexive responses in the spinal cord at the lowest level and the most complex types of control in the cortex at the highest level. Movement control illustrates this hierarchical organization.

The neuron is different from other cells of the body in that it is capable of carrying signals. Those signals take the form of electrical impulses, or action potentials, which involve the movement of electrically charged particles across the cell's membrane. These movements result in changes in the electrical balance across the membrane, carrying the impulses down the axon to the axon terminal, where, through synaptic transmission, the neuron sends messages to other cells. In synaptic transmission, minute quantities of chemical messengers called neurotransmitters flow across a tiny gap between cells. Upon reaching the cell that is receiving information, neurotransmitter molecules bind to special receptor sites and in that fashion affect the electrical balance of the receiving cell. Synaptic connections are significantly modified by learning.

Besides the nervous system, the other major mode of communication within the body is the hormonal system. Hormones are chemical messengers that are released from endocrine glands and other organs and are delivered to various target tissues through the bloodstream. They produce a variety of effects, playing important roles in the development of anatomical differences between males and females and in the body's response to stressful situations, for example.

The hormonal system and the nervous system are intimately related. In many ways, the hormonal system is under the control of the brain. Also, some hormones are chemically identical to neurotransmitters.

Drugs differ from hormones in that they are not produced inside the body but are introduced from outside. Like hormones, drugs are carried by the blood and taken up in target tissues of the body. Also like hormones, drugs can affect synaptic transmission, but the brain protects itself from some such substances by the blood-brain barrier. The phenomena of drug tolerance and withdrawal symptoms help explain the effects of drugs on physiology and behavior.

> *LOOK over the table of contents for this chapter in your textbook before you continue with your study*

> *Notice that there are focus questions in the margins of the text for your use in studying the material. The following chart lists which study guide questions relate to which focus questions.*

| Focus Questions | Study Guide Questions |
|---|---|
| Functional Organization of the Nervous System | |
| 1–4 | 1–12 |
| 5–6 | 13–20 |
| 7 | 21–23 |
| 8 | 24–29 |
| 9–13 | 30–38 |
| 14–18 | 39–50 |
| 19–21 | 51–53 |
| 22–24 | 54–58 |
| How Neurons Work and Influence Each Other | |
| 25–28 | 1–13 |
| 29 | 14–17 |
| 30–32 | 18–22 |
| How Hormones and Drugs Interact with the Nervous System | |
| 33–37 | 1–10 |
| 38–40 | 11–24 |

# The Integrated Study Workout

> *Complete one section at a time.*

## *Functional Organization of the Nervous System*
(pages 163–182)

> *CONSIDER these questions before you go on. They are designed to help you start thinking about the subject, not to test your knowledge.*

What is a neuron? Is it the same as a nerve?

How do messages get from my feet or eyes or tongue to my brain? or from my brain to my fingers?

How does the nervous system make your heart pound when you are scared? or make you want to get something to eat?

What part or parts of the brain are involved when you feel anger or joy?

How does the nervous system manage complex movement such as that involved in walking or skating?

> *READ this section of your text lightly. Then go back and read thoroughly, competing the Workout as you proceed.*

Despite the brain's rather unassuming appearance, the Roman physician Galen recognized it to be the organ of thought, feeling, and behavioral control. This represented a major break from the position of earlier Greek thinkers, who credited the heart with these responsibilities. Students are often surprised to see that a psychology text includes a chapter on the brain (and the nervous system of which it is a part) because they expect that subject to be reserved for biologists. But if psychology is the science of mind and behavior, shouldn't we understand the organ that makes mind and behavior possible? Psychologists have answered "yes" to that question from the beginning, and the "yes" becomes increasingly insistent as new research uncovers more and more of the secrets of this amazing organ.

Let's begin with an overview of the nervous system.

1.  Describe briefly the four kinds of work the nervous system must perform.

    a.

    b.

    c.

    d.

2. The central nervous system consists of the
_____ and the
_____ . The peripheral nervous
system includes the _____ that
connect the central nervous system to the rest of
the body.

3. Distinguish between a neuron and a nerve.

In order to understand the way the nervous system
works, you must have a solid understanding of individual cells.

4. The basic units, the "building blocks," of the nervous system are called _____ .

5. For what two jobs are these cells specialized?

6. List and briefly describe three functional types of
neurons. (By functional type we mean a group of
neurons that are all designed to carry out the
same basic type of work. See Figure 6.2 on text
page 164.)

a.

b.

c.

7. Different neurons have many of the same functional parts in common. Label the diagram of a
neuron below. (See Figure 6.3 on text page 165.)

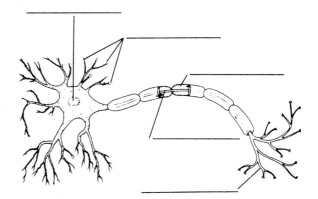

8. Each part of a neuron is specialized for some
function. Write the name of the part that performs each of the following functions.

_____ a. thin, branchlike extensions that
increase the surface area for
receiving incoming signals from
other neurons

_____ b. a small swelling that can release
a chemical substance onto anoth-
er cell, such as another neuron or
a muscle cell

_____ c. the widest part of the cell, which
contains the cell nucleus and
other structures that perform the
basic functions common to all
cells

_____ d. a thin, tubelike structure that carries electrical impulses to other
cells

_____ e. a fatty casing that wraps around
the axons of some neurons

9. Briefly compare interneurons to motor neurons in
terms of shape, size, location, and the type of cells
on which they synapse.

10. Briefly compare sensory neurons to motor neurons in terms of layout, nature of stimulation, and the location of the cells on which they synapse.

Actually, neurons are not the most numerous type of cell in the nervous system. That distinction belongs to another type of cell.

11. The most numerous type of cell in the nervous system is a _____ .

12. What are some functions of this type of cell?

The incredible capabilities of the nervous system depend on its complex organization. The nervous system is divided into the central and peripheral nervous systems; this division is a matter of both structural and functional organization. In learning about the nervous system's organization, try to keep in mind the main functions of each structure and try to relate each structure to others you've studied. We will begin by looking more closely at the peripheral nervous system, which consists of all of the body's nerves. (Refer back to Figure 6.3 on text page 165.) We can differentiate two categories of nerves. In all cases, the nerves exist in pairs, with one left and one right member.

13. Humans have _____ pairs of cranial nerves and _____ pairs of spinal nerves.

14. Distinguish between cranial and spinal nerves. Are these types of nerves exclusively sensory or motor? Explain.

The peripheral nervous system can be subdivided in terms of motor functions. The two subsystems affect different types of structures.

15. What is the skeletal system?

16. What is the autonomic system?

17. Point out an important functional difference between the skeletal and autonomic systems.

The autonomic portion of the peripheral nervous system can be further subdivided into two opposing systems.

18. What does the sympathetic division do?

19. What does the parasympathetic division do?

20. When you are conversing comfortably with a friend, the _____ division is probably predominating. When you are viewing the climax of a suspenseful movie, the _____ division is probably predominating.

The organization of the central nervous system with its billions of neurons and trillions of synapses is not nearly so straightforward as that of the peripheral nervous system. However, certain conceptual distinctions and organizational principles can help us to understand it.

21. Define these terms.

  a. tract

  b. nucleus

22. What is white matter? What is gray matter?

23. The neurons organized in a given nucleus
_____ (do/do not) tend to be
functionally related. Groups of nuclei located
near one another _____ (do/do
not) tend to be functionally related.

Now we will examine the various subdivisions of the central nervous system, starting with the spinal cord and moving up to the anatomical top of the system, the cerebral cortex. Remember to think about structure and function together and to relate one structure to another. Although the chapter focuses on the *human* central nervous system, we know that the central nervous systems of other mammals are similar.

24. In what sense is the spinal cord a conduit? What are ascending tracts? descending tracts?

25. How is the level of spinal cord injury related to the severity of the resulting deficit? (See Figure 6.1 on text page 164.)

26. What are pattern generators and what function do they serve?

In addition to serving as a conduit and generating rhythmic signals for locomotion, the spinal cord directly controls some reflexive behavior independent of the brain. These behaviors are called spinal reflexes.

27. How are such spinal reflexes studied?

28. What is a flexion reflex and why is it useful? Is it a response to pain? How do you know?

29. What is the general anatomical arrangement underlying this spinal reflex? (Refer back to Figure 6.2 on text page 164.)

Moving up from the spinal cord, we turn to the organization of the brain. All brain structures below the cerebral cortex are called subcortical structures. We will begin with those subcortical structures that lie nearest to the spinal cord—the brainstem and the thalamus. (See Figure 6.6 on text page 171.)

30. The parts of the brainstem are the

_____ , _____ ,

and _____ .

31. Explain the brainstem's anatomical and functional similarity to the spinal cord.

32. Two kinds of reflexes organized by the medulla and pons are the _____ reflex and the _____ reflex.

33. Characterize the brainstem's control of movement by describing the behavior of an animal after its central nervous system is severed above the midbrain.

34. Why is the thalamus considered a relay station?

Moving beyond the brainstem and thalamus, we come to the cerebellum and basal ganglia, both importantly involved in motor control.

35. Answer the following questions about the cerebellum.

    a.  The cerebellum's name comes from the Latin word for _____ and it is so called because of its appearance.

    b.  The cerebellum rests on the rear of the _____ .

    c.  Describe the most important function of the cerebellum and what happens when the cerebellum is damaged.

    d.  Why is the cerebellum especially well developed in birds and monkeys?

    e.  Does the cerebellum process sensory information? Explain.

36. Answer the following questions about the basal ganglia.

    a.  The basal ganglia are large masses of _____ matter lying on each side of the _____ .

    b.  How is their role in motor control complementary to that of the cerebellum?

    c.  Tremors and difficulty starting and stopping movements are symptoms of _____ , which results from deterioration of neurons connecting the _____ to the basal ganglia.

At the next level up are the limbic system and the hypothalamus.

37. Answer the following questions about the limbic system.

    a.  The term *limbic* comes from the Latin word for _____ .

    b.  What is the general anatomical pattern of the limbic system?

    c.  Two important substructures within the limbic system are the _____ and the _____ .

    d.  In general, structures of the limbic system help to regulate basic _____ and _____ .

    e.  Give a physiological explanation for the fact that smells can strongly influence our drives and emotions.

f. The _____ , a structure in the limbic system, is critical to the formation of memories.

38. Where is the hypothalamus? Why is it so very important and how does it accomplish its tasks?

The evolutionarily newest part of the brain lies at the top of the brain.

39. The Latin word _____ means "brain"; the Latin word _____ means "bark." Thus the term _____ refers to the "bark," or outer layer, of the brain.

40. In size, the cerebral cortex is the _____ part of the human brain, accounting for about _____ percent of the brain's entire volume. Much of its surface area lies deep in _____ and is thus not visible in an undissected brain.

41. The cerebral cortex is divided into left and right halves, or _____ . In turn, each of these can be divided into four _____ .

42. Identify the lobes of the brain in the drawing below. (See Figure 6.9 on text page 174.)

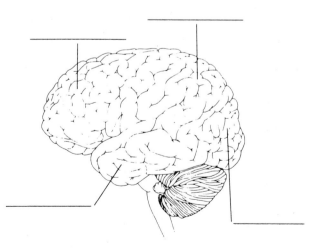

43. Identify the following different functional regions of the cortex by labeling the drawing below: primary sensory areas (including visual, auditory, and somatosensory areas) and primary motor areas.

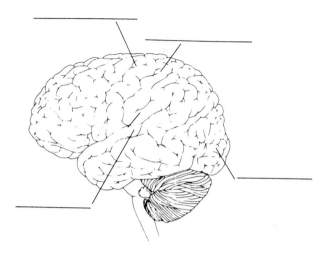

44. What are association areas and what are their functions?

One way of approaching the complexities of the cortex is to think in terms of principles of organization, rather than physical divisions like right and left hemisphere.

45. What is the principle of topographic organization? Give one example to illustrate this principle.

46. Look at the maps of the somatosensory and primary motor areas of the cortex in Figure 6.11 on text page 175. Why do some body parts have greater representation than others? Why would species differ in terms of which body part has the greatest representation in these areas?

Now, let's concentrate on a more in-depth understanding of how the cortex is involved in motor control.

47. The motor cortex, the basal ganglia, and the cerebellum are all involved in motor control. In what order do the structures exert their influence? How do we know?

48. Briefly describe the evidence showing that the motor cortex is critical for making delicate movements.

49. What role do the premotor and supplementary motor areas of the cortex play in motor control? How do we know?

50. What role in motor control is played by association areas in the frontal lobes? How do we know?

Movement is behavior, whether it is something as dramatic and complex as a balance-beam routine or as subtle as a shift of the eyes. It is therefore worth understanding how the entire nervous system works to manage movement. This function of the nervous system also illustrates hierarchical control.

51. How do evolutionarily older and newer systems relate in the movement-control hierarchy?

52. Figure 6.13 (text page 178) shows a functional hierarchy of movement control. Using this figure as an aid, describe what would be happening at the four levels of the hierarchy as a person thirsty after a long run spots a cool drink.

a. at the first level (the top):

b. at the second level:

c. at the third level:

d. at the fourth level:

53. Despite the elegance of a hierarchical explanation of nervous-system control over movement or some other activity, we do not have answers to all our questions. What type of question have we answered? What type of question have we not answered?

Even though the right and left hemispheres of the brain look like mirror images, their functioning is not the same in all regards.

54. Are the brain's two hemispheres isolated from one another? Explain.

55. In what ways are the hemispheres functionally symmetrical? functionally asymmetrical?

Split-brain studies provide some of the most compelling evidence for the functional differences between the hemispheres. These studies focus on individuals in whom the corpus callosum has been cut for medical reasons, thus effectively separating the hemispheres.

56. Describe a typical split-brain experiment and its results.

57. Are there individual differences in the right hemisphere's comprehension of language? Explain.

58. How do people who have had split-brain surgery manage in the everyday world?

### *How Neurons Work and Influence Each Other* (pp. 183–190)

> CONSIDER *these questions before you go on. They are designed to help you start thinking about the subject, not to test your knowledge.*

What actually happens when a neuron carries an electrical impulse?

How do neurons pass information among themselves?

Does experience have any effect on neurons and, if so, how does it affect them?

> READ *this section of your text lightly. Then go back and read thoroughly, completing the Workout as you proceed.*

As you have noted, neurons are designed to carry and to integrate information. Because these functions are so critical to everything we do—breathing, walking, smiling, writing, any activity you can name—it is important to understand them in greater detail.

1. Explain what it means to say that an action potential is "all or none."

2. What is the cell membrane? intracellular fluid? extracellular fluid?

3. Identify the electrically charged chemicals in the internal and external fluid environments of the inactive neuron. Also indicate their charge and location.

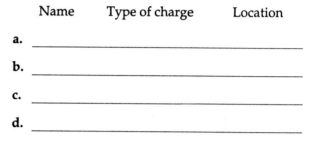

|  | Name | Type of charge | Location |
|---|---|---|---|
| a. | | | |
| b. | | | |
| c. | | | |
| d. | | | |

4. Now place chemical symbols (e.g., $Na^+$) representing the various chemicals named above on the following diagram of an inactive neuron.

5. What is the resting potential? How is it relevant to the action potential?

The action potential can be broken down into two major phases: depolarization and repolarization. Now let's trace the events of an action potential in detail.

6. Does the action potential occur in all parts of the axon simultaneously? Explain.

7. Answer the following questions about the depolarization phase of the action potential.

   a. What happens in the cell membrane to begin the action potential?

   b. This allows _____ ions to rush into the neuron.

   c. Two forces cause this movement to take place. They are a _____ and an _____ force.

   d. As a result of this movement, the electrical charge across the cell membrane becomes _____ .

8. Answer the following questions about the repolarization phase of the action potential.

   a. As the sodium channels close up, channels that permit only _____ ions to pass through open.

   b. Are these ions moving into or out of the cell? Why?

   c. As a result of this movement, the electrical charge across the cell membrane becomes _____ .

9. About how long does it take for an action potential to occur at a given point on the axon?

10. Why doesn't a cell "wear down" after a certain number of action potentials have taken place?

11. What is a cell's threshold?

The speed with which an action potential can travel down an axon is affected by several factors.

12. Larger-diameter axons will conduct an action potential _____ than thinner ones. Another factor that affects the speed of conduction is the presence or absence of a _____ . In cells with this type of insulation, the action potential does not move smoothly along the axon but rather _____ from one _____ to the next. The fastest neurons in the nervous system can carry an action potential at about _____ meters per second.

13. How could it be that you feel the pressure of a pinprick before you feel the pain of it?

Neurons are separated from one another and from muscle cells by tiny gaps. Synaptic transmission is the nervous system's special means of conveying information across those gaps.

14. Answer the following questions about structures involved in synaptic transmission.

   a. Neurons influence the action of other cells at _____ .

   b. The synaptic _____ is the tiny gap that separates the _____ membrane from the _____ membrane that it influences.

   c. The axon terminal of the presynaptic cell contains hundreds of minute globe-like _____ , which hold chemical _____ .

15. Answer the following questions about the events that take place in synaptic transmission.

   a. What happens when an action potential reaches the axon terminal?

**b.** What then happens if the postsynaptic cell is a muscle cell?

**c.** At a general level, what two results are possible if the postsynaptic cell is a neuron?

It is important to consider neural activity in terms of the information being sent. A necessary distinction is that between excitatory and inhibitory synapses. At each of these types of synapses, a different type of signal is sent to the postsynaptic neuron. The two types of signals are designed to produce opposite effects in the postsynaptic cell.

**16.** Explain the mechanism by which these two types of synapses influence the postsynaptic cell.

**a.** excitatory synapses

**b.** inhibitory synapses

**17.** Why is it important to remember that each neuron receives input from many different synapses, often involving many different neurons? What ultimately determines the rate of action potentials in the postsynaptic neuron?

As part of a living system, neurons can be modified by experience. They can change in size, shape, excitability, and patterns of connections. Though we can't grow new neurons after birth, we can establish new synapses.

**18.** What brain differences were found in rats raised in enriched, as compared to deprived, environments?

**19.** Why have scientists chosen to study *Aplysia*, the sea slug?

**20.** Answer the following questions about the gill-withdrawal reflex in *Aplysia*.

**a.** What is the neural mechanism underlying short-term sensitization?

**b.** What is the basis for long-term sensitization?

**c.** At the molecular level, how does classical conditioning of the gill-withdrawal reflex take place?

Though we cannot study complex forms of learning in the human brain as easily as in *Aplysia*, researchers have speculated about the mechanisms involved.

**21.** How did Kandel's *Aplysia* research confirm Donald Hebb's 1949 theory?

22. What is involved in neural network modeling?

## How Hormones and Drugs Interact with the Nervous System (pages 191–198)

> *CONSIDER these questions before you go on. They are designed to help you start thinking about the subject, not to test your knowledge.*

What are hormones and how do they affect the body's functioning?

How is the brain involved in hormonal effects?

How could a drug paralyze someone? affect someone's motor behavior? alter someone's mood?

Why do people sometimes need larger and larger doses of a drug?

What causes the unpleasant withdrawal symptoms associated with some drugs?

> *READ this section of your text lightly. Then go back and read thoroughly, completing the Workout as you proceed.*

Given that the heart is part of a vast circulatory system and that its vessels are easier to see than nerves, it is not surprising that early theorists considered it the seat of thought, emotion, and behavioral control. In fact, the circulatory system does play a communications role within the body. It is, however, a much slower messenger system than the nervous system.

1. _____ are chemical messengers secreted into the blood to act on specific _____ tissues.

2. Hormones, dozens of which have been identified, are secreted not only by _____ glands but also by other organs such as the brain and stomach.

3. What is a possible evolutionary explanation for the chemical similarities between hormones and neurotransmitters?

4. Explain how each of the following illustrates the chemical similarity between hormones and neurotransmitters.

   a. norepinephrine

   b. endorphins

   c. neurohormones

As you might guess, given the complexity of the hormonal system and of the brain's interaction with it, hormones affect behavior in a variety of ways.

5. Hormones can affect behavior by influencing growth processes. Explain how sex hormones can work in this way.

6. Hormones can also have shorter-term effects. How do adrenal hormones such as cortisol help in times of stress?

7. How do hormones exert an influence at the molecular level? How do peptides and steroids differ?

The hormonal system is not independent of the brain. In fact, it would be reasonable to say that the brain is the master of the hormonal system. (Refer to Figures 6.26, 6.27, and 6.28 on text pages 193–195.)

8. Why is the pituitary gland sometimes called the master endocrine gland? Where is it located?

9. Distinguish between the posterior and anterior lobes of the pituitary.

10. Briefly summarize a series of hormonal events that might occur in a frightening situation.

   a.

   b.

   c.

   d.

   e.

The blood can carry messengers other than hormones that affect the body's tissues, sometimes dramatically.

11. How are drugs similar to hormones? How are they different?

12. Identify several different ways in which drugs can be introduced into the body. Why might one method be preferred in a given set of circumstances?

13. What is the blood-brain barrier? What kinds of substances can generally pass easily through the barrier?

Drugs can have a variety of effects by altering synaptic transmission. Most drugs used by psychiatrists and neurologists to affect mood or behavior work in this way.

14. List the three ways that drugs can affect synaptic activity.

   a.

   b.

   c.

15. Explain how a lock-and-key analogy can help us to understand one of the above modes of influence.

Drugs can influence behavior by affecting activity at any level of the neural hierarchy.

16. What is curare? At what level of the hierarchy does it act? How does it have its effects?

17. What is L-dopa? What is it used to treat? Where in the hierarchy does it have its effects? Why isn't dopamine itself used?

18. What are psychoactive drugs? At what level of the hierarchy do they work? What can they affect?

Tolerance, withdrawal symptoms, and addiction are three phenomena of drug use that can occur with pharmacological drugs as well as illicit "street" drugs.

19. Describe the phenomenon of drug tolerance.

20. What are withdrawal symptoms?

21. Are the occurrence of drug tolerance and withdrawal symptoms linked in any way? Explain.

22. Present a general theory that can explain both tolerance and withdrawal symptoms.

23. Briefly show how this theory can help to explain tolerance and withdrawal symptoms in the use of amphetamines.

24. Explain what it means to say that someone is addicted to a drug. What are some factors that might underlie addiction?

> *Be sure to READ the Concluding Thoughts at the end of the chapter. Note important points in your Workout. Then consolidate your learning by answering the focus questions in the margins of the text.*

> *After you have studied the chapter thoroughly, CHECK your understanding with the self-test that follows.*

## Self-Test 1

*Multiple-Choice Questions*

1. Galen believed the _____ to be the organ of psychological functioning, thereby _____ Aristotle.
   a. heart; agreeing with
   b. heart; contradicting
   c. brain; agreeing with
   d. brain; contradicting

2. Where are nerves found?
   a. only in the peripheral nervous system
   b. only in the brain
   c. only in the spinal cord
   d. in all parts of the nervous system

3. In some cases, a myelin sheath is wrapped around a neuron's:
   a. dendrites.         c. cell body.
   b. axon.              d. cell nucleus.

4. The nervous system is made up of the _____ and the _____ .
   a. skeletal nervous system; autonomic nervous system
   b. central nervous system; peripheral nervous system

c. peripheral nervous system; autonomic nervous system

d. sympathetic nervous system; parasympathetic nervous system

5. An injury that severs the spinal cord will cause _____ ; the _____ the injury is, the more of the body it will affect.

a. paralysis but not sensory loss; higher
b. sensory loss but not paralysis; lower
c. paralysis and sensory loss; higher
d. sensory loss and paralysis; lower

6. A person's hand can be withdrawn from a hot stove before the brain ever receives pain signals because this behavior is based on:

a. an ascending reflex.
b. a flexion reflex.
c. cortical structures in the brain.
d. subcortical structures in the brain.

7. The medulla, pons, and midbrain are all parts of the:

a. limbic system.
b. brainstem.
c. thalamus.
d. cerebellum.

8. Parkinson's disease, which involves tremors and difficulty starting and stopping deliberate movements, stems from deterioration of neurons terminating in the:

a. basal ganglia.
b. cerebellum.
c. limbic system.
d. thalamus.

9. The part of the brain that plays a special role in the regulation of drives and emotions is the:

a. limbic system.
b. brainstem.
c. cerebellum.
d. corpus callosum.

10. The hypothalamus regulates the body's internal environment by:

a. influencing the autonomic nervous system.
b. controlling the release of some hormones.
c. affecting drive states such as hunger and thirst.
d. doing all of the above.

11. Association areas in the _____ lobe are critical to planning actions.

a. parietal        c. occipital
b. frontal         d. temporal

12. During the depolarization phase of the action potential, _____ rush into the neuron.

a. protein molecules     c. sodium ions
b. potassium ions        d. chloride ions

13. A neuron's threshold is defined as the:

a. strength of the action potentials that occur in that neuron.
b. critical level of depolarization that must be reached before an action potential is triggered.
c. number of action potentials that can take place in the neuron in a given unit of time.
d. place on the neuron where action potentials begin.

14. Within the axon terminals are _____ , which store the _____ needed for synaptic transmission.

a. vesicles; neurotransmitter
b. nodes; neurotransmitter
c. vesicles; sodium
d. nodes; sodium

15. Endorphins and norepinephrine help to illustrate the fact that:

a. hormones target only one tissue each.
b. hormones and neurotransmitters can be chemically identical.
c. some hormones have their effects exclusively in the brain.
d. neurohormones play an important role in the hormonal system.

*Essay Questions*

16. Explain the process of synaptic transmission. How do excitatory and inhibitory synapses differ?

17. Discuss drug tolerance and withdrawal symptoms. Show how a single theory might explain both phenomena. How might the existence of withdrawal symptoms be implicated in addiction?

*After you have assessed your understanding on the basis of Self-Test 1 and have tried to strengthen your preparation in any areas of weakness, GO ON to Self-Test 2.*

## Self-Test 2

*Multiple-Choice Questions*

1. The brain and spinal cord together comprise the:
   a. autonomic nervous system.
   b. central nervous system.
   c. peripheral nervous system.
   d. sympathetic nervous system.

2. The most basic unit of the nervous system is a:
   a. dendrite.        c. neuron.
   b. nerve.           d. tract.

3. In which type of neuron does stimulation come from a source other than neurons?
   a. motor neuron     c. sensory neuron
   b. interneuron      d. none of the above

4. Which part of the nervous system directly mediates the body's physiological response to a stressful situation by increasing heart rate, increasing blood pressure, releasing energy, and so on?
   a. excitatory nervous system
   b. sympathetic division of the autonomic motor system
   c. parasympathetic division of the autonomic motor system
   d. skeletal motor system

5. The mystery writer Agatha Christie often mentioned the little gray cells of her detective, Hercule Poirot. Gray matter actually consists of:
   a. nuclei in the central nervous system.
   b. nerves in the peripheral nervous system.

   c. tracts in the central nervous system.
   d. whole neurons in the brainstem.

6. The sustained cyclic movement of walking appears to be managed directly by:
   a. nuclei in the limbic system.
   b. pattern generators in the spinal cord.
   c. cranial nerves.
   d. the cerebellum.

7. The part of the brain located directly above the brainstem that serves as a major sensory relay station is the:
   a. pituitary.       c. amygdala.
   b. cerebellum.      d. thalamus.

8. Which part of the brain is considered a kind of computer or even a "little brain" that initiates and controls movements that are too fast to be guided by sensory feedback once begun?
   a. basal ganglia    c. frontal lobes
   b. cerebellum       d. brainstem

9. The cerebral cortex is divided into two _____ connected by _____ .
   a. lobes; the corpus callosum
   b. hemispheres; the corpus callosum
   c. primary sensory areas; lobes
   d. association areas; tracts

10. Studies of people who have had split-brain surgery have taught us a great deal about:
    a. the limbic system.
    b. cortical involvement in movement.
    c. topographic organization in the cortex.
    d. the asymmetry of the higher functions in the cortex.

11. When the neuron is inactive, the charge across the cell membrane is such that:
    a. the inside is about –70 millivolts relative to the outside.
    b. the inside is about –700 millivolts relative to the outside.
    c. the inside is about +70 millivolts relative to the outside.
    d. the inside is about +700 millivolts relative to the outside.

12. Neurotransmitters increase the rate of action potentials in the postsynaptic cell at _____ synapses.
    a. excitatory
    b. inhibitory
    c. cortical
    d. peripheral

13. The pituitary gland, located at the base of the brain:
    a. is often called the "master endocrine gland" because of its control over other glands.
    b. actually has no physiological relationship to the brain.
    c. does not actually manufacture any hormones but does direct the movement of many hormones.
    d. exerts its effects on the brain but not on any other part of the body.

14. The hormones that can pass through cell membranes and activate or inhibit specific genes there are:
    a. neurohormones.
    b. peptides.
    c. steroids.
    d. releasing factors.

15. Curare is a drug that paralyzes by blocking receptor sites in:
    a. muscle cells.
    b. nerves in the spinal cord.
    c. neurons in the cerebellum.
    d. neurons in the motor cortex.

### Essay Questions

16. What is meant by the term *hierarchical control of behavior*? How did such hierarchical control systems come to be?

17. At what level (or levels) of the behavior-control system do drugs work? Cite specific cases, where possible, to support your answer.

# Answers

*Functional Organization of the Nervous System*

2. brain; spinal cord; nerves
4. neurons
8. a. dendrites
   b. axon terminal
   c. cell body
   d. axon
   e. myelin sheath
11. glial cell
13. 12; 31
20. parasympathetic; sympathetic
23. do; do
30. medulla; pons; midbrain
32. postural; vital
35. a. little brain
    b. brainstem
36. a. gray; thalamus
    c. Parkinson's disease; brainstem
37. a. border (or edge)
    c. amygdala; hippocampus
    d. drives; emotions
    f. hippocampus
39. cerebrum; cortex; cerebral cortex
40. largest; 80; folds
41. hemispheres; lobes

*How Neurons Work and Influence Each Other*

3. **a.** soluble protein molecules (A⁻), negative, internal

   **b.** potassium ions (K⁺), positive, internal

   **c.** sodium ions (Na⁺), positive, external

   **d.** chloride ions (Cl⁻), negative, external

7. **b.** sodium

   **c.** concentration; electrical

   **d.** positive

8. **a.** potassium

   **c.** negative

12. faster; myelin sheath; skips; node; 100

14. **a.** synapses

   **b.** cleft; presynaptic; postsynaptic

   **c.** vesicles; neurotransmitters

*How Hormones and Drugs Interact with the Nervous System*

1. hormones; target

2. endocrine

*Self-Test 1*

1. **d.** Aristotle and many other ancient Greek thinkers believed that the heart was the seat of psychological functioning. (p. 163)

2. **a.** (p. 166)

3. **b.** (p. 165)

4. **b.** (p. 164)

5. **c.** Severing the cord will cut through both ascending and descending tracts and will thus produce both sensory and motor deficits. The higher up in the cord the injury lies, the greater the number of spinal nerves that are cut off from the brain, and thus the greater the area of the body affected. (p. 169)

6. **b.** The flexion reflex is an example of a spinal reflex. It is carried out independently of brain control. It makes adaptive sense that this defensive move should be handled by a spinal reflex since it can thus be accomplished faster, minimizing potential damage. (p. 170)

7. **b.** (p. 170)

8. **a.** (p. 172)

9. **a.** (p. 172)

10. **d.** (p. 173)

11. **b.** (p. 177)

12. **c.** (p. 184)

13. **b.** (p. 185)

14. **a.** (p. 186)

15. **b.** (pp. 191–192)

16. Synaptic transmission is the process through which a neuron sends a message to another cell, whether it be another neuron or a muscle or gland cell. When an action potential reaches the axon terminals of the "sending," or presynaptic neuron, it causes the release of the neurotransmitter from tiny vesicles in the axon terminals. The neurotransmitter acts as a chemical messenger that moves across the synaptic cleft, a tiny gap between the cells. When they reach the membrane of the "receiving," or postsynaptic cell—typically on the dendrites or cell body if the cell is a neuron—the molecules of the neurotransmitter are received at special binding sites. The process works something like fitting a key (the neurotransmitter molecule) into a lock (the binding site).

When the "key" fits into the "lock," the postsynaptic cell will contract if it is a muscle cell. If the postsynaptic cell is another neuron, the result is a change in the electrical balance across the cell's membrane. The direction of change depends on whether the synapse is excitatory or inhibitory. At an excitatory synapse, positively charged sodium ions enter the cell and slightly depolarize it, thus pushing it toward an action potential. At an inhibitory synapse, the entry of negatively charged ions moves the cell farther away from the threshold level of depolarization needed to trigger an action potential, thus making one less likely. Since any given postsynaptic cell has many synapses, its rate of action potentials depends on the balance of activity at the various synapses. (pp. 185–187)

17. Drug tolerance means that progressively larger doses of a drug must be taken in order to achieve the original effect. It occurs with repeated use of some drugs. Withdrawal symptoms are unpleasant and sometimes life-threatening effects that occur when use of some drugs is stopped. The symptoms are often the opposite of the effects produced by the drug. Both drug tolerance and withdrawal symptoms may arise as a result of a physiological response to prolonged use of the drug. The body appears to counteract the effect of those drugs that produce tolerance and withdrawal symptoms. When this happens, more of the drug is needed to override the body's own counteractive effect. And withdrawal symptoms occur because, when the drug is stopped, only

the counteractive force is left in effect. In the case of drugs that produce withdrawal symptoms, addiction may be due partially to continuation of the drug as a means of avoiding or alleviating withdrawal symptoms. (p. 196)

## Self-Test 2

1. **b.** (p. 164)
2. **c.** (p. 164)
3. **c.** Sensory neurons receive their input, directly or indirectly, from whatever type of sensory stimulation they are specialized to respond to. (p. 166)
4. **b.** (pp. 167–168)
5. **a.** (p. 169)
6. **b.** Of course, the pattern generators exert their control under orders from the brain. You might say they are "deputized." (p. 170)
7. **d.** (p. 171)
8. **b.** (p. 172)
9. **b.** (pp. 179–180)
10. **d.** (p. 181)
11. **a.** (p. 184)
12. **a.** (p. 187)
13. **a.** (p. 193)
14. **c.** (p. 193)
15. **a.** (p. 196)
16. In hierarchical control, multiple behavior-control systems play a role in regulating behavior, each acting within a kind of chain of command. At the lowest level are systems involved in the actual execution of some response. Lower-level systems may be capable of carrying out some simple functions independently or semi-independently. An example would be a spinal reflex like a flexion reflex. But lower-level systems are also subject to control from higher levels. At the highest level of the hierarchy are systems involved in planning and motivation. These higher-level systems achieve their effects by acting upon the lower-level systems. Both cortical and subcortical structures are involved at the top levels of the hierarchy. Hierarchical control may have come about as evolution created more complex and sophisticated systems. Rather than replacing older, more primitive systems, the newer ones took control over the older ones. (pp. 177–179)
17. Drugs can affect synaptic transmission at all levels of the behavior-control hierarchy. For example, they can alter what happens at the lowest level at which neurons synapse on muscle or glands cells. The case of curare illustrates action at this level. Curare paralyzes by blocking muscle binding sites, preventing the neurotransmitter from getting in to cause the muscle to contract. It is like having the wrong key stuck in a lock. There's no way to get the right key in until the wrong key is removed. Drugs can also affect behavior at intermediate levels of behavior control. For example, L-dopa works by aiding the formation of dopamine in the basal ganglia of Parkinson's patients. Drugs such as psychoactive drugs can work at still higher levels of behavior control in the cortex, affecting mood, thought processes, and more. (pp. 195–196)

# CHAPTER 7   MECHANISMS OF MOTIVATION, SLEEP, AND EMOTION

*Read the introduction below before you read the chapter in the text.*

We can think of psychological states as the slow-moving components of mental life that help modulate and direct the fast-moving parts, such as thoughts, perceptions, and actions. This chapter examines the physiological bases of several such states. One type of state—a motivational state or drive—is an internal condition that changes over time and orients an individual toward specific categories of goals, such as food, water, or a sexual partner. Physiological psychologists can learn about central (brain) states involved in drives by lesioning (destroying) brain tissue, stimulating an area of the brain, or recording electrical brain activity. They also study the influence of processes that are peripheral to (outside) the brain.

Hunger is one area in which such research has yielded major progress. It was once thought that the hypothalamus was a hunger control center in the brain, with activity in one area increasing hunger and activity in another area suppressing it. We now know that the control of hunger is more complicated than that, involving several types of peripheral factors as well as the hypothalamus. Research into obesity suggests that it may be related to heightened sensitivity to food cues or responses to stress, though it is not clear whether obesity is a cause or a consequence. Dieting may make permanent weight loss *less*, rather than more, achievable.

Physiological psychology has also helped us to understand the sex drive. In humans and other animals, sexual differentiation early in an individual's development is due to hormones. Experiences that affect the prenatal hormonal environment may affect the individual's later sexual behavior. Hormones also play a major role in the sex drive after puberty, although adult sexuality in humans is not strictly tied to hormones. Testosterone, popularly considered a strictly male hormone, may be a key factor in the sex drive in women as well as in men. While hormones provide the physiological *potential* for the sex drive in humans, the actual induction of the drive also requires sensory stimulation.

Another product of physiological research has been the discovery of systems in the brain that are responsible for pleasure or reward. These appear to be at least partly specific to different drives. Understanding their functioning may help us to better understand the mechanisms of drug addiction.

Another state—sleep—is both a drive and an altered state of consciousness. One of the most important tools in sleep research has been the electroencephalogram, or EEG, which provides a crude picture of brain activity. During the typical night's sleep, an individual goes through a well-ordered sequence of stages, each identifiable in part through the EEG pattern associated with it. Among the stages is REM sleep, so called because of the rapid back-and-forth eye movements that occur during this stage. It is during this stage that dreaming occurs. The restoration theory and the preservation and protection theory both help to explain why slow-wave sleep may have evolved. The first theory suggests that sleep is needed so that the body can recover from the day's wear and tear. The second suggests that sleep developed as a way for animals to conserve energy and to protect themselves at times of the day when activity would bring more risk than benefit. Sleep is an example of a circadian rhythm, an internally guided cycle that occurs on a 24-hour basis. Sleep deprivation affects some kinds of performance more than others and is a relative term, given that nonsomniacs function normally on very little sleep. Like hunger and sex, sleep is governed by specific brain mechanisms.

Arousal and emotion are the final states considered in this chapter. Arousal is a pattern of measurable physiological changes that helps prepare the body for "fight or flight." Prolonged exposure to intensely negative situations, whether physical or psychological in nature, may have adverse health consequences. Emotion is a subjective feeling often accompanied by physiological arousal. In fact, some of the central theoretical issues in the study of emotion concern the relationship between emotion and arousal. For example, one question asks whether arousal produces emotion, or vice versa. Some evidence suggests that the amount of physiological arousal we feel and even our facial expression may contribute to our emotional experience. Emotion also involves specific brain mechanisms.

> *LOOK over the table of contents for this chapter in your textbook before you continue with your study.*

> *Notice that there are focus questions in the margins of the text for your use in studying the material. The following chart lists which study guide questions relate to which focus questions.*

| Focus Questions | Study Guide Questions |
| --- | --- |
| Motivation and Reward | |
| 1 | 1–5 |
| 2–5 | 6–16 |
| 6–12 | 17–29 |
| 13–20 | 30–39 |
| 21–23 | 40–43 |
| Sleeping and Dreaming | |
| 24–26 | 1–10 |
| 27–30 | 11–18 |
| 31–32 | 19–24 |
| 33 | 25 |
| Emotion | |
| 34–35 | 1–4 |
| 36–41 | 5–14 |
| 42–43 | 15–19 |

## The Integrated Study Workout

> *Complete one section at a time.*

### Motivation and Reward   (pages 201–220)

> *CONSIDER these questions before you go on. They are designed to help you start thinking about the subject, not to test your knowledge.*

What internal factors cause a person to feel hungry?

What causes some people to become obese? What factors make it difficult for them to lose excess weight?

Does the sex drive work very differently in men and women? in humans and nonhuman animals?

Can sex hormones stimulate the sex drive?

How can the pleasure we experience when a need is satisfied be explained physiologically?

> *READ this section of your text lightly. Then go back and read thoroughly, completing the Workout as you proceed.*

The term *motivation*, as used in psychology, refers to a host of factors, some internal and others external, that cause particular behaviors at particular times. But this definition is really too broad to be theoretically useful. Psychologists who study motivation prefer more specific terminology.

1. Define motivational state. Give one example. What term is a synonym for motivational state?

2. How do psychologists determine when an individual is in a particular motivational state?

3. Define incentive. Give one example. What terms are synonyms for incentive?

4. How are drives and incentives related? Give an example to illustrate your point.

5. Do psychologists generally agree that basic drives like hunger and sex are all that motivate human behavior? Explain.

A motivational state is a hypothetical construct. Efforts to understand such states physiologically are efforts to make the hypothetical more concrete. Some psychologists have focused their attention on brain states. Others, such as Walter Cannon, described motivational states in terms of tissue needs.

6. Explain Cannon's concept of homeostasis. How, in Cannon's view, is homeostasis related to motivation? to motivated behavior?

7. Briefly summarize some evidence suggesting that individuals behave in ways that fit their tissue needs.

The idea of homeostasis turned out to be more useful for understanding some drives than others. Even for the drives to which the concept applied well, its usefulness was limited.

8. Homeostasis cannot explain certain types of drives, together classified as _____ drives. An example of this category of drives would be _____ .

9. Was it theoretically useful for psychologists to propose hypothetical needs for such drives? Why?

10. Explain the current distinction between regulatory and nonregulatory drives.

11. Why were definitions of drives based on tissue needs not entirely satisfactory even for regulatory drives?

Today, physiological psychologists generally think of drives in terms of brain states.

12. Explain the central-state theory of drives. What is a central drive system?

13. Describe the characteristics a set of neurons must have in order to serve as a central drive system.

14. What characteristics of the hypothalamus make it a suitable hub of many central drive systems?

Physiologists looking for concrete mechanisms of motivation within the body must have some methodological tools to find them.

15. Answer the following questions about lesions.

    a.  A lesion is an area of _____ .

    b.  Brain lesions can be produced in either of two ways: _____ , by delivering a current through an _____ ; or _____ , by injection through a _____ .

    c.  Why are lesions typically made bilaterally?

**d.** What can be concluded if an animal with bilateral lesions in some area no longer shows a particular drive (but does respond to other incentives)?

**16.** Answer the following questions about stimulation.

    **a.** Describe two methods used by physiological psychologists to stimulate specific brain areas.

    **b.** What can be concluded if stimulation of a specific brain area causes an animal to engage in motivated behavior it was not previously exhibiting?

Hunger is the drive that has received the greatest amount of attention from physiological psychologists. Our changing conception of the hypothalamus' role in hunger not only provides fascinating information about this important motivational system, it also vividly illustrates the scientific process. (See Figure 7.4 on text page 207.)

**17.** According to Stellar, the hunger center is located in the_____

and the satiety center is located in the

_____ .

**18.** What patterns of research data seemed to support this theory? What observations then suggested that reality was more complicated than the theory suggested?

**19.** Answer the following questions about current views on the central drive system for hunger.

    **a.** What is the function of the tract running from parts of the brainstem through the lateral hypothalamus to the basal ganglia? What happens if lesions are made anywhere along this tract?

    **b.** Is there evidence that some lateral hypothalamic neurons really do play a special role in hunger? How was this question approached through lesion studies? What research technique did Edmond Rolls use and what did he discover?

    **c.** What is the current explanation of why bilateral lesions in the ventromedial hypothalamus cause animals to eat to the point of obesity?

The central nervous system structures involved in hunger are sensitive to a variety of influences, though none by itself exerts total control.

**20.** Describe four types of influences on hunger.

    **a.**

    **b.**

    **c.**

    **d.**

Many people weigh more than they would like to. One aim of research on the motivational state of hunger has been to explain obesity.

21. A person whose weight is more than

    _____ percent above average for those of the same sex, height, and bone structure is generally considered obese.

22. How did Schachter explain obesity? Describe some evidence supporting Schachter's view.

23. What is the stress-eating theory of obesity? Describe some evidence supporting it.

24. Why are the stress-eating and cue-sensitivity theories still open to debate?

25. Explain why heredity is considered an important factor in who becomes obese and who does not.

26. How is the number of fat cells in the body related to obesity? What is the ratchet effect?

27. Dieting alone seems relatively ineffective as a means of keeping excess weight off. How do diet-related changes in basal metabolism help to explain the ineffectiveness of reducing diets?

28. What undesirable effect does yo-yo dieting have?

29. Does weight loss through exercise have the same effect as dieting on basal metabolism? Explain.

The sex drive has also received a great deal of attention from physiological psychologists. Most of the research has been conducted on laboratory animals, usually rats. Because humans differ from other animals in both social and biological aspects of sexuality, care must be taken in generalizing research findings to humans. One important finding has been the existence of separate neural systems for male and female sex drives.

30. Brain manipulation (lesion or stimulation) in the

    _____ area of the hypothalamus has shown it to be critical in the male, but not the female, sex drive. The area most critical to the female sex drive is the _____ area of the hypothalamus.

31. The male-female brain differences that affect adult sexual behavior are caused by the absence or presence of _____ during a critical prenatal period. One brain structure that is very much affected by this hormone is the _____ nucleus, which is five times larger in male than in female rats, and contributes to the male sex drive.

32. Describe how testosterone might produce sexual differentiation in the central nervous system.

33. How does prenatal stress affect the sexual development of male rats?

34. Why is a male rather than a female hormone critical to this early sexual differentiation?

35. What evidence suggests that prenatal influences may affect sexual orientation in humans? Why must we be cautious about causal conclusions?

Puberty marks a great increase in sex hormone production in humans as well as in other mammals. Motivational theorists are most interested in the effects of hormones on the sex drive after puberty.

36. Answer the following questions regarding hormonal effects on the sex drive in males.

    a. Castration, the removal of the male's
       _____ , and thus the supply
       of _____ , causes a
       _____ in the sex drive.

    b. The injection of testosterone (or the implantation of testosterone crystals in the medial preoptic area of the hypothalamus)
       _____ the sex drive.

37. Answer the following questions regarding hormonal effects on the sex drive in females.

    a. What is the menstrual cycle? What is the estrous cycle?

    b. Removal of the ovaries in rodents causes the
       _____ of the sex drive; subsequent administration of estrogen (or estrogen and progesterone) _____
       the sex drive.

    c. How do humans, nonhuman primates, and rodents differ in the role hormones play in sexual capability and sex drive?

    d. Describe evidence that testosterone may be the most important hormonal factor in women's sex drive.

As with other drives, the actual manifestation of the sex drive involves an interaction between incentive and motivational state. In fact, this interaction is even more important in the sex drive than it is in hunger.

38. What innately stimulates sexual interest among nonhuman species?

39. Are men more aroused than women by sexually visual stimuli? Support your answer with evidence.

Subjectively, we are aware of the relationship between a drive and the pleasure we feel upon satisfying that drive. Research in physiological psychology has advanced our understanding of the neural basis of pleasure and reward.

40. What did James Olds and Peter Milner discover in the 1950s?

41. How have people receiving such stimulation described the resulting feeling? Did they work compulsively for it?

42. What role is the nucleus accumbens thought to play in rats' responses to brain stimulation and drugs such as cocaine and opiates?

It is important to note that the brain areas underlying reward evolved to serve natural motivations—such as those directed toward sex or food—not motivations for electrical brain stimulation or drugs such as cocaine.

43. What evidence suggests that the neural circuitry involved in reward from brain stimulation also underlies natural drives?

*Sleeping and Dreaming*   (pages 220–229)

> CONSIDER *these questions before you go on. They are designed to help you start thinking about the subject, not to test your knowledge.*

What is sleep? Is it just a kind of "suspended animation" in which nothing much is going on?

How can psychologists learn anything about sleep, given that the sleeping person is, well, asleep?

What purpose does sleep serve? What physiological mechanisms cause us to sleep?

How do people differ in the amount of sleep they need?

What is dreaming and why does it happen? Does everyone do it?

What happens if a person goes without sleep for several days?

If people had no clues to night or day, would they still tend to sleep at the same time they ordinarily do?

> READ *this section of your text lightly. Then go back and read thoroughly, completing the Workout as you proceed.*

Sleep can be thought of as a drive, since people will go to some trouble to achieve it, but it is also an altered state of consciousness. Because sleep involves little overt behavior that can be used to infer internal processes, scientists have developed ways to tap more subtle behavioral and physiological information. One of the most important tools at their disposal has been the EEG.

1. Answer the following questions about the electroencephalogram (EEG). (See Figure 7.8 on text page 221.)

   a. What is the electroencephalogram (EEG)?

   b. What is it really measuring? What metaphor is presented in the text to characterize the quality of information the EEG provides?

   c. How can the EEG help sleep researchers to better understand sleep?

2. For each of the following EEG patterns, note the frequency and amplitude of the waves and when each is likely to occur. (See Figure 7.9 on text page 222.)

   a. alpha waves

   b. beta waves

   c. sleep spindles

   d. delta waves

3. What is the general relationship between the frequency and amplitude of EEG waves and the synchronization of neural activity?

The EEG follows a regular sequence of changes in a sleeping person. The changes, which are gradual and continuous, are used by researchers to divide sleep into four stages. (See Figures 7.9 and 7.10 on text pages 222 and 223.)

4. For each stage described below, identify the appropriate stage number.

   _____ a. the period in which sleep spindles appear, indicating the onset of sleep

   _____ b. the period in which 10 to 50 percent of the EEG consists of delta waves

   _____ c. the brief transitional stage between waking and sleeping, when alpha waves decline and neural activity becomes unsynchronized

   _____ d. the stage in which more than half of the EEG consists of delta waves

5. As a person moves from stage 2 to stage 4, sleep becomes successively _____ .
   At the same time, other physiological indices of arousal _____ .

6. What happens after a person gets to stage 4?

7. REM is an acronym for _____ .

8. In what sense are there conflicting indicators of arousal during REM sleep (emergent stage 1 sleep)?

9. Stages 2, 3, and 4 are collectively referred to as _____ sleep.

10. A person goes through _____ sleep cycles in a typical night. A cycle consists of a progressive deepening of sleep, then progressive lightening, followed by _____ sleep. Each cycle lasts about _____ minutes. The depth of sleep _____ (decreases/increases) with each successive cycle.

One of the mysteries that has interested not just scientists, but people generally, is why we have developed a need for sleep. Researchers have offered two possible explanations for the evolution of sleep.

11. Explain the restoration theory and present two types of evidence that support it.

12. Explain the preservation and protection theory and present two types of evidence that support it. How might this theory explain the typical 8-hour nighttime sleep pattern of adult humans?

We can generally understand more about a scientific phenomenon by looking at it in different ways. One useful way to think about sleep involves its nature as a biological rhythm. (See Figure 7.12 on text page 225.)

13. What happens when animals are kept in an environment in which they have no cues to time of day? What happens with humans when time cues are removed?

14. What is a circadian rhythm? What governs such rhythms?

15. Under normal environmental conditions, what cue resets the circadian clock daily? How can the cycle be artificially reset? Are there any possible practical applications of this technique?

Most students have at some time or other experienced some sleep deprivation, perhaps in studying for an exam or finishing a paper. (I hope that is not your current circumstance.)

16. What happens when people go 3 or 4 days without sleep? What kinds of tasks are most affected by sleep deprivation? What kinds are least affected?

17. What is the most reliable effect of sleep deprivation? Is this effect simply related to the amount of sleep deprivation? Explain.

18. Describe a nonsomniac. How does this disorder compare with insomnia?

Dreaming is one reason that sleep has long fascinated us. In dreams, we may become a different character, overcome the limitations of time and space, experience bizarre happenings, and more.

19. How did Sigmund Freud explain the purpose of dreaming?

20. How do scientists study dreams?

21. Describe a true dream. How are true dreams related to REM sleep? Does everyone dream?

22. What kind of mental activity do people sometimes report when awakened from slow-wave rather than REM sleep?

23. In the currently prevailing view, why do we have true dreams? Is there evidence consistent with this view? Explain.

24. Does the side-effect theory necessarily imply that dreams cannot be useful in understanding a person's mind?

Just as the hunger and sex drives are regulated by neurons in the brain, so too is sleep. Sleep is not, as researchers once believed, a state that the brain enters when external stimulation is low. After all, we sometimes sleep with considerable stimulation around us and sometimes fail to sleep when stimulation is minimal.

25. Research on animals has uncovered three separate but interacting brain systems involved in sleep. Identify and describe each, making sure to specify its role and indicate the evidence for that role.

a.

b.

c.

*Emotion*  (pages 230–238)

Do we perform better if we are super-relaxed, super-excited, or somewhere in between? Does the answer to the question depend on the kind of task we are performing?

Is emotion "all in the head" or does it have something to do with activity in the rest of the body as well?

Sometimes people who are feeling a little blue are told they will feel happier if they make themselves smile. Does this make any sense?

*READ this section of your text lightly. Then go back and read thoroughly, completing the Workout as you proceed.*

If a police car pulls up behind you as you drive down the highway, its lights flashing and spinning, you will probably have more than a cognitive awareness of the event. Among other things, your heart may pound and your muscles may tense. These changes are part of the physiological arousal response.

1. Define and describe the arousal response.

2. When would it be better for a person to have an audience—when the task is to design a better mousetrap or to count how many mousetraps are in a box?

3. Explain the Yerkes-Dodson law. (See Figure 7.16 on text page 230.)

4. Describe the effects of an arousal response that is too strong and prolonged.

The same stimuli that lead to high physiological arousal also lead to feelings. Arousal, emotions, and drives are all intimately related.

5. How does the text define emotion?

6. If someone asked you how many different emotions humans are capable of experiencing, what would be the wisest response?

One dimension of emotional experience is physiological. Psychologists have sought to understand the role that peripheral changes in heart rate, breathing rate, and muscle tension, for example, play in emotional feelings.

7. What position did William James take on this issue? Was his theory based on experimental data? Explain.

Stanley Schachter developed a theory of emotion similar to James's.

8. How is Schachter's theory like James's theory? How does it differ? How does each relate to the "common sense theory"? (See Figure 7.18 on text page 233.)

9. What laboratory evidence did Schachter provide to support his view?

10. How was George Hohmann's study of men with spinal cord injuries relevant? What did his results suggest?

11. Why should we be somewhat cautious in interpreting Hohmann's results? What did Bermond find in his replication study?

In an emotional situation, the autonomic nervous system automatically triggers certain bodily responses. Depending on the stimulus and on your reaction to it, you may also lower your eyebrows in anger or lift the corners of your mouth in a smile. Paul Ekman asked whether facial expressions can contribute to emotion.

12. What evidence suggests that "putting on" a particular facial expression can affect mood?

13. What findings indicate that facial feedback may produce bodily states similar to those associated with the emotion depicted?

14. How might facial feedback help to account for emotional contagion?

Emotion depends not just on peripheral processes, of course, but also on the brain.

15. In what ways is the brain central to emotional processes?

16. The _____ is thought to be central in assessing the emotional significance of a stimulus and producing an immediate response. The _____ is critical for conscious emotional experience and more deliberate emotional behavior.

17. Describe what happens to emotional responsiveness when the amygdala is destroyed.

18. How do the results of prefrontal lobotomy verify the importance of the frontal lobes to emotion?

19. What evidence suggests that the left and right frontal lobes may be specialized for different emotions?

---

*Be sure to READ the Concluding Thoughts at the end of the chapter. Note important points in your Workout. Then consolidate your learning by answering the focus questions in the margins of the text.*

---

*After you have studied the chapter thoroughly, CHECK your understanding with the self-test that follows.*

# Self-Test 1

## *Multiple-Choice Questions*

1. The term *motivational state* is synonymous with:
   a. emotion.
   b. drive.
   c. incentive.
   d. arousal.

2. According to Walter Cannon, tissue needs produce drives, which in turn produce behaviors that will restore:
   a. a central drive system.
   b. motivational states.
   c. incentive.
   d. homeostasis.

3. An example of a nonregulatory drive is the drive for:
   a. food.
   b. sex.
   c. both a. and b.
   d. neither a. nor b.

4. A brain structure that is the hub of many central drive systems is the :
   a. brainstem.
   b. cerebellum.
   c. thalamus.
   d. hypothalamus.

5. Which of the following statements is true of peripheral influences on hunger?
   a. Hunger is turned on or off exclusively by signals from the stomach.
   b. Despite popular belief, stomach distension actually plays no part in signaling satiety.
   c. Hunger levels are affected by the amount of food molecules in the blood.
   d. The hunger drive is influenced by external stimuli only in the case of obese individuals.

6. In rats and other nonhuman mammals, the critical brain system in the sex drive is:
   a. the medial preoptic area of the hypothalamus.
   b. the ventromedial area of the hypothalamus.
   c. the sexually dimorphic nucleus.
   d. a. in males and b. in females.

7. According to research described in the text, the hormonal changes that accompany a woman's menstrual cycle:
   a. cause her to experience peak sex drive during menstruation.
   b. cause her to experience a dramatically increased sex drive about the time of ovulation.
   c. cause her to experience an absence of sex drive during menstruation.
   d. have relatively little, if any, effect on her sex drive.

8. Electrical stimulation of reward mechanisms in the brain:
   a. has never been tried in humans.
   b. is not pleasurable enough to cause nonhuman animals to work for it.
   c. is effective only if electrodes are placed in the ventromedial hypothalamus.
   d. suggests that there are different reward systems serving different survival-related needs.

9. The electroencephalogram, or EEG, has proven especially useful in studying:
   a. sleep.
   b. hunger.
   c. sex.
   d. curiosity.

10. Which stage of sleep represents the actual onset of sleep?
    a. stage 1
    b. emergent stage 1
    c. stage 2
    d. stage 4

11. Physical exercise is typically followed by lengthier, deeper sleep. This fact supports the _____ theory of sleep.
    a. restoration
    b. preservation and protection
    c. side-effect
    d. common sense

12. Prolonged sleep deprivation in humans leads to:
    a. coma and death within 10 days.
    b. severe difficulty in the performance of tasks requiring physical skill or mental judgment.
    c. irritability, distorted perception, and difficulty carrying out simple, boring tasks.
    d. a paradoxical absence of sleepiness.

13. The pattern of measurable physiological changes that helps prepare the body for "fight or flight" is called:
    a. the circadian rhythm.
    b. the arousal response.
    c. emotion.
    d. the alertness mechanism.

14. According to the Yerkes-Dodson law, conditions of high arousal would be most likely to harm performance on a(n):
    a. high-energy physical task.
    b. instinctive or well-practiced task.
    c. task that demands persistence or endurance.
    d. task involving creativity or careful judgment.

15. Peripheral feedback contributes to the emotional experience, according to:
    a. James.          c. both a. and b.
    b. Shachter.       d. none of the above.

### Essay Questions

16. What is obesity? Explain three factors that may predispose a person to become and stay obese.

17. Discuss hormonal effects on the human sex drive after puberty. Be certain to deal with both the male and the female sex drive.

---

*After you have assessed your understanding on the basis of Self-Test 1 and have tried to strengthen your preparation in any areas of weakness, GO ON to Self-Test 2.*

## Self-Test 2

### Multiple-Choice Questions

1. A thirsty fan at a football game waits in line for a soft drink. In this example, the fan's thirst is a(n) _____ and the soft drink is a(n) _____ .
    a. reinforcer; incentive
    b. incentive; drive
    c. drive; incentive
    d. motivational state; drive

2. A set of neurons in which activity constitutes a drive is a:
    a. central drive system.
    b. motivational state.
    c. limbic system.
    d. homeostatic regulator.

3. Which of the following methods involves insertion of a cannula into the brain to destroy neurons whose cell bodies are near the cannula's tip?
    a. the electrical production of lesions
    b. the chemical production of lesions
    c. electrical brain stimulation
    d. chemical brain stimulation

4. Animals with bilateral lesions to the lateral hypothalamus neither seek food nor eat it if it is put in front of them. This is because:
    a. the lateral hypothalamus is the hunger center and, once destroyed, can no longer produce the hunger drive.

b. such lesions interrupt a tract serving general motor-activation functions for hunger and other drives.

c. lesions in the lateral hypothalamus cause changes in digestion and metabolism.

d. the brain can no longer send hunger signals to the stomach.

5. The amount of fat stored in fat cells under the skin tends to be conserved if an individual is:

a. above his or her set point, thus tending to stimulate hunger.

b. under his or her set point, thus tending to stimulate hunger.

c. above his or her set point, thus tending to reduce hunger.

d. under his or her set point, thus tending to reduce hunger.

6. Stanley Schachter and his colleagues found that obese subjects ate more peanuts if the nuts were brightly illuminated than if they were dimly illuminated, whereas nonobese subjects ate the same amount in either condition. These results supported the _____ theory of obesity.

a. side-effect          c. cue-sensitivity
b. restoration          d. stress-eating

7. In the area of sex, a basic difference between humans and other species is that:

a. humans are much more stereotyped in their sexual behavior.

b. the sex drive of human females is not limited to a specific time in their hormonal cycle.

c. humans are not sexually differentiated as a result of prenatal hormones.

d. the human sex drive typically remains strong in the absence of sex hormones.

8. Simon LeVay has reported that a structure homologous to the sexually dimorphic nucleus is:

a. the same size in homosexual and heterosexual men.

b. larger in homosexual men than in heterosexual men.

c. smaller in women and homosexual men than in heterosexual men.

d. destroyed by AIDS.

9. Injections of the hormone testosterone:

a. will fail to restore the sex drive in men who have been castrated or who produce abnormally low levels of the hormone.

b. will dramatically increase the sex drive of men who already produce normal amounts of the hormone.

c. will be rejected by the immune systems of women because testosterone is an exclusively male hormone.

d. will increase the sex drive in women who are experiencing low sex drive due to removal of the adrenal glands.

10. The administration of dopamine-blocking drugs will:

a. cause animals who have learned to lever press for food to nearly stop their lever pressing and eating behaviors.

b. enhance the effects of cocaine, amphetamines, and certain other illicit drugs.

c. help an animal learn faster how to stimulate its reward centers electrically.

d. cause animals who have learned to lever press for food to exhibit this behavior at unusually high rates.

11. The sleep cycle can be reset through carefully timed:

a. exposure to bright fluorescent light.
b. changes in temperature.
c. alterations in diet.
d. mild electrical shocks.

12. True dreams occur during _____ sleep.

a. slow-wave          c. stage 2
b. REM                d. stage 4

13. The circadian clock is located in a specific nucleus in the:

a. pons.              c. hypothalamus.
b. cerebral cortex.   d. medulla.

14. George Hohmann asked men paralyzed through spinal cord injury about their emotions. They reported that emotions with a major physiological arousal component, such as anger or fear, were no longer felt as acutely as they were prior to injury. For which of the following reasons must we question his results?

a. George Hohmann is not himself paralyzed and had some admitted difficulty in establishing rapport with his subjects.

b. Subjects may have been led to equate emotion with bodily arousal.

c. The same essential study has been carried out numerous times with other paralyzed individuals who report overall stronger emotional experiences.

d. Research by Stanley Schachter had indicated that high physiological arousal produced by the injection of epinephrine has no bearing on emotional intensity.

15. In terms of emotional experience, research suggests that the left and right frontal lobes:
    a. are not involved in emotion as was once thought.
    b. are responsible for immediate unconscious responses to emotional stimuli.
    c. differ in that one is specialized for positive emotions and one for negative emotions.
    d. are involved in emotional responses for women but not men.

## Essay Questions

16. What is the function of slow-wave sleep? Offer evidence for any theories that you present.

17. What is the arousal response? What role does it play in emotion? Support your position.

# Answers

## Motivation and Reward

8. nonregulatory; sex (or curiosity)
15. a. damage
    b. electrically; electrode; chemically; cannula
17. lateral area of the hypothalamus; ventromedial area of the hypothalamus
21. 20
30. medial preoptic; ventromedial
31. testosterone; sexually dimorphic
36. a. testes; testosterone; decrease
    b. restores
37. b. elimination; restores

## Sleeping and Dreaming

4. a. stage 2
   b. stage 3
   c. stage 1
   d. stage 4
5. deeper; decline
7. rapid eye movement
9. slow-wave
10. 4 or 5; REM; 90; decreases

## Emotion

16. amygdala; frontal lobe

## Self-Test 1

1. b. (p. 201)
2. d. (p. 203)
3. b. Nonregulatory drives are those whose purpose is other than to maintain internal bodily conditions within certain limits. In other words, nonregulatory drives exist for nonhomeostatic purposes. (p. 204)
4. d. (p. 205)
5. c. (p. 208)
6. d. (p. 213)
7. d. (p. 217)
8. d. (pp. 219–220)
9. a. (p. 221)
10. c. Stage 1 is a transitional stage between waking and sleep, and emergent stage 1, another name

for REM sleep, appears only after the first sleep cycle. (p. 222)

11. **a.** (p. 223)

12. **c.** In fact, the difficulty with simple, boring tasks may be due to brief episodes of sleep during the performance of the task. (p. 226)

13. **b.** (p. 230)

14. **d.** (p. 230)

15. **c.** (p. 232)

16. Obesity is a condition in which a person is more than 20 percent above the average weight for people of the same sex, height, and bone structure. Although it is not impossible for people to overcome the tendency to be obese, a number of psychological and physiological factors make it difficult. There is some evidence that obese individuals are more sensitive to external food cues and less sensitive to internal cues about the need for food. Since we know from the appetizer effect that external food cues increase the hunger drive, an excessive sensitivity to such cues would tend to exaggerate the hunger drive. This would be especially troublesome given a reduced sensitivity to internal cues signaling that no more food is needed. Even if the altered cue sensitivity of obese individuals is a product of their obesity or of their attempts to diet, this heightened sensitivity would make it hard for them to lose the weight once it was gained. Obese individuals also may be strongly influenced by hereditary factors. Evidence from adoption studies shows that adopted children resemble their biological parents more than their adoptive parents where weight is concerned. Another factor is the ratchet effect, a phenomenon in which the set point is raised with prolonged overeating but does not go down when intake is reduced over a long period. (Note: Other factors could be mentioned—for example, eating to cope with stress.) (pp. 209–211)

17. The hormone testosterone appears to be important for maintaining the sex drive in both men and women. Men who have been castrated or who produce abnormally low amounts of testosterone will show a decline in the sex drive and sexual behavior, though they will often not lose the drive entirely. If they receive injections of testosterone, their sex drive will be restored. At least in the case of men with abnormally low levels, the injection of testosterone specifically affects the desire for sex, not the ability to carry out sexual behavior. In men who already have sufficient testosterone, additional amounts of the hormone do not further increase the sex drive.

In women, the sex drive also appears to depend on some minimum level of testosterone in the body. Unlike females of other species, a woman's sex drive is not tied directly to cyclic fluctuations in the female hormones estrogen and progesterone. A woman whose ovaries have been removed, and who therefore is producing little estrogen and progesterone, will experience no decline in sex drive. However, a woman whose adrenal glands have been removed, and who therefore is producing no testosterone, will experience a decline in sex drive. As with men, injections of testosterone restore the sex drive in such women. (pp. 215–217)

### Self-Test 2

1. **c.** Remember that the drive, or motivational state, is the condition of the individual that causes it to orient toward some goal. The incentive is the external stimulus toward which motivated behavior is directed. (pp. 201–202)

2. **a.** (p. 204)

3. **b.** Cannulas are used in chemical methods of lesioning and stimulation, but only in lesioning is there destruction of brain tissue. Electrodes are used for electrically produced lesions and stimulation. (p. 205)

4. **b.** (p. 207)

5. **b.** The body of an individual under his or her set point acts to increase weight. It will not easily release stores of fat molecules into the blood, leaving the body with an energy deficit; this stimulates the hunger drive so that food will be consumed to meet current needs. (p. 209)

6. **c.** (pp. 209–210)

7. **b.** (p. 212)

8. **c.** Note that this correlational result does not allow us to conclude that this is a cause of male homosexuality. (p. 215)

9. **d.** (p. 217)

10. **a.** Apparently, the dopamine blockers prevent the usual rewarding consequence that eating naturally produces. (p. 220)

11. **a.** (p. 225)

12. **b.** Sleep thought, a type of mental activity different from true dreaming, occurs during slow-wave sleep, which includes stages 2 through 4. (p. 227)

13. **c.** Other neural controls for REM and slow-wave sleep are found in the brainstem, which includes the pons and medulla. (p. 229)

14. **b.** (pp. 233–234)

**15.** c. (p. 237)

**16.** There are two major theories on the functions of slow-wave sleep. The restoration theory suggests that sleep is needed for the body to recover physically after a day of wear and tear. Several lines of evidence support this notion. One is the fact that sleep really is a time of rest in which the muscles are relaxed and the metabolic rate is slowed. Another is the fact that extreme physical exertion causes sleep to be deeper and a little longer, as if more repair is needed following harder wear and tear.

The preservation and protection theory is also supported by several different kinds of evidence. The theory states that sleep came about in evolution to conserve energy and to keep an animal relatively safe during that part of a 24-hour period when activity would be more risky than beneficial. Evidence for this theory comes primarily from comparing different species. For example, the theory helps to make sense of the fact that variations in sleep time between species correspond to feeding habits and ways of avoiding predators. Animals who need to spend large amounts of time getting food and who are too big to hide easily during sleep do not sleep much. Animals who get all the food they need easily and who can sleep in a safely hidden place sleep for a good portion of a 24-hour period. (pp. 223–224)

**17.** The arousal response is a pattern of measurable physiological changes that occurs in response to some stimulus that provokes the individual to prepare for "fight or flight." The particular changes involved vary from individual to individual and from situation to situation, but may include such things as elevated heart rate, breathing rate, and blood pressure; diversion of blood to the skeletal muscles; the release of endorphins; and the narrow focusing of attention. James's peripheral feedback theory suggests that emotion—the subjective feeling we have—is simply our awareness of the bodily changes we experience. Schachter's theory proposes that emotion is a product both of the arousal we experience and of an emotionally significant stimulus that causes us to interpret the arousal in emotional terms. According to this theory, the more arousal there is, the more intense the emotion we experience.

Schachter found in a laboratory experiment that the intensity of his subjects' emotional response was heightened by epinephrine, which produces physiological arousal. (pp. 230–234)

# CHAPTER 8 SENSATION

*Read the introduction below before you read the chapter in the text.*

Sensation occurs when a physical stimulus produces physiological responses that lead to a subjective, psychological experience of that stimulus. Sensations, in the form of sights, sounds, tastes, smells, and so on, are necessary for us to know about the world around us and even about our own bodies. Vision may seem very different from hearing, and smell very different from pain, but sensory systems actually have much in common. For example, all of our sensory systems need certain types of neural structures: receptors, which respond directly to the stimulus; sensory neurons, which carry sensory information to the central nervous system; and still other cells that process sensory information in particular ways. Processes common to all of our senses include transduction (responding to a physical stimulus with electrical changes that can trigger neural impulses), coding (preserving information about the stimulus in patterns of neural activity), and adaptation (altering sensitivity to a stimulus with continued stimulation or lack of stimulation).

Sound waves—vibrations in the air or some other medium—are the stimuli that initiate responses in the ear. The chapter explains both the nature of sound waves and the workings of the human ear. Emphasis is placed on a structure called the cochlea, which is located in the inner ear, because it is in this coiled structure that transduction takes place. Two types of deafness—conduction deafness and sensorineural deafness—can occur, each resulting from a different type of malfunction in the ear. The basilar membrane, a structure in the inner ear, is the focus of theories of pitch perception; both the pattern and timing of its movement contribute to our ability to discriminate among pitches.

The discussion of vision begins with a description of the nature of the sensory stimulus—light—and the basic workings of the sense organ—the eye. The retina, the part of the eye that includes the receptor cells capable of responding to light, contains two types of visual receptors—rods and cones—each underlying a kind of visual subsystem with particular strengths and weaknesses. The rods enable us to see in very dim light, but we must rely on the cones to see color and fine detail. Color vision involves neural mechanisms in the eye and higher up in the nervous system that code information provided by the light stimulus. This section concludes by discussing how the visual system enhances contrast for sharper vision and how the brain processes information about visual features.

Pain is a sense we may at times wish we didn't have; yet it is one with real survival value. The receptors for pain are the sensory neurons themselves. There are two subsystems of pain—a slow one mediated by neurons called C fibers and a fast one mediated by faster neurons called A-delta fibers. Each subsystem has its own neural pathways and results in its own type of subjective experience. The gate-control theory helps to explain pain and its inhibition. Pain relief may come from a number of natural sources, including endorphins, acute stress, and even our beliefs.

The chapter concludes by introducing several questions addressed by the field of psychophysics, which attempts to relate characteristics of the stimulus to aspects of the resulting subjective experience. One question is: How weak can a stimulus be and still be detected? This question concerns the so-called absolute threshold. (Actually, it turns out to be a fairly arbitrary and unabsolute threshold, as you will see.) A second question is: How different do two stimuli have to be before we notice the difference? A third question is: How is the strength of the stimulus related to the strength of the sensation? For example, how does loudness change as we vary the physical intensity of a sound? Psychophysics has been a fruitful area for those who appreciate mathematical precision in their answers.

*LOOK over the table of contents for this chapter in your textbook before you continue with your study.*

*Notice that there are focus questions in the margins of the text for your use in studying the material. The following chart lists which study guide questions relate to which focus questions.*

| Focus Questions | Study Guide Questions |
|---|---|
| Overview | |
| 1–5 | 1–5 |
| Hearing | |
| 6–8 | 1–10 |
| 9–11 | 11–15 |
| Vision | |
| 12–14 | 1–4 |
| 15–17 | 5–11 |
| 18–23 | 12–19 |
| 24–28 | 20–28 |
| Pain | |
| 29–30 | 1–4 |
| 31–32 | 5–11 |
| Psychophysics | |
| 33–35 | 1–8 |
| 36–38 | 9–16 |

# The Integrated Study Workout

*Complete one section at a time.*

## Overview  (pages 242–246)

*CONSIDER these questions before you go on. They are designed to help you start thinking about this subject, not to test your knowledge.*

How can psychologists study a person's sensations, given that they're completely private experiences?

Are there really only five senses?

The eyes are certainly necessary for sight and the ears for hearing, but does seeing actually take place in the eyes? or hearing in the ears?

When we see a full moon or hear a train whistle or feel the touch of another person's hand, what are we really experiencing? After all, the moon, the whistle, and the hand exist only outside the body. So what exists inside the body that corresponds to those things?

How can the wonderful smell of fresh coffee seem so vivid at first but become barely noticeable after a short while?

*READ this section of your text lightly. Then go back and read thoroughly, completing the Workout as you proceed.*

Sensation, and the kinds of questions scientists ask about sensation, can be more clearly understood if the process is broken down into three classes of events.

1.  Indicate the three classes of events involved in sensation by filling in the diagram below.

    _____  →  _____

    →  _____

2.  Direct physical measurement is possible for the first two classes of events in sensation. How do psychologists measure the third?

Different domains of inquiry focus on different types or relationships in the chain of events above.

3.  Label each of the areas of study described below. (See Figure 8.1 on text page 243.)

    a.  _____ deals with the relationship between the physiological response and the sensory experience.

    b.  _____ concerns the relationship between the stimulus and the sensory experience.

    c.  _____ focuses on the relationship between the stimulus and the physiological response.

Though we have a number of different senses, each unique in important ways, all senses have some things in common. For example, all depend on certain types of physiological elements, which carry out particular types of functions. The senses also have some basic processes in common.

4.  Name the three types of physiological structures common to all senses and briefly state their respective functions.

    Structure            Function

    a.

Structure            Function

**b.**

**c.**

**5.** Define the following processes and give a specific example of each.

   **a.** transduction

   **b.** coding

   **c.** sensory adaptation

## *Hearing* (pages 246–252)

> *CONSIDER these questions before you go on. They are designed to help you start thinking about this subject, not to test your knowledge.*

Where in the ear does the neural response to sound occur?

What causes deafness? Why does a hearing aid help some deaf people and not others?

What makes some sounds high such as those of a piccolo and others low such as those of a tuba? What makes them loud or soft?

> *READ this section of your text lightly. Then go back and read thoroughly, completing the Workout as you proceed.*

Every sensory system is specialized to respond to a particular type of stimulation. In order to understand the workings of each sense, you must understand the nature of its stimulus.

**1.** Sound occurs when an object produces _____ of the air or some other medium, which can be described in terms of _____ with a given height and rate of movement.

**2.** We experience the intensity, or _____ , of the sound (measured in _____ ) as _____ .

**3.** The frequency of the sound waves (measured in _____ ) corresponds to what we hear as _____ . Humans hear sounds varying from 20 up to _____ .

**4.** Most natural sounds are more complex than a _____ tone, which is a constant-frequency wave of vibration that can be described as a simple sine wave.

In order to understand the sense of hearing, you must also know something about the parts of the ear. The ear is commonly divided into three major sections, each with its own functions. (See Figure 8.4 on text page 248.)

**5.** The outer ear, which consists of the _____ and the _____ , is separated from the middle ear by the _____ , which is also called the _____ . The function of the outer ear is to _____ sound inward.

**6.** The middle ear contains the _____ (more specifically called the _____ , _____ , and _____ ), whose main function is to increase the _____ of sound waves on the inner ear.

**7.** Identify and describe the following parts of the inner ear. (See Figures 8.4 and 8.5 on text pages 248 and 249.)

   **a.** cochlea

b.  basilar membrane

c.  hair cells

d.  auditory nerve

8.  Briefly describe the process of transduction in the inner ear.

Two types of deafness can occur, each stemming from a different physiological problem.

9.  What problem underlies conduction deafness? Is there any help for this problem? Explain.

10. What problem underlies sensorineural deafness? Is there any help for this problem? Explain.

A major task for scientists studying sensation is to understand how the nervous system codes various aspects of the stimulus. In the study of hearing, interest has centered on how frequency is coded to produce the experience of pitch.

11. How does the ear code various frequencies to allow pitch perception, according to Georg von Békésy? (See Figure 8.7 on text page 251.)

12. Explain how Békésy's traveling-wave theory partially accounts for asymmetry in auditory masking. (See Figure 8.8 on text page 251.)

13. How does his theory fit with the fact that aging reduces sensitivity to higher frequencies more than to lower frequencies?

14. Explain how the timing of activity in the basilar membrane plays a role in pitch perception of sounds below about 4000 Hz.

Information delivered to the brain by the auditory nerve receives extensive processing in the auditory cortex. Many cells there are specialized to respond only to very specific types of auditory information—a narrow range of frequencies, for example, or a brief burst of sound. Through the combined pattern of activity in these cells, the brain extracts information about different aspects of the sound.

15. Four types of information (in addition to loudness and pitch) that the brain extracts about sound are _____ ,

_____ , _____ ,

and _____ .

*Vision* (pages 253–269)

> *CONSIDER these questions before you go on. They are designed to help you start thinking about this subject, not to test your knowledge.*

What is light "made of"?

Which part of the eye is able to respond to light? What do the other parts do?

When you enter a dark, crowded movie theater, you may be unable to see the bucket of popcorn in your hand; yet, moments later you see well enough to find an unoccupied seat. Why is that?

How does the brain process the signals it receives from the eye in order to give us such incredibly detailed and subtle views of the world?

How do we see color? Why are some people color blind? What does a color-blind person "see"?

> *READ this section of your text lightly. Then go back and read thoroughly, completing the Workout as you proceed.*

With vision as with hearing, it is necessary to understand the nature of the stimulus for which the sense is specialized.

1. Light can be thought of in terms of particles called _____ . It can also be thought of in terms of _____ , which provides the most useful perspective for understanding vision.

2. Light varies in _____ from 400 to 700 nanometers (nm).

3. Visible light is a small range of wavelengths within the _____ spectrum, which also includes x-rays and radio waves.

The eye is an organ specialized for vision. Some of its parts are designed for responding to light with neural signals. Others are designed for focusing the light on the cells that are light sensitive.

4. Match the parts of the eye with their descriptions. (See Figure 8.11 on text page 254.)

| | |
|---|---|
| _____ a doughnut-shaped ring of muscle fibers that opens or closes to control the amount of light entering the eye | a. pupil<br>b. retina<br>c. cones<br>d. lens<br>e. fovea |
| _____ transparent tissue at the front of the eye whose curved surface begins to focus incoming light | f. rods<br>g. iris<br>h. cornea<br>i. optic nerve |
| _____ a thin membrane at the back of the eye that contains vision receptors | |
| _____ a hole that admits light into the eye | |
| _____ a structure that carries visual information from the eye to the brain and causes a blind spot where it leaves the eye | |
| _____ a retinal area specialized for high visual acuity | |
| _____ a flexible structure that can become rounder or flatter to focus on objects at different distances | |
| _____ receptor cell that permits sharply focused color vision in bright light | |
| _____ receptor cell that permits vision in dim light | |

The transduction of light occurs in rods and cones, the visual receptors in the retina. These photoreceptors contain chemicals that are sensitive to light—rhodopsin in the case of rods and other light-sensitive chemicals in the case of cones.

5. Put the following events in proper order to describe transduction in rods, writing the appropriate step number next to each statement.

| Step | Event |
|---|---|
| _____ | There is an electrical change across the rod's cell membrane. |
| _____ | Electrical changes are triggered in retinal cells other than the receptors. |
| _____ | Rhodopsin is struck by light. |
| _____ | Action potentials move down the optic nerve to the brain. |
| _____ | Rhodopsin molecules undergo a structural change. |

Rods and cones are the two types of visual receptors in the retina. They underlie two separate but coordinated systems.

6. Describe the difference between these two systems by filling in the table that follows.

| | Rods (scotopic vision) | Cones (photopic vision) |
|---|---|---|
| Sensitivity to light | | |
| Acuity | | |
| Color vision capability | | |
| Distribution over retina | | |

In light adaptation, the eyes become less sensitive; in dark adaptation, they become more sensitive. This is due primarily to changes in the photochemicals inside rods and cones.

7. What happens to the photochemicals in rods and cones in bright light?

8. Why are cones more sensitive than rods in bright light?

9. What happens to the photochemicals in rods and cones in darkness?

10. In what sense is dark adaptation a two-part process? How can that be demonstrated? (See Figure 8.15 on text page 256.)

Rods and cones send information on to bipolar cells, which in turn send information on to ganglion cells. The axons of ganglion cells form the optic nerve.

11. Using the concepts of receptive fields and convergence, explain how the increased sensitivity and reduced acuity of rods are really two sides of the same coin. (See Figure 8.17 on text page 258.)

The world we see is full of color. Our experience of color depends on the wavelengths of light reaching our eyes. An object absorbs some wavelengths from the light falling on it and reflects others, depending on its pigments.

12. Answer the following questions about subtractive color mixing. (See Figure 8.18 on text page 259.)

a. Subtractive color mixing involves mixing

_____ .

b. Under what circumstances would the mixture appear green?

13. Answer the following questions about additive color mixing. (Hint: For b. and c., it will help if you spend some time studying the standard chromaticity diagram in Figure 8.20 on text page 261.)

a. Additive color mixing involves mixing

_____ .

**b.** State the three-primaries law of color vision.

**c.** State the law of complementarity.

**d.** Why do we say that these two laws represent psychological, not physical, facts?

Two theories—trichromatic and opponent-process—have been advanced to explain the behavioral and physiological aspects of color vision.

**14.** Explain the trichromatic theory developed by Thomas Young and Hermann Helmholtz.

**15.** How well does the trichromatic theory account for the three-primaries law of color vision? Explain.

**16.** What is a dichromat? Why is a dichromat more likely to be male than female? What is red-green color blindness? How well does our understanding of red-green color blindness fit with the trichromatic theory?

**17.** What observation was Ewald Hering trying to explain with his opponent-process theory of color vision? What was Hering's explanation?

**18.** How does the opponent-process theory explain the complementarity of afterimages?

**19.** Are the trichromatic and opponent-process theories considered to be contradictory? Explain.

Our visual system is designed to provide us with the information we need to survive. For example, we need information about contour to identify objects around us. We also need to know such information as the direction in which a moving object is traveling, how fast it is going, and how far away it is. Contour is so important that the visual system enhances contrast to "sharpen" contours for us. Stephen Kuffler's work has helped us to understand how the receptive fields of ganglion cells help to accomplish this sharpening.

**20.** Diagram and explain the functioning of a ganglion cell's receptive field with an *on* center and an *off* surround. (See Figures 8.24 and 8.25 on text page 265.)

Using cats and monkeys as subjects, Hubel and Wiesel studied the receptive fields of cells in the visual area of the brain's cortex. They discovered that these receptive fields were arranged differently from those of retinal ganglion cells.

21. Briefly describe the retinal receptive fields for edge and bar detectors.

22. Explain how edge and bar detectors are sensitive to orientation.

23. What did Hubel and Wiesel find about orientation sensitivity as they moved from one column of cortical cells to another?

Cortical neurons are also sensitive to spatial frequency.

24. Which of the patterns below has higher spatial frequency?

a.

b.

25. Spatial frequency is defined as the number of _____ per unit distance in the pattern's retinal image.

26. List two reasons that vision researchers are interested in spatial frequency.

As you know, sensory information receives a great deal of processing after it arrives in the brain. Some cells in the brain serve a feature-detection function. Others serve to integrate information from feature detectors in various ways.

27. What is the process of surface interpolation and how might it be valuable?

28. How is it possible that people who have suffered brain damage in a particular area of the cortex might lose one specific aspect of vision (e.g., seeing color) but retain others?

*Pain*   (pages 269–273)

*CONSIDER these questions before you go on. They are designed to help you start thinking about this subject, not to test your knowledge.*

The usefulness—and the pleasures—of senses such as sight and hearing are obvious, but why should pain exist?

Is there a sense organ for pain? Where does this type of sensation originate?

Why might a person who has been badly injured not feel pain until later?

Can our beliefs affect pain? Are there mental techniques that can lessen pain?

*READ this section of your text lightly. Then go back and read thoroughly, completing the Workout as you proceed.*

Pain is a biologically useful, though generally unwanted, type of sensation. It is related to other cutaneous, or skin, senses such as the senses of touch and temperature. Like the receptors for these senses, pain receptors are actually specialized parts of sensory neurons, not separate cells. (See Figure 8.30 on text page 270.)

1. Pain neurons have sensitive terminals called _____ , which are found in _____ .

2. Distinguish between C fibers and A-delta fibers. Indicate the type of stimulus that activates each and specify the type of pain associated with each.

As with other senses, pain depends not only on specialized peripheral neurons, but also on specialized areas of the brain. A-delta and C fibers apparently send neural signals to different areas of the brain. (See Figure 8.31 on text page 271.)

3. Trace the pathway of pain information from A-delta fibers by answering the following questions.

   a. Input from A-delta fibers is received by the area of the thalamus called the

   _____ .

   b. The information is then sent to the

   _____ .

   c. Why is this part of the cortex organized as it is?

4. Trace the pathway of pain information from C fibers by answering the following questions.

   a. Input from C fibers is received by the area of the thalamus called the _____ .

   b. The information is then sent to the

   _____ .

   c. The fact that the experience of pain does not always come from pain receptors is illustrated by an experience called _____ .

Ronald Melzack and Patrick Wall proposed the gate-control theory to explain when pain will be felt and when it will not. The theory is well supported by physiological evidence.

5. Explain the basic premise of the gate-control theory.

6. Discuss the role of the PAG in gate control.

7. What happens to pain levels when the PAG is stimulated electrically? by morphine? by endorphins?

Nature has provided us with several natural mechanisms of pain reduction.

8. Describe the phenomenon of stress-induced analgesia.

9. Describe evidence suggesting that stress-induced analgesia is mediated by endorphins.

10. Can pain be reduced through the power of belief or faith? Explain.

11. What do endorphins have to do with placebo effects?

*Psychophysics*   (pages 274–280)

> CONSIDER *these questions before you go on. They are designed to help you start thinking about this subject, not to test your knowledge.*

What's the smallest amount of light a person can see? or the smallest amount of sound a person can hear?

How can we study human sensations (which are private experiences) precisely enough to make trustworthy measurements?

Are any general psychophysical relationships pretty much the same for everyone? Or is everyone so different that a scientific law would be impossible to establish?

Why does changing lighting from a 50- to a 100-watt bulb make a bigger difference in brightness than changing from a 150- to a 200-watt bulb?

> READ *this section of your text lightly. Then go back and read thoroughly, completing the Workout as you proceed.*

Psychophysics involves the relationship between physical characteristics of a stimulus and the psychological experiences that it produces. The physical characteristics of the stimulus can be measured directly, but experience must be measured indirectly. One major psychophysical question is: What is the weakest stimulus that can be detected in a particular sensory system, for example, vision?

1. What does the term *absolute threshold* refer to? Why is the absolute threshold not really "absolute"?

2. In general, how is a person's absolute threshold for a particular kind of stimulus determined? (See Figure 8.34 on text page 275.)

According to signal-detection researchers, stimulus detection depends on more than sensory sensitivity.

3. What is the other major factor? Why is it especially important in real-life tasks?

Psychophysicists use a procedure in which there are four categories of response—hits, misses, false alarms, and correct rejections—to obtain separate measures of sensory sensitivity and response bias.

4. Complete the following matrix of possible signal-detection outcomes by entering hit, miss, and so on in the appropriate box. (See Figure 8.35 on text page 276.)

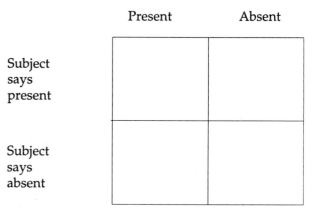

5. Why would both hits and false alarms increase with a liberal response strategy? decrease with a conservative response strategy?

6. To derive d', a true measure of sensitivity, researchers compare the proportion of

   _____ to _____ .

A second question asked by psychophysicists is: How different must two stimuli be in order to be noticeably different?

7. What is a difference threshold, or jnd? Is the difference threshold a statistical concept like the absolute threshold? Explain.

8. Express Weber's law as a formula, defining each element. Now state the same law verbally.

Another major interest in psychophysics has been the way sensation increases with increasing stimulus intensity. Gustav Fechner in the nineteenth century and S. S. Stevens in the twentieth century both produced elegant mathematical descriptions of this relationship.

9. On what theoretical unit did Fechner base his law? What important assumption did he make about this unit?

10. State Fechner's law mathematically. According to Fechner, to what is the magnitude of the sensory experience proportional?

11. Why is it useful that the law involves a logarithmic transformation?

Stevens went on to do what Fechner believed could not be done: He tested the validity of Fechner's work experimentally.

12. Describe the subject's task in Stevens's method of magnitude estimation.

13. If Fechner's law were correct, what relationship should Stevens have found in his subjects' magnitude estimations? What did he find instead?

14. What kind of mathematical relationship best describes Stevens's results?

15. Is the exponent ($p$) greater or less than 1 for most of the various types of stimuli Stevens investigated? When $p$ is less than 1, does a given increase in stimulus intensity produce equal sensory effects at the high and low ends of the scale? Explain. What about cases in which $p$ is greater than 1?

16. Why did Stevens think nature would produce senses that follow power laws?

*Be sure to READ the Concluding Thoughts at the end of the chapter. Note important points in your Workout. Then consolidate your learning by answering the focus questions in the margins of the text.*

*After you have studied the chapter thoroughly, CHECK your understanding with the self-test that follows.*

## Self-Test 1

*Multiple-Choice Questions*

1. The basic sequence of events in sensation is: (1) physical stimulus → (2) physiological response → (3) sensory experience. Sensory physiology is concerned with:
   a. only 2.
   b. the relationship between 1 and 2.
   c. the relationship between 2 and 3.
   d. the relationships among 1, 2, and 3.

2. The amplitude of a sound is:
   a. a dimension of psychological sensation.
   b. related to what the hearer experiences as loudness.
   c. the rate at which the sound waves are traveling.
   d. measured in units called hertz.

3. The main function of the ear's ossicles is to:
   a. transmit the pattern of sound waves from the outer to the inner ear without modification.
   b. decrease the pressure of sound waves before they reach the delicate inner ear.
   c. increase the pressure that incoming sound waves place on the inner ear.
   d. lower the frequency of incoming sound waves to reduce wear and tear on the auditory nerve.

4. Békésy found that high-frequency sounds cause:
   a. the basilar membrane to vibrate equally over its whole length.
   b. the basilar membrane to vibrate maximally near its proximal end, that is, near the oval window.
   c. the basilar membrane to vibrate maximally near its distal end.
   d. the two ends of the basilar membrane to vibrate more than the middle.

5. Conduction deafness occurs when the _____ become(s) rigid.
   a. basilar membrane    c. hair cells
   b. tectorial membrane    d. ossicles

6. The retina is designed to produce a neural response to light, while the rest of the eye is designed primarily to:
   a. focus light on the retina.
   b. filter incoming light.
   c. transduce light.
   d. separate light into different wavelengths.

7. Which of the following is true of dark adaptation?
   a. It involves reduced sensitivity with increased time in the dark.
   b. It involves changes in cones as well as rods.
   c. It is the direct result of local adaptation.
   d. It is due to the breakdown of photopigments in cones.

8. In the retina, _____ synapse on _____ , which in turn synapse on _____.
   a. rods; cones; ganglion cells
   b. photoreceptors; ganglion cells; bipolar cells
   c. rods and cones; bipolar cells; ganglion cells
   d. ganglion cells; photoreceptors; the optic nerve

9. A ganglion cell's receptive field consists of:
   a. those rods and/or cones from which it receives input.
   b. the portion of the stimulus from which it receives input.
   c. the part of the ganglion cell that synapses on other cells.
   d. an area in the cerebral cortex to which it sends sensory information.

10. The notion that color vision is mediated by three different types of receptors is known as:
    a. the law of complementarity.
    b. the three-primaries law.
    c. additive color mixing.
    d. trichromatic theory.

11. Hubel and Wiesel showed visual stimuli to cats while recording electrical activity in the cells of their visual cortex. They were interested in discovering how the visual system accomplishes:
    a. transduction.       c. coding.
    b. adaptation.         d. psychophysics.

12. Which of the following is true of pain receptors?
    a. They are the same as those for touch and temperature.
    b. They are found only in the skin and joints.
    c. They are specialized endings of sensory neurons.
    d. They are short, thick neurons with special encapsulated endings.

13. Which of the following statements is true of stress-induced analgesia?
    a. It is at least partially the result of endorphins in the brain.
    b. It is purely psychological and unrelated to physiological mechanisms of pain.
    c. It has not been found to occur under controlled laboratory conditions.
    d. It occurs in humans but not in other animals.

14. In signal-detection tasks, _____ and _____ are compared in order to derive a true measure of sensitivity called _____ .
    a. hits; false alarms; d'
    b. hits; misses; d'
    c. hits; false alarms; the absolute threshold
    d. hits; misses; the absolute threshold

15. In a room with 20 lit candles, we must add 2 to get a jnd. How many would Weber's law say we have to add to a set of 100 candles to get a jnd?
    a. 2       c. 10
    b. 5       d. 20

*Essay Questions*

16. Compare rods and cones in terms of acuity and then in terms of sensitivity. Explain how the concept of convergence can be used to explain these differences.

17. What is an absolute threshold? Why isn't it really "absolute"? How do we define the absolute threshold for a given type of stimulus?

*After you have assessed your understanding on the basis of Self-Test 1 and have tried to strengthen your preparation in any areas of weakness, GO ON to Self-Test 2.*

# Self-Test 2

*Multiple-Choice Questions*

1. Measurement of sensory experience is:
   a. not possible.
   b. irrelevant because sensory experience is a purely psychological creation with no objective reality.
   c. not only precise but also objective.
   d. accomplished indirectly by observing what the subject says and does.

2. The process by which a receptor cell produces a neural signal in response to a physical stimulus is called:
   a. sensory adaptation.
   b. coding.
   c. perception.
   d. transduction.

3. The function of the eardrum is to:
   a. vibrate in response to incoming sound waves.
   b. transduce sound.
   c. increase the frequency of incoming sound waves.
   d. relieve pressure created by waves in the cochlea.

4. A higher tone cannot mask a lower tone very effectively because:
   a. the basilar membrane vibrates more intensely for lower tones than for high ones.
   b. the area of the basilar membrane that responds to high tones is completely separate from the area that responds to low tones.
   c. the part of the basilar membrane that responds most to low tones is unaffected by higher tones and is thus "out of their reach."
   d. our ears are insensitive to higher frequencies.

5. The wavelength of visible light ranges from:
   a. 20 to 20,000 nm.      c. 100 to 1000 nm.
   b. 400 to 700 nm.        d. 700 to 1400 nm.

6. The receptors for vision are located in the:
   a. cornea.               c. lens.
   b. retina.               d. optic nerve.

7. Cones are concentrated _____ , whereas rods are found _____ .
   a. in the periphery of the retina; in the fovea
   b. in the retina; just beyond the retina
   c. in the fovea; everywhere in the retina except the fovea
   d. evenly over the retina; only in the fovea

8. Which of the following statements is true of people with red-green color blindness?
   a. They may be completely unaware that they have defective color vision.
   b. They are more likely to be female than male.
   c. They have a defective or missing blue cone.
   d. They can only distinguish colors in the red-to-green part of the spectrum.

9. The trichromatic and opponent-process theories of color vision:
   a. are contradictory and have both been proven wrong by recent physiological data.
   b. are contradictory and only trichromatic theory is supported by physiological data.
   c. are contradictory and only opponent-process theory is supported by physiological data.
   d. are complementary and both have been supported by physiological data.

10. The visual system is designed to:
    a. reduce contrast.
    b. preserve exact levels of physical contrast.
    c. exaggerate contrast.
    d. accomplish all of the above under different circumstances.

11. Hubel and Wiesel discovered cells in the cortex that are maximally responsive to:
    a. bars of light or dark at specific orientations.
    b. roughly circular spots of light at specific locations on the retina.
    c. simple shapes such as circles and triangles.
    d. contours that curve in a particular direction.

12. In the sensory system for pain, A-delta fibers are:
    a. fast-conducting.
    b. activated by chemical changes in damaged tissue.
    c. associated with diffuse, dull pain.
    d. the receptive endings for C fibers.

13. The PAG (periaqueductal gray):
    a. acts as a gate controller for pain.
    b. causes pain to be felt more intensely when it is activated.
    c. reduces pain when it is inhibited.
    d. gives pain its motivational and emotional facets.

14. The absolute threshold for a given type of sensation depends on all of the following except:
    a. particular characteristics of the test stimulus (such as the frequency of a sound when hearing is being tested).
    b. the conditions under which the test is made.
    c. the particular statistical definition of absolute threshold being used.
    d. the jnd for that particular type of sensation.

15. Signal detection theory suggests that, when you are in the shower, whether or not you think you hear the phone ringing depends on:
    a. your sensitivity.
    b. whether you are expecting a call.
    c. whether you are motivated not to miss the call.
    d. all of the above.

*Essay Questions*

16. Describe the theoretical concepts necessary to explain the full range of our ability to discriminate pitch.

17. What are endorphins? How do they have their effect? What evidence suggests that they are involved in stress-induced analgesia?

# Answers

*Overview*

3. a. sensory physiological psychology
   b. psychophysics
   c. sensory physiology

*Hearing*

1. vibrations; waves
2. amplitude; decibels; loudness
3. hertz; pitch; 20,000 hertz
4. pure

5. pinna; auditory canal; eardrum; tympanic membrane; funnel

6. ossicles; hammer; anvil; stirrup; pressure

15. location in space; timbre; onset and offset; inflection

## Vision

1. photons; waves

2. wavelength

3. electromagnetic

4. g; h; b; a; i; e; d; c; f

5. 3, 4, 1, 5, 2

12. a. pigments

13. a. colored lights

24. pattern a.

25. repetitions

## Pain

1. free nerve endings; all parts of the body

3. a. ventrobasal complex

   b. somatosensory cortex

4. a. midline nuclei

   b. frontal lobe of the cerebral cortex

   c. phantom-limb pain

## Psychophysics

6. hits; false alarms

## Self-Test 1

1. **b.** The major type of question asked by sensory physiologists is: If this stimulus is presented, what physiological response will be produced? For example, if a pure tone of 1000 hertz is presented, what part of the basilar membrane will move maximally? (p. 243)

2. **b.** Amplitude is the physical dimension of sound related to the psychological dimension of loudness. Frequency is the physical dimension of sound related to the psychological dimension of pitch. (p. 246)

3. **c.** (p. 248)

4. **b.** Békésy found that the effects of sounds of various frequencies differ in the total area of the basilar membrane stimulated and in the place of maximal vibration. For example, low sounds produce vibration in a larger portion of the mem-

brane and also produce peak vibration nearer the distal tip. (p. 250)

5. **d.** (p. 249)

6. **a.** (p. 254)

7. **b.** Dark adaptation involves increasing sensitivity with time in the dark. Improvement over the first 10 minutes or so results from a change in cones, whereas further and even greater improvements result from changes in the rods. (p. 256)

8. **c.** Photoreceptors (rods and cones), bipolar cells, and ganglion cells essentially make up three different layers of the retina. (p. 257)

9. **a.** (p. 257)

10. **d.** According to trichromatic theory, there are three types of receptors, each responding to a broad range of wavelengths but more sensitive to some than to others. It is the balance of activity over the three types of cells that helps to determine what color we experience. (pp. 261–262)

11. **c.** (p. 266)

12. **c.** (p. 270)

13. **a.** (pp. 272–273)

14. **a.** (p. 276)

15. **c.** Weber believed that the amount that must be added to the original stimulus to produce a jnd was a constant proportion of the original stimulus. So, if we had to add 2 to 20, the proportion would be 1/10. This proportion would also apply to 100 candles. Thus, we would need to add 1/10 of 100, or 10. (p. 277)

16. Rods are more sensitive than cones, but cones have higher acuity than rods do. Different levels of convergence help to produce both the sensitivity and the acuity difference. Convergence refers to the way that many receptor cells feed information to fewer sensory neurons. If many photoreceptors feed information to a single ganglion cell, there is high convergence. This is typical of rods. By contrast, if only a few receptors feed information to a single ganglion cell, there is low convergence. This is typical of cones. With high convergence, a single ganglion cell will benefit from the combined sensitivity of a number of receptors. However, it will also lose acuity for the following reason. If only a few receptors are feeding information to each ganglion cell, as with cones, the distinct spatial layout of the stimulus can be preserved. For example, if ganglion cell X responds, it had to get its stimulation from receptors A, B, or C. If there is high convergence, however, the ganglion cell's firing doesn't "tell" the brain as

much about what spatial location on the retina was the source of that stimulation. It could have been any of twenty different receptors. So spatial detail is lost. (pp. 255–257)

17. An absolute threshold is not truly absolute—clear and permanently fixed—for several reasons. For one thing, different people have different absolute thresholds. For example, an older person might have a higher absolute threshold for hearing than a younger person, who might in turn have a higher absolute threshold than some of her peers. Also, other aspects of the stimulus besides intensity may play a part in determining the threshold. In hearing, it depends on the frequency of the sound, for example. The conditions under which the test is made, such as the amount and type of background noise, can also make a difference. And finally, since we depend on behavior to infer the absolute threshold and since behavior is variable, we define the absolute threshold statistically. Since we cannot say that one level of intensity produces no detections and another level just above it produces 100 percent detections, we must arbitrarily define the absolute threshold as the level of stimulus intensity that produces 50 percent correct detection. (pp. 274–275)

*Self-Test 2*

1. **d.** (p. 242)

2. **d.** (p. 244)

3. **a.** The eardrum performs an important function, but the nature of its response to sound is merely mechanical, not neural. It is the middle ear that serves to increase the pressure exerted by sound waves on the inner ear. (p. 248)

4. **c.** One tone masks another when the wave it sets up in the basilar membrane interferes with the wave set up by the masked tone. Higher tones affect only the near portion of the basilar membrane. Therefore, they cannot disrupt the distal area of the membrane, the region that responds maximally to low tones. (p. 251)

5. **b.** (p. 253)

6. **b.** (p. 254)

7. **c.** (p. 254)

8. **a.** People who are red-green color blind are generally male because of the nature of the genetic transmission of the defect. Red-green color blind people are one type of dichromat. The defective or missing cone is either a red or a green one; its absence produces abnormalities in the way these people see colors in the red-to-green part of the color spectrum. But because what we actually see is private, they cannot compare their color vision directly with that of normal individuals and thus may not realize there is a problem. (p. 262)

9. **d.** (p. 264)

10. **c.** The visual system, through such mechanisms as ganglion receptive fields, sharpens contrast. (p. 264)

11. **a.** (pp. 266–267)

12. **a.** Alternatives b. and c. describe C fibers, not A-delta fibers. (p. 270)

13. **a.** The PAG, when it is activated, blocks the progress of pain messages at the point where they would enter the central nervous system. (p. 272)

14. **d.** (pp. 274–275)

15. **d.** (pp. 275–276)

16. Two kinds of theories of pitch discrimination are necessary. Békésy's traveling-wave theory suggests that sounds produce traveling waves in the basilar membrane, with different frequencies having maximal effects in different areas. The waves produced by high frequencies create maximal vibration in the near, or proximal, portion of the basilar membrane and, in fact, produce maximal vibration there. The brain can then interpret sounds as higher or lower depending on the location of the most rapid firing. For sounds below 4000 Hz, the *timing* of the activity in the basilar membrane also determines the pitch we hear. Basically, frequency of firing in the auditory neurons will match the frequency of the incoming stimulus. (pp. 250–252)

17. Endorphins are chemicals produced by the body that play an important role in pain reduction. They behave much like drugs such as morphine. In fact, *end* comes from "endogenous" and *orphin* refers to the similarity to morphine. We believe endorphins reduce pain by stimulating the PAG, a site also responsive to morphine. Activation of the PAG inhibits pain signals at the point where they enter the central nervous system. Endorphins are also thought to act in the spinal cord and lower brainstem where pain neurons enter. Experimental evidence that endorphins mediate the phenomenon of stress-induced analgesia comes from a study of rats that were shocked for 30 minutes (the stressor) and were then shown to be insensitive to pain for a short time after (the analgesia). Rats that had been given a drug that blocks endorphins did not show any such analgesic effect of stress. (pp. 272–273)

# CHAPTER 9  PERCEPTION

*Read the introduction below before you read the chapter in the text.*

Chapter 9 examines perception, the ability to extract meaning from the patterns of stimulation received by the sense organs. Discussion focuses primarily on visual perception. Pattern perception and object recognition involve both top-down and bottom-up processing. In top-down processing, our knowledge helps us to interpret incoming information; it often involves utilizing information about the whole to help us interpret parts. In bottom-up processing, we begin with parts and construct from them a perception of the whole. At the most elementary level, these parts are called features. Although top-down and bottom-up processing may appear to be mutually exclusive, and although different theorists may emphasize one over the other, the perception of patterns and objects consists of a continuous interaction of top-down and bottom-up processing. The Gestalt school of psychology was the first to emphasize holistic perception, as demonstrated in their principles of grouping.

A vast array of stimuli are available to us at any given moment, yet we cannot perceive them all with equal clarity and completeness. How do we select what we perceive? Selective attention is our ability to focus on stimuli that are currently relevant. Theorists are interested not only in our ability to focus our attention selectively but also in our ability to divide attention over several different tasks simultaneously, within limits, of course. With practice, we can actually make some processes automatic. A number of theories have been proposed to explain attention. Though they differ in important ways, they generally contain these basic components: first, a large-capacity compartment that does an automatic preliminary analysis of sensory input; then a selection mechanism that determines which input goes on for further process-ing; and finally, a limited-capacity compartment in which input receives more thorough, effortful processing.

The chapter concludes by considering the spatial perception of objects. We use various cues to help us make determinations about depth, size, and motion. For example, binocular disparity—the slight difference in the views our two eyes receive—is a major cue to depth. In general, the closer an object is, the more different the two views will be. In some cases, the study of spatial aspects of perception has progressed through the study of visual illusions. For example, psychologists have gained a better understanding of how we perceive size by studying errors in judgment. A case in point is the moon illusion, in which the moon looks much larger near the horizon than high in the sky, even though the size of the retinal image cast by the moon remains the same. Theorists try to explain this and other systematic errors in spatial perception not just to uncover the reasons for the illusions but to reveal something about the normal mechanisms of perception. An underlying theme worth following carefully is the perceptual system's use of information about relationships among various aspects of a scene. For example, frames of reference are critical to motion perception. We perceive that something has moved if its position changes relative to the earth or some stationary object such as a building or a tree. The chapter presents two views of the way we make use of relational information. The unconscious-inference theory hypothesizes that unconscious mental "calculation" is necessary. The direct-perception theory maintains that we are biologically designed to pick up such relational information effortlessly.

*LOOK over the table of contents for this chapter in your textbook before you continue with your study.*

*Notice that there are focus questions in the margins of the text for your use in studying the material. The following chart lists which study guide questions relate to which focus questions.*

| Focus Questions | Study Guide Questions |
|---|---|
| Perceiving Patterns and Recognizing Objects | |
| 1–5 | 1–12 |
| 6–11 | 13–22 |
| Attention: The Selectivity of Perception | |
| 12–15 | 1–7 |
| 16–19 | 8–13 |
| 20–23 | 14–19 |
| Perceiving Depth, Size, and Motion | |
| 24–28 | 1–6 |
| 29–32 | 7–10 |
| 33–35 | 11–15 |
| 36–38 | 16–18 |

# The Integrated Study Workout

*Complete one section at a time. .*

## Perceiving Patterns and Recognizing Objects
(pages 288–299)

*CONSIDER these questions before you go on. They are designed to help you start thinking about this subject, not to test your knowledge.*

How do we decide whether the object we're looking at is a tree, a trumpet, or a teapot?

Since the typical visual scene is full of many parts—lines, curves, textures—how do we know what goes with what?

Which, if anything, is more important in perception, the details or the "big picture"?

Can anything other than the "objective facts" of a stimulus affect the way we perceive it?

*READ this section of your text lightly. Then go back and read thoroughly, completing the Workout as you proceed.*

Perception is usually studied from a cognitive perspective, because the processes involved are too complex for us to understand at a physiological level.

1.  What is perception?

The study of pattern perception and object recognition has often employed ideas that are in some sense opposites. For example, some theorists emphasize that perception involves breaking wholes down into parts. Others emphasize that perception involves putting parts together to make wholes.

2.  Define the following terms.

    a.  bottom-up processes

    b.  top-down processes

    c.  holistic perception

Gestalt psychologists were among those who took a strong stand on the issue of wholes and parts in perception. They were active in the early part of this century, but their influence has lasted.

3.  What is perception, according to the Gestalt view?

4.  The Gestalt psychologists are responsible for a well-known saying: "The whole is different from the sum of its parts." Explain this statement. Try to produce an example that illustrates the point.

5. Identify the following principles of grouping by writing the correct term in the blank provided. (See Figure 9.2 on text page 290.)

_____ **a.** Elements closer to one another are grouped together as part of the same object.

_____ **b.** When lines cross, line segments are put together perceptually so that smooth, unbroken lines are formed.

_____ **c.** Stimuli are perceptually organized in ways that maximize symmetry, simplicity, and completeness.

_____ **d.** Gaps in a form's border are ignored.

_____ **e.** Like objects are grouped together, separate from unlike objects.

_____ **f.** Stimuli moving in the same direction at the same rate are seen as part of a single object.

The Gestalt psychologists also pointed out our tendency to automatically divide a scene into a more important part (the object to which we attend) and a less important part (the background).

6. The object to which we attend is called the _____ , while the rest of the scene is the _____ .

7. This automatic process is guided by certain cues in the stimulus. For example, _____ is a cue that will cause a surrounded form to be seen as the _____ and the surrounding form as the _____ .

8. When cues are insufficient, object and background may exchange roles, sometimes at the will of the perceiver. This is what occurs in _____ figures. (See Figure 9.4 on text page 291.)

The stimulus itself—such as the letter or the face we're trying to identify—is not the only factor that determines what we perceive. Top-down processes that make use of our knowledge to generate perceptual expectations can be very powerful determinants of our experience. For example, we may use the general topic of a conversation to identify a muffled word. Or we may use holistic aspects of a visual scene to help us identify an individual object.

9. What is perceptual set? Give an example of how set could affect perception in everyday life. (See Figure 9.5 on text page 291.)

Through the operation of top-down processing, context can lead to compelling illusions.

10. In the visual stimulus above, you may see a white triangle even though there is no continuous edge outlining this "triangular" area. This phenomenon is called _____ . The illusion may be due to the Gestalt principle of _____ .

11. Context can also create auditory illusions. Suppose that someone spliced out the first "c" sound in a tape of the phrase "introductory psychology" and that listeners insisted they heard the "c" anyway. This would demonstrate the psychological effect called _____ .

12. Why are phonemic restoration and illusory contours considered especially powerful demonstrations of top-down precessing?

Bottom-up processing theorists have tried to understand how parts are put together to form higher-level structures in perception. Anne Treisman, for example, has studied the most primitive low-level parts called features.

13. Identify the two steps in Treisman's feature-integration theory. Which comes first?

14. Distinguish between serial and parallel processing. When is feature processing serial and when is it parallel, according to Treisman? What is her evidence? (See Figure 9.7 on text page 294.)

15. Treisman has pointed out a phenomenon that she calls *illusory conjunctions*. What are illusory conjunctions and why do they occur?

16. How has Treisman recently modified her theory?

Like Treisman, Irving Biederman has produced a bottom-up theory of perception. But Biederman has investigated structures at an intermediate level of complexity, rather than simple features. Biederman is interested in how components are perceptually combined into whole, real-world objects like faces, houses, or flowers.

17. Explain the basic idea behind Biederman's recognition-by-components theory.

18. Define the term *geons*. What role do they play in perception? How many different geons are in Biederman's suggested list?

19. Briefly describe two pieces of evidence that support Biederman's theory.

Eleanor Gibson proposes that our ability to perceive and discriminate can be altered through experience and is related to feature perception.

20. Define the term *distinctive features*. What part does Gibson suggest they play in perceptual learning?

21. Think of two professions in which a high degree of perceptual learning must underlie the skill demonstrated. Briefly explain each choice. (See page 137 for sample answers.)

    a.

    b.

22. Does being able to use distinctive features effectively necessarily mean that one can describe them? Explain.

## Attention: The Selectivity of Perception
(pages 299–308)

> CONSIDER these questions before you go on. They are designed to help you start thinking about this subject, not to test your knowledge.

What is attention and what does it mean to say that it is selective?

How does the psychologist's use of the term *attention* fit with the everyday expression *paying attention*?

When a person really attends to something, what happens to all the information being ignored? Does it get into the system at all?

Why is it that sometimes we can easily pay attention to two or three things at once and other times we can't seem to do this without slowing down or making mistakes?

Is there any way to improve our ability to process a lot of information at once?

> READ this section of your text lightly. Then go back and read thoroughly, completing the Workout as you proceed.

Attention is defined as the process or set of processes by which the mind chooses from among the various stimuli available to it, allowing some stimuli to receive higher levels of processing.

1. We can try to learn more about how we

   _____ attention on a single source of stimulation to the apparent exclusion of other sources. Alternatively, we can investigate our ability to _____ non-attended stimuli.

Psychologists have learned a good deal about attention from studies of selective listening.

2. Describe the cocktail-party phenomenon.

3. What is shadowing?

4. Describe the dichotic-listening procedure.

5. What factors affect our ability to listen selectively?

6. In studies of selective listening, what happens to the unattended message? Is there any evidence that it is processed for meaning?

Studies of selective viewing have provided findings analogous to those of selective-listening studies.

7. How do the methods and findings of selective-viewing studies compare to the methods and findings of selective-listening studies?

Up to this point, we have been talking about focused attention. Now we turn to divided attention. One of the most practical findings in research on attention concerns the effects of practice on our ability to process information.

8. Describe the evidence provided by Ulrich Neisser to support the view that perceiving and responding to a great deal of information involves skill.

9. How did Harold Pashler demonstrate a limit to dual-task performance?

10. When is the first stage (perception) in the three-stage performance sequence more likely to involve interference—when both stimuli are in the *same* sensory system (e.g., both visual) or when they are in *different* systems (e.g., visual and auditory)? (Circle same or different.)

11. What does it mean to say that a perceptual skill has become automatic?

12. Walter Schneider and his colleagues have studied the development of automatic processing. Briefly describe their method and explain their conclusions.

13. Though automaticity has obvious advantages, the Stroop interference effect illustrates a major disadvantage. In the Stroop technique, subjects are shown a series of color names, each printed in a particular ink color. For example, the word "blue" might be printed in red ink. (See Figure 9.16 on text page 305.)

    a. Describe the subject's task.

    b. What sort of difficulty does the subject encounter?

c. What disadvantage of automaticity is illustrated?

A number of theories of selective attention have been proposed. Although most have some basic ideas in common, they differ in particulars.

14. A general model of attention has two main information-processing compartments and a selector. Explain the roles of these components. (See Figure 9.17 on text page 306.)

    a. first information-processing compartment

    b. second information-processing compartment

    c. selector

15. In general, how do the various theories of attention differ?

16. Describe Broadbent's filter theory of attention. What findings can it account for? What can it not account for?

17. How do early- and late-selection theories differ?

18. How does each type of theory explain the ability to respond to the meaning of a stimulus that was not consciously perceived?

19. Explain how the distinction between explicit and implicit tests is related to the distinction between conscious and unconscious perception.

*Perceiving Depth, Size, and Motion*
(pages 308–323)

CONSIDER *these questions before you go on. They are designed to help you start thinking about this subject, not to test your knowledge.*

How can people tell how far away or how big a given object is?

Why does a person who has the use of only one eye, perhaps because of blindness or having to wear an eyepatch, find it harder to perceive depth?

Why is the experience of depth partly missing in paintings, photographs, and movies? On the other hand, what allows them to give as much of an impression of depth as they do?

Can the eye be fooled in judging such things as size or motion?

Why does the perceptual world look fairly stable and sensible even when our eyes and all sorts of objects in the world are moving around?

READ *this section of your text lightly. The go back and read thoroughly, completing the Workout as you proceed.*

As modern psychologists have attempted to understand how we perceive depth, size, and motion, they have found Helmholtz's nineteenth-century notions about unconscious inferences consistently valuable.

1. Explain the concept of unconscious inference.

The retina directly represents only two dimensions—an up-down dimension and a side-to-side dimension. Where do we get the information that allows us to see depth? The answer lies in a variety of depth cues that fall into two categories—binocular cues and monocular cues.

2. What makes a depth cue binocular? What makes it monocular?

3. Define the following two binocular depth cues, making sure to note which is more important. (See Figure 9.18 on text page 310 for help with binocular disparity.)

   a. eye convergence

   b. binocular disparity

4. What is a stereoscope? What depth cue do we depend on when we experience stereopsis?

Motion parallax is an important monocular depth cue that is present only when the eyes are moving through real three-dimensional space.

5. Answer the following questions about motion parallax.

   a. Define motion parallax in general terms. Now describe a specific scene in which a person has a clear experience of motion parallax and a consequent impression of depth.

   b. How is motion parallax similar to binocular disparity?

Most monocular depth cues can help to convey a sense of depth in pictures. Monocular cues that function in this way are called pictorial cues.

6. Name the monocular cue represented in each of the following descriptions. (See Figures 9.19 and 9.20 on text page 312.)

   _____ a. A tree appears closer to the horizon than the house it shades.

   _____ b. Railroad tracks appear to get closer and closer together with increasing distance.

   _____ c. The bricks in a campus side-walk look smaller and more densely packed together the farther away they are.

   _____ d. A person sees a car and a bill-board and, because the retinal image of the car is bigger, the car appears closer.

   _____ e. A vase in the middle of a table is partially hidden by a hat, so we see the hat as being closer to us.

The perception of size is closely related to the perception of distance. People are in fact unable to judge the size of unfamiliar objects without cues to distance.

Psychologists have often tried to understand size perception by seeking to explain size illusions. In these illusions, normal perceptual mechanisms cause us to make systematic errors in judging size.

7. Briefly describe the following size illusions or draw a rough sketch of each, as you prefer. (See Figures 9.22 and 9.25 on text pages 314 and 316, respectively.)

   a. Müller-Lyer illusion

   b. Ponzo illusion

   c. moon illusion

Several explanations of these size illusions have been offered. Not all explanations work equally well for all illusions, however. Sometimes a theory must be modified if it is to remain feasible. (See Figures 9.23, 9.24, and 9.25 on text pages 314, 315, and 316, respectively.)

8. What is the depth-processing theory? How does it explain the following illusions?

   a. Ponzo illusion

   b. Müller-Lyer illusion

   c. moon illusion

9. Why is the depth-processing theory problematic as an explanation of the Müller-Lyer and moon illusions? How do proponents defend the depth-processing explanation?

10. What is assimilation theory? What is the frame illusion and how is it explained by the assimilation theory? (See Figure 9.26 on text page 316.) How does assimilation theory explain the Müller-Lyer illusion? the moon illusion?

You might think that the detection of motion is simply a matter of registering an image as it crosses over different locations in the retina. But, in fact, it is more complicated than that.

11. Why is motion perception more complex than simply sensing an image moving across the retina?

12. What are two possible solutions to this perceptual puzzle?

13. What is a frame of reference? Why is it important in the perception of movement? What is the evidence that a frame of reference is important?

14. What is movement within movement? How is it related to the ability to establish different frames of reference?

15. Point out some evidence that perceiving movement patterns can help us identify people or objects.

In the perception of depth, size, and motion, it seems that information about relationships is often critical. Two theoretical approaches to the issue of relational information have informed much of the thought on perceptual issues.

16. What is the major premise of Helmholtz's unconscious-inference theory? Explain how the theory can be applied to size, shape, or lightness constancy.

17. What is the major premise of Gibson's direct-perception theory? Explain how the theory can be applied to size, shape, or lightness constancy.

18. How can the two theoretical perspectives be seen as complementary? What type of research does each theory promote?

> *Be sure to READ the Concluding Thoughts at the end of the chapter. Note important points in your Workout. Then consolidate your learning by answering the focus questions in the margins of the text.*

> *After you have studied the chapter thoroughly, CHECK your understanding with the self-test that follows.*

# Self-Test 1

## Multiple-Choice Questions

1. Suppose you discovered a mysterious, humanlike creature who accurately reports (in English, no less!) on his own perceptual processes. Suppose he told psychologists he saw first a collection of various straight lines and curves, then intermediate structures like "wheel," "chain," and "handlebars," and finally he put all these together to see a bicycle. This creature would be describing _____ perception.
   - **a.** top-down
   - **b.** bottom-up
   - **c.** holistic
   - **d.** either a. or c.

2. Suppose you are waiting for a friend. At about the time your friend is due, you think you see her walking toward you. But when you look closer, you see it isn't your friend. You mistakenly perceived this stranger to be your friend because of:
   - **a.** a reversible figure.
   - **b.** closure.
   - **c.** selective viewing.
   - **d.** perceptual set.

3. A biologist watches a group of twenty penguins moving toward the water for feeding. The group then splits into two groups, some moving to the left and some to the right. What Gestalt principle helps the biologist to perceive that there are two groups now instead of one?
   - **a.** good continuation
   - **b.** similarity
   - **c.** good form
   - **d.** common movement

4. In _____ , figure and ground may switch roles.
   - **a.** the Ponzo illusion
   - **b.** the Müller-Lyer illusion
   - **c.** a reversible figure
   - **d.** illusory conjunctions

5. Anne Treisman has developed a theory about the bottom-up aspect of form perception. She proposes that there are two different steps, first _____ and then _____ .
   - **a.** feature detection, which involves parallel processing; feature integration, which involves serial processing
   - **b.** feature detection, which involves serial processing; feature integration, which involves parallel processing
   - **c.** feature integration, which involves parallel processing; feature detection, which involves serial processing
   - **d.** feature integration, which involves serial processing; feature detection, which involves parallel processing

6. If a person is searching for a red horizontal line among distractors that are either red or green, and either vertical or horizontal:
   - **a.** the target will appear to "pop out" at the perceiver.
   - **b.** the target will be undetectable even with effort.
   - **c.** the number of distractors will not affect the time it takes to find the target.
   - **d.** the time it takes to find the target will increase as the number of distractors increases.

7. The distinctive features that we use in skilled perceiving:
   - **a.** are necessarily available to consciousness.
   - **b.** depend on the types of distinctions we need to make.
   - **c.** are not attended to any more than other features.
   - **d.** are primitive features that we need not learn to detect.

8. Studies of selective listening and viewing have typically found that subjects can later report:
   - **a.** absolutely nothing about the unattended material.
   - **b.** physical characteristics of the unattended material.
   - **c.** only the meaning of the unattended material.
   - **d.** none of the above, since selective listening and selective viewing have virtually opposite patterns of results.

9. Suppose that Stroop stimuli, such as the word "red" printed in green ink, are presented to a variety of subjects. Who among the following should be *most* susceptible to the Stroop effect in this case?
   - **a.** a normal adult reader of English
   - **b.** a young child who is just beginning to read English
   - **c.** a Chinese person who speaks English but does not read it
   - **d.** a normal adult reader of English who is looking at the stimuli with her head tilted 90 degrees to the side

10. The visual world we attempt to see has _____ dimensions and the retinal image of this world has _____ dimensions.
    a. three; only one
    b. two; three
    c. three; all three
    d. three; only two

11. If we simultaneously view pictures of the same object taken from slightly different angles, looking at one picture with the left eye and the other with the right eye, we may see the object in depth. Our ability to perceive depth in this case is dependent upon:
    a. occlusion.
    b. convergence.
    c. binocular disparity.
    d. pictorial cues.

12. When you're riding through the countryside, telephone poles move by at a pretty fast clip; trees some distance from the road move more slowly; and hills in the distance pass by more slowly still. This experience is a product of:
    a. binocular disparity.
    b. linear perspective.
    c. occlusion.
    d. motion parallax.

13. The depth-processing theory most *easily* explains the _____ illusion.
    a. moon
    b. Ponzo
    c. Müller-Lyer
    d. frame

14. Perceiving motion is a complex undertaking. An image moving across the retina could arise from movement of our eyes or movement of environmental stimuli. Apparently, we handle this complication by:
    a. unconsciously "calculating" which part of the motion is due to eye movement and which to the object's motion.
    b. setting up a stable frame of reference for a visual scene.
    c. doing both of the above.
    d. doing neither of the above.

15. Which theorist most vigorously promoted the idea that perception must be considered ecologically?
    a. Gibson
    b. Helmholtz
    c. Treisman
    d. all of the above

*Essay Questions*

16. Present the basic idea of assimilation theory and show how it can explain either the frame illusion or the Müller-Lyer illusion.

17. What is the meaning of the Gestalt psychologists' statement that "the whole is different from the sum of its parts"? What is the status of the *whole* in the Gestalt conception of object perception?

*After you have assessed your understanding on the basis of Self-Test 1 and have tried to strengthen your preparation in any areas of weakness, GO ON to Self-Test 2.*

# Self-Test 2

*Multiple-Choice Questions*

1. The Gestalt psychologists believed that, in the course of perceiving an object, we see _____ first.
    a. features
    b. the whole
    c. components
    d. sometimes a., sometimes b., sometimes c.

2. When you see a highway sign for a deer crossing, the deer symbol appears to pop out at you as the object of interest while the rest of the sign

appears to exist behind the symbol. This exemplifies:

- a. perceptual set.
- b. illusory contours.
- c. the figure-ground relationship.
- d. relative size.

3. Sometimes a photocopy may be missing a fraction of an inch of text on the right edge, but we can fill in the missing letters or words by using:

- a. context.
- b. feature integration.
- c. good continuation.
- d. serial processing.

4. The most primitive, low-level elements of a visual stimulus are its:

- a. components.
- b. features.
- c. contours.
- d. visual forms.

5. If the time to locate a target increases in direct proportion to the number of distractors, this indicates that the perceiver is:

- a. doing serial processing, that is, attending to one item at a time.
- b. doing parallel processing, that is, attending to all items at the same time.
- c. doing parallel processing, that is, attending to one item at a time.
- d. doing serial processing, that is, attending to all items at the same time.

6. An entomologist can easily distinguish among many types of beetles that would look alike to most people. According to Eleanor Gibson, the entomologist has learned the _____ of these insects.

- a. distinctive features
- b. primitive features
- c. shape constancy
- d. geons

7. In Biederman's theory of object perception, geons are:

- a. primitive features.
- b. complex shapes such as flowers and faces.
- c. basic geometric forms that can be combined to create more complex forms.
- d. irregular, almost random shapes.

8. Theories of attention frequently differ in:

- a. whether they include any preattentive processing.
- b. whether they include a selector mechanism.
- c. the amount or kind of processing they say occurs preattentively.
- d. both b. and c.

9. Subjects in the Becklen and Cervone study of selective viewing saw two videotapes of men playing basketball, one videotape superimposed over another. They were instructed to attend to one of these videotapes. The investigators found that:

- a. most subjects noticed when an odd event occurred in the unattended videotape, indicating that irrelevant material is not screened out very well.
- b. few subjects noticed when an odd event occurred in the unattended videotape, indicating that irrelevant material is screened out quite well.
- c. most subjects were unable to attend to one videotape as opposed to the other because they were thematically related, indicating that we use meaning as our primary basis for selection.
- d. few subjects noticed when an odd event occurred in the unattended videotape, indicating that irrelevant material is not screened out very well.

10. We would have an implicit test of perception if we asked someone to:

- a. identify a telephone by name.
- b. pick the telephone from an array of several objects.
- c. answer an incoming phone call.
- d. do any of the above.

11. Which of the following statements is true of depth perception?

- a. It is possible only with two eyes.
- b. It is possible with one eye, but better with both eyes.
- c. It is equally good with both eyes or with just one.
- d. None of the above is true.

12. Eye convergence is:

- a. a monocular depth cue in which lines move closer together, thus giving an appearance of depth.
- b. a binocular depth cue in which we unconsciously rotate the eyes inward as we focus on an object.
- c. poorer for closer objects than for more distant ones.
- d. the most powerful binocular depth cue available to us.

13. Which of the following statements regarding size perception is true?

- a. When dealing with familiar visual objects such as a car, a telephone, or a person, previous knowledge of the object's size surprisingly plays no part in size perception.

b. We can accurately judge the size of objects, familiar or unfamiliar, with or without depth cues.

c. We judge size directly from the size of the retinal image, with a larger image meaning a larger object and a smaller image meaning a smaller object.

d. We cannot accurately perceive the size of unfamiliar objects if depth cues are effectively removed.

14. The direct-perception theory emphasizes the _____ of stimulus information, whereas the unconscious-inference theory emphasizes its _____ .

a. static nature; dynamic nature
b. absolute qualities; relative qualities
c. richness; relative lack of information
d. lower-level structure; higher-level structure

15. The unconscious-inference theory is most closely associated with:
a. James Gibson.
b. Anne Treisman.
c. Donald Broadbent.
d. Hermann von Helmholtz.

## Essay Questions

16. Explain Broadbent's filter theory of attention and broadly describe findings from attentional studies that fit well with this theory. Similarly, describe findings that convince us that the theory is nevertheless wrong as it stands.

17. Give a general definition of a visual constancy. Then discuss shape constancy specifically. How is shape constancy explained by unconscious-inference theory? by direct-perception theory?

# Answers

*Perceiving Patterns and Recognizing Objects*

5. a. proximity, b. good continuation, c. good form, d. closure, e. similarity, f. common movement

6. figure; ground

7. circumscription; figure; ground

8. reversible

10. illusory contours; good form

11. phonemic restoration

21. Examples of professions that require a high degree of perceptual learning include musicians, who must learn to recognize and distinguish chords; dog breeders, who must learn to distinguish a champion from an also-ran; radiologists, who must learn to distinguish a pattern in images that are cause for concern from those that are not.

*Attention: The Selectivity of Perception*

1. focus; monitor

10. same

*Perceiving Depth, Size, and Motion*

6. a. position relative to the horizon

b. linear perspective

c. texture gradient

d. relative image size for familiar objects

e. occlusion

*Self-Test 1*

1. **b.** (p. 288)

2. **d.** (p. 291)

3. **d.** (p. 290)

4. **c.** (p. 291)

5. **a.** According to Treisman, serial processing (as compared with parallel processing) is indicated when the time it takes to find a target increases proportionally with the number of distractors. (pp. 294–295)

6. **d.** (pp. 295–296)

7. **b.** Distinctive features are attended to more than other features, and they become less and less available to consciousness with increased skill levels. (pp. 297–298)

8. **b.** For example, subjects in a dichotic-listening study may be able to say that they heard a male talking but they won't be able to tell you what he said or even the gist of the message. They might, however, notice especially meaningful stimuli such as their own names. (pp. 300, 301)

9. **a.** This should make sense to you in view of the fact that Stroop interference comes from the obligatory nature of a well-practiced, and hence automatic, process like reading. Since reading has become automatic process, but reading sideways has not, d. cannot be correct. (p. 305)

10. **d.** (pp. 308–309)

11. **c.** (p. 310)

12. **d.** Motion parallax and binocular disparity are somewhat related, but motion parallax arises because the two eyes of a stationary perceiver occupy different positions. Also note that motion parallax as described in the question would be experienced monocularly. (p. 311)

13. **b.** (p. 314)

14. **c.** (pp. 317–318)

15. **a.** (p. 321)

16. According to assimilation theory, we don't necessarily restrict ourselves to an object's boundaries when judging the object's size. Rather, we incorporate elements close to the object. In the frame illusion, a square surrounded by a frame looks larger than an identical square without the frame. Assimilation theory suggests that the frame is incorporated into our perception of the square's boundary, drawing the eye outward and thus making the square seem larger. (pp. 316–317)

17. When Gestalt psychologists said, "the whole is different from the sum of its parts," they meant something is added. The whole cannot be reduced to a catalog or a "line-up" of parts. It is an organization of those parts into a pattern or form. In fact, the Gestalt psychologists believed the whole that is created by the arrangement of parts is the first thing we see when we perceive an object. To them, it is the primary—the most important—thing. They believed we are biologically designed to be able to perceive incoming information in simple, holistic ways. (p. 289)

*Self-Test 2*

1. **b.** (p. 289)

2. **c.** (pp. 290–291)

3. **a.** (pp. 291–292)

4. **b.** (p. 294)

5. **a.** This makes sense because, for example, it takes twice as long to check 10 items serially (one item at a time) as it does to check 5. If parallel processing were being used, all 5 or all 10 items would be checked simultaneously and the number of items would not affect processing time. (p. 294)

6. **a.** (p. 298)

7. **c.** (p. 296)

8. **c.** (p. 306)

9. **b.** (p. 301)

10. **a.** (p. 308)

11. **b.** It is possible with one eye, but without binocular disparity, we are lacking a powerful cue to depth. (p. 309)

12. **b.** (p. 310)

13. **d.** (p. 312)

14. **c.** (p. 321)

15. **d.** (p. 320)

16. Broadbent proposed that there is an attentional filter that acts as a kind of gatekeeper between the first, or preattentive, processing compartment and the second, or attentive, processing compartment. He suggested that information at the preattentive stage is only processed for gross physical characteristics such as color or location or loudness. Stimuli with the "right" physical characteristics are selectively allowed into the next compartment for further processing; other stimuli cannot get through the filter. This theory fits with the research finding that people can successfully

select a message based on its physical characteristics, such as pitch. But it can't explain the findings that show some aspects of meaning coming through from the unattended message. (pp. 306–307)

17. We are dealing with a visual constancy when some aspect of the retinal image changes and yet our perception stays the same. In shape constancy, for example, the shape of the retinal image of an object changes as its orientation in three-dimensional space changes. Yet, we perceive its shape as remaining the same. Unconscious-inference theory would say that we mentally calculate how far different parts of the object are from us in various orientations and take this into account, with the result that perceived shape stays the same. Direct-perception theory would say that we directly pick up higher-order information that easily and consistently tells us about the shape of the object regardless of its rotation in space. For example, in the case of a square rotated in space, we would be picking up not only the borders of the square but also textural information about the surface itself. (pp. 320–322)

# CHAPTER 10 MEMORY

*Read the introduction below before you read the chapter in the text.*

Memory holds a central place in cognitive psychology. All of our cognitive activities—such as reasoning, understanding, speaking, perceiving, planning—and indeed most of our physical activities depend on memory. The most influential and widely accepted theory of memory, the modal model, proposes that memory consists of a sensory store, a short-term store, and a long-term store, each with its own function, capacity, and duration. The model also describes control processes, which handle information within stores or transfer information from one store to another.

The sensory store is the first component of the memory system in which incoming information is registered. It holds a good deal of information, but very briefly—just long enough for basic physical characteristics of stimuli to be processed. Each sensory system has its own sensory store. Visual sensory memory is also called iconic memory and auditory sensory memory is also called echoic memory.

The short-term store is the component of memory in which conscious thought occurs. Information enters the short-term store from either the sensory store or the long-term store and can be maintained there through rehearsal. Short-term memory is limited in the number of items it can hold at a given moment.

Long-term memory is the more permanent large-scale repository of knowledge. Long-term memory for information is best achieved through elaboration, which involves thinking about the information. Memory can be made more efficient through chunking and other organizational strategies. For example, by packaging information so that each item is a larger unit called a chunk, we can fit more information into memory. Techniques involving visualization, such as the key word method for learning foreign language vocabulary, can also help.

How is information represented and organized in long-term memory? (Representation refers to the abstract relationship between a memory and the experience that originally produced the memory.) One debate centers on the nature of image representation. The evidence suggests that visual images are in some ways like pictures. Theorists have also focused on the way we represent concepts in long-term memory. The mental relationships among concepts are often represented as networks.

What causes us to forget? Decay theory suggests that memory just fades with time and disuse. Interference theories maintain that other information in memory may get in the way of our remembering the information we want. Retrieval-cue theories suggest that the memories we want may be stored but cannot be accessed because we lack the appropriate cues. As the chapter makes clear, remembering is not just the passive replaying of some sort of mental "tape." Rather, it is a constructive process in which retrieved information is pieced together and inferences are drawn. This constructive nature of memory makes it efficient, but also opens the door to potential distortion. Research has shown that hypnosis is ineffective as a way of enhancing recall; furthermore, it increases the chances of memory being distorted.

While the modal model described at the beginning of the chapter works well for explicit memory, it is not so useful for implicit memory. Explicit memory involves making the remembered information consciously available. Implicit memory, in contrast, influences perception, thought, or behavior without the stored information itself entering consciousness. Evidence for the existence of these two broad classes of memory—explicit and implicit—includes findings from neuropsychological research with humans and monkeys.

*LOOK over the table of contents for this chapter in your textbook before you continue with your study.*

*Notice that there are focus questions in the margins of the text for your use in studying the material. The following chart lists which study guide questions relate to which focus questions.*

| Focus Questions | Study Guide Questions |
|---|---|
| An Information-Processing Model of Memory | |
| 1 | 1–4 |
| 2–4 | 5–13 |
| 5–8 | 14–20 |
| 9–11 | 21–26 |
| Memorizing: Encoding into Long-Term Memory | |
| 12 | 1–2 |
| 13 | 3–4 |
| 14–16 | 5–8 |
| 17 | 9–11 |
| Representation and Organization in Long-Term Memory | |
| 18 | 1–3 |
| 19–20 | 4–5 |
| 21–23 | 6–10 |
| 24–27 | 11–16 |
| Remembering and Forgetting: Problems of Retrieval from Long-Term Memory | |
| 28 | 1–3 |
| 29 | 4–8 |
| 30–32 | 9–14 |
| 33–35 | 15–19 |
| 36 | 20–22 |
| Multiple Memory Systems: Beyond the Modal Model | |
| 37–39 | 1–3 |
| 40–41 | 4–8 |
| 42–44 | 9–11 |

# The Integrated Study Workout

*Complete one section at a time. B*

## An Information-Processing Model of Memory
(pages 327–336)

*CONSIDER these questions before you go on. They are designed to help you start thinking about this subject, not to test your knowledge.*

What is memory?

How is it that a person can remember some informa-

tion for a lifetime and forget other information seconds after acquiring it?

How can psychologists begin to "get a handle on" something as abstract as memory?

*READ this section of your text lightly. Then go back and read thoroughly, completing the Workout as you proceed.*

The dominant theory of memory for more than 20 years—the modal model of memory—proposes that memory is made up of several interacting components. The model has led to intensive study of those proposed components, of their interactions, and of the very idea that memory is actually divided in such a fashion. Keep in mind as you study that the model is just that—a model—not reality itself.

1. What is a model and how is it useful? What does it mean to call a model "modal"?

2. The three components of memory proposed by the modal model are the _____, _____, and _____ stores.

3. The modal model characterizes each store in terms of its _____, _____, and _____.

4. What do control processes do?

Sensory memory is so fleeting that we are generally unaware of it. The sensory store is the component of memory that holds this brief memory trace.

5. What do psychologists consider to be the function of the sensory store?

6. Another name for the sensory store is the
_____ store.

Each sensory system appears to have its own form of
sensory memory. Psychologists have investigated
visual and auditory sensory memory much more than
any others.

7. *Visual* sensory memory is also called
_____ and the trace it holds is
called the _____ .

8. According to Sperling, the icon lasts for about
_____ of a second.

9. How did Eriksen and Collins demonstrate the
picturelike nature of iconic memory?

10. Another name for *auditory* sensory memory is
_____ and the trace it holds is
called the _____ .

11. Briefly describe some early evidence for echoic
memory.

12. How long is the echo estimated to last? Why
might it last longer than the icon?

13. What does the phonemic restoration effect suggest about echoic memory?

Short-term memory refers to information held in the
short-term store and to the mind's ability to store
information there.

14. Why is short-term memory also called working
memory?

15. Information flows into the short-term store from
_____ and _____ .

Though a great deal of information passes through
the short-term store, it can hold only a very limited
amount at one time. Just as time and space are related
in physics, duration and capacity turn out to be related aspects of short-term memory.

16. What do psychologists mean by the *span of short-
term memory*? What is a common estimate of the
span of short-term memory for simple, easily
repeated items?

17. Explain why the span of short-term memory
depends on the time a single item can remain
there without repetition. What analogy does the
text use to depict this relationship?

18. Briefly state the question Lloyd and Margaret
Peterson asked, their method for answering it,
and what they found. (See Figure 10.3 on text
page 332.)

As noted earlier, control processes are mental
processes that control or manipulate information.

19. Identify the following control processes involved
in moving information from one store to another.

_____ a. controls the movement of
information from the short-
term into the long-term store

_____ **b.** controls which information in the sensory store will flow into the short-term store

_____ **c.** controls the flow of information from the long-term store into the short-term store

20. Are there control processes involved in manipulating or processing information within a memory store? Explain.

The long-term store is the third component of the mind, according to the modal model.

21. Characterize long-term memory and contrast it with short-term memory.

List-learning experiments have provided some of the evidence that supports the short-term/long-term distinction at the heart of the modal model. In particular, experiments designed to clarify primacy and recency effects have suggested that there may indeed be two functionally different stores. (See Figure 10.4 on text page 334.)

22. Define the following terms.

    **a.** primacy effect

    **b.** recency effect

23. How are these effects explained by the modal model?

24. What evidence supports the two-part explanation for primacy and recency effects?

Neuropsychological evidence has also helped us to assess the validity of the distinction between short-term and long-term memory.

25. Who was H.M. and what happened to his memory following surgery for epilepsy?

26. How does the case of H.M. help to illuminate the issue of a short-term/long-term distinction in memory?

### Memorizing: Encoding into Long-Term Memory (pp. 336-343)

_CONSIDER these questions before you go on. They are designed to help you start thinking about this subject, not to test your knowledge._

How can we improve our memory performance?

In what ways is an expert's memory different from a novice's?

_READ this section of your text lightly. Then go back and read thoroughly, completing the Workout as you proceed._

One of the most interesting areas of research on memory—and one especially relevant to students—concerns the kind of processing that can help to encode information into long-term memory.

1. What important point was made by the experiment by Fergus Craik and Michael Watkins?

2. The process by which information is held in short-term memory is _____ rehearsal. The process of encoding information into the long-term store involves _____ rehearsal.

3. What is elaboration (or elaborative rehearsal)? What is its immediate goal? How could you put this concept to practical use?

4. Briefly describe two examples of experimental evidence that elaboration is valuable.

Organizing information—which requires elaboration, of course—is a useful strategy for increasing the efficiency of memory.

5. What is chunking and how is it related to memory efficiency?

6. Describe the dramatic effects of chunking on the digit span of a young man studied by Ericsson and Chase. Did chunking actually change the capacity of his short-term store? Explain.

7. Using the case of chess masters, show how chunking is related to expertise.

8. What is hierarchical organization? How can this type of organization improve long-term memory?

Visualization has also been found to be an important aid to memory.

9. How does Paivio explain the value of imagery in long-term memory performance?

10. Why else might mental imagery be a way to improve memory?

11. Describe the key word method. If you have any foreign language vocabulary, show how the key word method could be applied to learning a specific word. (See Figure 10.8 on text page 342.)

### Representation and Organization in Long-Term Memory   (pages 343–349)

*CONSIDER these questions before you go on. They are designed to help you start thinking about this subject, not to test your knowledge.*

When we hear or read verbal information, do we generally retain the actual words or only their meaning?

How does the memory system represent pictorial information? conceptual information?

How might information in the long-term store be organized, given its tremendous amount and variety?

> READ this section of your text lightly. Then go back and read thoroughly, completing the Workout as you proceed.

Who was your first-grade teacher? What is one of your favorite books? How many times have you read it? Who is the main character? What does the word *stirrup* mean? What countries border France? Our long-term memories allow us to answer innumerable questions, skip from topic to topic, make sensible associations, and much more. Try to imagine a filing system that could match the performance of your own memory! In what form would the information be stored? How would it be organized? Psychologists studying long-term memory have tried to understand both the ways that information is represented in this store and how that information is organized.

1. What is meant by the term *representation*?

2. When we take in verbal information, what do we generally retain—the actual wording or the meaning? Summarize the evidence on this issue from research by Jacqueline Sachs.

3. Under what circumstances are we most likely to remember statements verbatim?

One of the major issues of representation in long-term memory deals with how we store visual information.

4. Compare the propositional and analogue theories.

5. Although some researchers do not believe the theories are testable, others believe they are. Briefly describe research by Stephen Kosslyn and Martha Farah, respectively, that supports analogue theory.

Another important question concerns the representation of conceptual knowledge.

6. Complete the following sentences.

   a. _____ provide the basis for categorizing objects and events; that is, they are the basic units of a person's general knowledge.

   b. A _____ is the way a concept is mentally represented.

   c. A _____ involves schemas that organize events in time rather than objects in space.

7. How is a schema characterized by the feature theory?

8. How is a schema characterized by the prototype theory?

9. Describe Eleanor Rosch's work on typicality. Which theory does it tend to support? Can the alternative theory possibly account for typicality effects?

10. Are feature and prototype theories necessarily black-and-white alternatives? Explain.

The manner in which information is organized determines what will and what will not be an effective way to find that information in the system. The sophisticated organization of memory largely explains our flexible retrieval abilities. Some of the basic principles of association were originally proposed by Aristotle.

11. State Aristotle's principle of association by contiguity. What ability can it help to explain?

12. What was Aristotle's principle of association by similarity?

13. In what sense is the principle of similarity more complicated than the principle of contiguity?

14. Describe William James's views on the roles of contiguity and similarity in the organization of memory.

A common way of portraying the mind's vast store of knowledge is a network in which concepts are linked by pointers (association). (See Figure 10.10 on text page 349.)

15. What led Allan Collins and Elizabeth Loftus to develop their model? Briefly describe the model.

16. Why is the term *spreading activation* used to describe the model?

### Remembering and Forgetting: Problems of Retrieval from Long-Term Memory
(pages 350–358)

*CONSIDER these questions before you go on. They are designed to help you start thinking about this subject, not to test your knowledge.*

What is the pattern of forgetting? Does it occur at a constant pace? Does it occur more rapidly or more slowly right after learning?

Why do we forget?

What kinds of cues can help us to probe our memories most effectively?

Can a memory be altered by information learned later? For example, could an attorney's misleading questions affect a witness' memory of an accident?

Can hypnosis help us remember buried memories?

*READ this section of your text lightly. Then go back and read thoroughly, completing the Workout as you proceed.*

Somehow we are more likely to complain about the occasional failures of our memories than to applaud the frequent successes. Psychologists have tried to discover some of the reasons underlying those failures—the kind we tend to notice, such as the outright inability to retrieve desired information, as well as the less detectable cases of distortion in memory.

1. What do Ebbinghaus's forgetting curves teach us about the relationship between time and forgetting? what about the work of H. P. Bahrick and colleagues on memory for former high-school classmates?

2. Define the terms below.

   a. decay theory

   b. interference theories

   c. retrieval-cue theories

3. How well accepted is decay theory today? Why?

4. What did Jenkins and Dallenbach find in their study of memory for nonsense syllables? Which theory did this tend to support?

5. Define the following two types of interference. (See Table 10.1 on text page 351.)

   a. retroactive interference

   b. proactive interference

6. Indicate whether each case below represents retroactive interference (RI) or proactive interference (PI).

   _____ a. A student who has studied French and now studies Spanish cannot recall the Spanish verb "to know" because the French verb keeps coming to mind.

   _____ b. An engineer who has just moved to a new firm slips and calls the new boss by the old boss' name.

   _____ c. A senior dormitory resident cannot remember the name of a freshman-year roommate.

7. Give one explanation of interference effects and provide evidence to support it.

8. Can interference be demonstrated in a real-life situation? Support your answer.

Retrieval cues are apparently critical to our ability to gain access to long-term memories. In fact, this factor can help to explain why some tests of memory are harder than others.

9. What is a recall test? Give an example.

10. What is a recognition test? Give an example.

11. Identify each of the following as involving either recall or recognition.

    _____ a. You meet an acquaintance on the street and try to remember the individual's name.

    _____ b. You look down a column in the phonebook to see whether your doctor, whose last name is "Smith" and whose first name you can't quite think of, is listed.

    _____ c. Your history professor asks you to summarize the causes of World War I.

    _____ d. You are given a true-false test in geography.

12. Which is harder, recall or recognition? Why is this the case?

13. What is the encoding-specificity principle? Identify some observations that it can help explain.

14. Define the following and cite a research example for each.

    **a.**  context-dependent memory

    **b.**  state-dependent memory

    **c.**  mood-dependent memory

Remembering is an active rather than a passive process. It is not like replaying a tape recording, or even like reading words we have written down.

15. Explain what it means to say that memory entails construction. What are some of the consequences of memory's constructive nature?

16. Briefly describe how Frederick Bartlett used "The War of the Ghosts." What did he discover?

17. How did Elizabeth Loftus and J. C. Palmer show that the construction of memories can be affected by information acquired after the original experience?

18. Why would findings such as those of Loftus and Palmer be of practical importance?

19. How was Loftus's interpretation challenged by Michael McCloskey and Maria Zaragoza? How did they test their hypothesis and what did they find?

Popular literature and the media often depict hypnosis as a valuable tool for uncovering memories that are not accessible in other ways. Just as with other claims, scientists must approach this claim skeptically, asking for evidence, not merely assertions.

20. How do psychologists characterize hypnosis?

21. Does hypnosis facilitate retrieval? Support your answer with evidence.

Another reported effect of hypnosis on memory is amnesia.

22. Describe the phenomenon of post-hypnotic amnesia, being careful to indicate whether it represents real inability to remember or merely a pretense of inability.

## Multiple Memory Systems: Beyond the Modal Model  (pp. 358–365)

> CONSIDER these questions before you go on. They are designed to help you start thinking about this subject, not to test your knowledge.

Can all knowledge in memory potentially be made conscious?

Isn't there something fundamentally different about memory for the meaning of dancing and memory for how to dance?

Why is it that we can sometimes fail to recall someone's phone number verbally and yet can quickly dial the number?

> READ this section of your text lightly. Then go back and read thoroughly, completing the Workout as you proceed.

Though the modal model accounts well for many memory phenomena, it falls short when we consider memory that does not involve the conscious mind.

1. Label the following types of memory.

_____ a. memory in which the remembered information enters consciousness; tested by directly asking the person to recall or recognize the information. It includes:

_____ memory of the person's own specific past experiences and

_____ knowledge of word meanings, facts, and ideas that are part of the person's general understanding of the world.

_____ b. previously acquired information that affects behavior or thought without itself entering consciousness. It includes:

_____ motor skills, habits, and unconsciously learned rules.

2. Identify each of the following as illustrating procedural (P), semantic (S), or episodic (E) memory.

_____ Norman remembers that he ate spaghetti three times last week.

_____ Hannah recalls that the sympathetic nervous system is involved in producing the fight-or-flight response.

_____ Gordon plays a piano sonata.

_____ Sally knows how to pitch a curve ball.

_____ Gene remembers seeing an article about how to invest in mutual funds.

3. How do implicit and explicit memories differ in terms of their dependence on the immediate situation?

4. What is priming?

5. Briefly describe a typical perceptual priming experiment.

6. Does elaborative rehearsal improve perceptual priming? What does this indicate?

7. How can conceptual priming be demonstrated in the laboratory?

8. What purpose might conceptual priming serve?

Evidence that explicit and implicit memory involve different neural systems is available from neuropsychological studies.

9. How do studies of amnesic patients suggest that the hippocampus and neural connections with it are critical for creating new explicit memories but not new implicit memories in long-term memory?

10. Describe Mortimer Mishkin's work showing separate memory systems in monkeys that parallel the procedural/declarative distinction in humans.

11. Describe some neuropsychological evidence suggesting that episodic and semantic memory involve different neural systems.

---

*Be sure to READ the Concluding Thoughts at the end of the chapter. Note important points in your Workout. Then consolidate your learning by answering the focus questions in the margins of the text.*

*After you have studied the chapter thoroughly, CHECK your understanding with the self-test that follows.*

## Self-Test 1

*Multiple-Choice Questions*

1. According to the modal model of memory, memory is made up of:
   a. the attentive store, the short-term store, and the long-term store.
   b. the sensory store, the working store, and the attentive store.
   c. the sensory store, the short-term store, and the long-term store.
   d. the episodic store, the procedural store, and the semantic store.

2. Information passes into the short-term store from:
   a. working memory.
   b. the sensory store.
   c. the long-term store.
   d. both b. and c.

3. A brief, picturelike trace of a visual stimulus is held in _____ memory.
   a. episodic
   b. implicit
   c. context-dependent
   d. iconic

4. On average, how many simple repeatable items can be held in short-term memory?
   a. two            c. seven
   b. five           d. ten

5. The Petersons asked subjects to retain three consonants in memory while engaging in a distraction task. They found that:
   a. when subjects were prevented from rehearsing in this way, information in short-term memory disappeared in less than 20 seconds.
   b. when subjects were prevented from rehearsing in this way, information in short-term memory took about 90 seconds to disappear.
   c. subjects could not perform the distractor task under these circumstances because the three consonants fully occupied the short-term store.

d. subjects were able to rehearse the consonants and perform the distractor task, thus indicating that concurrent tasks can be performed in short-term memory.

6. A woman receives a secret identification number for using her bank's cash machines. She remembers the number, 111621, as 11 (the month of her birth), 16 (sweet sixteen), and 21 (the age of majority). This woman is using _____ to enhance her memory performance.
   a. episodic memory
   b. a prototype
   c. chunking
   d. verbatim recall

7. A boy studying Spanish mentally pictures a cart full of letters in order to remember *carta*, the Spanish word for "letter." This student is employing:
   a. the key word method.
   b. the primacy effect.
   c. echoic memory.
   d. a prototype.

8. If your schema for birds is essentially a list of characteristics such as "has feathers," "can fly," and "has wings," then the _____ theory correctly describes your representation of concepts.
   a. prototype
   b. feature
   c. retrieval-cue
   d. analogue

9. According to the Collins and Loftus network model of memory organization, hearing "table" facilitates subsequent recognition of a "chair" through the process of:
   a. visualization.
   b. elaborative rehearsal.
   c. spreading activation.
   d. procedural memory.

10. A type of schema that organizes events in time rather than objects in space is called a(n):
   a. script.
   b. procedural memory.
   c. proposition.
   d. pointer.

11. Suppose a subject is given a list of words for later recall. Next to each word is another word, which the subject is simply asked to read. One of the words to be recalled is "jam" and the word beside it is "strawberry." Considering the principle of encoding specificity, what would make the best retrieval cue for "jam" at recall time?
   a. grape
   b. traffic
   c. strawberry
   d. All of the above would be equally effective.

12. The idea that unused memories are forgotten with the passage of time is known as _____ theory and is _____ accepted today.
   a. decay; widely
   b. decay; not well
   c. interference; widely
   d. interference; not well

13. Frederick Bartlett asked subjects to listen to "The War of the Ghosts" and later retell the story from memory. He found that subjects:
   a. had excellent verbatim memory.
   b. distorted the story in accordance with their own schemas.
   c. used their schemas to accurately relate the meaning of the story in different words.
   d. could not retain any aspect of the story.

14. Michael McCloskey and Maria Zaragoza showed subjects slides, then gave some subjects misleading information, and finally tested memory with one of two tests. Test 1 pitted misleading information against original information; Test 2 did not. They found that:
   a. subjects remembered the original information despite misleading information and regardless of which test was used.
   b. misled subjects performed worse than other subjects in both tests, indicating that the misleading information had replaced the original information.
   c. misled subjects performed better than other subjects on both tests because they had been put on their guard by the misleading information.
   d. misled subjects performed worse than other subjects only on Test 1, showing that the original information had not been replaced.

15. Neuropsychological studies have provided evidence suggesting that:
   a. there really is no distinction between short-term and long-term memory.
   b. procedural and declarative memories are encoded by way of different neural paths.
   c. episodic and semantic memories are encoded through precisely the same neural mechanisms.
   d. both a. and b. are true.

*Essay Questions*

16. Distinguish between explicit and implicit memory, giving examples of each. Present one piece of evidence to support the reality of this distinction.

17. Hypnosis is widely believed to aid recall. Why would this theory make sense? What does research on this subject suggest?

---

*After you have assessed your understanding on the basis of Self-Test 1 and have tried to strengthen your preparation in any areas of weakness, GO ON to Self-Test 2.*

## Self-Test 2

*Multiple-Choice Questions*

1. Which of the following statements regarding sensory memory is true?
   a. Apparently, only vision and hearing have sensory memory systems.
   b. All information in the sensory store is passed on to the short-term store.
   c. Information in the visual sensory store is still in sensory form.
   d. Rehearsal can help to keep information in sensory memory longer.

2. Encoding is the control process that:
   a. maintains information in the short-term store.
   b. maintains information in the sensory store.
   c. transfers information from the sensory store to the short-term store.
   d. transfers information from the short-term to the long-term store.

3. Suppose subjects who are given a list of words to study one at a time are then asked to do mental arithmetic for a short time before recalling the words in any order. This procedure should:
   a. prevent a primacy effect.
   b. prevent a recency effect.
   c. produce both primacy and recency effects.
   d. prevent both primacy and recency effects.

4. Which of the following statements concerning rehearsal is true?
   a. Maintenance rehearsal is the best means of accomplishing encoding.
   b. Maintenance rehearsal and encoding rehearsal are one and the same.
   c. Rote rehearsal is the preferred method of accomplishing elaboration.
   d. Elaborative rehearsal promotes encoding better than rote rehearsal.

5. A young man studied by Ericsson and colleagues used _____ to increase his digit span to about _____ .
   a. chunking; 30
   b. chunking; 80
   c. the key word method; 30
   d. the key word method; 80

6. If you were to study by outlining a chapter using several levels of headings, from more general to more specific, you would be using _____ to aid your memory.
   a. the key word method
   b. prototypes
   c. feature theory
   d. hierarchical organization

7. The idea that long-term memory represents visual information in a way that is functionally equivalent to a picture is called the:
   a. propositional theory.
   b. feature theory.
   c. analogue theory.
   d. encoding-specificity theory.

8. Eleanor Rosch found that subjects can more quickly verify that a robin is a bird than that a chicken is a bird. This typicality effect tends to support the _____ theory.
   a. feature
   b. dual-coding
   c. prototype
   d. propositional

9. The notion that forgetting occurs because other memories get in the way of our ability to retrieve a given memory is the essence of:
   a. analogue theory.
   b. dual-coding theory.
   c. interference theory.
   d. decay theory.

10. If you get a new phone number and have trouble remembering it because your old phone number keeps getting in the way, you are experiencing the problematic effects of:
    a. retroactive interference.
    b. proactive interference.
    c. state-dependent memory.
    d. echoic memory.

11. A true-false test would be a(n) _____ test of memory, while an essay exam would be a _____ test of memory.
    a. rote; recognition
    b. recall; retroactive
    c. recognition; recall
    d. interference; retrieval

12. Gail routinely greeted her professors by name when she met them on campus. But when she encountered one of them at the local movie theater, she couldn't think of the person's name. In fact, she wasn't quite sure it was the same person. What could best explain this?
    a. context-dependent memory
    b. a recency effect
    c. proactive interference
    d. Korsakoff's syndrome

13. Hypnosis has generally been shown to be:
    a. effective as a means of aiding the retrieval of verbal information.
    b. effective as a means of helping people remember pictorial or spatial information.
    c. effective in helping subjects retrieve many kinds of information, though they are generally not confident about what they remember.
    d. ineffective as a means of facilitating retrieval.

14. What kind of information in your memory allows you to be a skillful dancer?
    a. procedural
    b. declarative
    c. semantic
    d. episodic

15. Priming is a type of _____ memory.
    a. explicit
    b. implicit
    c. propositional
    d. short-term

*Essay Questions*

16. What is the span of short-term memory? How does chunking affect the amount of information that can be held in short-term memory? Can chunking make a substantial difference in the amount of information short-term memory can hold? Explain.

17. Discuss alternative views on the representation of concepts in long-term memory.

# Answers

*An Information-Processing Model of Memory*

2. sensory; short-term; long-term
3. function; capacity; duration
6. preattentive
7. iconic memory; icon
8. one-third
10. echoic memory; echo
15. sensory store; long-term store
19. a. encoding, b. attention, c. retrieval

*Memorizing: Encoding into Long-Term Memory*

2. maintenance; encoding

*Representation and Organization in Long-Term Memory*

6. **a.** concepts, **b.** schema, **c.** script

*Remembering and Forgetting: Problems of Retrieval from Long-Term Memory*

6. **a.** PI, **b.** PI, **c.** RI

11. **a.** recall, **b.** recognition, **c.** recall, **d.** recognition

*Multiple Memory Systems: Beyond the Modal Model*

1. **a.** explicit memory; episodic memory; semantic memory

   **b.** implicit memory; procedural memory

2. E, S, P, P, E

### Self-Test 1

1. **c.** (p. 328)

2. **d.** Information coming in from the outside world passes through the sensory store before it can be transferred to the short-term store. Information in the long-term store must enter the short-term store in order to be consciously processed. For example, in order to think about an event that happened to you last week or to form a mental image of a friend's face, you must process information from the long-term store in the short-term store. Remember that working memory is another name for short-term memory, which highlights its role as the active workplace of the mind. (pp. 330–331)

3. **d.** (p. 329)

4. **c.** This question is, of course, referring to the span of short-term memory. (p. 331)

5. **a.** In fact, they had virtually zero memory for the consonants after 18 seconds of engaging in the distractor task. (p. 332)

6. **c.** (p. 339)

7. **a.** This particular technique is the key word method described in the text. (p. 342)

8. **b.** (p. 346)

9. **c.** (p. 349)

10. **a.** (p. 347)

11. **c.** (p. 353)

12. **b.** (p. 350)

13. **b.** (p. 355)

14. **d.** (p. 356)

15. **b.** Neuropsychological research has suggested that all of the distinctions mentioned in the alternatives (short-term and long-term memories, procedural and declarative memories, and episodic and semantic memories) have some physiological basis. (pp. 363–365)

16. Explicit memory is memory in which the remembered information enters consciousness. It is tested by asking a person to recall or recognize the information of interest. Explicit memory is well accounted for by the modal model. Implicit memory involves stored information that can influence behavior or cognitive processes without entering consciousness. Implicit memory is not yet as well understood as explicit memory, perhaps because most laboratory studies have focused on explicit memory. Episodic memory, such as your memory for the last movie you saw, is a type of explicit memory. Procedural memory, such as your knowledge of how to drive a car, would be considered implicit. One kind of evidence for the distinction comes from amnesic patients who cannot create new long-term memories of the explicit type but can create new implicit ones. (pp. 359–365)

17. The idea that hypnosis might help people to retrieve memories more effectively makes some apparent sense. Perhaps the focusing of attention that occurs in hypnosis would help to keep a person's search for information from being sidetracked by distractions. However, research indicates that hypnosis does not aid retrieval. In laboratory experiments in which people learn material and are then tested on it either with or without hypnosis, hypnosis does not make a difference in memory performance. Field research also shows no beneficial effect of hypnosis on memory. In fact, because hypnosis involves a state of heightened suggestibility, it can lead to increased distortion in memory. It can also lead subjects to express greater confidence in their reported memories, even though they are not objectively more accurate. (pp. 357–358)

### Self-Test 2

1. **c.** (p. 329)

2. **d.** (p. 333)

3. **b.** The recency effect depends on short-term memory, which in this procedure is required for the arithmetic task. The result is that items in short-term memory, and thus the recency effect, are lost. (p. 334)

4. **d.** (p. 337)

5. **b.** (p. 340)

6. **d.** (pp. 340–341)

7. **c.** (pp. 344–345)

8. **c.** (pp. 346–347)

9. **c.** (p. 350)

10. **b.** (p. 351)

11. **c.** (p. 353)

12. **a.** (p. 354)

13. **d.** (pp. 357–358)

14. **a.** (p. 360)

15. **b.** (p. 361)

16. The term *span of short-term memory* refers to the number of items that can be held in short-term memory at one time. In general, the span of short-term memory is about 7 items. Even though the number of items that can be held stays roughly the same, the effective capacity of this store can be improved by increasing the amount of information packed into each item. This is called chunking. For example, the letters c, i, a, f, b, i could be remembered not as six individual letters but as two acronyms—CIA and FBI. With this method, it is possible to dramatically improve memory performance. One man, after weeks of practice, managed to increase his digit span (the number of digits he could repeat after hearing them just once) to 80. His incredible performance was achieved by grouping digits together in meaningful chunks that he classified as running times, dates, etc. Chunking also seems to be a consequence of becoming an expert. Expert chess players can reproduce a briefly displayed layout of a chess game better than people less experienced at chess. This ability was attributed to the fact that they could chunk meaningful combinations of pieces on the board. When a random layout of chess pieces was shown, in which no such meaningful combinations would be likely, experts did no better than other players. (pp. 331, 339–340)

17. Concepts are used to categorize objects and events in the world. Cognitive psychologists suggest that conceptual information is represented in schemas. The nature of a schema, however, has been the subject of debate. The feature theory proposes that a schema consists of a set of defining features or characteristics. For example, the schema for cow might include the facts that such an animal "is large," "eats grass," "makes a mooing noise," and "is raised for milk." A problem with the theory is that it is difficult to identify those defining features for many categories.

An alternative theory is the prototype theory, which suggests that a schema consists of a holistic, picturelike representation of a typical or average member of the category. Eleanor Rosch has shown that typical members of a category are treated differently than less typical members. For example, people can more easily verify that a robin (a typical bird) is a bird than that a chicken (an atypical bird) is a bird. This kind of finding is more easily interpreted in terms of prototype theory. It should be noted that both theories can be modified to account for such findings, and in fact some theories have been presented that combine the characteristics of feature and prototype theories. (pp. 346–347)

# CHAPTER 11 THE HUMAN INTELLECT

*Read the introduction below before you read the chapter in the text.*

Chapter 11 provides a multifaceted examination of the human intellect. The chapter opens with a discussion of intelligence as it is defined and studied from four major perspectives—the psychometric, information-processing, neuropsychological, and ecological approaches. The psychometric approach attempts to understand intelligence by analyzing patterns of scores on mental tests. It is the approach most strongly associated with standardized IQ tests. The first of these was developed by Alfred Binet; later modifications and alternative tests were created by Lewis Terman and David Wechsler. Other adherents of a psychometric approach, such as Charles Spearman and Louis Thurstone, have used factor analysis to learn more about the structure of intelligence. The information-processing approach focuses on the steps involved in carrying out mental tasks. Robert Sternberg, for example, has sought a comprehensive understanding of how various cognitive components constitute intelligence. Some investigators have bridged the information-processing and psychometric approaches as they attempt to find basic correlates of intelligence such as short-term memory capacity and speed of information processing. The neuropsychological approach attempts to relate specific mental abilities to specific areas of the brain. Howard Gardner's concept of multiple intelligences has arisen largely from neuropsychological evidence. Finally, the ecological approach emphasizes the importance of considering intelligence in its environmental context. This approach has been valuable in pointing out that standard IQ tests may fail to adequately measure intelligence exhibited on the job and may incorrectly represent the intelligence of people from other cultures, particularly non-Western cultures.

A major function of the human intellect involves solving problems that depend on logical reasoning. Inductive reasoning entails reasoning from the specific to the general. Research on inductive reasoning has identified several kinds of biases in thinking.

Deductive reasoning involves reasoning from the general to the specific. Research suggests that people who reason successfully on deductive problems often use visual imagery to aid their thinking. Problem solving can include many types of problems—syllogisms used to test deductive reasoning, math story problems, a game of chess, crossword puzzles, even how to write a novel or be a happier person. Psychologists have described several ways in which people can be more effective problem solvers, such as avoiding rigid thinking patterns (called mental set), using analysis, and establishing subgoals.

Language is an important topic because it underlies so much of our problem solving, memory, perception, and thought. The work of Noam Chomsky was a major stimulus to the study of language as a cognitive ability. Chomsky's theory emphasizes the rule-based nature of grammar and specified how meaning might be related to the surface structure of a sentence (the sentence as spoken or written). Psychologists have learned much about language by analyzing the kinds of speech errors people make. Merrill Garrett's theory of sentence generation is based largely on such data. Psychologists have also learned something about the brain areas involved in language through the study of individuals with aphasia—a loss of language ability resulting from brain damage. A major issue in the study of language is that of linguistic relativity, the notion that thought may be shaped and even limited by the language of the thinker.

*LOOK over the table of contents for this chapter in your textbook before you continue with your study.*

*Notice that there are focus questions in the margins of the text for your use in studying the material. The following chart lists which study guide questions relate to which focus questions.*

| Focus Questions | Study Guide Questions |
| --- | --- |
| Conceptions of Intelligence | |
| 1–4 | 1–11 |
| 5–7 | 12–18 |

| | |
|---|---|
| 8–13 | 19–23 |
| 14–17 | 24–27 |
| 18–20 | 28–30 |

Logical Reasoning and Problem Solving

| | |
|---|---|
| 21–26 | 1–6 |
| 27–28 | 7–9 |
| 29–34 | 10–22 |

Language and Its Relationship to Thought

| | |
|---|---|
| 35–41 | 1–12 |
| 42–43 | 13–17 |
| 44–47 | 18–23 |

# The Integrated Study Workout

*Complete one section at a time.*

## *Conceptions of Intelligence*   (pages 369–386)

*CONSIDER these questions before you go on. They are designed to help you start thinking about this subject, not to test your knowledge.*

How did IQ tests originate? What do they really measure? What aspects of intelligence do they tend to miss?

Is intelligence a single ability that a person simply has more or less of? Or is intelligence a collection of several qualitatively different abilities?

What is the truth behind the popular notion that the right and left brains have different capabilities?

How might one's culture affect one's performance on an intelligence test?

*READ this section of your text lightly. Then go back and read thoroughly, completing the Workout as you proceed.*

When Mark Snyderman and Stanley Rothman asked over 1000 experts what abilities they considered important aspects of intelligence, they found considerable agreement on some aspects (such as abstract reasoning and problem solving) and much less on others (such as sensory acuity and goal directedness). Historically, there have been different approaches to the study of intelligence, each with its own view of what intelligence is. A recurring theme is the issue of whether intelligence is unitary or a collection of different abilities. The chapter discusses four different approaches, beginning with the psychometric approach.

1. Define psychometrics.

The psychometric approach was pioneered by Sir Francis Galton, whose interest in intelligence began with his interest in heredity.

2. Answer the following questions about Galton's work.

   a. How did Galton's interest in heredity affect his approach to the study of intelligence?

   b. Describe the kinds of measures taken in Galton's Anthropometric Laboratory. What did Galton expect to show with regard to these measures?

   c. What was a practical goal of this research?

   d. What kind of statistical procedure did Galton invent in connection with his anthropometric research? Why did he invent it?

   e. Did Galton's research turn out as he expected? Explain.

Today's intelligence tests can be traced back not to Galton's work but to the work of Alfred Binet and his assistant Theophile Simon.

3. Answer the following questions about the work done by Binet and Simon.

   a.  How did Binet's view of intelligence differ from Galton's?

   b.  What was the original purpose of the Binet-Simon Intelligence Scale?

   c.  What kinds of items did Binet and Simon include on their test? How were items selected? Were the kinds of items used consistent with the purpose of the test? Explain.

   d.  Explain the concept of mental age.

In North America, the first widely used intelligence test was Lewis Terman's modification of the Binet and Simon scale. It was called the Stanford-Binet Scale because the work was conducted at Stanford University.

4. The formula for IQ is _____ . IQ stands for _____ .

Revisions of the Stanford-Binet Scale are widely used today, but revisions of David Wechsler's test are even more commonly used. Both are individually administered intelligence tests.

5. Why did Wechsler design his test?

6. The acronyms *WAIS-R* and *WISC-III* stand for _____ and _____ , respectively.

7. How is the meaning of IQ in Wechsler's test different from its original meaning? Why would the original meaning have been absurd in an adult test?

Psychometricians in the field of intelligence testing must ask themselves whether their tests provide useful and trustworthy information—that is, whether they really tell us about a person's intelligence.

8. The extent to which a test measures what it is supposed to measure is its _____ .

9. How well do IQ scores correlate with school grades?

10. How did Terman attempt to uncover the relationship between IQ and achievement outside of school? What were his findings and why were they suspect?

11. What evidence suggests that IQ can help to predict on-the-job performance?

Does it make sense to summarize intelligence with a single number as in an IQ score? Or does this misrepresent something as complex as the intellect? The answer depends on whether one believes intelligence to be unitary or a collection of separate abilities. The primary psychometric tool for studying the structure of intelligence is factor analysis, a method invented by Charles Spearman. (See Figures 11.2 and 11.3 on text pages 375 and 376.)

12. Explain the basic rationale underlying factor analysis.

13. What did Spearman refer to as *g*? What suggested to him that *g* existed?

14. What did Spearman refer to as *s*? What suggested to him that there was such a thing as *s*?

Louis Thurstone came to different conclusions about the intercorrelations among different tests.

15. What observation led Thurstone to pursue a different means of factor analysis? Describe his procedure.

16. Define Thurstone's concept of a primary mental ability and contrast his model of the mind with Spearman's. In order to facilitate comparison of Thurstone's view of intelligence with the views of other theorists, list the seven primary mental abilities he identified. (See Figure 11.4 on text page 377.)

Since Thurstone's work, psychologists have used new batteries of tests and new factor-analytic techniques to develop different theories about the structure of intelligence. (See Figure 11.5 on text page 377.)

17. How is the mind commonly depicted in recent theories? What aspects of Spearman's and Thurstone's ideas are preserved in these theories? In what way do the theories differ from one another?

18. Identify the two second-level abilities proposed by Philip E. Vernon. In what way does the scoring of the Wechsler tests fit well with Vernon's conception?

The information-processing approach to the study of intelligence can be regarded as complementary to the psychometric approach.

19. Compare and contrast the goals of the psychometric and information-processing approaches.

One goal of the information-processing approach is to find elementary cognitive correlates of intelligence. Research in this area bridges the information-processing and psychometric approaches, as it searches for correlations between IQ scores and performance on very simple cognitive tasks. Many of the research findings in this area highlight the importance of the speed of information processing, a notion that echoes Galton's idea of mental quickness.

20. Summarize evidence that general intelligence is correlated with the speed of information processing.

21. Why might one think that short-term memory capacity underlies differences in intelligence? How is short-term memory capacity related to speed of processing? What evidence supports this hypothesis?

22. How is the issue of inferring causality from correlations relevant to discussion of this area of research?

Robert Sternberg sees intelligence as "mental self-government."

23. Answer the following questions about Sternberg's work.

    a. What does Sternberg mean by "mental self-government"?

    b. What are metacomponents? What does the term *meta-* mean in this context? Give some examples of tasks performed by metacomponents.

    c. Name and describe the two groups of lower components in Sternberg's theory.

    d. In Sternberg's experiments, people who performed well consistently differed from those who performed poorly in a way that tends to support his theory. How did they differ?

    e. How does Sternberg explain $g$?

Neuropsychology is an approach to the study of intelligence that complements the two already discussed. This approach seeks to relate intelligence to specific areas of the brain.

24. Since the 1970s, it has become popular to describe people as being left-brained or right-brained. What are some problems with this classification scheme?

25. Is there evidence that the left and right hemispheres are associated with different aspects of intelligence? Explain.

26. What does the pattern of intellectual capabilities and deficits in people with brain damage imply?

Using a good deal of neuropsychological evidence, Howard Gardner has suggested that there is no such thing as a general intelligence that applies to all mental tasks. His theory is called the multiple intelligences theory.

27. Answer the following questions about Gardner's work.

    a. What are the various types of evidence on which Gardner has based his conclusions?

    b. List the seven separate intelligences suggested by Gardner.

    c. How have some critics responded to Gardner's inclusion of such things as "musical" intelligence and "interpersonal" intelligence? How has Gardner responded to the critics?

    d. Identify another, more damaging criticism of Gardner's theory.

The last approach to intelligence discussed in the text is the ecological approach.

28. What is the focus of the ecological approach?

29. Describe evidence that intelligence as expressed on the job may not be reflected by scores on standard tests.

30. Researchers who take an ecological perspective have concluded that culture affects an individual's approach to an intelligence test. What kinds of results have led to this conclusion?

31. Summarize the evidence that a cultural group's environment and lifestyle may be related to its members' performance on different subtests of a standard IQ test.

*Logical Reasoning and Problem Solving*
(pages 387–396)

> CONSIDER *these questions before you go on. They are designed to help you start thinking about this subject, not to test your knowledge.*

How do people reason? Do people in different cultures approach reasoning problems in the same or different ways?

What specific biases have psychologists identified in people's judgments?

How can we improve our problem-solving performance?

> READ *this section of your text lightly. Then go back and read thoroughly, completing the Workout as you proceed.*

Reasoning as a subject of psychological inquiry has come in and out of favor. With behaviorism and psychoanalysis, it went out; more recently, with the rise of cognitive psychology, it has come into favor again.

1. We distinguish between two kinds of logical reasoning. Deciding whether a specific conclusion follows from one or more general premises is called _____ reasoning. Inferring a general rule from specific items or observations is called _____ reasoning, or hypothesis construction.

Psychologists such as Amos Tversky and Daniel Kahneman have explored inductive reasoning with problems that resemble those people face in everyday life. They have been especially interested in identifying the kinds of information people tend to use or tend to ignore in making judgments.

2. Explain the concepts below and illustrate each in terms of the librarian-or-salesperson problem in the text.

 a.  representativeness

 b.  base rate

3. What evidence suggests that people tend to ignore base rates?

4. How does availability bias thinking?

5. What is confirmation bias and how was it demonstrated in Wason's experiment?

6. Could confirmation bias occur because it is adaptive in daily life? Explain.

Psychological research often uses syllogisms to study deductive reasoning.

7. What is a syllogism and what is a person's task when confronted with one?

8. Does research suggest that people solve syllogisms through formal rules of logic? Explain.

9. In the view of Philip Johnson-Laird, how do people successfully solve syllogisms? What evidence tends to support his view?

Problem solving has been another major focus in cognitive psychology.

10. Define the term *problem.*

11. The three elements that all problems have in common are _____ , _____ , and _____ .

12. What must one do to solve a problem? Which of these steps are most critical for many problems?

Habits are often helpful results of learning, but they can sometimes set up barriers to effective problem solving.

13. Define the concept of mental set and show how it applies to the nine dot problem.

14. Define the type of mental set known as functional fixedness and show how it applies to the candle problem.

15. What did the Gestalt psychologists believe was involved in solving a problem such as the nine dot or candle problem? What does their view suggest about ways of solving problems more effectively? Describe research evidence consistent with this view.

Analogies can be powerful aids to problem solving; some famous examples of successful problem solving, such as Darwin's theory of natural selection, illustrate this point nicely.

16. What are analogies and how can they help a problem solver?

Sometimes a problem is difficult because the problem solver must deal with a great deal of information and find some way to represent it efficiently.

17. How do experts differ from novices with regard to selecting and representing information?

18. What general point about organizing information is illustrated by the stick-configuration problem, presented in Figure 11.12 on text page 394?

19. Distinguish between an algorithm and a heuristic.

Sometimes the gap between a problem's initial state and its goal state is too great to be negotiated in a single step. Subgoals provide a useful means of bridging such a gap.

20. Explain and give an example of the concept of subgoals.

21. Distinguish between well-defined and ill-defined problems. Would balancing your checkbook be an example of a well-defined or an ill-defined problem? what about achieving financial security?

22. How is it possible for subgoals to impede progress toward a goal?

### Language and Its Relationship to Thought
(pages 396–407)

*CONSIDER these questions before you go on. They are designed to help you start thinking about this subject, not to test your knowledge.*

What mental steps are involved when people produce sentences?

How can slips of the tongue help psychologists to learn more about language use?

What can the study of people who have suffered brain damage tell us about the brain's involvement in language?

How are thought and language related? Can the language we speak affect our thoughts or make some thoughts more likely than others?

Can sexist language, such as the use of *man* to mean both people in general and men in particular, promote sexist thinking?

> *READ this section of your text lightly. Then go back and read thoroughly, completing the Workout as you proceed.*

Humans are unique in possessing verbal language. The ability to use this abstract, symbolic mode of communication has enormous implications for human life. Language allows us to span distance, time, and the limitations of our personal experience. It is the means by which cultures are developed and passed on. Cognitive psychologists are interested in language because it is a cognitive ability itself and because it is closely connected with other cognitive abilities.

1. Given that there are about 3000 distinct languages in the world today, how is it possible to speak of human language in the singular?

2. Entities that stand for other entities are _____ . These entities take the form of pronounceable sounds called _____ , which are the smallest meaningful units in a language. For example, the word *unhappiness* has _____ of these units.

3. Answer the following questions about morphemes.

   a. Distinguish between content words and grammatical morphemes.

   b. What does it mean to say that a morpheme is arbitrary? Why is arbitrariness important?

   c. What does it mean to say that a morpheme is discrete?

   d. Explain how arbitrariness and discreteness distinguish linguistic symbols from nonverbal communication signals.

4. Answer the following questions about the structure of language.

   a. Explain why language is said to be hierarchical.

   b. In what sense is this type of organization powerful?

   c. The elementary vowel and consonant sounds of a language are called _____ .

   d. The rules that specify permissible ways to arrange units at one level of structure in order to produce the next higher level constitute the _____ of the language.

5. Is grammar something one learns in school? Support your answer.

6. How is tacit knowledge of grammar demonstrated?

Noam Chomsky has had a major influence not only on his own field of linguistics but also on cognitive psychology. In his 1957 book *Syntactic Structures*, Chomsky set out to describe a model of grammar that could apply to any language.

7. Answer the following questions about Chomsky's theory.

    a. In what way did Chomsky's work represent an attack on the behaviorist perspective then dominant in psychology?

    b. What is the surface structure of a sentence? How did Chomsky relate the surface structure to the meaning of the sentence? How in Chomsky's view does a person produce a sentence?

    c. Chomsky's theory is called the _____ _____ theory.

Chomsky's theory stimulated cognitive psychologists to investigate empirically the sorts of issues Chomsky had approached in a purely theoretical manner. Psychologists have learned how people produce and comprehend sentences by studying the errors they make. Error patterns can help to reveal the steps in language processing of which we are normally unaware.

8. What is a spoonerism? Give an example.

9. If the speaker intended to say, "Then the big guy climbed the tree," which of the following two sentences would be the more likely slip of the tongue? Why?

    a. Then the big tree climbed the guy.
    b. Then the tree guy climbed the big.

10. Suppose a speaker intended to say, "An owl gave a hoot" and instead accidentally switched the words *hoot* and *owl*. Is the first word of the sentence more likely to be *An* or *A*? Why?

11. Why would you be unlikely to hear a slip of the tongue like "The pogger ran three times around the jark"?

12. Describe Merrill Garrett's model of sentence generation and show how it explains observations about slips of the tongue. (See Figure 11.15 on text page 401.) Be sure to define the functional and positional stages of sentence generation in your answer.

The neuropsychological approach to language has advanced our understanding through the study of people who have aphasia.

13. Define the term *aphasia*.

14. Describe the language of someone with Broca's (nonfluent) aphasia. What area of the brain is damaged in such cases and where is that area located? (See Figure 11.16 on text page 402 for this question and for item 15.)

15. Describe the language of someone with Wernicke's (fluent) aphasia. What area of the brain is damaged in such cases and where is that area located?

16. State Carl Wernicke's hypothesis about the functions of Broca's and Wernicke's areas.

17. What is the new view of the role of Broca's area and Wernicke's area in speech comprehension and production? (See Figure 11.17 on text page 403.) What is the status of this view among researchers?

Psychologists have theorized about the relationship between language and thought for many years, producing a wide range of opinions on the subject.

18. What was John B. Watson's view of the relation of language to thought? How was it put to the test and what was the outcome of the test?

19. Discuss Lev Vygotsky's theory about the dependence of thought on language.

Benjamin Whorf, an expert on Native American languages, proposed the theory of linguistic relativity, a conception of thought's relation to language that has inspired considerable psychological research.

20. What is suggested in Whorf's theory of linguistic relativity? What observations led Whorf to this theory?

21. Do linguistic differences in color naming coincide with differences in how colors are perceived?

    a. Explain in terms of Eleanor Rosch's work with the Dani tribe. Do Rosch's results support or contradict the theory of linguistic relativity?

    b. What evidence suggests that language does affect subtler aspects of color judgments?

22. Interpret the results from studies of bilingual speakers in terms of the theory of linguistic relativity.

The possibility exists that we can deliberately affect our thinking by altering our language. That idea provides part of the motivation for the current attempt to eliminate certain sexist constructions in the English language. An example of such a construction is the use of *man* to mean both humans in general and human males in particular.

23. Describe research by Joseph Schneider and Sally Hacker showing that this double use of the term *man* does, in fact, affect thinking.

---

*Be sure to READ the Concluding Thoughts at the end of the chapter. Note important points in your Workout. Then consolidate your learning by answering the focus questions in the margins of the text.*

*After you have studied the chapter thoroughly, CHECK your understanding with the self-test that follows.*

## Self-Test 1

*Multiple-Choice Questions*

1. Snyderman and Rothman asked specialists in the field of intelligence to indicate those human abilities that were important elements of intelligence. Nearly everyone in the study indicated all of the following *except*:
   a. abstract reasoning.
   b. problem solving.
   c. sensory acuity.
   d. capacity to acquire knowledge.

2. Asking whether a test really measures what it is supposed to measure is a question about the test's:
   a. standardization.   c. factor analysis.
   b. validity.   d. *g*.

3. The technique known as *factor analysis* is a powerful means of determining the _____ of intelligence.
   a. biological basis   c. degree
   b. ecological validity  d. structure

4. After analyzing intercorrelations among different tests, Louis Thurstone concluded that intelligence consists of:
   a. *g* alone.
   b. *g* and a number of *s*'s.
   c. seven primary mental abilities.
   d. the capacity for mental self-government.

5. Researchers looking for basic cognitive correlates of intelligence have often converged on _____ in one form or another.
   a. the speed of information processing
   b. the size of long-term memory
   c. problem-solving ability
   d. metacomponents

6. Studies of the on-the-job intellectual performance of electricians would most probably be conducted in the context of the _____ approach to intelligence.
   a. psychometric
   b. information-processing
   c. anthropometric
   d. ecological

7. Amos Tversky and Daniel Kahneman have suggested that people tend to _____ base rates.
   a. overestimate
   b. underestimate
   c. ignore
   d. pay too much attention to

8. A person who reasons from the premises *All birds can fly* and *Chickens are birds* that *Chickens can fly* has:
   a. engaged in deductive reasoning.
   b. engaged in inductive reasoning.
   c. fallen prey to the availability bias.
   d. fallen prey to the confirmation bias.

9. Consistent with Philip Johnson-Laird's hypothesis, research has shown that college students reason better with syllogisms that are easier to:
   a. pronounce.
   b. visualize.
   c. state in terms of a mental set.
   d. combine into one sentence.

10. Charles Darwin's use of selective breeding by horticulturists to help him understand natural selection illustrates the power of:
    a. subgoals.
    b. algorithms.
    c. metacomponents.
    d. analogies.

11. A strategy for solving an anagram (a scrambled-word problem) that involves producing all possible sequences of the letters in the anagram is a(n):
    a. heuristic
    b. analogy.
    c. algorithm.
    d. morpheme.

12. The physical structure of morphemes need not be similar to the concept they stand for; in other words, morphemes are:
    a. discrete.          c. arbitrary.
    b. grammatical.       d. transformational.

13. In Merrill Garrett's theory of sentence production, slips of the tongue that involve switching whole content words take place in:
    a. the functional stage.
    b. the positional stage.
    c. both the functional and positional stages.
    d. a stage earlier than either the functional or positional stage.

14. The Soviet psychologist Lev Vygotsky suggested that:
    a. thought involves a hidden form of the muscular movements that are part of speech.
    b. language is separate from thought in very young children, but they gradually come to use it for private thought.
    c. language plays little or no role in the development of thought.
    d. thought cannot occur in the absence of some linguistic symbol system.

15. The idea that language can affect thinking is known as _____ and has received_____ research support.
    a. linguistic relativity; no
    b. linguistic relativity; some
    c. arbitrariness; no
    d. arbitrariness; some

### Essay Questions

16. What is aphasia? How do the symptoms of Broca's and Wernicke's aphasia differ? What do the symptoms suggest about the functions of Broca's area and Wernicke's area?

17. How is intelligence portrayed in Howard Gardner's theory of multiple intelligences? On what kind of data is the theory primarily based? What other theory of intelligence is Gardner's theory most similar to? How has Gardner responded to critics claiming that he has stretched the meaning of intelligence too far?

*After you have assessed your understanding on the basis of Self-Test 1 and have tried to strengthen your preparation in any areas of weakness, GO ON to Self-Test 2.*

# Self-Test 2

### Multiple-Choice Questions

1. Francis Galton believed that intelligence:
    a. was unrelated to heredity, a fact that he succeeded in demonstrating in his research.
    b. would be reflected in simple sensory and motor abilities, but he found only weak correlations among such measures.
    c. must be studied through tests similar to those encountered in the academic environment.
    d. could only be interpreted sensibly in the context of tasks people routinely perform in their everyday lives.

2. Alfred Binet and Theophile Simon developed the Binet-Simon Intelligence Scale by trying out items similar to those found in schoolwork and:
    a. keeping only those that could be answered by about 50 percent of the children.
    b. making them easier or harder to accommodate children of different mental ages.
    c. dropping those that did not correlate well with simple measures of mental speed and sensory acuity.
    d. keeping only those that yielded results similar to teachers' ratings.

3. Which of the following correctly represents the *original* meaning of IQ?
   a. mental age divided by chronological age times 100
   b. chronological age divided by mental age times 100
   c. mental age divided by the number of items correctly answered times 100
   d. the number of items correctly answered divided by chronological age times 100

4. IQ scores on standard intelligence tests are most highly correlated with:
   a. school grades.
   b. job success.
   c. achievement motivation.
   d. brain weight.

5. Most recent factor-analytic theories of intelligence combine _____ with _____ .
   a. Sternberg's idea of mental self-government; Spearman's idea of separate mental abilities
   b. Thurstone's idea of ecological intelligence; Spearman's idea of academic intelligence
   c. Spearman's idea of *g*; Thurstone's idea of separate mental abilities
   d. Vernon's idea of practical-mechanical inteligence; Sternberg's idea of metacomponents

6. Classifying people as left-brained or right-brained is problematic because:
   a. people who are above average in logical reasoning also tend to be above average in spatial skills.
   b. there is no direct means of left- versus right-brained development.
   c. factor analysis shows no evidence that different abilities are located in different hemispheres.
   d. of both a. and b.

7. Howard Gardner has based his theory of multiple intelligences in large part on:
   a. the intercorrelations among subtests in a large battery of tests.
   b. people with especially high general intelligence.
   c. case histories of rare individuals such as idiots savants.
   d. the methods of the information-processing approach.

8. Researchers have found that the Kpelle people of Nigeria:
   a. were unable to sort by taxonomic category as Westerners typically do.
   b. could sort by taxonomic category but preferred to sort in another way.
   c. typically sorted by taxonomic category just as Westerners do.
   d. could not sort at all unless they were given a set of categories.

9. Alan believes that a classmate who is a somewhat flamboyant nonconformist is an English major when in fact he is a chemistry major. Alan's error illustrates:
   a. overreliance on representativeness.
   b. overreliance on base rates.
   c. a faulty major premise.
   d. availability bias.

10. Carrie is nervous about boarding her flight to Denver because of a highly publicized plane crash the previous week. We could best explain her apprehension in terms of:
    a. mental set.
    b. availability bias.
    c. a syllogism.
    d. an analogy.

11. A problem, by definition, has all of the following *except*:
    a. a goal state.
    b. an initial state.
    c. possible operations.
    d. algorithms.

12. Suppose a person going to a birthday party needs something to protect a carefully wrapped present from the rain, but overlooks an unused plastic trash bag lying on the counter. This person has illustrated the problem of:
    a. functional fixedness.
    b. representativeness.
    c. induction.
    d. spoonerisms.

13. The set of rules that determines how units at one level can be arranged to form the next-higher level constitutes a language's:
    a. hierarchy.          c. morphemes.
    b. grammar.            d. phonemes.

14. According to Chomsky, underlying the words we speak is an abstract, mental representation of the meaning of those words. This representation is called the:
    a. generative grammar.
    b. transformation.
    c. deep structure.
    d. surface structure.

15. An individual whose speech is meaningful but labored and made up almost entirely of content words fits the pattern of someone:
    a. with linguistic relativity.
    b. with Wernicke's aphasia.
    c. with Broca's aphasia.
    d. who is an idiot savant.

## Essay Questions

16. What is confirmation bias? Give an example from laboratory research.

17. What is deductive reasoning? Explain Philip Johnson-Laird's hypothesis about why some people solve syllogisms better than other people. What evidence suggests that Johnson-Laird's hypothesis might be correct?

# Answers

## Conceptions of Intelligence

4. (mental age/chronological age) × 100; intelligence quotient

6. Wechsler Adult Intelligence Scale, Revised; Wechsler Intelligence Scale for Children, Third Edition

8. validity

## Logical Reasoning and Problem Solving

1. deductive; inductive

11. an initial state; a goal state; operations

## Language and Its Relation to Thought

2. symbols; morphemes; 3

4. c. phonemes, d. grammar

7. c. generative-transformational

## Self-Test 1

1. c. (p. 369)

2. b. (p. 374)

3. d. (p. 375)

4. c. (pp. 376–377)

5. a. This represents a revival of Galton's earlier thinking, which is now supported by research data. (pp. 378–379)

6. d. (p. 385)

7. c. (p. 388)

8. a. (pp. 390–391)

9. b. (p. 392)

10. d. (p. 394)

11. c. (p. 395)

12. c. (p. 397)

13. a. (p. 401)

14. b. (p. 404)

15. b. (pp. 404–406)

16. Aphasia is any loss of language ability resulting from brain damage. Broca's and Wernicke's aphasia are two categories of aphasia, each associated with damage to a particular area of the brain.

    Damage to Broca's area in the left frontal lobe typically produces a tendency to speak in a labored way. The speech that the individual with this type of aphasia struggles to produce is generally telegraphic; that is, it contains mostly content words and grammatical morphemes such as *and*, *the*, or past-tense endings. Broca's aphasics show relatively good language comprehension, but often have difficulty understanding grammatically complex sentences. A sentence in which meaning cannot be inferred from content words alone will not be understood by the person with Broca's aphasia.

The person with Wernicke's aphasia can speak with apparent fluency, but the speech is really only gibberish. It is full of nonsense words and has few content words. The speech retains its grammatical structure but loses its meaning. This kind of aphasia is associated with damage to Wernicke's area in the left temporal lobe. The current view is that Wernicke's area is critical for connecting words with their meanings both in production and comprehension. (pp. 402–403)

17. Howard Gardner's theory depicts intelligence as a collection of relatively separate kinds of intelligence. He argues against the existence of something like Spearman's *g*. His conception of the structure of intelligence is somewhat similar to that of Louis Thurstone, who proposed seven primary mental abilities. Gardner produced his theory of multiple intelligences largely on the basis of case histories of people who were normal or superior in one intellectual ability and otherwise generally deficient intellectually.

Gardner has tentatively suggested a set of seven types of intelligence. Some, such as language ability, are similar to the kinds of abilities commonly tested on intelligence tests in the psychometric tradition. Others, such as musical or bodily-kinesthetic intelligences, have not been traditionally considered aspects of intelligence. Critics argue that Gardner has stretched the meaning of intelligence too far in the case of these intelligences. Gardner has answered by saying that there is no good basis for discriminating between these intelligences and others that are considered more acceptable by the critics. According to Gardner, the tradition has excluded some forms of valuable and complex behaviors while overemphasizing others. (pp. 383–384)

*Self-Test 2*

1. **b.** (p. 370)

2. **d.** Binet realized the circular nature of this selection procedure, but also saw the advantages of a single standard test that could be used on many different children in different circumstances.

Further, since he was trying to produce a valid test of academic ability, he needed to compare it with an accepted measure of such ability. (p. 371)

3. **a.** Don't forget that Wechsler, in developing his adult intelligence test, kept the term IQ because of its familiarity to the public but changed its meaning. An IQ score was no longer produced by dividing mental age by chronological age. Rather, 100 was the IQ score associated with whatever level of performance was average for a particular age group; better or poorer performance received correspondingly higher or lower scores. (p. 372)

4. **a.** (p. 374)

5. **c.** These hierarchical theories of intelligence differ chiefly in what they propose as the abilities at the second level of the hierarchy. (p. 377)

6. **d.** (pp. 382–383)

7. **c.** (p. 383)

8. **b.** The Kpelle clearly had a different notion of what constituted intelligent behavior, since they would sort by taxonomic category only when they were asked to sort the way a stupid person would. (p. 386)

9. **a.** (p. 388)

10. **b.** (p. 389)

11. **d.** (p. 392)

12. **a.** Mental set is a situation in which we have difficulty breaking free of existing habits of thought to find a solution. Functional fixedness is a special case of mental set in which a habit of thought makes it harder to think of using objects for unaccustomed purposes. (p. 393)

13. **b.** (p. 398)

14. **c.** (p. 399)

15. **c.** The current view holds that Broca's area is critical to syntax. The person with Broca's aphasia does not simply have a language production problem, as researchers once thought. Rather, the person also suffers difficulties in comprehension whenever understanding depends critically on syntactic analysis and not just on content words and context. (p. 402)

16. Confirmation bias is the tendency to look for confirmation rather than disconfirmation of a hypothesis. This is despite the fact that, logically, no amount of confirmation can prove a hypothesis true and that disconfirmation has the power to rule *out* a hypothesis. Peter Wason asked subjects to guess the rule that the experimenter was using to generate sequences of three numbers, such as

5-7-9. The subjects could test their hypotheses by generating sequences of their own and having the experimenter say whether they fit his rule or not. Subjects tended to generate sequences consistent with their own hypotheses rather than sequences that could tell them if their sequence was wrong. (p. 389)

17. Deductive reasoning involves reasoning from the general to the specific. It is often tested in syllogisms, which contain two general premises and a specific conclusion. The person solving the syllogism must indicate whether the conclusion logically follows from the premises. An example would be "All fish are scaly (major premise); Cedric is a fish (minor premise); therefore, Cedric is scaly (conclusion)." In this case, the conclusion does follow logically from the premises. Johnson-Laird suggested that people who solve such problems successfully do so by creating a visual image to represent what is said in the premises and inspecting it to see if the conclusion is valid. Research evidence to support this idea comes from studies in which people have been shown to do better with syllogisms in which the major premise is easy to visualize. Another line of evidence comes from psychometric research. The ability to solve syllogisms is more strongly correlated with visual-spatial ability than with verbal ability. (pp. 390–392)

# CHAPTER 12 COGNITIVE DEVELOPMENT

*Read the introduction below before you read the chapter in the text.*

Chapter 12 explores the development of mental abilities during infancy and childhood. It begins by examining four questions fundamental to the study of human development. How orderly is developmental change? Researchers who emphasize consistency across individuals are interested in normative development—the typical sequence of developmental changes. Psychologists interested in individual development emphasize the developmental differences among individuals. How coherent is development across different cognitive domains? Some theorists contend that the mind develops as a whole, others say that specific abilities develop independently, and still others say that the truth lies somewhere in between. What is the pattern of change? Some theorists suggest that change is gradual and continuous, while others talk about development in terms of stages. What are the sources of developmental change? The maturationist perspective emphasizes nature and the learning perspective emphasizes nurture, but most developmentalists consider themselves interactionists, stressing the combined influence of biological and environmental factors.

Babies are born with certain sensory and perceptual capabilities, which develop further during infancy—roughly the first 18 to 24 months of life. For example, their visual acuity and their ability to perceive patterns improve. Studies using the visual cliff apparatus have shown that infants learn to fear and thus to avoid apparent drop-offs through experience in self-produced locomotion. Self-produced actions play a central part in the theory of Jean Piaget, a major theorist in the area of cognitive development. Piaget also emphasizes the infant's development of object permanence, the understanding that objects continue to exist even when they are no longer in view.

The child's acquisition of language is one of the most amazing aspects of cognitive development. In general, developmentalists believe that it depends both on innate mechanisms that predispose the child to learn language and on an environment that supports such learning. Young infants can distinguish phonemes, the basic units of speech sound. Early in life, infants begin to coo and babble, two forms of vocalization that prepare them for later speech and which appear to be types of play. Children move on to acquire words, slowly at first and then at a faster pace. At first they speak one word at a time, but they soon learn to produce progressively longer utterances that are meaningful and indicate some understanding of the rules of grammar. A number of observations suggest that children do not simply mimic the speech around them, but infer the underlying rules of language. Efforts to teach nonvocal forms of language to common chimpanzees have generally shown that, while they can learn to use symbols in a referential way, they cannot acquire more than a slight knowledge of grammar. More recent research with pygmy chimps suggests that they have somewhat greater facility with language than common chimpanzees do.

Using a variety of intellectual tasks, Jean Piaget has suggested that the growth of the child's ability to think logically occurs in four stages: sensorimotor, preoperational, concrete operational, and formal operational. The movement from one stage to the next involves the emergence of new types of schemes in the child's thinking. Schemes are something like mental blueprints for organized patterns of action. Theorists from the information-processing perspective attempt to understand cognitive development in terms of developmental changes in the components of the mind, such as short-term memory. Theorists from the sociocultural perspective emphasize that cognitive development occurs in a particular cultural and social context. Lev Vygotsky, the theorist generally credited with originating this perspective, stressed the importance of the relationship between language and thought in human cognitive development.

*LOOK over the table of contents for this chapter in your textbook before you continue with your study.*

*Notice that there are focus questions in the margins of the text for your use in studying the material. The following chart lists which study guide questions relate to which focus questions.*

| Focus Questions | Study Guide Questions |
|---|---|
| Some Basic Questions in the Study of Development | |
| 1–3 | 1–10 |
| Development of Perception and Knowledge in Infancy | |
| 4–7 | 1–5 |
| 8–10 | 6–10 |
| Development of Language | |
| 11–15 | 1–14 |
| 16–18 | 15–22 |
| 19–22 | 23–28 |
| Development of Logical Thought | |
| 23–29 | 1–9 |
| 30–33 | 10–12 |
| 34–37 | 13–19 |

# The Integrated Study Workout

*Complete one section at a time.*

## Some Basic Questions in the Study of Development (pages 413–416)

*CONSIDER these questions before you go on. They are designed to help you start thinking about this subject, not to test your knowledge.*

What kinds of questions do developmental psychologists ask and how do they answer them?

Does development take place gradually and continuously or in a series of stages?

What causes the child to develop? Is development the unfolding of the child's genetic plan? Is it the net result of the child's experience in the world? Or is it something more complex than either of these possibilities?

*READ this section of your text lightly. Then go back and read thoroughly, completing the Workout as you proceed.*

Development is the process of change that begins at conception and lasts throughout life. It is shaped not only by what occurs during an individual's lifetime, but also by evolutionary and cultural history. Developmental psychologists seek to understand the changes in abilities and behaviors that come with increasing age. They have most often focused their efforts on childhood, but adult development has recently received a greater share of attention than it once did. Critical questions involved in the study of development concern the nature and causes of change.

1. Explain the assumption of orderliness that underlies most research in developmental psychology.

2. Some theorists emphasize the typical sequence of developmental changes for a group of people, which is called _____ development. Others emphasize _____ development, which concerns the differences among people in developmental paths.

3. How can orderliness help psychologists to understand the nature of more advanced abilities?

4. Explain why some developmentalists prefer to emphasize individual development.

Developmentalists use two different methods to compare people at different ages.

5. Describe the cross-sectional method. Is it more useful for studying normative or individual development?

6. Describe the longitudinal method. Is it more useful for studying normative or individual development?

A central theoretical question in developmental psychology asks how coherent mental development is.

7. Briefly outline three positions on this question.

Parents often remark that their children are going through a stage. The notion of developmental stages is a matter of dispute among theorists.

8. Contrast continuity and stage theories of development.

Developmental psychologists also want to understand the sources of developmental change.

9. Those who see development as the product of experience in the world represent the
_____ perspective. Those who see development as the result of genetically programmed growth, particularly brain growth, represent the _____ perspective. Most developmental psychologists would be considered _____ because they emphasize the combined influence of experience and biological growth.

10. Explain what it means to say that it is the *whole person* who interacts with the environment.

## Development of Perception and Knowledge in Infancy   (pages 416–422)

> CONSIDER *these questions before you go on. They are designed to help you start thinking about this subject, not to test your knowledge.*

How can psychologists learn about an infant's perception or knowledge if the infant can't tell them about what it perceives or knows?

If you and an infant look at the same object, do you perceive the same thing?

Does an infant know better than to crawl over a sudden drop-off? Must an infant have experience with falling before it will avoid such a drop-off?

Can an infant who sees an interesting object—say, a bright red ball—continue to think about it once it has disappeared?

> READ *this section of your text lightly. Then go back and read thoroughly, completing the Workout as you proceed.*

The term *infancy* refers to the first 18 to 24 months of life. Despite the fact that infants cannot speak for much of this period, developmental psychologists have devised ingenious ways to learn about infants' perceptual abilities and knowledge. At the time of birth, infants have some basic sensory capabilities and respond to sensory stimulation by orienting toward some kinds of stimuli (such as a blinking light) and away from others (such as an unpleasant smell). However, the sensory systems of newborn infants are not fully developed.

1. Answer the following questions about the development of visual acuity in infancy.

   a. How have psychologists exploited infants' preference for patterned over unpatterned stimuli in studying visual acuity?

**b.** Is the infant's visual acuity still developing at the age of 1 day? 2 months? 8 months? How does acuity at 8 months compare to the acuity of an adult?

**c.** The infant's improvement in acuity is at least partly due to continued maturation of the _____, receptor cells in the retina.

2. Answer the following questions about the development of pattern recognition in infancy. (See Figure 12.2 on text page 417.)

**a.** What evidence indicates that young infants prefer human faces to other stimuli? What evidence suggests that even infants a few days old can recognize faces?

**b.** Describe the phenomenon of habituation.

**c.** Explain how habituation can be used to test infants' perceptual and memory abilities. What has such research shown about infants' ability to develop and retain mental concepts?

When infants begin to move around on their own, they face a new set of potential opportunities for learning and new dangers as well—electric outlets, hot ovens, sharp-edged tables, and sudden drop-offs. Psychologists use the visual cliff to study the growth of infants' wariness of heights. The visual cliff allows researchers to safely investigate whether an infant will move in a direction that visually suggests a sharp drop-off. (See Figure 12.3 on text page 418.)

3. What did Eleanor Gibson and Richard Walk discover about crawling infants' reactions to height in their experiment with the visual cliff?

4. In other experiments, noncrawling and crawling infants have shown different heart-rate responses to the visual cliff. How did noncrawlers and crawlers differ and how was the difference interpreted? Was the difference a result of age or of experience in crawling?

5. Is the experience of falling necessary for infants to develop fear of the visual cliff? Support your answer and then provide an evolutionary interpretation.

Perception and the avoidance of visual cliffs and physical obstacles imply that infants have knowledge of their physical world.

6. What is the origin of such knowledge? Describe three contrasting views on this matter.

**a.** empiricist philosophers

**b.** nativist philosophers

**c.** Piaget

Active exploration figures prominently in Jean Piaget's conception of infant cognitive development.

7. Describe some evidence that infants are in many ways "little scientists."

8. Why does Piaget characterize infancy as the sensorimotor stage of intellectual development? In your answer, focus on his view of the role of action in infant cognition.

A 3-month-old baby may watch fascinated as you dangle a rattle just out of reach, but then, when you hide it behind your back, act as if the rattle never existed. One of the most important early developments in the child's growing ability to represent the world mentally is object permanence, the knowledge that objects continue to exist even when out of view. According to Piaget, object permanence develops gradually during the first year and a half of life.

9. Briefly describe Piaget's three hidden-object tasks, the new level of object permanence each requires, and the age at which infants typically succeed at each. (See Figure 12.4 on text page 421.)

   a. simple hiding problem

   b. changed hiding-place problem

   c. invisible displacement problem

10. Piaget's position on the development of object permanence and knowledge of other physical principles has been challenged by recent research.

   a. What findings led investigators such as Baillargeon and Spelke to believe young infants know more about the physical world than Piaget suggested they do?

   b. How do they interpret infants' failure on Piaget's tasks?

## Development of Language (pages 422–432)

> CONSIDER these questions before you go on. They are designed to help you start thinking about this subject, not to test your knowledge.

Can children respond to language even before they are born?

What do the babbling and cooing of young infants have to do with language development?

How is it possible that children who have not mastered the intricacies of dressing themselves or using eating utensils can produce and understand something as complex as language?

Why do children say things like "Jimmy goed over there" or "She runned up to the fence"?

How does language learning compare across different language groups?

Is there any evidence that nonhuman animals are capable of learning language?

> READ this section of your text lightly. Then go back and read thoroughly, completing the Workout as you proceed.

Perhaps the most incredible feat of the developing human mind is its rapid progress toward the mastery of language. Children typically acquire considerable facility with their native language before they can manage many other, simpler tasks.

1. Most developmentalists agree that language learning requires a combination of

   _____ mechanisms that pre-

   dispose children to it and an _____

   that provides models and opportunities for prac-

   tice.

2. Summarize evidence that infants are sensitive to and interested in speech stimuli as soon as they are born and possibly even while they are still in the womb.

3. Describe one experimental technique used in research on infants' abilities to distinguish phonemes. What do such experiments suggest about the abilities of infants between 1 and 6 months of age? What happens to their abilities after the age of 6 months?

A familiar (sometimes all-too-familiar) form of infant vocalization is crying. Another type of infant vocalization consists of cooing and babbling.

4. Repeated, drawn-out vowel sounds, such as

   oooh-oooh, are called _____ ;

   _____ consists of repeated

   consonant-vowel sounds, such as baa-baa.

5. Cooing and babbling occur most often when the infant is happy and seem to be forms of

   _____ that have evolved to

   _____ the vocal apparatus.

6. Are cooing and babbling influenced by the speech sounds infants hear around them? Explain by comparing the development of deaf and hearing children.

A child's first words are generally greeted with great parental excitement and pride. The psychologist studying language development, however, must be somewhat more rigorous than the typical parent in deciding what counts as a word!

7. Distinguish between a performative and a true word.

8. Describe the rate of growth of the child's vocabulary. Do children acquire most of their new words through explicit instruction? Explain.

9. How do children determine what aspect of the environment a new word refers to?

10. Answer the following questions about the child's extension of words to new referents.

    a. A child's application of the term *car* to a truck or bus would be an instance of

       _____ .

    b. A child who fails to include a picture of a chicken in a stack of pictures of birds is showing evidence of an _____ of the term *bird*.

A major step in language development is taken when the child begins to put words together to form rudimentary sentences.

11. Do infants express multiword ideas with one-word statements? Explain.

12. When do children begin to put two words together? What kinds of words do children tend to include in these early sentences? Do they use word order correctly to indicate their meaning?

13. What evidence has shown that young children learn grammatical rules? (See Figure 12.7 on text page 426.)

14. What does it mean to say that children *discover* the rules of their language?

The process of language development is promoted by both internal and external supports. Nativist theories emphasize the role played by innate biological preparedness.

15. Identify some ways in which humans are specially equipped for language.

16. The LAD stands for _____
_____ , our innate grammar-learning aids. This concept was developed by
_____ .

17. Describe the approach to understanding the LAD exemplified by Dan Slobin's work. What has Slobin's work suggested about the LAD?

18. What has Derek Bickerton concluded from studying the development of creole languages?

19. What is developmental dysphasia and how does it indicate the existence of an innate grammar-learning mechanism?

20. Describe evidence for the critical-period hypothesis.

21. Describe the view of language learning offered by social learning theory. Define the LASS.

22. What evidence supports the social learning perspective? How can social learning theorists make sense of language development in Kalikuli infants?

Language is considered uniquely human. Many people have wondered whether it is possible for other species to acquire language under certain circumstances. Most efforts to answer this question have focused on chimpanzees, the species most closely related to humans. Because chimpanzees lack the vocal apparatus for speech, most efforts have used nonvocal language systems.

23. Allen and Beatrix Gardner successfully taught a chimp named Washoe to communicate with ASL, or _____ .

24. Summarize Herbert Terrace's research and conclusions.

25. In working with chimps, Sue Savage-Rumbaugh used an invented language in which the words were geometric figures called _____ , with Kanzi, a _____ chimp.

27. For each of the following chimps, what training methods were used, and how did the training conditions compare to the usual conditions of children's language learning?

    a. Washoe

    b. Nim

    c. Kanzi

27. What evidence suggests that Washoe, Kanzi, and other chimps used words as symbols, not merely as operant responses?

28. How do the chimps compare to children in terms of sentence length? in terms of grammar?

## Development of Logical Thought
(pages 432–445)

*CONSIDER these questions before you go on. They are designed to help you start thinking about this subject, not to test your knowledge.*

If a 5-year-old child is shown a tall, narrow container of liquid, will the child realize that the amount of liquid remains the same when it is poured into a short, wide container?

How does a child's understanding of cause-effect relationships differ from an adult's?

What aspect of the child's experience promotes the development of new capabilities in logical thinking?

How are changes in a child's memory related to changes in the child's ability to think logically?

What role does language play in the development of thought?

*READ this section of your text lightly. Then go back and read thoroughly, completing the Workout as you proceed.*

As they grow older, children become increasingly logical in their thinking. Developmental psychologists want to know how to describe these changes in logical capabilities, and how to explain their occurrence. Jean Piaget is widely regarded as the most influential theorist in this area of research.

1. What did Piaget mean when he referred to himself as a genetic epistemologist? What was his goal? What was his basic approach?

2. What is a scheme? How does the nature of schemes change with development?

3. Characterize each of the following stages, being careful to indicate the kind of scheme associated with each and the kinds of abilities they support. (Define new terms such as conservation, operation, and hypothetico-deductive reasoning where appropriate.)

   a. sensorimotor stage (birth to about 2 years old)

   b. preoperational stage (about 2 to 7 years old)

   c. concrete-operational stage (about 7 to 12 years old)

   d. formal-operational stage (about 12 years old through adulthood)

In Piaget's theory, transition to a given stage is based on the child's thoughts and activities at the previous stage. The schemes of the previous stage are modified through experience until something altogether new and revolutionary in the child's thinking has developed. Assimilation and accommodation are the complementary processes that produce this development.

4. Complete the following sentences.

   a. _____ is the process by which experiences are incorporated into existing schemes.

   b. _____ is the change in an existing scheme or set of schemes that results from the assimilation of an event or object.

5. Identify each of the following descriptions as focusing primarily on assimilation or accommodation. (Note that each example involves both processes.)

   _____ A child sees a woodcarving of a human figure and thinks of it as a doll.

   _____ A child discovers that the pencil scribblings she has produced can be erased.

   _____ A child is surprised to hear a neighbor's cat "meow" given that it looks a lot like a "doggy."

6. Why does a spider's web provide a better analogy for the growth of the mind than a brick wall?

7. What kinds of experiences are children most fascinated by, in Piaget's view?

Like any scientific theory, Piaget's theory of cognitive development has its critics. The process whereby theories are developed, criticized, defended or modified, and so on, is part of the nature of the scientific endeavor.

8. List and explain three types of criticisms of Piaget's theory. Where possible, describe evidence supporting the critics' point of view.

   a.

**b.**

**c.**

9. What contributions have caused Piaget's work to be so widely admired despite the criticism?

The information-processing perspective approaches cognitive development not in terms of the whole mind, as Piaget did, but rather in terms of interacting mental components. These mental components are organized as a system for handling information. From this perspective, cognitive development can be explained in terms of changes in the components, for example, changes in the memory stores/control processes or changes in processing rules.

10. Answer the following questions about the developmental importance of increased short-term memory capacity.

   **a.** Why are developmental changes in short-term, or working, memory thought to be particularly important?

   **b.** Summarize Juan Pascual-Leone's theory.

**c.** Describe evidence that appears to support Pascual-Leone's theory.

**d.** Describe evidence that increases in short-term memory are due more to experience than to maturation, contrary to Pascual-Leone's view. (See Figure 12.10 on text page 440.)

**e.** How might short-term memory improvements be due to an increase in processing speed?

11. Summarize Robert Siegler's work on the development of the ability to solve balance-beam problems. How does Siegler's account illustrate the fundamental difference between the information-processing and Piagetian approaches? (See Figure 12.11 on text page 441.)

12. What kinds of cognitive changes occur in adulthood? How can these changes be explained from an information-processing perspective?

Still another view of cognitive development is offered by the sociocultural perspective. Lev Vygotsky is usually regarded as the originator of this perspective.

13. Compare and contrast the views of Vygotsky and Piaget on the aspects of the environment most relevant to development.

14. What was Vygotsky's view of the child's relationship to the social world? How did he define cognitive development?

15. What did Piaget mean by the term *egocentric speech*? How did Vygotsky reinterpret this phenomenon? Describe some evidence consistent with Vygotsky's view.

16. Why are language in general and the internalization of speech in particular so important to cognitive development, in Vygotsky's view?

The developing child's thought occurs not in a void but rather in a particular social and cultural context. The child's experience is structured by a variety of social routines—making a purchase at a store, getting ready for bed, and going to the movies, for example.

17. Explain Vygotsky's notion that the child is an apprentice. How does Barbara Rogoff's research support Vygotsky's view?

18. How does Sudbury Valley School illustrate Vygotsky's conceptualization of apprenticeship?

19. What does the apprenticeship analogy suggest about the goal of cognitive development?

> Be sure to READ the Concluding Thoughts at the end of the chapter. Note important points in your Workout. Then consolidate your learning by answering the focus questions in the margins of the text.
>
> After you have studied the chapter thoroughly, CHECK your understanding with the self-test that follows.

# Self-Test 1

*Multiple-Choice Questions*

1. To say that a psychologist is interested in age-related changes that occur in a consistent order in most individuals means that he or she is specifically interested in:
   a. stage theories of development.
   b. normative development.
   c. individual development.
   d. maturation.

2. With regard to the question of the sources of development, most developmental psychologists would consider themselves:
   a. advocates of the maturationist perspective.
   b. advocates of the learning perspective.
   c. interactionists.
   d. cross-sectionalists.

3. Young infants will generally look longer at _____ than at _____.
   a. homogeneous stimuli; patterned stimuli
   b. novel stimuli; familiar stimuli
   c. dark, rounded shapes; bright, angular shapes
   d. stimuli that are controlled by others; stimuli they control themselves

4. Eleanor Gibson and Richard Walk showed that infants who had learned to crawl would:
   a. refuse to crawl across the deep side of the visual cliff apparatus unless their mothers called to them.
   b. crawl more slowly and carefully across the deep side of the visual cliff apparatus than across the shallow side.
   c. refuse to crawl across both the shallow and the deep sides of the visual cliff apparatus.
   d. crawl across the shallow side of the visual cliff apparatus but refuse to crawl across the deep side.

5. Piaget refers to the child's ability to think of an object that is not immediately present as:
   a. object permanence.
   b. invisible displacement.
   c. egocentric speech.
   d. overextension.

6. Which of the following is true of infants tested shortly after birth for their response to speech sounds?
   a. They show a preference for human speech over instrumental music.
   b. They show a preference for the sound of their own mother's voice over the voice of another woman.
   c. They show a preference for a prose passage recited daily during their last 6 weeks in the womb as compared to an unfamiliar passage.
   d. All of the above are true.

7. A child's application of the term *kitty* to cats, dogs, and stuffed bears can be described as:
   a. overextension.          c. a performative.
   b. underextension.         d. a LAD.

8. With regard to children's language acquisition, Noam Chomsky contends that:
   a. children's general intelligence is enough to help them acquire language.
   b. children have a set of innate learning aids that specifically help them to acquire language.
   c. learning is not involved in the acquisition of language.
   d. children do not acquire language rules, but merely learn to repeat what they hear and are reinforced for producing the sounds.

9. Which of the following is true of young children's early word combinations?
   a. They typically use only content words.
   b. They put words together themselves after they can comprehend multiword statements.

   c. Their word order is essentially random.
   d. They generally use the passive voice before the active voice.

10. Attempts to teach language to common chimpanzees:
    a. have repeatedly shown that they are incapable of using language symbolically and of learning rules of grammar.
    b. have recently led researchers to conclude that they are fully capable of both basic symbolic usage and grammar.
    c. have consistently shown that they are capable of learning grammar but incapable of using language symbolically.
    d. have led to the general conclusion that they can use language symbolically but have only the slightest capacity for grammar.

11. Piaget's theory has been criticized for:
    a. lack of evidence for qualitatively different stages.
    b. overspecifying the process of change.
    c. overestimating the role of the social environment.
    d. all of the above.

12. In Piaget's theory, true logic develops when children:
    a. reach the formal-operational stage.
    b. develop schemes.
    c. understand reversible actions.
    d. are capable of egocentric speech.

13. Which approach attempts to understand specific changes in the child's cognitive abilities in terms of specific changes in the mind's components?
    a. the Piagetian approach
    b. the information-processing approach
    c. the sociocultural approach
    d. all of the above approaches

14. The view that a broad range of problems can be solved through general principles of logic once the appropriate stage of development has been reached is held by _____ and disputed by _____.
    a. Piaget; information-processing theorists
    b. Piaget; sociocultural theorists
    c. information-processing theorists; Piaget
    d. information-processing theorists; learning theorists

15. Lev Vygotsky used the analogy of a(n) _____ to characterize the developing child.
    a. scientist          c. apprentice
    b. sponge             d. computer

*Essay Questions*

16. Describe the development of the young infant's abilities to distinguish and produce phonemes.

17. Discuss Jean Piaget's beliefs about the role of action in cognitive development during the sensorimotor stage. Be sure to include in your discussion the concept of schemes.

---

*After you have assessed your understanding on the basis of Self-Test 1 and have tried to strengthen your preparation in any areas of weakness, GO ON to Self-Test 2.*

# Self-Test 2

*Multiple-Choice Questions*

1. In order to study individual development, a researcher:
   a. must employ the cross-sectional method.
   b. must employ the longitudinal method.
   c. must employ both the cross-sectional and longitudinal methods and then compare the results of the two methods.
   d. may employ either the cross-sectional or longitudinal method.

2. _____ theories maintain that development involves plateaus of stable behavior separated by transitional periods of rapid growth.
   a. Normative
   b. Stage
   c. Continuity
   d. Maturational

3. What leads to wariness of heights as indicated by the visual cliff?
   a. physical maturation reached by 9 months
   b. experience with falling
   c. experience with self-produced locomotion
   d. social experience, such as seeing parental concern when the infant is near a dropoff

4. Piaget used hiding problems to test the development of:
   a. conservation.
   b. reflexive actions.
   c. object permanence.
   d. operations.

5. Which of the following statements is *not* true of babbling?
   a. It consists of consonant-and-vowel sounds such as *baa-baa-baa*.
   b. Deaf infants begin to babble at the same age and with the same variety of sounds as infants who can hear.
   c. Infants babble only the sounds heard in their own native language.
   d. It helps to prepare the infant for speech.

6. An infant who reliably produces a wordlike sound in a particular context, but does not use the word as a symbol, is producing a(n):
   a. overextension.
   b. lexical contrast
   c. performative.
   d. lexigram.

7. The fact that children overgeneralize the past tense *-ed* ending to create such utterances as "He comed over" helps to illustrate the fact that they:
   a. prefer their own egocentric speech patterns to adult speech patterns.
   b. tend to overextend more than underextend.
   c. must reach the stage of formal operations before they can acquire an understanding of syntax.
   d. learn grammatical rules rather than simply mimicking what they hear.

8. The case of the girl known as Genie provides evidence _____ the idea that _____.
   a. for; children acquire language rules
   b. against; children acquire language rules
   c. for; there is a critical period for some aspects of language acquisition
   d. against; there is a critical period for some aspects of language acquisition

9. The language-development theorist who would be most likely to point out that adults speak much more simply and clearly to young children than they do to other adults would be a(n):
   a. social learning theorist.
   b. maturationist.
   c. nativist theorist.
   d. information-processing theorist.

10. In Piaget's theory, as children become mentally free from the strict control of the here-and-now, they enter which stage of cognitive development?
    a. sensorimotor          c. concrete-operational
    b. formal-operational    d. preoperational

11. According to Piaget, hypothetico-deductive reasoning appears in the _____ stage of intellectual development.
    a. preoperational
    b. concrete operational
    c. formal operational
    d. sensorimotor

12. Piaget refers to change in an existing scheme that results from incorporating new experiences as:
    a. an operation.        c. accommodation.
    b. assimilation.        d. horizontal décalage.

13. Juan Pascual-Leone proposed that the most significant change underlying cognitive development is a gradual, maturational increase in the:
    a. speed of retrieval from long-term memory.
    b. capacity of short-term memory.
    c. tendency to use rote rehearsal.
    d. speed of problem solving.

14. Robert Siegler's research on children's ability to solve balance-beam problems showed that the children could:
    a. not profit from feedback regardless of which rule it disconfirmed.
    b. profit from feedback regardless of which rule it disconfirmed.
    c. profit from feedback that disconfirmed their current rule and confirmed the next rule in the developmental sequence.
    d. profit from feedback that disconfirmed their current rule and also disconfirmed the next rule in the developmental sequence.

15. Barbara Rogoff's research shows that children learn better when they work on problems:
    a. alone.
    b. with peers.
    c. with a younger child.
    d. with parents or older children.

*Essay Questions*

16. Describe the visual cliff apparatus. How do crawling infants respond to the shallow side? to the deep side? Can infants too young to crawl see the visual cliff? How do we know?

17. Discuss the opposing views of Lev Vygotsky and Jean Piaget on the phenomenon of egocentric speech.

# Answers

*Some Basic Questions in the Study of Development*

2. normative; individual

9. learning; maturationist; interactionists

*Development of Perception and Knowledge in Infancy*

1. c.  cones

*Development of Language*

1. innate, environment

4. cooing; babbling

5. play; exercise

10. **a.** overextension

    **b.** underextension

16. language-acquisition device; Noam Chomsky

23. American Sign Language

25. lexigrams; Pygmy

*Development of Logical Thought*

4. **a.** assimilation

   **b.** accommodation

5. assimilation; accommodation; accommodation

*Self-Test 1*

1. **b.** (p. 413)

2. **c.** (p. 416)

3. **b.** This fact is interesting in its own right, but it is also important because it provides a methodological tool. The infant's preference for novelty can be used to test the infant's ability to discriminate between the familiar stimulus and the novel one. If the infant prefers the new stimulus, it must be able to tell that it is different from the previous stimulus or, in other words, novel. (p. 417)

4. **d.** Infants will crawl across the shallow side, indicating that they are able and willing to crawl in the test situation, but they will refuse to crawl across the deep side. The fact that this refusal persists even when the infants' mothers call to them and that they show an increased heart rate when placed face-down on the deep side indicates that they are fearful of the visual drop-off. (p. 418)

5. **a.** (p. 420)

6. **d.** (pp. 422–423)

7. **a.** (p. 425)

8. **b.** Chomsky dubbed this set of special language-learning aids the LAD, or language-acquisition device. (p. 427)

9. **a.** (p. 426)

10. **d.** (p. 432)

11. **a.** (pp. 437–438)

12. **c.** (p. 435)

13. **b.** (p. 439)

14. **a.** Piaget's approach is holistic, referring to global changes in the mind that allow wide-ranging and new problem-solving capabilities. Information-processing theorists, in contrast, are concerned with changes in individual components of the mind and believe that children learn specific rules that better equip them to handle particular classes of problems. (p. 441)

15. **c.** (p. 444)

16. Even very young infants are able to distinguish among phonemes, the individual vowel and consonant sounds that make up speech. Infants between 1 and 6 months of age can detect differences between very similar speech sounds. After the age of 6 months, they start to lose the ability to distinguish subtly different sounds that belong to the same phoneme category in their native language.

    Infants can also produce a wide variety of phonemes in their cooing and babbling. Cooing consists of the repetition of long, drawn-out vowels (such as *ooooh-ooooh*). Babbling involves consonant-and-vowel combinations (such as *gaaa-gaaa* or *paatooo*). Both are forms of vocal play that help to exercise the vocal apparatus in preparation for speech. The phonemes that the infant produces initially do not appear to come from experience, but rather are genetically based. Evidence for this comes from the fact that deaf infants coo and babble as many different sounds as hearing babies, and from the fact that infants' sounds are not much influenced by the particular language they hear. A baby who hears English spoken in the home will produce not only the phonemes of English, but will also produce the phonemes of other languages. By about 10 months, babbling increasingly reflects the child's native language. (pp. 422–424)

17. In Piaget's view, action is synonymous with knowledge during infancy. The infant is initially incapable of representing objects and events in terms of mental symbols. During the sensorimotor period, he or she internalizes actions as schemes so that they can be thought of without actual physical movement. In other words, the infant can think about objects and events in terms of action schemes, such as schemes for sucking, kicking, grasping, and so on. Piaget called the infant's stage of cognitive development the sensorimotor stage because the infant engages in motor behavior and then learns the consequences of its actions through sensory feedback. (pp. 432–433, 436–437)

*Self-Test 2*

1. **b.** (p. 414)

2. **b.** (p. 415)

3. **c.** (pp. 418–419)

4. **c.** (p. 420)

5. **c.** (p. 423)

6. **c.** (p. 424)

7. **d.** (p. 426)

8. **c.** (p. 428)

9. **a.** (p. 428)

10. **d.** (p. 433)

11. **c.** (p. 436)

12. **c.** Assimilation is something that one does to an object. It is a recognition process, a matching to an existing scheme. Accommodation is something that happens to one's schemes; when the object assimilated does not quite fit the scheme to which it is matched, the scheme must be modified accordingly. (p. 437)

13. **b.** Pascual-Leone referred to this capacity as *M* space, or mental space. (p. 439)

14. **c.** Siegler suggested that children move sequentially through a series of four rules and that they cannot use feedback that would require them to skip over the next rule in the sequence. (p. 441)

15. **d.** (p. 444)

16. The visual cliff apparatus is a glass-topped table with a board across the middle. On the shallow side, a checkerboard pattern is placed right underneath the glass top, so that there does not appear to be a drop-off. On the deep side, the checkerboard pattern is placed some distance below the glass, so that there does appear to be a cliff or steep drop-off. Infants are typically placed on the board, and experimenters watch to see if they will crawl across the deep side. Infants who are experienced crawlers will crawl across the shallow side but not the deep side. They will refuse to crawl over the visual cliff even when their mothers call to them. The reason for the avoidance of the visual cliff is apparently fear, as indicated by their increased heart rate when placed face-down directly on the deep side. Infants who are too young to crawl respond to the deep side with interest rather than fear, judging by their decreased heart rate when similarly placed. The fact that they show interest obviously demonstrates that they can perceive the visual cliff. (pp. 418–419)

17. Piaget observed that kindergarten children often produce speech that does not take other people into account. What they say is not tailored for the comprehension of another person. For example, the topic of one child's speech may have no relation to the topic of another child's speech, even though they are working or playing side by side. Or one child may say something that has no apparent referent, such as "I see where it is." Piaget labeled this uncommunicative speech of young children egocentric speech because he felt it was simply another display of the child's basic egocentrism—the inability to take another person's perspective.

Vygotsky, on the other hand, felt that language (rather than action, as in Piaget's theory) was the foundation of thought, and thus of cognitive development. He believed that the child's speech was truly communicative from the start. In his view, what Piaget considered egocentric speech was the child's thinking out loud, using language as a support to thought. He noted that egocentric speech was most likely to occur under the conditions in which Piaget had observed it—a situation in which children were working side by side on separate projects. Vygotsky pointed out that children who were simply talking to one another or were working jointly on some project used speech communicatively. Vygotsky explained the decline in egocentric speech in terms of the child's progress at internalizing language. By the age of 7, the child could depend on inner speech, rather than audible speech, to aid thinking. (p. 443)

# CHAPTER 13 SOCIAL DEVELOPMENT

*Read the introduction below before you read the chapter in the text.*

We are all social beings who must continue to adapt to the social environment throughout our lifetimes. Several theoretical approaches offer different perspectives on social development. Psychoanalytic theorists, such as Sigmund Freud and Erik Erikson, emphasize the role of drives, biological maturation, and universal sequences in social development. Social learning theorists, such as Urie Bronfenbrenner, emphasize the role of the social environment and cross-cultural differences. Cognitive theorists, such as Jean Piaget, stress the role of intellectual growth in social development.

Attachment is a major focus of infant social development. The term *attachment* refers to the emotional bonds that infants develop toward principal caregivers, usually their mothers. John Bowlby, on the basis of his studies of children orphaned as a result of World War II, suggested that attachment in infancy significantly influences later psychological development. Research on humans and other primates indicates that physical contact with the caregiver is an important element of attachment. Human infants first show signs of attachment at about the time they begin to crawl, which makes evolutionary sense. Secure attachment in infancy is associated with greater confidence and sociability, and better emotional health and problem-solving performance later in childhood. Cross-cultural differences in infant care are considerable. Western cultures are in many ways less indulgent of infants' desires.

Childhood, which lasts from age 3 to the end of puberty, is a time when powerful forms of socialization are at work. Three major sources of socialization during this period are parenting, play, and school. Theorists have devised ways of categorizing different styles of parental discipline and have argued that some styles are more effective than others. Theorists generally agree that play serves developmental functions, but disagree about what they are. Some theorists emphasize its value as a means of learning about social roles and rules and about morality; others, its usefulness in working through emotional crises. The experience of schooling serves to socialize the child. Traditional schools exert pressure to compete and to conform to strict schedules, curricula, and rules. Some alternative schools have pursued other types of social atmosphere—often one more free and accepting of individuals. Gender is also a factor in socialization. Gender enters into treatment of boys and girls by parents, by teachers, and by children themselves.

Adolescence lasts from the first signs of puberty until an individual is accepted as a full member of adult society. During adolescence, individuals typically become more independent of parents and more dependent on peers. Peer relationships are closer and more intimate than in childhood and serve in part to help individuals deal with issues of dating and romance. Problems of emerging sexual relationships are compounded by the continuing sexual double standard. Adolescents build on the self-concept that has been developing since infancy, coming to a greater understanding of their psychological makeup and social relationships. They may or may not go through an identity crisis. Adolescence is also a time in which individuals may have gained the intellectual capabilities that permit sophisticated moral reasoning, as described in Lawrence Kohlberg's and Carol Gilligan's theories of moral reasoning.

Adulthood centers largely around the themes of love and work. In many ways, adult romantic love is similar in form to infant attachment. Research suggests that mutual liking, commitment, good communication, and understanding are among the characteristics of happy marriages. Parenthood is a role that many adults assume, one that changes them in a variety of significant ways. Because work is such a large part of adult life, job satisfaction is very important to life satisfaction. In fact, unemployment may have devastating effects. The chapter concludes with a look at old age and points out that life satisfaction in later years is often greater than younger people would predict. Older people are apparently happier with their lives if they can stay actively involved, if they feel they have some control over their environment, and if they have someone to confide in.

> LOOK over the table of contents for this chapter in your textbook before you continue with your study.

> Notice that there are focus questions in the margins of the text for your use in studying the material. The following chart lists which study guide questions relate to which focus questions.

| Focus Questions | Study Guide Questions |
|---|---|
| Perspectives on Social Development | |
| 1–2 | 1–3 |
| 3–4 | 4–5 |
| 5 | 6–7 |
| Infancy | |
| 6–11 | 1–12 |
| 12–14 | 13–17 |
| Childhood | |
| 15–18 | 1–3 |
| 19–21 | 4–9 |
| 22–23 | 10–11 |
| 24–28 | 12–21 |
| Adolescence | |
| 29–33 | 1–8 |
| 34–36 | 9–16 |
| 37–40 | 17–25 |
| Adulthood | |
| 41–44 | 1–6 |
| 45–47 | 7–10 |
| 48–50 | 11–18 |

# The Integrated Study Workout

> Complete one section at a time.

## Perspectives on Social Development
(pages 449–453)

> CONSIDER these questions before you go on. They are designed to help you start thinking about this subject, not to test your knowledge.

What forces "propel" and direct social development?

Are people expected to adhere to any kind of timetable of social development?

> READ this section of your text lightly. Then go back and read thoroughly, completing the Workout as you proceed.

Through all the phases of life, an individual is enmeshed in a social world to which he or she must adapt. Social development has been approached from three theoretical perspectives. One perspective emphasizes innate drives, biological maturation, and the notion that there are universal patterns of development.

1. Answer the following questions about Sigmund Freud's psychoanalytic approach to social development.

   a. Freud emphasized universal human drives, particularly the _____ and _____ drives.

   b. What type of learning is at the heart of social development in his view? When do the most critical aspects of this learning take place?

   c. Give some examples of situations in which conflict might arise between the child's drives and society's expectations. What provides the basis for the developing person's future interaction with others?

2. Answer the following questions about Erik Erikson's psychosocial approach to social development. (See Table 13.1 on text page 450.)

   a. How is Erikson's approach fundamentally like Freud's? How is it fundamentally different? Whose approach is better accepted by today's developmental psychologists?

b. What is a psychosocial stage? In what sense is conflict involved in each stage?

a. What does the term *social ecology* mean?

c. List Erikson's stages.

Stage 1

Stage 2

Stage 3

Stage 4

Stage 5

Stage 6

Stage 7

Stage 8

d. Do individuals typically emerge from a stage at one extreme or another? Explain. Briefly discuss how the resolution of the conflict at one stage affects subsequent development.

b. The concentric rings in Bronfenbrenner's model are listed below, beginning with the innermost circle and moving outward. Provide a brief description next to each term.

immediate environment

interrelation among immediate environments

social context

cultural context

c. How does *scarification* illustrate the importance of cultural context?

3. How does John Bowlby illustrate the influence of ethology on developmental psychology?

5. Describe Bernice Neugarten's concept of a social clock. Do you think Erikson's psychosocial stages would apply to cultures very different from his own? Why or why not?

Another perspective on social development emphasizes the influence of the social environment. This sociocultural perspective often focuses on cross-cultural differences.

4. Answer the following questions about Urie Bronfenbrenner's social ecology theory. (See Figure 13.1 on text page 452.)

A third approach emphasizes the impact of cognitive growth on the individual's social thought and behavior.

6. Explain Piaget's argument that social growth depends on cognitive growth.

7. How did Vygotsky's developmental theory combine the cognitive, sociocultural, and biological perspectives?

Physical contact with caregivers is important for the normal development of human and other mammalian infants.

2. Briefly describe the observations and conclusions from René Spitz's study of orphans.

3. Discuss the method and results of Harry Harlow's experiment on infant monkeys' attachment to surrogate mothers. (See Figures 13.2 and 13.3 on text pages 454 and 455.)

## Infancy   (pages 453–460)

> CONSIDER *these questions before you go on. They are designed to help you start thinking about this subject, not to test your knowledge.*

What happens when an infant is deprived of a caring person to look after his or her welfare?

How does day-care affect an infant's attachment to his or her parents?

How do Western cultures compare to other cultures in terms of infant care?

Why do some infants cling to a security blanket?

> READ *this section of your text lightly. Then go back and read thoroughly, completing the Workout as you proceed.*

Infants are born with a biological preparedness for developing an emotional bond with their caretaker. They quickly learn to recognize and prefer their caretaker, and they can express a range of emotions. The concept of such bonding, or attachment, is central to John Bowlby's theory of development.

1. What observations led Bowlby to focus on the concept of attachment?

The first overt signs of infants' attachments to their primary caregivers occur at about 8 months of age. Because these behaviors have been noted in a variety of cultures, they are thought to have a strong biological basis.

4. Describe the behaviors that, according to Bowlby, first indicate infants' attachment to primary caregivers.

5. Discuss the emergence of these behaviors from an evolutionary perspective.

6. As infants explore their world after learning to crawl or walk, they often look to their mother or another familiar adult for cues, a phenomenon known as _____ . Studies involving the visual cliff indicate that these cues can take the form of _____ .

Some means of measuring attachment is needed in order to study it objectively.

7. Name and describe the most commonly used method for measuring attachment. How do the responses of securely attached infants differ from those of infants who are not securely attached?

8. What are some limitations of the strange-situation test?

Psychologists have attempted to learn more about both the causes and the effects of attachment.

9. What behaviors in the caregiver are correlated with secure attachment?

10. How are these correlations interpreted by Bowlby and Ainsworth? What are some alternative interpretations?

Human infants can develop attachments to more than one caregiver, though the strongest attachment is typically still to the mother, perhaps because mothers tend to be gentler and more affectionate toward them. Researchers are interested in how the tendency for mothers to be employed outside the home affects the development of attachment.

11. Do we currently have firm conclusions about the effects of day-care on infants' attachment to parents? Explain.

Many psychologists have suggested that the quality of an infant's early attachment has long-term consequences.

12. What is some evidence that early attachment influences psychological functioning in later childhood and young adulthood? Why must we be cautious about cause-effect conclusions?

Cross-cultural studies show large differences in the way infants are cared for. In contrast to other cultures, Western culture is notable for its relative lack of physical contact between infant and caregiver. For example, infants and young children in Western society typically sleep alone, whereas infants in nonindustrialized cultures typically sleep with their mothers or other related adults.

13. How did Mayan and American women differ in beliefs as well as in sleeping practices?

14. How might sleeping arrangements be related to attachments to an inanimate object?

15. Why have some psychologists chosen to study hunter-gatherer societies?

**16.** How are infants cared for in !Kung society? in Efe society? Does infant indulgence produce spoiled or helpless children? Explain.

**17.** Do the positive results of !Kung infant-care practices mean that Western society should adopt the !Kung methods? Explain.

## Childhood  (pages 461–471)

> CONSIDER these questions before you go on. They are designed to help you start thinking about this subject, not to test your knowledge.

Is it better to be a firm, no-nonsense, no-explanations-given type of parent or are other styles of discipline more effective?

What functions are served by children's play?

If you could design the ideal school, what would it be like?

In what ways do adults treat boys and girls differently? What are some of the consequences of this differential treatment?

> READ this section of your text lightly. Then go back and read thoroughly, completing the Workout as you proceed.

During childhood, defined as the period from about age 3 to puberty, powerful forces of socialization are at work. Parents in all cultures are concerned that their children should develop the knowledge, habits, skills, and values that will lead to physical and emotional health, social acceptance, and economic success. The ways that parents try to promote this development differs from culture to culture. Most research on parental influence in our culture, however, has concentrated on styles of discipline.

**1.** Answer the following questions about Martin Hoffman's work on discipline.

**a.** Label the following techniques of discipline identified by Hoffman.

_____ the use or threatened use of punishment and reward to control the child's behavior

_____ a form of verbal reasoning in which the parent leads the child to think about his or her actions and their consequences for others

_____ a style in which parents often unconsciously express disapproval of the child, not just of the undesirable behavior

**b.** Which technique does Hoffman favor? Is power assertion ever necessary? Explain.

**c.** In what sense is Hoffman's theory cognitive? Why might this be relevant in our culture?

**d.** Describe evidence from a study of seventh graders that supports Hoffman's theory.

**2.** Answer the following questions about Diana Baumrind's work.

**a.** Label the three discipline styles identified by Diana Baumrind.

_____ parents were the most tolerant of their children's disruptive behaviors and least likely to discipline them

_____ parents were more concerned with helping the child to acquire and use principles of right and wrong than in pure obedience

_____ parents wanted obedience for its own sake and often used power assertiveness to get it

b. What was Baumrind's main finding? How might the results be interpreted?

c.

d.

5. What is the purpose of play, according to Groos?

3. Explain why one must exercise caution when interpreting correlations between parenting styles and children's behavior.

Cognitive theories emphasize the importance of play in the development of thinking. Piaget, for example, proposed that social play helps the child to better understand rules and morality.

6. According to Piaget, how does play allow the child to develop the ability to reason about right and wrong?

Play—what children do when their needs are met and they are free to choose their own activities—is one way that children actively promote their own development. As development progresses, play changes to meet the changing needs of the child. Play occurs in comparable forms in every culture studied, and theorists such as Karl Groos have suggested that it is based on instinctual drives.

4. List and briefly describe four types of play.

a.

7. Briefly discuss Lev Vygotsky's view of play.

8. Describe evidence that supports Vygotsky's view.

a.

b.

b.

Psychoanalytic theorists such as Erikson emphasize the value of play in learning to deal with emotional crises.

9. According to Eisen's account, how did play help children in Nazi death camps cope with their lives and perhaps even survive?

School is another major source of socialization.

10. Describe the traditional school environment. How well do children adjust to these conditions? Are there differences across cultures?

11. Summarize the philosophy and practice of the Sudbury Valley School in Massachusetts. What do follow-up studies of the school's graduates indicate about their ability to succeed? Given that students at Sudbury are not required to study, what factors seem to account for their learning?

In every culture studied, boys and girls differ, and so do their experiences of life.

12. Can hormones explain all the differences between boys and girls? Explain.

13. Distinguish between the terms *sex* and *gender*.

Differential treatment of boys and girls by adults begins very early indeed.

14. List some examples of how adults respond differentially to (a) boy and girl infants and (b) older boys and girls.

15. Discuss the findings that teachers have different expectations of boys and girls and treat them in accordance with those expectations. How might such differential treatment cause boys and girls to develop differently?

Children play a significant part in shaping their own gender-related behavior.

16. What is gender identity? How do children actively assert their own gender identity?

Children reinforce gender distinction through their peer groups. Boys and girls interact more with members of their own gender.

17. Discuss the findings of Jacklin and Maccoby on gender segregation in 33-month-olds.

18. Some have suggested that the peer groups of boys and girls are really different subcultures. Describe each of the following:

   a.  the world of boys

   b.  the world of girls

19. Does the degree of segregation vary across settings? Explain.

20. How do children maintain gender segregation? Are the efforts to enforce gender segregation equally strong for boys and girls? Explain.

21. How might adults influence the degree of gender segregation?

## Adolescence  (pages 471–480)

> CONSIDER *these questions before you go on. They are designed to help you start thinking about this subject, not to test your knowledge.*

Is the classic image of the adolescent as a rebel really accurate?

What role do peers play in the lives of adolescents?

Is there still a double standard of sexuality for adolescent girls and boys?

What factors contribute to the occurrence of date rape?

Do all adolescents go through an identity crisis?

What is the developmental basis of morality and of moral reasoning? Do the two genders have a different approach to morality?

> READ *this section of your text lightly. Then go back and read thoroughly, completing the Workout as you proceed.*

Adolescence, a bridge between childhood and adulthood, begins at the onset of puberty and ends when a person is considered a full member of adult society. In Western societies, the end of adolescence is less clearly marked than in traditional societies.

1. How have changing views of adolescence been linked with social and economic conditions?

2. Adolescence as a time of rebellion is a popularly accepted notion. In what sense do adolescents "rebel"? In what sense do they not?

3. Summarize the results of studies that track the changes in patterns of family conflicts as children enter adolescence.

As adolescents move toward independence from their parents, they become increasingly dependent upon their peers.

4. How is the meaning of friendship in adolescence different from the meaning of friendship for younger children?

5. Basing your answer on Dexter Dunphy's work, describe how peer groups can help to break down the gender barrier put up in childhood.

Many individuals become sexually active during adolescence.

6. Is there still a double standard of sexual behavior for adolescent boys and girls? Support your answer.

7. Discuss factors that may lead some boys and young men to exert unwanted sexual pressure, even to rape.

8. Is sexual orientation something that one chooses or something one discovers? What percentage of the population is exclusively homosexual in orientation?

The adolescent's attempt to arrive at an adult identity obviously depends on the existence of a self-concept.

9. How do the individual's self-descriptions change as he or she proceeds from early childhood to adolescence?

10. What did Erikson consider to be the main task of adolescence? Does research support his view that adolescence is a time of particular emotional turmoil?

11. What two dimensions did Marcia use in defining the concept of identity? What technique did Marcia develop in classifying people in terms of their identity status?

12. Label each of Marcia's identity status categories.

   a. _____ The person lacks commitments and is not concerned about them.

   b. _____ The person actively thinks about and questions various occupational paths and values.

   c. _____ The person has gone through a period of active thinking and questioning and has established firm commitments.

   d. _____ The person accepts unquestioningly career and ideological commitments from parents and other authority figures.

13. The identity-status category that corresponds with Erikson's identity-crisis phase is

   _____ .

14. Are people who go through the moratorium better off, as Erikson suggests? Support your answer.

15. Discuss some ways that identity formation may differ for women as compared to men.

16. Discuss the role of culture in identity formation.

The roots of morality lie in empathy, according to some theorists, and in the ability to reason logically, according to others. Lawrence Kohlberg has produced a comprehensive theory based on the latter view. (See Table 13.2 on text page 478.)

17. Briefly describe Kohlberg's research method. What aspect of people's responses was of greatest interest to Kohlberg?

18. Answer the following questions about Kohlberg's theory of the development of moral reasoning.

    a. Explain the nature of the progression from Stage 1 to Stage 5.

    b. In what sense do the stages represent a true developmental progression, according to Kohlberg?

    c. What is the motivating force that pushes a person on to the next stage of moral reasoning?

    d. Does everyone eventually reach Stage 5? Explain.

19. Is moral reasoning necessarily related to moral behavior? Explain.

20. Why do some critics argue that Kohlberg's theory is biased toward Western notions of morality?

Carol Gilligan has offered one of the best-known alternatives to Kohlberg's view of the development of moral reasoning.

21. What limitation in Kohlberg's research motivated Gilligan's research?

22. How does Gilligan study moral reasoning?

23. What are the two voices Gilligan describes?

24. Do the genders differ in their use of the two voices?

25. When the dilemma under consideration is personal and real rather than hypothetical, the _____ voice becomes relatively stronger.

### Adulthood (pages 480–488)

CONSIDER *these questions before you go on. They are designed to help you start thinking about this subject, not to test your knowledge.*

What makes some marriages happy and others unhappy?

How important is a successful career to general life satisfaction?

How does becoming a parent change a person? How does it change a marriage?

Why do women in the United States tend to live longer than men?

What can make old age a happier time of life?

Do elderly people fear death more than others?

---

*READ this section of your text lightly. Then go back and read thoroughly, completing the Workout as you proceed.*

---

Love and work are the joint themes of adult development. In the study of love relationships, psychologists have sought to understand why some marriages work while others do not.

1. List the characteristics that seem to be common both to romantic love and infant attachment.

2. Describe the three dimensions of Robert Sternberg's triangular model of love. What is each dimension critical to? How do these dimensions differ in their time course?

3. What do interviews of happily married couples reveal about them?

4. How do the communication patterns of unhappily married couples compare with those of happily married couples, according to John Gottman?

Changing dirty diapers, worrying about falls and fevers, and making countless decisions on behalf of a new person at some point become a daily part of life for most adults. Parenthood seems to be the event most likely to convince people that they really are adults.

5. In what ways do people change when they become parents?

6. How is marital satisfaction affected by parenthood?

A job is a fact of life for most adults but it is a happier fact for some than for others.

7. What are some factors associated with job satisfaction? In what way does job satisfaction change with increasing age, as shown by large-scale statistical studies? What are some possible explanations for this finding?

Women who work outside the home often have two roles—their outside employment and their work at home. And they often feel torn between the two sets of obligations.

8. Among couples in which husband and wife both work outside the home, are household duties evenly divided? Explain your answer.

9. How does work outside the home tend to affect a woman's level of stress? Why might this be true?

Job loss often has far-reaching effects.

10. What are some effects of men's job loss, independent of the loss of income this entails? Do these effects occur for both blue- and white-collar workers? How do wives suffer when their husbands are unemployed?

Given current estimates of life expectancy, today's college student can reasonably hope to live well past retirement age.

11. Give a partial explanation for the fact that women in the United States live an average of 7 years longer than men.

12. Old age is undeniably a period that involves loss, but is old age as bad as it seems to the young? Explain.

13. Is disengagement a natural consequence of growing older? Support your answer with evidence. What seems to be the key to a happy old age for most people?

14. Distinguish between the young-old and the old-old. Briefly describe evidence that retaining some personal control contributes to happiness and even to longevity in the latter group.

Having a confidant seems to be particularly important to a happy and healthy old age.

15. In a study of memory in nursing home patients, one of the conditions was called reciprocal self-disclosure. Briefly describe this experimental condition and its effects.

16. The loss of a spouse can have dramatic negative effects on elderly people. List some of these negative effects. Why are the effects greater for men than for women?

Death awaits everyone eventually, but with advancing age one grows ever closer to that point.

17. Do the elderly fear death more than people in other age groups? Explain.

18. Does everyone approach death in essentially the same way—by going through a sequence of stages, for example, or by reviewing his or her life? Support your answer.

*Be sure to READ the Concluding Thoughts at the end of the chapter. Note important points in your Workout. Then consolidate your learning by answering the focus questions in the margins of the text.*

*After you have studied the chapter thoroughly, CHECK your understanding with the self-test that follows.*

# Self-Test 1

*Multiple-Choice Questions*

1. Freud's and Erikson's theories of development are similar in that they:
   a. are both life-span theories, emphasizing the importance of continued development in adulthood.
   b. both give sexuality a central role in development.
   c. both portray social development as involving drives and conflicts.
   d. both propose that development occurs in stages that may take place in different orders in different individuals.

2. Bernice Neugarten suggests that the social clock:
   a. is an internal, biologically based "clock" that governs the social needs and crises people experience at different ages.
   b. is an internalized sense of what one's culture expects of individuals at different ages.
   c. allows one to predict the developmental patterns of individuals within a society based on the age of that society.
   d. is our sense of the pace of cultural change, which may dramatically affect individual development, especially in childhood and adolescence.

3. Mary Ainsworth's strange-situation test is used to:
   a. measure the developing child's ability to become involved in various kinds of play.
   b. promote the developing adolescent's resistance to peer pressure.
   c. enhance the developing child's ability to engage in moral reasoning.
   d. measure the developing infant's attachment to a person or object.

4. Cross-cultural research has shown that Western culture is atypical in that Western parents generally:
   a. require young children to sleep in a different room from adults.
   b. employ an authoritarian style of parenting.
   c. use power assertion to gain behavioral compliance from children.
   d. give in most readily to demands for attention from young children.

5. Martin Hoffman described one type of parental discipline in which parents use verbal reasoning to lead the child to think about his or her actions and their consequences. He called this type of discipline:
   a. authoritarian.
   b. permissive.
   c. induction.
   d. power assertion.

6. In the view of Lev Vygotsky, the most important function of play is that it:
   a. promotes spontaneity and creativity.
   b. provides a time of relaxation and release for children, who outside of play experience considerable pressure to learn and to become socialized.
   c. allows children to express deep, unconscious wishes and conflicts and thereby helps to alleviate emotional problems.
   d. gives children a context for learning about rules and social roles.

7. In their study of 33-month-old children, Jacklin and Maccoby found that mixed-sex pairs played together less than same-sex pairs, primarily because _____ withdrew on account of _____.
   a. girls; the unresponsiveness of the boys to their requests and suggestions
   b. girls; the verbal and physical aggressiveness of the boys
   c. boys; the unresponsiveness of the girls to their requests and suggestions
   d. boys; the failure of girls to enter into aggressive, competitive play

8. Studies show that adolescent rebellion is primarily directed against:
   a. school authorities rather than parents.
   b. peers rather than authority figures.
   c. ethical or political injustices in society rather than family matters.
   d. parental constraints on personal freedom rather than parental values.

9. Research suggests that there _____ a double standard of sexual behavior for boys and girls and that this may tend to _____ acts of sexual aggression.
   a. is still; contribute to
   b. is still; prevent
   c. is no longer; contribute to
   d. is no longer; prevent

10. Phil is a recent college graduate who has known from the time he was in high school that he wanted to go into the family automotive business. He has never wavered from his plan and has almost always seen "eye to eye" with his family on important issues. Phil appears to fit the

_____ category of James Marcia's identity-assessment scheme.

a. achieved
b. moratorium
c. foreclosure
d. diffusion

11. In his studies of moral development, Lawrence Kohlberg was mainly interested in:

a. the decision someone reached about resolving a dilemma.
b. the reasoning involved in reaching a decision about a dilemma.
c. the action someone had taken in a real-life moral dilemma.
d. the empathy people expressed for those involved in the dilemma.

12. In trying to learn what makes a marriage work, researchers studied communication between husbands and wives. They found that:

a. men in unhappy marriages respond to their wives' unspoken emotional needs as well as men in happy marriages do.
b. women in unhappy marriages respond to their husbands' unspoken emotional needs as well as women in happy marriages do.
c. men in happy marriages respond to their wives' unspoken emotional needs better than men in unhappy marriages do.
d. both b. and c. are true.

13. In most lines of work, as a person ages from 20 to 60, job satisfaction tends to:

a. peak in the 30s and then decline.
b. peak and decline about once every decade.
c. increase continuously.
d. decline continuously.

14. Which of the following does *not* generally appear to promote a healthy, happy old age?

a. disengagement
b. having a confidant
c. having some control over one's environment
d. All of the above generally contribute to a healthy, happy old age.

15. The loss of a spouse is generally coped with better by surviving _____, one reason being that they _____.

a. wives; keep closer social ties to relatives and friends
b. wives; tend to be younger than men who are widowed
c. husbands; know better how to take care of themselves
d. husbands; are less emotionally dependent than women

## Essay Questions

16. What is infant attachment? Describe research evidence suggesting that it is important to healthy development. What factors promote attachment?

17. What are the three components of love, according to Sternberg's triangular model of love? How are different types of relationships defined in terms of combinations of these? What is each component critical for? What is the time course of each component's development?

*After you have assessed your understanding on the basis of Self-Test 1 and have tried to strengthen your preparation in any areas of weakness, GO ON to Self-Test 2.*

# Self-Test 2

*Multiple-Choice Questions*

1. In contrast to Freud, Erikson emphasizes:

a. drives for sex and aggression.
b. social drives.
c. the biological basis for drives.
d. early childhood experience.

2. Bronfenbrenner uses the term *social ecology* to mean:
   a. the whole network of people as well as the social setting to which a developing person must adapt psychologically, which varies across cultures.
   b. those essential aspects of any social environment that underlie social development and that are the same across cultures.
   c. only those aspects of society that affect the developing child without the child actually coming into direct contact with them.
   d. the set of beliefs, values, and accepted ways of behaving that characterize the historically connected group of people to which the child and the child's family belong.

3. In Harry Harlow's study of attachment in infant monkeys, attachment:
   a. was based purely on whichever surrogate "mother" provided nutrition.
   b. developed toward the wire "mother" but not the cloth "mother."
   c. developed toward the cloth "mother" but not the wire "mother."
   d. was based on whichever surrogate "mother" the infant was first exposed to.

4. Bowlby believes that infant attachment is based on:
   a. sociocultural learning.
   b. biological factors arising through natural selection.
   c. the earlier phenomenon of social referencing.
   d. instruction from the mother or other caregiver.

5. Angela promptly comforts her infant son whenever he shows signs of distress. Research suggests that this is likely to:
   a. spoil the child.
   b. develop an unhealthy dependence in the child.
   c. promote secure attachment.
   d. promote insecure attachment.

6. Martin Hoffman uses the term *love withdrawal* to refer to a disciplinary style in which parents:
   a. use their superior strength or control of resources to induce the child to behave in ways they find acceptable.
   b. express disapproval of the child, not just of the child's specific unacceptable actions.
   c. use verbal reasoning to lead the child to think about his or her actions and the consequences of those actions.
   d. ignore or excuse their children's misbehavior without any attempt at correcting it.

7. Diana Baumrind found that nursery-school children were most likely to show positive qualities if their parents applied a disciplinary style she called:
   a. authoritative.         c. power assertion.
   b. authoritarian.         d. permissive.

8. Erik Erikson and other psychoanalytic theorists considered the major function of play to be:
   a. development of the ability to cope with emotional crises.
   b. the acquisition of an understanding of social rules, which are necessary for the maintenance of social order.
   c. encouragement of planning, decision making, and creativity in the child's thought.
   d. specific learning about a variety of social roles.

9. Which of the following is *not* emphasized as a key element in the educational effectiveness of the Sudbury Valley School?
   a. age mixing
   b. self-initiated and self-directed learning
   c. organized group activities
   d. an atmosphere of respect for each child

10. Which of the following correctly describes a research finding about the ways that teachers respond differently to boys and girls?
    a. Teachers give girls and boys the same general types of criticism in the same general circumstances, but criticize girls more often.
    b. Teachers give girls and boys the same general types of criticism in the same general circumstances, but criticize boys more often.
    c. Criticism of boys is more likely than criticism of girls to contain the implication that poor performance is due to lack of effort.
    d. Criticism of girls is more likely than criticism of boys to contain the implication that poor performance is due to lack of effort.

11. The self-concept of preschoolers is organized around:
    a. the physical self.       c. social relationships.
    b. the psychological self.  d. parental models.

12. In James Marcia's categorization of identity status, individuals in the _____ category are in the midst of an identity crisis.
    a. diffusion              c. foreclosure
    b. moratorium             d. achieved

13. Which dimension of Sternberg's triangular model of love is considered critical to the relationship's longevity?
    a. passion
    b. intimacy
    c. commitment
    d. both a. and b.

14. The 40-year-old first-time mother, the 51-year-old college senior, and the 25-year-old corporate vice president are not nearly as rare as they once were. Bernice Neugarten could use such observations as indications of the:
    a. increasing importance of the social clock to adult life in contemporary society.
    b. relative "clocklessness" of adult life in contemporary society.
    c. speeding up of the social clock for adults in contemporary society.
    d. fluctuating speed of the social clock for adults in contemporary society.

15. Research suggests that life satisfaction in old age is _____ younger people would expect it to be.
    a. much lower than
    b. somewhat lower than
    c. about what
    d. higher than

*Essay Questions*

16. What is the major function of play, according to Lev Vygotsky? Is there evidence to support his view? Explain.

17. Discuss Lawrence Kohlberg's theory of the development of moral reasoning. Be sure to include in your answer the primary goal of the theory, Kohlberg's methodology, the basic tenets of the theory, and some criticisms of the theory.

# Answers

*Perspectives on Social Development*

1. a. sexual; aggressive

*Infancy*

6. social referencing; facial expressions

*Childhood*

1. a. power assertion; induction; love withdrawal
2. a. permissive; authoritative; authoritarian

*Adolescence*

12. a. identity diffusion
    b. moratorium
    c. identity achieved
    d. foreclosure

13. moratorium

25. caring

*Self-Test 1*

1. c. Though they both emphasized inner drives and conflicts, Freud focused on sexual and aggressive drives, and Erikson on a set of social drives. (p. 450)

2. b. (p. 452)

3. d. Critics of this test as a measure of attachment charge that results depend too much on the

infant's temperament and that responses to the test vary cross culturally. (p. 456)

4. **a.** This may be related to a research finding that blanket attachments are more common in North American infants than in infants of other cultures who generally sleep in the same room with a mother or grandmother. (p. 459)

5. **c.** Induction is also the style that Hoffman most favors. (p. 462)

6. **d.** (p. 464)

7. **a.** Think about this research finding and how it relates to studies of communication and marital satisfaction discussed later in the chapter. (p. 470)

8. **d.** (p. 472)

9. **a.** (p. 474)

10. **c.** (p. 476)

11. **b.** Kohlberg, whose work was influenced by that of Piaget, was interested in the development of the ability to *think* about moral situations. He was therefore most interested in the thought processes involved in reaching a conclusion, not the conclusion itself. (p. 478)

12. **d.** (p. 482)

13. **c.** (p. 484)

14. **a.** (p. 486)

15. **a.** (p. 487)

16. Attachment is the emotional bond that an infant develops toward a primary caregiver. Evidence for the developmental importance of such a bond comes from a variety of sources. Studies of orphans by John Bowlby in Europe and René Spitz in Canada and the United States suggest that lack of a primary caregiver can result in enduring emotional scars. Spitz's work indicates that infants may even die if they lack the opportunity for such emotional bonds.

Touch seems to be an important factor in the development of attachment. Harry Harlow showed that what he called contact comfort is so important that rhesus monkey infants will develop an attachment to a soft cloth surrogate mother even if they are being nourished with a bottle on a wire surrogate mother.

Longitudinal research indicates that infants who consistently receive contact comfort and prompt responsive reactions when they cry are more likely to be securely attached, as indicated by the strange-situation test. Early measures of attachment are correlated with positive outcomes later in childhood, such as greater confidence, problem-solving ability, and emotional health.

The warmth and security of romantic attachment in adulthood may also be related to early attachment. Such findings do not show a causal role of attachment in producing such outcomes, however. (pp. 454–458)

17. On the basis of a statistical analysis of questionnaire data, Sternberg concluded that love and friendship relationships involve three fundamental components: passion, which includes sexual feelings and a desire to be with the beloved; intimacy, which includes a sense of closeness, mutual understanding, and shared thoughts and feelings; and commitment, the conscious, rational decision to support and maintain the relationship. Different relationships can be described in terms of the relative proportions of each component. Passion is critical to romance, intimacy to friendship, and commitment to the endurance of any relationship. Passion tends to develop most quickly, while intimacy and commitment develop more slowly. (pp. 481–482)

## Self-Test 2

1. **b.** (p. 450)

2. **a.** The social ecology includes c., which is the social context, and d., which is the cultural context. (pp. 451–452)

3. **c.** Harlow concluded that the contact comfort afforded by the cloth, but not the wire, "mother" was more important to attachment than feeding was. (p. 454)

4. **b.** (p. 455)

5. **c.** (p. 457)

6. **b.** (p. 461)

7. **a.** Be sure you can distinguish between authoritarian and authoritative parenting styles. Authoritar*ian* parents value control for its own sake and use a high degree of power assertion. Authoritat*ive* parents value good behavior more than control itself and prefer induction, but will use power assertion when necessary. (p. 462)

8. **a.** (p. 465)

9. **c.** (pp. 466–467)

10. **c.** Teachers' criticisms of girls, on the other hand, often imply that poor performance is due to lack of ability. (p. 469)

11. **a.** (p. 475)

12. **b.** (p. 476)

13. **c.** (p. 481)

14. **b.** (p. 481)

15. **d.** (p. 486)

16. Vygotsky, who generally emphasized the importance of the social world to development, felt that social play is critical to the socialization process. He argued that play is not the context in which children are most free and spontaneous, as popular belief would have it. Rather, play is a context in which children learn to govern their behavior according to rules of social behavior and according to the social roles they act out. A child playing the role of a robber in cops and robbers, for example, would be forced to think about what it means to be a robber—what behavior makes a person a robber, how a robber interacts with other people such as police, and so on. The child would also have to fit his or her behavior to that role as it is understood. This ability to assume roles later spills over into the child's nonplay activities, as the child begins to move into such social roles as student or junior gardener or pet caretaker. Research consistent with Vygotsky's position suggests that children actually do think about and enforce rules in their social play. Further, the amount of sociodramatic play children engage in is correlated with their social competence. (pp. 464–465)

17. Kohlberg recognized that moral development is at least in part the development of the ability to think logically about moral situations. He sought to understand this aspect of moral development by asking people what the protagonists of hypothetical moral dilemmas should do and why. His interest was not so much in the conclusions subjects reached but in the nature of the reasoning they used to reach those conclusions.

On the basis of such research, Kohlberg proposed that there is an invariant sequence of stages through which moral development proceeds. Initially, an individual thinks only of him- or herself. In the fifth and highest stage, which is not attained by everyone, universal moral principles are the basis of judgment. Progression from the first to the fifth stage involves a growing inclusiveness of others in the social world. As the limitations of one stage become evident, the individual is drawn toward the next stage.

Kohlberg's theory has been criticized on a number of grounds. Some critics say that Kohlberg is wrong about the invariance of stages. Others point out that it represents a moral perspective that is culturally biased toward the West. Still others insist that it embodies a bias toward males. These last two criticisms share the view that Kohlberg's conception of morality is too limited; the type of morality he places at the pinnacle of his developmental sequence—one based on abstract principles of justice—is not without alternatives. One alternative is morality based on caring and responsibility in the context of personal relationships. This kind of morality may be more prevalent in non-Westerners and women. Another criticism you could have mentioned is that Kohlberg places too much emphasis on thought alone and not enough on social learning. (pp. 477–480)

# CHAPTER 14 SOCIAL COGNITION

*Read the introduction below before you read the chapter in the text.*

Social cognition is the study of the mental processes and systematic biases underlying beliefs about the social world. Just as we form schemas for trees, modes of transportation, and furniture, we form schemas—organized sets of information or beliefs—for people. The person schema we have for an individual helps us to interpret and organize new information about that individual, though it can also distort our perceptions of the person. This distortion often occurs because we rely too heavily on first impressions and surface characteristics.

When we use a person's behavior in order to form a person schema for that individual, we are inferring something about the cause of the behavior. A decision about the cause of a behavior is called an *attribution.* Fritz Heider, a pioneer in this area, claimed that we have a natural tendency to attribute behavior to the stable, inner characteristics of the person behaving, although we sometimes attribute behavior to the situation. Harold Kelley has built on Heider's ideas to develop a model of the logic involved in making attributions.

Our attributions are not always logical or correct, however. Here, too, we have biases. Stereotypes, which are schemas about groups of people, can distort our impressions of individual members of those groups even if we consciously combat the influence of cultural stereotypes in our thinking. We tend to see groups of which we are members, called ingroups, differently from other groups. In some cases, we form prejudices—negative views—about members of these "outgroups." You may be surprised to learn that we have negative views of the victims of misfortune—victims of crime or illness, for example—often blaming them for their own misfortune.

In a variety of ways, we come to see ourselves by looking at the social world around us. Charles Cooley called this the looking-glass self. Our self-concepts and behavior are affected by other people's expectations of us, which can become self-fulfilling prophe-cies. Further, we all have multiple selves based on our various social roles. In some cultures, social roles are especially important in the creation of a self-concept. While our self-concepts are to some extent imposed on us, they also result from our active comparison of ourselves to others. The reference group to which we compare ourselves may affect how smart, ethical, or talented we think we are. We also try to project a certain view of ourselves to others, which is referred to as impression management. Self-monitoring is a personality variable related to impression management. People high in self-monitoring are especially concerned with others' opinions and have the confidence to try to manipulate those opinions.

Attitudes—beliefs or opinions that have an evaluative component—link the individual and society at large. The attitudes we have toward objects, events, people, concepts, and so on serve several functions. The formation and modification of our attitudes depends on such factors as reference groups, the kind of processing we give to persuasive messages, and cognitive dissonance. Cognitive dissonance is the psychological discomfort that exists when there is disagreement among our beliefs, attitudes, and/or behaviors. For example, if we freely perform some behavior contrary to our attitudes, with no obvious incentive, we may change our attitudes to be more consistent with the behavior. The relationship between attitudes and behaviors is not as simple and straightforward as psychologists once thought.

*LOOK over the table of contents for this chapter in your textbook before you continue with your study.*

*Notice that there are focus questions in the margins of the text for your use in studying the material. The following chart lists which study guide questions relate to which focus questions.*

# The Integrated Study Workout

*Complete one section at a time.*

## Perceiving Others   (pages 493–503)

*CONSIDER these questions before you go on. They are designed to help you start thinking about this subject, not to test your knowledge.*

How do we mentally represent other people? How do we use those representations to deal with new information about people?

If someone throws a tantrum, gives a lot of money to charity, or trips on the stairs, how do we decide what caused this behavior—is it the individual's personal characteristics, the situation, or something else?

Are our perceptions of other people unduly influenced by such factors as physical appearance?

How do our culture's stereotypes of certain groups—of women, blacks, students, or southerners, for example—affect the way people perceive individual members of those groups? How does a prejudiced person's thinking differ from that of an unprejudiced person?

How are our perceptions of people colored by misfortunes they have suffered? For example, do we view rape victims differently because they have been raped? or cancer victims differently because they have developed cancer?

*READ this section of your text lightly. Then go back and read thoroughly, completing the Workout as you proceed.*

Our cognitive capabilities are used not only for solving math problems, planning our days or our lives, or engaging in logical argument. They are constantly being applied to the social world in which we find ourselves. The study of the mental processes and systematic biases underlying our social beliefs is called *social cognition*. One area of investigation in social cognition concerns the ways we perceive other people.

1. Briefly explain Solomon Asch's Gestalt view of person perception.

2. The organized set of information or beliefs that we have about a person is called a

   _____ .

3. How does a schema change as new information is acquired?

A person schema is used to interpret new information received about that person. This is an instance of top-down processing. Although it is an efficient way to process information, it may at times lead to distortion.

4. Briefly describe the method and results of Harold Kelley's experiment on student perceptions of a guest lecturer.

A person's appearance is often the first information we have about him or her. It may influence the construction of our initial schema of the person and thereby have undue influence on our perception of that person.

5. Define the term *primacy effect* and give an example.

**6.** Briefly summarize two lines of evidence suggesting that physical appearance can have undue influence on our perceptions of people.

As we build a schema of a particular person, we must interpret that person's behavior. We must decide what, if anything, a given behavior indicates about the person's internal characteristics. The study of attributions—inferences about the causes of behavior—was pioneered by Fritz Heider.

**7.** What kind of attribution do we intuitively tend to make, according to Heider? What would be an alternative attribution and when would we tend to make it?

Heider's work was elaborated upon by Harold Kelley, who produced a model of the logic that might be involved in the attribution process.

**8.** What are the three types of causes to which you might attribute a given behavior, according to Kelley? Illustrate each type of cause in terms of the textbook's example of Susan getting angry in a traffic jam.

**a.**

**b.**

**c.**

**9.** Could you attribute a behavior to a combination of the above types of causes? Explain.

**10.** There are three types of information people would ideally take into account in making an attribution. Write three general questions that you might ask to obtain this information. (See Figure 14.3 on text page 497.)

**a.**

**b.**

**c.**

**11.** For each of the examples below, indicate the kind of attribution (e.g., personality, situation, etc.) that would logically be made on the basis of the information provided.

Attribution

_____ **a.** Ruth is arguing with her mother, something she often does. Ruth rarely argues with other people and other people rarely argue with Ruth's mother.

_____ **b.** Cally has missed her bus home. She is usually a few minutes early for the bus.

_____ **c.** Gene has criticized his friend for not trying hard enough in his classes. Gene regularly criticizes this friend—and his sisters, and the president, and the janitor, and the clerk at the record store, and. . . .

_____ **d.** Richard almost always slows down and looks both ways before driving through a particular intersection, even when he has the green light. So do many other drivers.

Several biases in attribution depend on whether the behavior in question is our own or someone else's and on whether the outcome is positive or negative.

12. Answer the following questions about the fundamental attribution error.

   a. What is the fundamental attribution error? Give an example.

   b. Explain Daniel Gilbert's view on the nature of this error and describe research evidence consistent with this view.

   c. Explain the cultural-norm hypothesis and present evidence that supports it.

13. Answer the following questions about the actor-observer discrepancy.

   a. What is the actor-observer discrepancy? Give an example.

   b. Explain the knowledge-across-situations hypothesis and describe an observation consistent with it.

   c. Explain the visual-orientation hypothesis and briefly summarize experimental support for it.

When our preconceptions influence our evaluation of a person, we are falling prey to prejudice in its most general sense. Usually, we use the term more narrowly to mean the negative views that people have of members of a particular group.

14. What are stereotypes? Can they bias our perceptions? Support your answer.

Patricia Devine has proposed a theory of stereotypes that employs the distinction between automatic and controlled mental processes.

15. Explain Devine's theory, being careful to state how prejudiced and unprejudiced people are alike and how they differ.

16. How did Devine show that both prejudiced and unprejudiced people can be influenced by their stereotypes when they are unaware that these stereotypes have been activated?

17. What does Devine's work imply about overcoming prejudice?

The kinds of schemas we develop about groups are affected by whether or not we are members of those groups.

18. A group to which a person belongs is an
_____ , while a group to which
he or she does not belong is an

_____ .

19. How do our perceptions of these two groups differ?

20. Define *ethnocentrism*. State two different views about the reasons that ethnocentrism arises.

21. Present one real-world and one laboratory example of blaming the victim.

22. Give two reasons for the occurrence of victim blaming.

*Perceiving and Presenting the Self*
(pages 503–514)

*CONSIDER these questions before you go on. They are designed to help you start thinking about this subject, not to test your knowledge.*

How do we arrive at a sense of who we are as individuals? Are we influenced by the ways others view us? Do we compare ourselves to others to see how we "measure up"?

How are our social roles related to our self-concepts? Was Shakespeare right when he wrote that "All the world's a stage, and all the men and women merely players"?

In what ways do we manipulate others' impressions of us?

Why do some people seem to be the same regardless of who they are with, while others seem to change like chameleons to reflect their social surroundings?

*READ this section of your text lightly. Then go back and read thoroughly, completing the Workout as you proceed.*

Unlike the members of most other species, we humans have a fairly rich conceptual representation of ourselves.

1. Describe the rouge test and how it has been used to demonstrate species differences in the existence of a self-concept.

We are obviously not born with a self-concept and we do not pluck one out of thin air. Instead, our views of ourselves arise from the social world of which we are a part.

2. Explain Charles Cooley's concept of the looking-glass self.

3. Summarize three lines of evidence suggesting that our self-concepts and behavior can be affected by others' expectations of us.

   a.

   b.

c.

William James suggested that each of us has not just one self but many. This idea has been further developed by psychologists who stress the relationship between self-concept and social roles.

4. Describe weblike models of the self-concept in which self-perceived traits are associated with particular social roles. Show how such an idea might apply to your own self-concept.

5. Does having multiple self-concepts associated with different roles add to psychological stress? Explain.

The culture in which people develop influences their self-concepts.

6. Contrast independent and interdependent views of the self.

7. Describe research using the Twenty Statements Test to show that this distinction is related to culture.

The self-concept is produced in part through the process of social comparison, in which we actively measure ourselves against others to determine how smart we are, how good-looking, how happy, how resourceful, and so on.

8. Define the term *reference group*. Why is it important to take reference groups into account when considering the self-concept?

9. Do children tend to describe themselves in ways that make them seem most like others in their group or in ways that most distinguish them? How can we interpret such findings?

10. How can our selection of a reference group affect our self-esteem? What reference group do you use when thinking of your athletic ability? of your academic ability? of your appearance?

When comparing themselves to others, people may show biases that reflect their culture.

11. Explain self-enhancing and self-effacing biases and show how they are related to culture.

For a variety of reasons, we are interested in others' impressions of us, and we do not generally leave those impressions to chance.

12. What is meant by the term *impression management*?

13. What analogy did Erving Goffman use to describe impression management? In what sense might his analogy be misleading?

We engage in impression management both to look good and to assert and validate our self-concept.

14. Discuss research showing that the "self" we project depends on the audience.

15. How do people tend to react when someone else challenges their self-concept and why do they do so? Support your answer.

16. Define *self-handicapping* and give an example. What purpose does this strategy serve? When does it tend to be used?

Sometimes, the two functions of impression management—looking good and asserting a consistent self-concept—are in conflict. People apparently differ in their tendencies to emphasize one or the other function in such cases.

16. The personality characteristic called

_____ is defined as sensitivity to other people's immediate reactions to oneself, combined with a desire and ability to control those reactions.

17. How do high self-monitors differ from low self-monitors?

18. How do high self-monitors differ from people who are shy?

## Attitudes  (pages 514–527)

> CONSIDER *these questions before you go on. They are designed to help you start thinking about this subject, not to test your knowledge.*

What are attitudes? Why and how do we form them?

Are our attitudes influenced by the attitudes of groups that we want to think well of us, such as fraternity brothers, fellow English majors, or people in the photography club?

If you don't really like someone but do him or her a favor anyway, could it change your attitude toward that person?

How well can we predict someone's behavior by knowing his or her attitudes?

> READ *this section of your text lightly. Then go back and read thoroughly, completing the Workout as you proceed.*

The study of attitudes is of central importance in social cognition because attitudes tie individuals to the whole social world. One can have attitudes toward birthday parties, police, justice, the man at the corner market, aerobic dance, fruitcake, and so on, ad infinitum. Attitudes develop from our experience in the social world and affect our behavior in that world.

1. Define the term *attitude*.

2. Name the function of the attitude described in each case below.

_____ a. Attitudes can serve a role in impression management. If Helen wants an environmentalist group to think well of her, she may be quick to proclaim her aversion to nonrecyclable materials.

_____ **b.** We may adopt an attitude because it helps us to feel better about ourselves or to feel less anxious or upset. If Sam is told by an insensitive kindergarten teacher that he has no sense of rhythm, he may develop a negative attitude toward music or dance.

_____ **c.** An attitude toward some particular object can help to determine our behavior toward that object. If Josh has a negative attitude toward boxing, he doesn't need to question whether he should spend money for tickets to a boxing match.

_____ **d.** Attitudes can help us to define who we are and to assert ourselves. If Roberta has a strong sense of herself as an actively involved citizen, her attitude toward voting is likely to be strongly positive.

3. Describe some evidence for the validity of this classification of attitude functions.

Reference groups play an important part in shaping and maintaining our attitudes.

4. Why might people tend to have attitudes similar to those of the people with whom they live or interact?

5. Describe the method and findings of the Bennington College study.

6. How might attitude change and self-interest be related?

Persuasive messages are not all given the same type of processing.

7. Distinguish between the central and peripheral routes to attitude change. What are some specific examples of handling information by way of the peripheral route?

8. What two propositions about persuasion are made in the elaboration likelihood model? Describe research supporting each.

a.

b.

We all have attitudes about many, many things. Sometimes, our attitudes and beliefs fit harmoniously with one another and with our behavior—but sometimes they do not.

9. Define the term _cognitive dissonance_ and state the fundamental tenet of Leon Festinger's theory of cognitive dissonance.

10. Describe research evidence showing that people sometimes avoid dissonant information.

11. Do people usually feel more confident of a decision just before or just after they have made it? Why?

12. Answer the following questions about the insufficient-justification effect.

   a.   What is the insufficient-justification effect? Give an example.

   b.   Describe four conditions that promote the insufficient-justification effect.

   c.   How can the insufficient-justification effect be explained in terms other than cognitive dissonance?

13. What does the existence of the insufficient-justification effect suggest about the relationship between attitudes and behavior?

14. Briefly summarize Richard LaPiere's early study involving attitudes and behavior toward Asians in the United States.

15. Were attitudes toward cheating correlated with cheating behavior in Corey's study? Explain.

The information-processing perspective points out that, in order to affect behavior, attitudes must be retrieved from memory at the time the behavior is produced.

16. How might this perspective help to explain the results of the LaPiere and cheating studies?

17. Briefly describe evidence showing that attitude-behavior correlations are stronger when people are required to think about their attitude shortly before behaving.

When social scientists first began to study attitudes, they assumed that attitudes would predict behavior. Early research profoundly challenged this assumption, but later research has suggested that attitudes are indeed related to behavior. The relationship is not simple and direct, however.

18. When are attitude-behavior relationships strongest, according to Russell Fazio? What is his reasoning?

Another complication in the attitude-behavior relationship is that attitudes are, of course, not the only cognitions involved in the decision to behave in a certain way.

19. According to Icek Ajzen, the conscious intention to behave in a particular way depends on:

    a. one's _____ , which is one's desire to act in a certain way;

    b. _____ , defined as one's beliefs about what important others might think; and

    c. _____ , one's sense of being able to carry out the action.

20. Briefly describe two findings consistent with Ajzen's view.

The apparent lack of congruence between attitudes and behavior may result in part from biases in the assessment of attitudes.

21. Describe evidence that the wording used in measuring attitudes may affect responses.

22. Discuss the 1989 Virginia governor's race to illustrate the idea that impression management can distort psychological measurements.

Attitudes conflict not only with other types of cognitions; they may conflict with one another. For example, if you have a strongly positive attitude toward freedom of speech and a strongly negative attitude toward racial bigotry, how will you feel about the right of a racist organization to engage in inflammatory rhetoric? How will you vote if you are on a jury asked to assess monetary damages for someone injured as an indirect result of such rhetoric?

23. How did Milton Rokeach approach the problem of conflicting attitudes? Did his approach help him to better predict behavior in specific situations?

24. How did Phillip Tetlock analyze political positions in terms of two potentially conflicting values?

---

*Be sure to READ the Concluding Thoughts at the end of the chapter. Note important points in your Workout. Then consolidate your learning by answering the focus questions in the margins of the text.*

*After you have studied the chapter thoroughly, CHECK your understanding with the self-test that follows.*

## Self-Test 1

*Multiple-Choice Questions*

1. An organized set of information or beliefs about someone is called a:
   a. personal stereotype.
   b. person perception.
   c. personality attribution.
   d. person schema.

2. According to Harold Kelley, if John regularly feels happy in situation *A*, and if most other people also feel happy in situation *A*, then John's happiness in situation *A* will be attributed to:
   a. his personality.
   b. extraneous factors, such as chance.
   c. situation *A*.
   d. a combination of a. and c.

3. The primacy effect in social cognition refers to the fact that:
   a. we remember our early encounters with people better than our later encounters.
   b. early information weighs more strongly than later information in forming an impression of a person.
   c. surface characteristics such as facial appearance are given less weight in person perception than are more relevant characteristics.
   d. we tend to like people we have known longer better than those we have known for a shorter time.

4. When we watch someone carry out an action, we are looking more at the person than at the environment; but when we ourselves carry out an action, we see the environment, not ourselves. This point has been used as a possible explanation of:
   a. the self-effacing bias.
   b. the actor-observer discrepancy.
   c. differences between perceptions of ingroups and outgroups.
   d. the knowledge-across-situations hypothesis.

5. Gilbert has suggested that attributions to internal characteristics are carried out through _____ processing.
   a. automatic
   b. controlled
   c. comparative
   d. defensive

6. Patricia Devine has theorized that:
   a. only prejudiced people have cultural stereotypes.
   b. both prejudiced and unprejudiced people have cultural stereotypes, but the stereotypes are automatically activated only in prejudiced people.
   c. both prejudiced and unprejudiced people have cultural stereotypes, but the stereotypes are automatically activated in prejudiced people and consciously activated in unprejudiced people.
   d. both prejudiced and unprejudiced people have cultural stereotypes that are automatically activated, but only prejudiced people consciously accept them.

7. In an experiment, women who could see themselves in a mirror while hearing about a rape were more likely to blame the victim than women who could not see themselves, a finding that tended to support _____ as an explanation of victim blaming.
   a. the just-world bias
   b. the fundamental attribution error

   c. stereotyping
   d. the undue influence of surface characteristics

8. The idea that we learn about ourselves by looking at the social world around us is referred to as:
   a. self-handicapping.
   b. self-monitoring.
   c. reference grouping.
   d. the looking-glass self.

9. The _____ view of self is characteristic of people in Asia, Africa, Latin America, and parts of Southern Europe.
   a. independent
   b. interdependent
   c. social comparison
   d. attributional

10. Because we construct the self-concept in part through social comparison, the self-concept depends on:
    a. the primacy effect.
    b. the reference group.
    c. the actor-observer discrepancy.
    d. impression management.

11. Swann's research suggests that a person will tend to project the characteristic of dominance more strongly if this trait is:
    a. important to the person's self-concept and if another person perceives him or her as dominant.
    b. important to the person's self-concept and if another person perceives him or her as submissive.
    c. relatively neutral in the person's self-concept and if another person perceives him or her as dominant.
    d. relatively neutral in the person's self-concept and if another person perceives him or her as submissive.

12. People high in self-monitoring should be most influenced by persuasive messages that appeal to _____ function of attitudes.
    a. the utilitarian
    b. the social-adjustive
    c. the value-expressive
    d. either the a. or c.

13. The Bennington College study demonstrated that:
    a. reference groups play an important part in changing attitudes.
    b. reference groups play little part in changing attitudes.
    c. cognitive dissonance plays an important part in changing attitudes.
    d. cognitive dissonance plays little part in changing attitudes.

14. People tend to use the _____ route to attitude construction except when messages have high personal relevance.
    a. effortful peripheral
    b. relatively effortless peripheral
    c. effortful central
    d. relatively effortless central

15. In an early study of the relationship between attitudes and behavior, researchers found that college students:
    a. with strong anti-cheating attitudes were just as likely to cheat as those with weak anti-cheating attitudes.
    b. with strong anti-cheating attitudes were less likely to cheat than those with weak anti-cheating attitudes.
    c. who cheated were likely to change their attitudes to be less negative toward cheating.
    d. who did not cheat were likely to believe that other students were also unlikely to cheat.

## Essay Questions

16. How is the self-concept affected by other people's expectations? Cite research evidence to support your answer.

17. What is impression management and why do people do it? Describe (a) a personality characteristic associated with individual differences in impression management, and (b) two different circumstances that you think might increase the tendency toward impression management.

---

*After you have assessed your understanding on the basis of Self-Test 1 and have tried to strengthen your preparation in any areas of weakness, GO ON to Self-Test 2.*

# Self-Test 2

## Multiple-Choice Questions

1. An inference about the cause of a particular behavior is called a(n):
    a. impression.     c. schema.
    b. attribution.    d. expectation.

2. Subjects in an experiment were given evidence regarding an individual charged with either a crime of negligence or a crime of deliberate deception. Baby-faced defendants were:
    a. generally found innocent of either charge.
    b. found innocent more often than mature-faced defendants, but only when the evidence was weak.
    c. more likely to be found guilty of a crime of negligence than a crime of deliberate deception.
    d. more likely to be found guilty of a crime of deliberate deception than a crime of negligence.

3. People are more likely to judge their friends' behavior as dependent on the situation than they are to judge a stranger's behavior as dependent on the situation. This supports the _____ as an explanation of the _____.
   a. visual-orientation hypothesis; fundamental attribution error
   b. fundamental attribution error; visual-orientation hypothesis
   c. knowledge-across-situations hypothesis; actor-observer discrepancy
   d. actor-observer discrepancy; knowledge-across-situations hypothesis

4. Adults in India were _____ likely than American adults to attribute behaviors to personality, a finding that _____ the fundamental attribution error.
   a. more; supports     c. less; supports
   b. more; challenges   d. less; challenges

5. People tend to view members of outgroups as _____ homogeneous than members of ingroups and to regard them _____ favorably.
   a. more; equally     c. more; less
   b. less; more        d. less; equally

6. The just-world bias may help to explain:
   a. the influence of cultural norms.
   b. self-monitoring.
   c. the use of reference groups in attitude formation.
   d. blaming the victim.

7. By placing a dot of rouge on a child's or animal's face before they look in a mirror, researchers have found that:
   a. only humans recognize themselves.
   b. only humans and higher primates, such as chimpanzees, recognize themselves.
   c. most vertebrates, including cats and dogs, recognize themselves.
   d. most species that exhibit social organization recognize themselves.

8. Which of the following messages to children has been shown experimentally to produce the greatest improvements in math performance?
   a. telling the children why math is important
   b. telling the children they should try to become good at math
   c. telling the children they are good at math
   d. telling the children they should try to do their best in everything

9. Self-handicapping is a strategy for:
   a. making accurate attributions about one's behavior.
   b. impression management.
   c. forming a self-concept.
   d. self-monitoring.

10. High self-monitors are people who have:
    a. little concern about other people's impressions of them.
    b. the ability to manipulate other people's impressions of them.
    c. a strong concern about other people's impressions of them.
    d. both b. and c.

11. The role of attitudes in guiding behavior with respect to the object of the attitude is referred to as the _____ function.
    a. defensive           c. utilitarian
    b. social-adjustive     d. value-expressive

12. Logical analysis of the message content:
    a. characterizes the central route to attitude construction.
    b. characterizes the peripheral route to attitude construction.
    c. can characterize either the central or the peripheral route to attitude construction, depending on the nature of the message.
    d. characterizes neither the central nor the peripheral route to attitude construction.

13. An awareness of disagreement or lack of harmony among the attitudes or beliefs in one's mind creates psychological discomfort. This concept is called:
    a. fundamental attribution error.
    b. cognitive distinctiveness.
    c. cognitive dissonance.
    d. cognitive bias.

14. If a person is induced to behave in a way that is contrary to his or her attitude, and lacks any obvious way to justify that behavior, the person's attitude will tend to:
    a. move in a direction consistent with the behavior.
    b. become strengthened in the direction of the original attitude.
    c. remain unchanged because of the conflict between thought and behavior.
    d. become neutralized so that it is neither positive nor negative.

15. Milton Rokeach attempted, with some success, to predict people's _____ by asking them to _____ their values.
    a. attitudes; rank order
    b. attitudes; discuss
    c. behavior; rank order
    d. behavior; discuss

## Essay Questions

16. Discuss self-enhancing and self-effacing biases in the context of culture.

17. Discuss psychology's changing view of attitudes as predictors of behavior.

# Answers

## Perceiving Others

2. person schema

11. a. person-situation combination
    b. extraneous factor
    c. personality
    d. situation

18. ingroup; outgroup

## Perceiving and Presenting the Self

16. self-monitoring

## Attitudes

2. a. social-adjustive
   b. defensive
   c. utilitarian
   d. value-expressive

19. a. attitude
    b. subjective norm
    c. perceived control

## Self-Test 1

1. d. (p. 494)
2. c. (p. 495)
3. b. (p. 495)
4. b. (p. 499)
5. a. (pp. 498–499)
6. d. According to Devine's theory, stereotypes are automatically activated in both prejudiced and unprejudiced people. However, only prejudiced people consciously accept the stereotype; unprejudiced people consciously reject it. Devine's theory has been supported by research evidence. (p. 501)
7. a. Women who could see themselves in the mirror were more aware of themselves. Thus, they were presumably more strongly motivated to think in terms of a just world, a world in which people get what they deserve. If one has not done something to cause oneself harm, then nothing harmful will happen. This view leads to blaming the victim as a way of protecting the illusion of personal control. It is defensive. (p. 503)
8. d. (p. 504)

9. **b.** (p. 507)

10. **b.** (p. 508)

11. **b.** (pp. 511–512)

12. **b.**   Because high self-monitors are inordinately concerned with the opinions of others and with favorably impressing others, this kind of message will be most effective for them. (pp. 512–515)

13. **a.**   At least partly because the Bennington College students continued to have a liberal reference group after college, their liberal attitudes persisted. (pp. 516–517)

14. **b.** (pp. 517–518)

15. **a.** (p. 523)

16. Charles Cooley introduced the term *looking-glass self* to indicate that the self-concept depends on the individual looking outward at the social world to "see" the self. One way in which the social world influences the self-concept is through the expectations other people have of us. Someone's beliefs about us can affect his or her behavior toward us, which can affect how we see ourselves and how we behave. In other words, other people's expectations of us can set up self-fulfilling prophecies.

    One kind of research finding consistent with this view has come from studies of people talking on the phone. In these studies, Person *A* was led to believe that Person *B*, the unknown individual on the other end of the phone conversation, had certain characteristics—that he or she was attractive, bright, and friendly, for example. Person *B* then tended to behave in accordance with those expectations, even though unaware that such expectations had been established.

    In other studies, longer-term expectations have been found to have significant effects on such behaviors as academic performance and neatness. In Rosenthal and Jacobson's study, elementary-school teachers were told that a group of students were about to undergo an intellectual growth spurt when in reality these children were just randomly selected. Several months later, these children showed superior gains in academic performance and IQ. Further research showed that the teachers' expectations caused them to act differently toward the children, by praising their work more often or giving them more challenging assignments, for example. This different treatment caused the children to regard themselves more positively and to act in ways consistent with their improved self-concept. (pp. 504–506)

17. Impression management is all the ways we consciously or unconsciously attempt to influence other people's impressions of us. One possible goal of impression management is to control the way other people treat us. For example, if we can get people to think of us as trustworthy or capable or likeable, they will presumably act more favorably toward us. Another goal is to get others to react to us in a way that boosts our self-esteem. Yet another goal is to get people to validate who we think we are. For example, if we think we are intelligent, we may be motivated to get other people to agree with that assessment, since a stable, consistent self-concept is apparently something we strive for.

    Self-monitoring is a personality characteristic related to impression management. People high in self-monitoring have a stronger concern about the way others view them and have enough confidence to try to manipulate those views. They seem to be motivated to engage in impression management in order to look good. People low in self-monitoring are more concerned with maintaining a consistent self-concept and are less likely to behave differently to please different audiences.

    We might be induced to engage in impression management if we are with a group of people we particularly want to appeal to. We also might engage in more impression management if we feel we have something valuable to lose, such as a reputation for being a good conversationalist or a fair-minded person. People have been found particularly likely to use the self-handicapping strategy for impression management if they fear they cannot live up to their reputation. (pp. 510–514)

### Self-Test 2

1. **b.** (p. 497)

2. **c.** Because people tend to perceive baby-faced individuals as more naive, honest, helpless, kind, and warm than mature-faced individuals of the same age, it is easier to believe them guilty of a crime of negligence than a crime of deliberate deception. (pp. 496–497)

3. **c.** (p. 499)

4. **d.** (p. 499)

5. **c.** (p. 502)

6. **d.** (p. 503)

7. **b.** (pp. 503–504)

8. **c.** When children are led to believe that they are good at math, they apparently incorporate that belief into their self-concept. They expect more of themselves and try to live up to those expectations. (pp. 505–506)

9. **b.** (p. 512)

10. **d.** (pp. 512–513)

11. **c.** (p. 514)

12. **a.** (p. 517)

13. **c.** (p. 519)

14. **a.** This is termed the insufficient-justification effect. (p. 521)

15. **c.** (p. 526)

16. People often demonstrate a bias in their perception when comparing themselves to others. However, the direction of the bias—favoring the self or favoring others—depends at least in part on culture. People in North America and Western Europe tend to see themselves as better than they actually are in comparison to others. This is called a self-enhancing bias. This bias is so prevalent in the United States that failure to demonstrate it is considered by some psychologists a sign of depression. Japanese subjects, in contrast, seem to be biased in the opposite direction at times. When administered the Twenty Statements Test, Japanese students gave twice as many negative as positive self-statements, the reverse of what American students in the study did. (pp. 509–510)

17. Initially, psychologists believed that knowing someone's attitudes would allow them to predict that person's behavior. However, early research soon proved the matter was not so simple. In the 1930s, LaPiere traveled around the country with a young Chinese couple, seeking service in hotels, restaurants, and so on. At that time, many people in the United States were quite prejudiced against Asians. Yet, LaPiere and his companions were refused service in only one of many establishments and were generally treated with reasonable courtesy. When these very establishments were asked in a survey whether they would house or serve Chinese customers, the great majority said no. Other studies also showed a lack of correlation between the attitudes people expressed and their behavior. Many people became convinced that attitudes do not correlate with behavior because they do not guide behavior. Others sought to look more closely at the attitude-behavior relationship, analyzing it more carefully and specifically.

As a result of this closer look, we have improved the ability to predict behavior from expressed attitudes and have arrived at a better understanding of why the relationship is not perfect. If people are aware of their attitudes, they are more likely to behave in ways consistent with those attitudes. In one study, people who could see themselves in a mirror while rating pornographic material were more likely to give ratings consistent with their previously expressed attitudes toward pornography. We must also acknowledge that attitudes are not the sole cognitive determinants of behavior; behavior is also affected by a person's sense of perceived control in a given situation or sensitivity to subjective norms of behavior. This might help to account for LaPiere's data, for example. Individual waitresses or innkeepers may have felt they were not in a position to refuse service, even if their attitudes were prejudiced against Asians. Further, attitudes may conflict with one another. When Rokeach had people rank order their values (central attitudes), he found that he could predict their behavior in specific situations fairly well. For example, if someone valued equality very highly, that person was more likely to participate in a rally for equal rights. (pp. 522–527)

# CHAPTER 15 SOCIAL INFLUENCES ON BEHAVIOR

*Read the introduction below before you read the chapter in the text.*

As participants in a social world, we are all influenced by a host of pressures, called social forces, which may take a variety of forms—such as direct or indirect requests, commands, expectations, and so on. These forces need not be real, only perceived, in order to affect us. Kurt Lewin, a pioneer in this area of social psychology, viewed these pressures holistically, as a field of forces that act together to push or pull individuals in various directions. His field theory is a foundation for much of the other work described in Chapter 15, such as Latané's social impact theory, which specifies the variables that can increase or decrease the impact of social forces.

Social psychologists have found that people have a general tendency to comply with requests, although they can be more or less compliant depending on a number of factors. A variety of techniques can induce greater compliance and are sometimes exploited by people whose job it is to persuade us to behave in certain ways, such as to buy a given product. For example, in the four-walls technique, the customer is influenced to make statements that are consistent with the idea that owning the product is a good thing.

People may be particularly likely to comply when the request is perceived as an order from an authority. A classic series of experiments by Stanley Milgram revealed that ordinary people will under some circumstances obey orders that they consider wrong, even if they believe another person will be seriously harmed as a result. Some theorists have applied these experimental results to real-world situations such as the Nazi Holocaust. The ethics of the experiments themselves have, however, been questioned.

Our behavior can be affected by the mere presence of other people. In social facilitation, performance with onlookers present is superior to performance when alone. In social interference, performance suffers when others are present. Robert Zajonc has explained both phenomena in terms of the effects of arousal on different kinds of tasks. The unrespon-sive-bystander phenomenon, in which people fail to help someone in apparent trouble, is more likely if there are multiple witnesses than if there is only one. In other cases, being part of a large group stimulates rather than inhibits behavior. As part of a crowd, people may carry out actions they would never carry out on their own—such as baiting a potential suicide, raping, or murdering.

Why do people conform? Solomon Asch expected to find that people would not conform to the judgment of a majority when a simple perceptual task was involved. To his surprise, he found that people often *did* conform to the opinion expressed by the majority—even if they knew it was wrong. Other research shows that consistently expressed minority opinions can also sway others.

Many decisions are the product not of individuals but of groups working together. Group discussion can change perceived social norms. It can also polarize attitudes; if people who agree on some matter get together to discuss it, they will generally emerge with a more extreme version of their original opinion. Groupthink is a faulty mode of thinking that may result when members of a cohesive group place unanimity above the realistic appraisal of alternatives.

People's lives are interdependent. Positive interdependence is a situation in which one person's success depends on others' success. Negative interdependence is a situation in which one person's success depends on others' failure. In social dilemmas, the situation can be viewed in terms of either positive or negative interdependence. Cooperation is more likely if there is an opportunity to establish reciprocity or if people share a group identity.

*LOOK over the table of contents for this chapter in your textbook before you continue with your study.*

*Notice that there are focus questions in the margins of the text for your use in studying the material. The following chart lists which study guide questions relate to which focus questions.*

# The Integrated Study Workout

*Complete one section at a time.*

## A Perspective: The Person in a Field of Social Forces  (pages 531–534)

*CONSIDER these questions before you go on. They are designed to help you start thinking about this subject, not to test your knowledge.*

What kinds of social pressures might affect a person's decision to either go to medical school or become a high school biology teacher?

Can social pressures be studied through experiments?

What factors tend to increase a person's stage fright?

*READ this section of your text lightly. Then go back and read thoroughly, completing the Workout as you proceed.*

The individual living in the midst of the social world is subject to a multitude of pressures from that world, some real and others imagined. We may feel pressure to be polite, to marry, to go into the family business, to wear a certain style of clothing, or to buy a specific product. Such pressures are called social forces. Kurt Lewin, a native of Germany who was strongly influenced by Gestalt psychology, provided the conceptual foundation for the study of social influence.

1.  State the basic premise of Lewin's field theory.

2.  What was Lewin's theoretical goal? What kind of research methodology did he advocate?

Bibb Latané's social impact theory elaborates on Lewin's concept of social force.

3.  How does Latané define *social impact*?

4.  State the three general propositions of social impact theory.

    a.

    b

    c.

The results of Latané's research on stage fright were consistent with all three propositions of his theory.

5.  Indicate whether each factor below produced an increase or a decrease in stage fright.

    a.  increased status of audience ＿＿＿＿＿＿＿

    b   increased size of audience  ＿＿＿＿＿＿＿

    c.  increased number of performers on stage                ＿＿＿＿＿＿＿

**6.** Which finding in Latané's stage-fright research was consistent with the second proposition of his social impact theory?

## *Influence of Others' Requests*   (pages 534–542)

*CONSIDER these questions before you go on. They are designed to help you start thinking about this subject, not to test your knowledge.*

How can salespeople sometimes manipulate us into buying what we don't want or need?

Why do people obey the orders of authorities even when they believe those orders to be wrong, even unethical? What factors help people to resist obeying such orders?

*READ this section of your text lightly. Then go back and read thoroughly, completing the Workout as you proceed.*

Both research and everyday experience reveal that most people have a tendency to comply with direct requests. In fact, they seem to need a good excuse before they feel free to refuse a request. As you learned, people are motivated to reduce cognitive dissonance, the discomfort experienced when one's beliefs clash with one another or with one's behavior. Robert Cialdini has shown that cognitive dissonance is the basis for several techniques that people use to increase compliance to their requests.

**1.** For each of the following techniques, give a general description, an example, and an explanation for its effectiveness.

   **a.** four-walls

   **b.** low-ball

   **c.** foot-in-the-door

Another basis for gaining compliance is the reciprocity norm.

**2.** Describe the reciprocity norm and give an example of how it can be exploited to gain compliance.

**3.** Answer the following questions about the door-in-the-face technique.

   **a.** Describe the door-in-the-face technique.

   **b.** How can the effectiveness of this technique be partially explained by the reciprocity norm?

   **c.** The door-in-the-face technique is the opposite of the _____ technique.

   **d.** Why is it important that the downward negotiation in the door-in-the-face technique occur immediately?

Obedience is defined as compliance to a request that is perceived as an order from an authority figure. Though obedience is often positively valued as necessary to social order, it can in some cases lead to nightmarish behavior, such as that exhibited in the Nazi Holocaust or the My Lai massacre in Vietnam. Stanley Milgram carried out a classic study of obedience—one that had disturbing results.

4. Describe the method and result of Milgram's study.

5. How consistent is this finding? Is it dependent on using a particular type of subject? Explain.

6. State four factors that are important in explaining the obedience found in experiments such as Milgram's. Where possible, indicate evidence that supports these explanations.

   a.

   b.

   c.

   d.

7. Summarize the *ethical* criticisms of Milgram's obedience studies. Are these criticisms valid? Support your answer.

8. Summarize criticisms of the *validity* of Milgram's obedience studies. Are these criticisms correct? Support your answer.

9. What happens when the subject works with another teacher (actually a confederate of the experimenter) who refuses to obey? What happens if the other teacher continues to the most severe shock level?

10. The chapter describes two experiments in which nurses were ordered by a "doctor" to give a patient what they knew to be an overdose. In one experiment, 95 percent would have obeyed had they not been stopped. In the other experiment, only 11 percent would have obeyed. What is thought to have made the difference?

*Influence of Others' Presence or Examples*
(pages 542–552)

CONSIDER *these questions before you go on. They are designed to help you start thinking about this subject, not to test your knowledge.*

Do people perform better or worse if onlookers are present?

How can people stand by and watch someone in trouble—someone apparently having a heart attack or being robbed, for example—without doing anything to help?

Why do people in a crowd sometimes behave in ways that they would not on their own?

Can the opinions expressed by a majority cause people to say things that are contrary to their beliefs just so they will fit in? Can the majority cause them to change their minds about what is true?

What kinds of conditions can lead to poor group decision making? What can promote good group decision making?

What are the roots of intergroup conflict? How can such conflict be reduced?

---

*READ this section of your text lightly. Then go back and read thoroughly, completing the Workout as you proceed.*

---

Our behavior can be affected by the mere presence of others. In social psychology's first published experiment, Norman Triplett reported that children wound fishing reels faster when they worked in pairs than when they worked alone. Similar results have been found in nonhuman species.

1. Were results like those of Triplett due to the competition that can arise when individuals work on the same task together? Explain.

2. Complete the following statements.

   a. _____ is the tendency to perform a task better in front of others than when alone.

   b. _____ is a decline in performance when others are present as compared to performance when alone

3. How did Robert Zajonc relate the occurrence of social facilitation at some times and social interference at other times to the nature of the task?

4. How are social facilitation and interference related to the effect of high arousal on performance, according to Zajonc?

5. Explain how the presence of others might lead to increased arousal in humans.

6. By examining World Series records, Baumeister and Steinhilber found that home teams usually lost the decisive championship games. How might this be explained in terms of Zajonc's arousal theory? What alternative explanation do Baumeister and Steinhilber favor?

The American public was shocked to learn of the circumstances of Catherine Genovese's murder. Thirty-eight people watched while the young woman was stabbed to death on a New York City street. This and similar incidents prompted social psychologists to study what has come to be called the *unresponsive-bystander phenomenon*.

7. Is a person who witnesses an emergency more likely to come to the victim's aid when alone or when other witnesses are present? Use research evidence to support your answer.

8. Researchers have proposed three interrelated explanations for such results. Present these explanations and describe evidence supporting each.

   a.

**b.**

**c.**

Being part of a crowd can sometimes lead individuals to behave in ways they would not behave on their own—even to loot, rape, torture, or kill in extreme cases.

9. The state of reduced personal responsibility that can occur when acting as part of a group is called

_____ .

10. One possible explanation of crowd-induced deindividuation is that being in a crowd reduces individual accountability through anonymity. Describe evidence to support this view.

11. Another possible explanation of deindividuation is that attention is shifted away from the self toward the extremely arousing external stimulation of the mob's action. Describe evidence to support this view.

12. Briefly describe one laboratory demonstration of increased aggression as a result of deindividuation.

How are people who are asked to express a view influenced by the views expressed by others around them? Does the majority opinion alter what people believe? Or does it only change what they say? These

questions concern the phenomenon of conformity, the focus of a classic series of experiments by Solomon Asch.

13. Briefly describe Asch's basic procedure and his results.

14. Distinguish between informational and normative influences on conformity. How did Asch test the relative importance of these influences and what did he find?

15. The relative importance of informational and normative influences on conformity may depend on the difficulty of the task. Explain.

In Asch's basic research, the confederates were unanimous in giving the wrong answer. Other experiments have examined the influence of a minority opinion.

16. What happens to conformity if one of the confederates disagrees with the rest? Does this also occur if the dissenting confederate simply gives a different wrong answer?

17. Serge Moscovici and others have studied the effect of an incorrect minority on the majority. Answer the following questions about the effects of a minority opinion.

   a. Can an incorrect minority affect the responses of a majority?

**b.** In what ways does a minority affect the majority?

**b.** group stereotyping

**c.** one-upmanship

Other studies of decision making in groups have used more natural conditions. Sometimes these studies have been related to real, practical problems. For example, during World War II the U.S. government wanted citizens to buy visceral meats because of the meat shortage. Citizens resisted the government's efforts at persuasion, however. Kurt Lewin saw in this situation a chance to explore the importance of social norms.

**d.** ingroup-outgroup

**18.** What was Kurt Lewin's explanation for the public's refusal to buy visceral meats?

Group decision making sometimes, but not always, leads to bad decisions. Irving Janis explored causes of bad group decisions by studying some notorious government decisions, such as those involved in the Bay of Pigs invasion and the Watergate cover-up.

**19.** How did he test his hypothesis and what did he find?

**22.** Explain Janis's concept of groupthink.

A well-documented phenomenon in group discussion is the polarization of attitudes.

**23.** Specify two conditions that tend to lead to sound group decision making.

**20.** Give an example of how group polarization could have important consequences in everyday life.

## Social Interdependence: Forces for Conflict or Harmony  (pages 553–559)

**21.** Describe four hypotheses about the cause of group polarization.

**a.** informational influence

CONSIDER these questions before you go on. They are designed to help you start thinking about this subject, not to test your knowledge.

What causes conflict between groups of people?

What makes people work together?

READ this section of your text lightly. Then go back and read thoroughly, completing the Workout as you proceed.

People have a variety of goals in life. Sometimes their goals are shared and other times their goals conflict.

1. What is positive interdependence? negative interdependence? Can people be both positively and negatively interdependent at the same time? Explain.

2. What are social dilemmas? How might such dilemmas be a matter of human survival?

Psychologists have often studied people's choices in social dilemmas through prisoner's dilemma games.

3. Explain the basic premise of a prisoner's dilemma game. How do players tend to play if they are anonymous? Does this serve them well? Explain.

4. Why are players more likely to cooperate in an iterative (repeated) prisoner's dilemma game?

5. Why was Rapoport's TFT program so successful?

6. How might the TFT strategy be related to reciprocity?

7. How is group identity related to the tendency to cooperate?

8. How do groups differ from individuals when playing social dilemma games?

Muzafer Sherif and colleagues conducted the Robbers Cave experiment in order to study conflict and ways of resolving that conflict.

9. How did the experimenters establish groups?

10. What resulted from the series of competitions between the groups?

11. List some methods tried in this and similar experiments that did *not* work as a means of reducing intergroup hostility.

12. What strategy for reducing intergroup hostility was successful? Explain.

In response to a real-life racial desegregation situation, social psychologist Elliot Aronson and his colleagues developed the jigsaw classroom.

13. What was the jigsaw classroom and how did it illustrate the importance of positive goal interdependence?

---

*Be sure to READ the Concluding Thoughts at the end of the chapter. Note important points in your Workout. Then consolidate your learning by answering the focus questions in the margins of the text.*

---

*After you have studied the chapter thoroughly, CHECK your understanding with the self-test that follows.*

---

# Self-Test 1

*Multiple-Choice Questions*

1. Bibb Latané's social impact theory is an elaboration of:
   a. Leon Festinger's cognitive dissonance theory.
   b. Kurt Lewin's field theory of social forces.
   c. Robert Zajonc's theory of social facilitation and inhibition.
   d. Robert Cialdini's work on social compliance.

2. Jackson, who suffers from stage fright, is about to deliver a dramatic speech. Which of the following circumstances would tend to *minimize* Jackson's stage fright, according to Latané's research?
   a. having only a few people in the audience
   b. being alone on stage rather than having other actors present
   c. having respected local actors in the audience rather than just fellow students
   d. both a. and b.

3. In social impact theory, the immediacy of a source:
   a. depends on the extent of the target's fear, admiration, respect, or need for that person.
   b. can increase if the source is physically near or has simply been brought to mind.
   c. refers to how recently the target has been exposed to the source.
   d. is unrelated to the amount of social force that source exerts.

4. A salesperson who gets potential customers to say things consistent with the idea that owning the product would be a good thing is using the _____ technique.
   a. door-in-the-face    c. foot-in-the-door
   b. low-ball            d. four-walls

5. In Milgram's classic study _____ percent of subjects went all the way to the most severe shock.
   a. 5      c. 35
   b. 15     d. 65

6. The opposite of the foot-in-the-door technique is the _____ technique.
   a. low-ball
   b. four-walls
   c. door-in-the-face
   d. reciprocity

7. Researchers have suggested that the My Lai massacre in Vietnam and the killing of millions of people in the Nazi Holocaust may be partially understood in terms of:
   a. Cialdini's work on principles of compliance.
   b. Zajonc's work on social interference and facilitation.
   c. Asch's work on conformity.
   d. Milgram's work on obedience.

8. Which of the following has *not* been supported as a partial explanation of the obedience shown in experiments such as those conducted by Stanley Milgram?
   a. the subjects' prior beliefs about authority
   b. the sequential nature of the task
   c. the experimenter's acceptance of responsibility
   d. the sadistic tendencies of the subjects

9. Studies of the unresponsive-bystander phenomenon have found that bystanders who know each other well are _____ likely to experience an inhibitory effect; this finding provides evidence for explanations of the phenomenon based on the _____.
   a. more; diffusion of responsibility
   b. more; normative influence
   c. less; diffusion of responsibility
   d. less; normative influence

10. Suicide baitings have been found to be most likely in large cities, at night, when a large crowd has gathered. This finding illustrates the:
   a. role of anonymity in crowd-induced deindividuation.

b. informational influences in the unresponsive-bystander phenomenon.

c. social facilitation of conformity.

d. phenomenon of group polarization.

11. In studies of conformity, Serge Moscovici showed that an incorrect minority:

a. can affect the judgment of some majority subjects through normative influence.

b. can affect the judgment of some majority subjects through informational influence.

c. is incapable of affecting the judgment of subjects in the majority because of group polarization.

d. is incapable of affecting the judgment of subjects in the majority because of social facilitation.

12. If Lewin's analysis was correct, people were unwilling to buy visceral meats earlier in this century because of:

a. perceived norms.

b. ingroup-outgroup differences.

c. previous conditioning, which led to an automatic negative response to such meats.

d. group polarization, which emerged from discussions with their neighbors about the pros and cons of such meats.

13. People who share the same view initially will tend to hold a more extreme version of that view after discussing the subject with one another. This phenomenon is called:

a. social facilitation.

b. normative influence.

c. group polarization.

d. groupthink.

14. In the laboratory study of responses to the prisoner's dilemma games, the situation is:

a. more likely to be interpreted as competitive by groups than by individuals.

b. less likely to be interpreted as competitive by groups than by individuals.

c. more likely to be interpreted as competitive by children than by adults.

d. less likely to be interpreted as competitive by children than by adults.

15. In Aronson's jigsaw classroom, _____ goal interdependence led children of different races to _____ with one another.

a. positive; compete

b. positive; cooperate

c. negative; compete

d. negative; cooperate

*Essay Questions*

16. How did Solomon Asch study conformity in the laboratory and what was his basic finding? What factor was found to help subjects resist conformity? Why did subjects conform?

17. What are two possible explanations of group polarization? Indicate whether each explanation is normative or informational.

*After you have assessed your understanding on the basis of Self-Test 1 and have tried to strengthen your preparation in any areas of weakness, GO ON to Self-Test 2.*

# Self-Test 2

*Multiple-Choice Questions*

1. According to Latané's social impact theory, _____ increases with an increase in the number of _____ .

a. social facilitation; sources

b. social facilitation; targets

c. social force; sources

d. social force; targets

2. The reciprocity norm can help to explain:
   a. the foot-in-the-door technique.
   b. the door-in-the-face technique.
   c. cooperation in an iterative prisoner's dilemma game.
   d. both b. and c.

3. An interviewer conducting a survey asks Max for a few seconds of his time and Max consents. Then Max is asked to respond to ten yes-or-no questions and he agrees. Finally, the interviewer works up to the primary aim, asking for a half-hour interview in Max's home. The interviewer is using the _____ to gain compliance.
   a. low-ball technique
   b. reciprocity norm
   c. foot-in-the-door technique
   d. door-in-the-face technique

4. Which of the following pairs of sales techniques are believed to work on the principle of cognitive dissonance?
   a. foot-in-the-door and door-in-the-face
   b. reciprocity and low-ball
   c. reciprocity and door-in-the-face
   d. foot-in-the-door and low-ball

5. Students who were asked to produce philosophical counterarguments did worse when in the presence of other people than when alone. This experimental result illustrates:
   a. diffusion of responsibility.
   b. the occurrence of cognitive dissonance.
   c. social interference.
   d. the phenomenon of groupthink.

6. Deindividuation seems to be due to:
   a. reduced accountability that comes from anonymity in the crowd.
   b. attention being shifted away from the self toward arousing external stimulation.
   c. the informational influence of the crowd.
   d. both a. and b.

7. Researchers have found that the relative amount of informational as compared to normative influence on conformity varies depending on the:
   a. personal persuasiveness of individuals in the majority.
   b. difficulty of the task.
   c. gender of confederates and subjects.
   d. amount that subjects are being paid.

8. Jim, Anne, and Karen believe that the workers in their factory should unionize. They believe this

even more firmly after talking together about the issue. This could be explained in terms of:
   a. groupthink.
   b. group polarization.
   c. social facilitation.
   d. none of the above.

9. Group polarization results because people tend to conform to a mentally exaggerated version of their group's opinion, according to the _____ hypothesis.
   a. one-upmanship
   b. group-stereotyping
   c. informational
   d. reciprocity

10. The kind of thinking that arises when people immersed in a cohesive ingroup strive for unanimity more than for realistic appraisal of alternatives for action is called:
    a. groupthink.
    b. deindividuation.
    c. diffusion of responsibility.
    d. obedience.

11. Garrett Hardin's "The Tragedy of the Commons" illustrates the relevance of _____ to _____ .
    a. positive interdependence; world peace
    b. outgroup stereotyping; environmental safety
    c. social dilemmas; human survival
    d. compliance; economic success

12. In one-shot social dilemma games, players tend to _____ ; in iterative games, they _____ .
    a. compete; cooperate
    b. cooperate; compete
    c. compete; do the same
    d. cooperate; do the same

13. A general term for the condition that led to intergroup hostility in Sherif's Robbers Cave experiment is:
    a. positive goal interdependence.
    b. negative goal interdependence.
    c. psychological reactance.
    d. the reciprocity norm.

14. In his Robbers Cave experiment, Sherif successfully ended intergroup hostilities between the boys by:
    a. arranging for joint participation in pleasant activities.
    b. setting up individual rather than group competitions.

c. establishing superordinate goals.

d. arranging peace meetings between group leaders.

15. Aronson's jigsaw classroom illustrated the power of positive interdependence to help overcome:

a. racial hostility.

b. conformity.

c. groupthink.

d. downward negotiation.

## Essay Questions

16. Summarize the method and results of Stanley Milgram's classic study of obedience. Give two explanations that have been offered for these results.

17. Define the terms *social facilitation* and *social interference*. How did Zajonc explain these phenomena and thereby predict when each would occur?

# Answers

### A Perspective: The Person in a Field of Social Forces

5. **a.** increase, **b.** increase, **c.** decrease

### Influence of Others' Requests

3. **c.** foot-in-the-door

### Influence of Others' Presence or Examples

2. **a.** social facilitation

**b.** social interference

9. deindividuation

### Self-Test 1

1. **b.** (p. 532)

2. **a.** Social force increases as the number of sources increases and as the number of targets decreases. Thus, the circumstance described in a. would tend to make things easier for Jackson, while those described in b. and c. would tend to worsen his stage fright. (p. 533)

3. **b.** (p. 532)

4. **d.** (p. 535)

5. **d.** (p. 539)

6. **c.** The foot-in-the-door technique involves working up from smaller requests to a larger one, whereas the door-in-the-face technique involves starting with a large request and moving down to a smaller one. The foot-in-the-door technique works because people try to reduce cognitive dissonance; they believe that their compliance to earlier, small requests must mean that they are favorably disposed toward this person, product, or cause. So why don't people come to the opposite conclusion after saying no to an initial large request in the door-in-the-face technique? Well, they do, if there is time for them to reduce cognitive dissonance. That is why the downward negotiation must occur immediately if the technique is to work. (p. 537)

7. **d.** Although the results of Milgram's studies are often discussed in reference to such events as these, critics have suggested that the connection is not very strong. They maintain that subjects in an experiment cannot truly believe that a sane experimenter would ask them to shock a learner to the point of danger. Therefore, their behavior cannot be realistically compared to that of people

who saw their victims suffer and die. (pp. 537–538, 541)

8. **d.** The subjects did not comply because they enjoyed harming the "learner"; they clearly showed evidence of distress as they carried out the experimenter's orders. The impact of Milgram's finding stems from the fact that these *were* normal subjects. Their behavior is something that normal people are capable of. (pp. 539–540)

9. **d.** (pp. 545–546)

10. **a.** (p. 546)

11. **b.** (p. 549)

12. **a.** (pp. 549–550)

13. **c.** (p. 550)

14. **a.** One possible explanation is that people overcome inhibitions about competitiveness when they are part of a group. Another is that, through prior experience, people have come to associate groups with competition. (pp. 556–557)

15. **b.** (p. 559)

16. Solomon Asch started out by trying to demonstrate that people will not conform. He arranged for each subject to join a group of people who appeared to be fellow subjects but who were in reality confederates of the experimenter. On each trial, subjects (real and fake alike) were to compare a standard line to a set of three comparison lines and to indicate the one line that was the same length as the standard. The task was extremely simple. The real subjects were seated so that they were the next to last to give their answers. The confederates had been instructed beforehand to give the same wrong answer on certain trials.

Most subjects were influenced by the clearly wrong answers of the confederates, at least sometimes. Some conformed to the unanimous wrong answer on every one of these trials. Recent research suggests that conformity is due mostly to normative influence on easy tasks but mostly to informational influence when the task is difficult.

Subjects apparently conformed primarily because of the normative influence of the group. When subjects were led to believe that they were late and should therefore give their answers in writing rather than aloud, the level of conformity dropped dramatically. The fact that some conformity existed even in this circumstance suggests that subjects were also doubting their own judgment on some trials and using the confederates' responses as useful information. (pp. 547–548)

17. Group polarization may be due to the tendency of like-minded people to present arguments favoring their own position but not the opposite view. As a result, each member will only be persuaded to hold his or her original position more firmly. This is an informational effect. The one-upmanship hypothesis, a normative hypothesis, suggests that people may try to outdo one another in the extremity of their support for the common view. People have been found to admire views that agree with their own but are more extreme. (pp. 550–552)

*Self-Test 2*

1. **c.** (p. 532)

2. **b.** (p. 537)

3. **c.** (pp. 535–536)

4. **d.** (pp. 535–536)

5. **c.** According to Robert Zajonc, the presence of others can lead to either social facilitation or social interference, depending on the task. If the task is well-learned, simple, or instinctive, social facilitation results. Zajonc explains the difference in terms of the increased arousal produced when others are present. High arousal typically improves performance on simple, well-learned tasks and harms performance on complex, poorly learned tasks. (p. 543)

6. **d.** (p. 546)

7. **b.** (p. 548)

8. **b.** (p. 550)

9. **b.** Both a. and b. are normative hypotheses about the causes of group polarization. (p. 551)

10. **a.** (p. 552)

11. **c.** (p. 554)

12. **a.** (p. 555)

13. **b.** (pp. 557–558)

14. **c.** This is another way of saying that he established positive goal interdependence. (p. 558)

15. **a.** (p. 558)

16. Stanley Milgram had subjects take the role of teacher, while the role of learner—supposedly played by another subject—was actually played by a confederate of the experimenter. The learner was placed in a separate room and the real subject stayed with the experimenter. The subject's job was to read questions on a verbal-memory test and to shock the learner when he made an error. (The shocks were, of course, not real.) As

the experimental session progressed, the shock level was increased and the learner began to show signs of distress, then to scream for the shocks to stop, and finally to fall silent. If the subject hesitated to continue the shocks at any point, the experimenter responded with firm prompts demanding cooperation.

Sixty-five percent of subjects continued to the highest level of shock, despite apparent reluctance to do so. This result has been partially explained in terms of subjects' preexisting beliefs about the appropriateness of obeying authorities. Another factor that seems to be important is the degree to which the experimenter appears to accept responsibility. In a similar experiment in which subjects were told they should accept responsibility for the learner's welfare, obedience was sharply reduced. (pp. 537–540)

17. In a variety of tasks, the presence of others has been found to improve performance relative to performance when subjects are alone. This well-established effect is known as social facilitation.

However, another well-established effect appeared at one time to contradict social facilitation. Social interference is a frequently replicated phenomenon in which the presence of others causes performance to worsen relative to performance when subjects are alone.

Robert Zajonc suggested that the task determines which phenomenon will result. Social facilitation will occur when tasks are dominant (for example, well-learned or simple), whereas social interference will occur when tasks are nondominant (for example, unfamiliar or complex). The underlying explanatory concept is arousal. The presence of other people increases physiological arousal. High arousal is known to affect simple or well-learned tasks positively and complex or unfamiliar tasks adversely. According to Zajonc, subjects are innately aroused by the presence of other members of their species. Other psychologists believe the increased arousal in humans is due to evaluation anxiety. (p. 543)

# CHAPTER 16 THEORIES OF PERSONALITY

*Read the introduction below before you read the chapter in the text.*

Psychologists use the term *personality* to mean an individual's general style of interacting with the world, especially with other people. Theories of personality are efforts to systematically describe and explain variations among people in this general style of behaving. Some personality theories depend primarily on clinical information, others on laboratory experiments, and still others on psychometric tests.

Freud's personality theory and his approach to psychotherapy are both called psychoanalysis, which is considered a psychodynamic theory—that is, one that focuses on mental forces. In this theory, unconscious motivation is the main cause of behavior; people are often unaware of or wrong about their true motivations because sex and aggression—the chief forces motivating us, according to Freud—are unacceptable to the conscious mind. However, free association, dreams, and mistakes such as speech errors (Freudian slips) can give clues to the contents of the unconscious.

The mind, in Freud's view, consists of three often conflicting divisions—the pleasure-oriented id; the reality-oriented ego; and the superego, which incorporates an internalized version of societal rules. One job of the ego is to reduce anxiety, sometimes through self-deceptive defense mechanisms. Freud regarded personality in terms of people's characteristic ways of channeling their mental energy. He described five psychosexual stages of personality development, the first three of which (oral, anal, and phallic) were considered the most critical.

Some of Freud's followers, such as Alfred Adler, Karen Horney, Carl Jung, and Erik Erikson, eventually split off to develop theories of their own. These theories, collectively called post-Freudian psychodynamic theories, retain Freud's core idea of unconscious mental forces, but differ in their emphasis on social needs, self-esteem, and psychological wholeness.

All psychodynamic theories are unified by a central idea—that people are powerfully influenced by the interplay of unconscious mental forces. They collectively criticized for the limitations of their clinical data and for their vague terms and untestable concepts.

Humanistic theories of personality were born out of a conviction that behaviorism and Freudian psychoanalysis, considered dominant forces at the time, dehumanized people. Humanistic theories emphasize those characteristics of people that are uniquely human. They typically have a phenomenological orientation, which means that they emphasize subjective mental experience; they are generally holistic; and they are concerned with people's tendency to actualize themselves, that is, to grow and to realize their potential. Carl Rogers and Abraham Maslow are pioneers of this approach. Critics of these theories tend to point out their scientific shortcomings and romanticized view of human nature.

Social cognitive theories of personality are distinguished by their strong connections to traditional areas of laboratory research, such as learning, cognition, and social influence. These theories emphasize objective behavioral data, use cognitive constructs as personality variables, assert the importance of learning in the social environment, and insist on considering personality variables in the context of specific situations. Julian Rotter's concept of locus of control, the tendency to believe that rewards are or are not usually controllable by one's own efforts, is an example of a cognitive construct used as a personality variable. A related idea is Albert Bandura's concept of self-efficacy, the belief in one's own ability to perform specific tasks. Research suggests that a positive, optimistic outlook is associated with various benefits. Social cognitive theories tend to be criticized for lacking holism and for emphasizing cognition at the expense of drives and emotions.

Unlike the theories just discussed, trait theories focus on describing individual differences; to do so, they attempt to specify the most fundamental traits underlying personality. A trait is a relatively stable predisposition to behave in a certain manner. Trait

238

theorists distinguish between surface traits, which are linked directly to observable behaviors, and source traits, which are the most basic dimensions of personality. Trait theorists typically collect data using paper-and-pencil questionnaires and subject the results to factor analysis. Using this general approach, Raymond Cattell has described personality in terms of sixteen dimensions, while Hans Eysenck has claimed that only two dimensions are really necessary. Many trait researchers today believe that there are five basic traits, which they call the Big Five. Three major issues for trait theorists are the consistency of traits over situations, their consistency over time, and their heritability. Trait theories have been criticized for problems of measurement validity, oversimplification, and an overemphasis on biological determinism.

> LOOK over the table of contents for this chapter in your textbook before you continue with your study.

> Notice that there are focus questions in the margins of the text for your use in studying the material. The following chart lists which study guide questions relate to which focus questions.

# The Integrated Study Workout

> Complete one section at a time.

## Psychodynamic Theories   (pages 566–579)

> CONSIDER these questions before you go on. They are designed to help you start thinking about this subject, not to test your knowledge.

Are we generally aware of why we do what we do?

Can our dreams tell us anything about ourselves that we don't already know?

Why do people experience mental conflict?

We all use the term *ego*, but what does it really mean?

What needs besides those involving sex and aggression have been considered important motivators of people's thoughts and behaviors?

Is Freud's theory truly scientific?

> READ this section of your text lightly. Then go back and read thoroughly, completing the Workout as you proceed.

George is shy, Susan reckless, and Sam friendly. As social beings, we are constantly making judgments about people's personalities—that is, about their style of interacting with the world in general and other people in particular. Psychologists seek to understand personality in a more formal, systematic way.

1. What is a personality theory?

   *It is a formal attempt to describe & explain the ways in which people differ in their general style of behavior*

2. List four elements that are included in most personality theories.

   a. *motivating forces / drives - underlie behavior*
   MOTIVATION

   b. *mental structures / components of the mind, interpret environment & make decisions that guide behavior*
   COGNITION

   c. *the ways in which personalities/traits can differ from one another, motivating force or mental structure*
   INDIVIDUAL DIFFERENCES

   d. *ways in which such personality differences develop from birthhood to adult-hood*
   DEVELOPMENT

3. One way to categorize personality theories is in accordance with the kinds of evidence on which they are based. Identify the category of theory described in each of the following cases.

*Laboratory based* a. theories based on experimental studies of learning, cognition, and social influence

*Clinical-Based* b. theories developed primarily by psychotherapists on the basis of their intimate knowledge of clients

*Psychometrically based-theories* c. theories that result from statistical analyses of responses to questionnaires

Sigmund Freud's theory of personality and his approach to psychotherapy are both referred to as psychoanalysis. It would be difficult to exaggerate the impact of Freud's thought on modern psychology.

4. Freud's psychoanalysis is the prime example of a psychodynamic theory. What does the term *psychodynamic* mean?

*force/energy - personality theories that emphasize the interplay of mental forces*

5. Explain the most basic idea in Freud's theory.

*the main causes of behavior lie deeply buried in the unconscious mind - the part of the mind that affects the individual's conscious thought & action.*

6. Define the term *libido* and describe its function. Why does it have such broad importance in human life, according to Freud?

*Instinctive force - that under lies the pleasure seeking & life seeking drive becomes redirected & provides the mental energy that motivates a wide range of thoughts & actions that at the surface do not appear to be sexual.*

7. Freud was also interested in the drive of *aggression*.

In Freud's view, a patient could be helped only if the contents of his or her unconscious mind were revealed.

8. Characterize Freud's general approach for revealing the unconscious. What aspects of thought and behavior did he consider to be the best clues?

*analyzing certain aspects of their speech - psychoanalysis - treat behavior as clues to the unconscious.*
*elements of thought & behavior that are least logical would provide best clue*

9. Complete the following statements about specific techniques Freud used to obtain clues.

a. In the technique of *free association*, Freud had his patients relax and report without reservation every image or idea that came to mind.

b. Why did Freud regard dreams to be informative? Distinguish between the manifest and latent content of a dream. Are all dream symbols Freudian symbols? Explain.
*- conventional logic is largely absent & forces that normally hold down unconscious role as are weakened.*
*- latent - underlying unconscious meaning*
*- manifest - as it is consciously experienced & remembered by the dreamer*
*- no - only the ones which are universal*

c. Freud also followed another route to the unconscious—by analyzing everyday behaviors, especially *mistakes - slips of the tongue*

Freud proposed that the mind is divided into three interacting, and often conflicting, components.

10. Describe each of these divisions of the mind, including its content, origin, and general function.

a. id *- mental energy, set of drives which person is born, only goal gratification pleasure principle (avoid pain) - no wrong/right. reality & fantasy not different. primary process.*

b. ego *- reality principle.*

c. superego

11. Distinguish between the primary and the secondary process. With which division of the mind is each associated?

12. Briefly describe the relationship between the divisions of the mind and the conscious-unconscious distinction. (See Figure 16.2 on text page 570.)

According to Freud, the ego has the greatest direct control of conscious thought and behavior.

13. How does the ego exert its influence?

14. Label the following.

_____ a. the unpleasant feeling accompanying the ego's sense of impending danger

_____ b. the ego's fear of threats in the real world

_____ c. the ego's fear of the id's irrational wishes

_____ d. the ego's fear of the guilt that the superego can produce

15. What is a defense mechanism? Does the ego have alternative means of accomplishing the same purpose? Explain.

16. Define each of the following defense mechanisms.

a. repression

b. displacement and sublimation

c. reaction formation

d. projection

e. rationalization

17. Which is considered the most fundamental defense mechanism? Why is it regarded as such?

18. Indicate which defense mechanism each of the following individuals is using.

_____ a. Garth is partying too much to get his studying done. He tells himself that he needs a lot of relaxation in order to handle the pressure of school.

_____ b. Yolanda is a sculptor who loves to take a piece of stone and carefully chisel it into a smooth, curving form.

_____ c. Eric unconsciously harbors great hostility but instead perceives that his brother Joe is hostile.

Freud saw personality as emerging from the interaction of children's wish-fulfilling behaviors and the reactions those behaviors elicit from parents and other people. He described the development of personality in terms of a series of five psychosexual stages, the first three being the most important.

19. By what age is an individual's basic personality fixed, according to Freud? Does behavior continue to change after that point? Explain.

20. What is an erogenous zone?

21. Define the term *fixation*. What can produce fixation?

22. Describe each of the following psychosexual stages and, where appropriate, indicate the consequences of fixation.

    a.  oral

    b.  anal

    c.  phallic (for boys)

    d.  phallic (for girls)

    e.  latency

    f.  genital

Freud's ideas sparked the imaginations of many and quickly led to the formation of an international society of psychoanalysts. However, some of those who were counted among his followers later became his theoretical opponents.

23. What were some of the objections that led these theorists to split from Freud and develop their own theories?

24. List three core elements of Freudian theory retained by post-Freudians.

    a.

    b.

    c.

25. What characteristics shared by these post-Freudian psychodynamic theories differentiate them from Freud's theory?

Freud believed that people are essentially asocial, being held together in society only because of their needs. Most post-Freudian psychodynamic theorists instead regard people as fundamentally social and as motivated by needs that go beyond the sexual and aggressive drives that Freud emphasized.

26. Define the term *ego-social needs*.

27. Describe two concepts in Karen Horney's theory that illustrate her emphasis on ego-social needs.

28. How did ego-social needs fit into Erikson's theory?

The need for self-esteem, which can be counted as a social need, is given special emphasis by post-Freudian psychodynamic theorists, particularly by Alfred Adler and Karen Horney.

29. Briefly discuss Adler's concept of inferiority and superiority complexes.

30. Define Horney's concepts of the ideal self and the real self and discuss how they affect self-esteem.

Psychological wholeness is another central concept of post-Freudian psychodynamic theories.

31. Briefly discuss Carl Jung's notion of the self (similar to the ego) as a force for personality integration.

A major avenue of personality research inspired by the psychodynamic approach involves the exploration of people's defensive styles.

32. Briefly summarize the method and results of Robert Sears's study of projection.

33. What are repressers and how do they respond differently from others to emotional stimuli?

34. How is defensive style related to a healthy, satisfying life, according to George Vaillant's research?

35. Discuss two broad criticisms of psychodynamic theories in general, and Freud's theory in particular.

a.

b.

36. Present three positive effects of Freud's theory.

a.

**b.**

**c.**

*Humanistic Theories*   (pages 580–585)

> *CONSIDER these questions before you go on. They are designed to help you start thinking about this subject, not to test your knowledge.*

What do people mean when they say such things as "I just want to know who the real me is"?

How can parents and educators promote learning and creativity?

What does a person need in order to fulfill his or her own potential?

> *READ this section of your text lightly. Then go back and read thoroughly, completing the Workout as you proceed.*

The founders of humanistic psychology objected to what they saw as the dehumanizing conceptions of people inherent in behaviorism and Freudian psychoanalysis, then considered the dominant forces in psychology. Theorists from this alternative perspective proposed to counter with a "Third Force" concentrating on the uniquely human aspects of the person.

1. Explain each of these themes of humanistic psychology.

    **a.** phenomenological approach

    **b.** holistic view of the person

    **c.** the actualizing tendency

The personality theory of Carl Rogers, one of the most influential representatives of humanistic psychology, often is called *self theory* because of its focus on the individual's sense of self.

2. In Rogers's view, the most general goal that people have when they enter therapy is to become

_____ .

3. Explain how incongruence and conditions of worth can cause one not to be oneself.

4. What is the main goal of psychotherapy, according to Rogers? How does the therapist help the client toward this goal?

5. How would ideal parents respond to their children, in Rogers's view?

6. Explain the implications of Rogers's views for education and for the development of creativity. Is there any research support for Rogers's position? Explain.

As a humanistic psychologist, Abraham Maslow is distinguished by the fact that he was not a psychotherapist. Like psychotherapists, however, he sought to gain a deep understanding of particular individuals; unlike psychotherapists, he devoted his attention to psychologically healthy people. His main interest was in self-actualization.

7. Complete the five levels of Maslow's hierarchy of needs.

highest level  _____

                      _____

                      _____

                      _____

lowest level  _____

8. With regard to the hierarchy of needs, what must one do in order to become a self-actualizing person?

9. How do Maslow's needs fit with those emphasized by psychodynamic theorists?

10. In what sense do Maslow and Freud disagree about the prerequisites for creativity?

11. How did Maslow attempt to understand the characteristics of the self-actualizing person? List a few of the characteristics that Maslow felt were shared by self-actualizers. (See Table 16.1 on text page 584.)

12. Why is Maslow's work vulnerable to the charge of being unscientific?

Humanistic psychology has had widespread cultural influences, affecting views on education, parenting, and psychotherapy, and inspiring the human-potential movement. It has been criticized on a number of grounds, however.

13. Describe the main criticisms of humanistic psychology.

a.

b.

c.

## Social Cognitive Theories  (pages 586–591)

*CONSIDER these questions before you go on. They are designed to help you start thinking about this subject, not to test your knowledge.*

How could personality be studied in the laboratory?

Who experiences more anxiety—people who believe that their own efforts determine their rewards or those who believe that rewards are controlled by external factors?

Does a person's belief about his or her ability to perform a task affect actual performance?

READ *this section of your text lightly. Then go back and read thoroughly, completing the Workout as you proceed.*

Social cognitive theories (also called social learning or social cognitive learning theories) are closely tied to laboratory research on learning, cognition, and social influence. In general, this approach is informed not by the perspective of a clinician, but by that of a laboratory scientist interested in objective measurement and prediction of behavior. Pioneers in this approach to personality are Julian Rotter, Albert Bandura, and Walter Mischel.

1. Explain the basic tenets of social cognitive theories by elaborating on the following phrases.

   a. cognitive constructs as the basis for personality

   b. learning in the social environment

   c. situational specificity of personality variables

The cognitive constructs most often studied in the social cognitive approach to personality involve expectancies. An example is Rotter's locus of control.

2. What led Rotter to conclude that people's beliefs about their ability to control rewards affects their behavior?

3. Explain locus of control as a personality trait.

4. Describe some correlational data consistent with the concept of locus of control.

Another cognitive construct in social cognitive theory is Bandura's concept of self-efficacy.

5. Define the term *self-efficacy* and distinguish it from locus of control. Do the two usually go hand in hand (for example, internal locus of control and high self-efficacy)? Give an example of a case in which they don't.

6. Is self-efficacy positively correlated with performance on tasks? Does it play a causal role? Support your answer.

Many people believe that positive thinking has numerous benefits.

7. Does psychological research support this notion?

8. What is some evidence that a positive outlook correlates with other positive outcomes?

9. How might positive thinking produce positive effects?

The social cognitive perspective on personality has many strong points, including its emphasis on the situational specificity of personality characteristics, its focus on conscious beliefs, and the objectivity of its data. However, two criticisms arise from the limitations of the laboratory method (which is, ironically enough, also an important advantage of these theories).

10. Present the two most common criticisms of social cognitive theory.

   a.

   b.

## Trait Theories and Psychometric Research
(pages 591–601)

*CONSIDER these questions before you go on. They are designed to help you start thinking about this subject, not to test your knowledge.*

Is a person either honest or dishonest? friendly or unfriendly? conscientious or not conscientious?

Can the fundamental ways in which personalities differ be efficiently summarized in terms of two dimensions? in terms of five? Or does it take many more dimensions to do the job?

Can we predict that a person who is polite in dealing with employers will be polite with store clerks? with children? with coworkers?

Will a person who is suspicious today tend to be suspicious 20 years from now?

How much of a role does heredity play in determining the personality differences among individuals?

*READ this section of your text lightly. Then go back and read thoroughly, completing the Workout as you proceed.*

Unlike the personality theories covered so far, trait theories have the description of individual differences in personality as their main purpose. They provide formal ways of describing and measuring such differences. Though the other theories consider individual differences, they are primarily designed to explain behavior in terms of human motives and goals.

1. Define the term *trait* and distinguish traits from states. Are traits all-or-none characteristics—that is, does a person have a trait or not have a trait? Explain.

2. How can we tell if someone has a trait? Are traits directly observable?

3. Distinguish between surface and source traits. Give an example of each and explain how source traits can be identified.

4. What is the goal of most trait theorists? What means do they generally use to achieve this goal?

Raymond Cattell, a pioneer of the trait approach to personality, describes personality in terms of sixteen dimensions, or source traits. (Hint: See Table 16.3 on text page 594.)

5. What are L-data and Q-data? How did Cattell collect and use them in developing his theory?

**6.** Describe the results of Cattell's research.

Hans Eysenck took an approach similar to Cattell's, but used factor analysis differently and produced a theory involving far fewer source traits.

**7.** Describe the two dimensions of Eysenck's theory and indicate the surface traits associated with each extreme on the continuum.

  **a.** introversion-extroversion

  **b.** neuroticism-stability

**8.** The Eysenck Personality Inventory classified people into four groups: _____ ,

_____ , _____ ,

and _____ . (See Figure 16.7 on text page 595.)

**9.** Eysenck contended that personality differences among people are related to inherited physiological characteristics. In what way? How did he explain the underlying reasons for differences in introversion-extroversion? Cite evidence supporting this view.

Some trait theorists consider Cattell's theory too complex and Eysenck's too simple. Factor-analytic studies using more sophisticated procedures have produced results that are remarkably consistent, even when testing was conducted in different countries, with different languages, or with children rather than adults.

**10.** What are the "Big Five"? What do they have in common with Eysenck's two dimensions?

If you are honest when you detect a bank error in your favor, does that necessarily mean that you will be honest on tests or with your doctor? A point of controversy in trait theories concerns the consistency of traits across situations. The position of trait theorists is that they are consistent, a view disputed most adamantly by social cognitive theorists.

**11.** State the basic premise of trait theories that underlies their position on the issue of consistency.

**12.** Summarize Walter Mischel's argument against the trait theorists' position.

**13.** How did the results of a study by Hartshorne and May support Mischel?

**14.** How did Mischel and Peake study the trait of conscientiousness? What did they conclude? Explain.

**15.** What counterarguments to Mischel's position have trait theorists presented?

**16.** How would you assess the outcome of the debate overall?

A second theoretical issue concerns consistency of traits over time. The question is essentially whether our personalities will remain the same a year from now, 5 years from now, or even 40 years from now. Longitudinal studies are needed to answer this type of question.

**17.** What general conclusion have researchers reached about the consistency of traits over time? Describe some specific findings that support this view.

How heritable are personality traits? As with the heritability of other characteristics, such as intelligence, twin and adoption studies have been key to answering the question.

**18.** Describe the most common approach to studying the heritability of personality traits. What is the usual finding? What possible flaw in methodology calls into question the results of such studies?

**19.** How did David Lykken and his colleagues get around the methodological pitfalls of other twin studies? Were their results consistent with other studies? What were two surprising findings?

Like every other approach to personality, trait theories have been the target of criticism.

**20.** Present the major criticisms of trait theory by elaborating on the following phrases.

**a.** the problem of measurement validity

**b.** traits as oversimplifications

**c.** overemphasis on biological determinants

*Be sure to READ the Concluding Thoughts at the end of the chapter. Note important points in your Workout. Then consolidate your learning by answering the focus questions in the margins of the text.*

*After you have studied the chapter thoroughly, CHECK your understanding with the self-test that follows.*

# Self-Test 1

*Multiple-Choice Questions*

1. A personality theory based on paper-and-pencil questionnaires and statistical procedures for compiling and analyzing the results of those questionnaires is said to be:
   a. laboratory-based.
   b. clinically based.
   c. psychometrically based.
   d. psychodynamically based.

2. In Freud's theory, the instinctive force underlying the main pleasure-seeking and life-seeking drive is:
   a. the superego.
   b. sublimation.
   c. libido.
   d. basic anxiety.

3. Freud believed that the best clues to the contents of a person's unconscious are those elements of thought and behavior:
   a. that are least logical.
   b. that are most logical.
   c. for which the person can offer no explanation.
   d. that most clearly signal a lack of self-esteem.

4. According to Freud, reality and fantasy are not differentiated in dreams, which thus represent the closest we come to consciously experiencing:
   a. the primary process.
   b. the secondary process.
   c. reaction formation.
   d. the superego.

5. Brian believes that he intensely dislikes Alicia because his real love for her is unacceptable to him. Brian is using a defense mechanism called:
   a. sublimation.          c. reaction formation.
   b. projection.           d. fixation.

6. Most post-Freudian psychodynamic theories are similar to one another and different from Freudian psychoanalysis in their emphasis on:
   a. early childhood experiences.
   b. social needs.
   c. the role of anxiety.
   d. unconscious mental forces.

7. An emphasis on phenomenology is especially characteristic of _____ theories of personality.
   a. psychoanalytic       c. trait
   b. social cognitive      d. humanistic

8. According to humanistic psychology, the overriding, holistic purpose of individuals is:
   a. actualization, the direction for which must be environmentally determined.
   b. actualization, the direction for which must be determined from within the individual.
   c. the development and maintenance of self-esteem, which is possible only in a humane environment.
   d. the development and maintenance of self-esteem, which must come from within the individual, regardless of the environment.

9. Which of the following statements about theoretical views of creativity is correct?
   a. Both Freud and Maslow believed that people create because they have been unable to satisfy a more basic need.
   b. Both Freud and Maslow believed that people are free to create only after their more basic needs are relatively satisfied.

   c. Unlike Freud, Maslow believed that people are free to create only after their more basic needs are relatively satisfied.
   d. Unlike Maslow, Freud believed that people are free to create only after they have rejected lesser needs, such as those for social acceptance.

10. The theoretical approach to personality that has been criticized for having an overly romantic view of human nature is:
    a. humanistic psychology.
    b. post-Freudian psychodynamic theories.
    c. social cognitive theories.
    d. Freudian psychoanalysis.

11. Louise believes that whether she gets into graduate school depends primarily on her own efforts; she also believes that she can succeed in this endeavor. Louise appears to have an _____ locus of control and to be _____ in self-efficacy.
    a. external; high        c. external; low
    b. internal; low         d. internal; high

12. The approach to personality that has most emphasized the situational specificity of personality variables is:
    a. post-Freudian psychodynamic theory.
    b. trait theory.
    c. social cognitive theory.
    d. humanistic theory.

13. Which of the following is true of traits as they are seen from the perspective of trait theory?
    a. A trait is a characteristic that a person either has or doesn't have in all-or-none fashion.
    b. Trait and state are equivalent terms, but the former is applied to cognitive characteristics, whereas the latter is applied to motivational and emotional characteristics.
    c. Traits are characteristics of the person rather than of the environment.
    d. Traits are temporary, changeable characteristics that can be inferred from current behavior patterns.

14. What technique did trait theorists Raymond Cattell and Hans Eysenck apply to the questionnaire data they collected?
    a. factor analysis
    b. free association
    c. projection
    d. neuropsychological assessment

15. Research generally shows that central personality traits such as introversion-extroversion:

a. are quite stable over the course of adult life.

b. are not at all stable over the course of adult life.

c. are stable prior to middle age but relatively unstable thereafter.

d. are relatively unstable prior to middle age but stable thereafter.

## Essay Questions

16. Discuss Abraham Maslow's approach to the study of personality and describe his views on the hierarchy of needs and on self-actualization.

17. Describe the aims of trait theorists. How do the "Big Five" fit in with these aims? Discuss two criticisms of trait theories.

*After you have assessed your understanding on the basis of Self-Test 1 and have tried to strengthen your preparation in any areas of weakness, GO ON to Self-Test 2.*

# Self-Test 2

## Multiple-Choice Questions

1. A personality theory that emphasizes the importance of mental energy or forces in shaping personality and determining thought and behavior would by definition be a _____ theory.
   a. social learning
   b. psychodynamic
   c. trait
   d. psychoanalytic

2. In order to gain information about the contents of a patient's unconscious mind, Freud used all of the following as sources of data *except*:
   a. dreams.
   b. questionnaires.
   c. free association.
   d. instances of forgetting.

3. According to Freud, the division of the mind that includes an internalization of society's moral rules is the _____ and that which includes a conscious understanding of reality is the

   _____ .

   a. id; superego
   b. ego; id
   c. ego; superego
   d. superego; ego

4. In Freud's psychoanalytic theory, fixation occurs when a person:
   a. consciously experiences the conflict associated with a given stage of psychosexual development.
   b. experiences too little gratification at a particular stage of psychosexual development.
   c. experiences too much gratification at a particular stage of psychosexual development.
   d. does either b. or c.

5. According to Alfred Adler, an inferiority complex represents:
   a. an inability to overcome the normal feeling of inferiority that accompanies the dependence of early childhood.
   b. a mask for unacceptable feelings of superiority that arise from sexual and aggressive drives.
   c. a failure to recognize the difference between one's real self and one's ideal self.
   d. an exaggerated tendency to compare ourselves to others and an overreliance on other people's judgments of our worth.

6. A major criticism leveled against Freud's psycho-analytic theory is that it:
   a. lacks holism.
   b. overemphasizes cognitive constructs.
   c. is unscientific.
   d. overemphasizes the social environment.

7. Carl Rogers believed that when people feel they are not themselves (as they often do), it is because they sense:
   a. incongruence between their self-concept and their actual thoughts or behavior.
   b. incongruence between their own ideal self and that most respected by their culture.
   c. conflict between the anima (the female side of the person) and the animus (the male side of the person).
   d. conflict between the phenomenological self and the actualizing self.

8. Maslow differed from other humanistic psycholo-gists in that he:
   a. based his theory primarily on factor-analytic studies.
   b. devoted his attention to psychologically healthy people.
   c. produced objectively testable scientific hypotheses.
   d. did not see needs as primary determinants of personality.

9. The theoretical approach to personality that most emphasizes objective observations of people's actual behavior is _____ theory.
   a. psychoanalytic    c. social cognitive
   b. trait             d. humanistic

10. Suppose experimenters give subjects a series of problems that are, unbeknownst to the subjects, unsolvable. Some subjects are led to believe that they are able to solve the problems but others are not manipulated in this way. The results show that those who are led to believe that they can succeed work longer on the problems. This exper-iment illustrates the effects of:
    a. locus of control.
    b. self-efficacy.
    c. self-actualization.
    d. self-esteem.

11. Social cognitive theories have been criticized for:
    a. a lack of scientific testability.
    b. a lack of holism.
    c. the influence of personal bias.
    d. an overemphasis on drives and emotions.

12. Which of the following statements about traits is correct?
    a. Only source traits are linked directly to specif-ic, observable behaviors.
    b. A number of related surface traits must be identified in order to infer the existence of a given source trait.
    c. Source traits are biological predispositions, whereas surface traits are those traits due pri-marily to learning.
    d. Source traits are enduring characteristics, whereas surface traits are transitory states.

13. Hans Eysenck proposed that differences in the arousability of the central nervous system cause the observed differences in _____ , which he considers one of the two basic dimensions of personality.
    a. neuroticism-stability
    b. openness-nonopenness
    c. introversion-extroversion
    d. dominance-submissiveness

14. Hartshorne and May studied dishonesty in chil-dren in a variety of situations. They found that children tended to behave:
    a. consistently both within a given type of situa-tion and across situations, a finding that sup-ports the views of trait theorists.
    b. consistently both within a given type of situa-tion and across situations, a finding that sup-ports the views of social cognitive theorists.
    c. consistently within a given type of situation but not across different situations, a finding that supports the views of trait theorists.
    d. consistently within a given type of situation but not across different situations, a finding that supports the views of social cognitive the-orists.

15. David Lykken and his colleagues have studied _____ and found evidence of high heritability for _____ .
    a. twins raised apart, as well as twins raised together; virtually every personality trait assessed
    b. twins raised apart, as well as twins raised together; very few of the personality traits assessed
    c. families that have adopted two children, some twin and some nontwin biological siblings; virtually every personality trait assessed
    d. families that have adopted two children, some twin and some nontwin biological siblings; very few personality traits assessed

*Essay Questions*

**16.** What is the purpose of anxiety, according to Freud? Distinguish among reality anxiety, neurotic anxiety, and moral anxiety. Define the term *defense mechanisms* and describe two specific defense mechanisms, providing examples for each.

**17.** Describe two characteristics shared by Freudian and post-Freudian psychodynamic theories and two characteristics that differentiate post-Freudian psychodynamic theories from Freud's psychoanalysis.

# Answers

*Psychodynamic Theories*

**3. a.** laboratory-based, **b.** clinically based, **c.** psychometrically based

**7.** aggression

**9. a.** free association

**c.** mistakes (especially slips of the tongue)

**14. a.** anxiety

**b.** reality anxiety

**c.** neurotic anxiety

**d.** moral anxiety

**18. a.** rationalization

**b.** sublimation

**c.** projection

*Humanistic Theories*

**2.** their real selves

**7.** highest to lowest: self-actualization needs; esteem needs; belongingness and love needs; safety needs; physiological needs

*Trait Theories and Psychometric Research*

**8.** introverted-neurotic; introverted-stable; extroverted-neurotic; extroverted-stable

*Self-Test 1*

**1. c.** (p. 565)

**2. c.** (p. 567)

**3. a.** Freud wanted to learn what lay behind the consistent, rational explanations so readily offered by the conscious mind. He assumed that what was *least* logical in a person's speech or behavior was most likely to represent the irrational, sometimes troubling contents of that person's unconscious.  (p. 567)

**4. a.** (p. 569)

**5. c.** In reaction formation, an individual perceives his or her true feelings as their opposites—experiencing hate where there is love or love where there is hate, for example. In projection, the feeling is perceived accurately but is attributed to someone else. Sublimation is a redirection of unacceptable urges into culturally valued channels. (p. 572)

**6. b.** (p. 575)

**7. d.** (p. 580)

**8. b.** (p. 581)

**9. c.** Freud believed that creativity stems from libido that is not satisfied in more basic ways, such as sex. Maslow believed that creativity is only possible once more basic needs are relatively satisfied. (p. 584)

10. **a.** (p. 585)

11. **d.** Louise believes that her success in graduate school admission will be determined by her own efforts; that means she has an internal locus of control. She also believes that those efforts will be enough to gain her admission; that means she has high self-efficacy. (pp. 587–589)

12. **c.** The position of the social cognitive theorists is most strongly disputed by the trait theorists, who rest their entire approach to personality on the existence of stable, enduring traits—behavioral predispositions that remain essentially the same across situations. (pp. 587, 597)

13. **c.** (p. 592)

14. **a.** (pp. 594–595)

15. **a.** (p. 599)

16. Abraham Maslow, unlike many other humanistic psychologists, was not a psychotherapist. His approach to personality research was clinical in that he sought to understand people through prolonged in-depth contact; he differed from many clinically based theorists in choosing to study psychologically healthy people rather than troubled people.

    Maslow's hierarchy of needs ranks different categories of needs from the lowest to the highest: physiological needs, such as the need for food; needs for safety, such as the need for shelter from rain or snow; belongingness and love needs, such as the need for family or friendship; esteem needs, such as the need for respect from others; and needs for self-actualization, such as the need for self-expression. Maslow felt that people must essentially meet these needs in order, seeing that lower needs are at least relatively satisfied before moving on to other needs.

    Like other humanistic psychologists, Maslow was particularly interested in self-actualization, the ability to use one's potential to the fullest. Maslow attempted to characterize the self-actualizing person by selecting people he felt to be clearly in this category and studying them through interviews or, when necessary, through biographies and public documents. He drew up a list of characteristics that seemed to be common among such self-actualizers. Some have criticized Maslow's approach as a circular one in which he chose subjects based on his prior approval of their personal qualities, such as democratic values or identification with all of humanity. (pp. 583–584)

17. Most personality theorists wish to describe human personality in terms of the inner drives, beliefs, and goals that shape it. For them, explaining individual differences in these terms is secondary. Trait theorists, in contrast, are primarily interested in individual differences. Their aim is to discover the most basic dimensions along which personality varies, to efficiently describe individual differences in terms of a limited set of characteristics or traits. Traits are assumed to be relatively stable predispositions to behave in a particular way.

    The usual method for revealing these traits involves the factor analysis of questionnaire data. Different theorists have collected data in somewhat different ways and have identified different numbers and types of basic dimensions. The "Big Five" are a set of five dimensions that have consistently turned up in modern factor-analytic studies. Introversion-extroversion is an example of one of the Big Five. There is fairly good consensus among trait theorists that individual differences in personality can be described in terms of differences along these different dimensions.

    Trait theories have been criticized for their failure to show that what people say on questionnaires is reliably and sensibly related to actual behavior. For example, if I check off a number of adjectives or otherwise rate myself in ways that indicate I am honest, does that mean I will try to return a wallet packed with cash or report all my tip income on my tax return? In fact, trait theories have paid little attention to this issue. A second criticism is that trait theories oversimplify what is really a very complex matter; perhaps personality cannot be adequately described in the way trait theorists attempt to describe it. (pp. 591–592, 596, 600–601)

*Self-Test 2*

1. **b.** Psychoanalytic theories are one type of psychodynamic theory. (p. 566)

2. **b.** Questionnaires are used by trait theorists. (pp. 567–568)

3. **d.** (pp. 569–570)

4. **d.** (p. 572)

5. **a.** Adler suggested that the need to overcome the sense of inadequacy can in some cases lead to a superiority complex. (p. 576)

6. **c.** (p. 579)

7. **a.** (p. 582)

8. **b.** (p. 583)

9. **c.** Though trait theorists systematically collect data, it is typically questionnaire data. They do

not generally attempt to make connections between what people *say* on questionnaires and how people actually *behave*. (p. 586)

10. **b.** Studies like this suggest that self-efficacy may have some causal effect on performance. (p. 589)

11. **b.** (pp. 590–591)

12. **b.** (pp. 592–593)

13. **c.** (pp. 595–596)

14. **d.** (p. 597)

15. **a.**  By including identical twins reared apart, Lykken and his colleagues avoided the methodological pitfall of some other studies of identical twins. If identical twins are reared together, they are not only genetically identical, but may also be treated more alike than fraternal twins are; thus, it would be hard to separate genetic and environmental contributions to their similarities in personality. (pp. 599–600)

16. In Freud's model of personality, the ego has the job of responding to the demands of the world, the id, and the superego. These demands are felt by the ego in terms of anxiety, a feeling of impending danger. The attempt to reduce anxiety causes the ego to direct thought or behavior in particular ways. Thus, anxiety essentially propels the ego. Reality anxiety is produced by the demands of the real world, such as the need to avoid being locked outdoors during a blizzard. Neurotic anxiety is the ego's sense of danger posed by the irrational demands or desires of the id, such as the desire to strike someone who has angered us. Moral anxiety represents the ego's fear of the guilt that the superego can produce, such as the guilt that might arise from lying.

Defense mechanisms are one means through which the ego reduces anxiety. All defense mechanisms involve some form of self-deception. The most basic defense mechanism is repression, in which the ego exerts pressure to push anxiety-provoking material out of consciousness. Reaction formation is a defense mechanism in which we perceive our true feelings as their opposite. For example, if someone is jealous of his brother's accomplishments, he may behave as if he is excessively proud of or happy about those accomplishments. (pp. 570–572)

17. The personality theorists who developed post-Freudian psychodynamic theories generally retained some essential elements of Freud's psychoanalysis. One such element was an emphasis on the unconscious. Both Freud and those followers who broke away from his theory held that a person's conscious thought and behavior are determined by unconscious mental forces. The post-Freudians also shared with Freud the view that unconscious mental forces exert their influence through the production of anxiety.

Post-Freudian psychodynamic theorists differ from Freud in several regards. A major difference is their emphasis on social needs. Whereas Freud believed that the drives of sex and aggression were at the root of virtually all human thought and behavior, the post-Freudians believed that this emphasis neglected important aspects of personality. They viewed people as inherently social beings and attempted to explain personality in terms of specifically social drives. For example, Karen Horney discussed the need for security, which is fulfilled socially, usually through the influence of the child's parents. The post-Freudians also placed a stronger emphasis than Freud did on psychological wholeness. Freud's theory was most explicit about the conflicts among different divisions of the personality, whereas the post-Freudians tried to explain the integration of the personality. (pp. 574–576)

# CHAPTER 17 MENTAL DISORDERS

▌ *Read the introduction below before you read the chapter in*
▌ *the text.*

The concept of a mental disorder is not sharply or clearly defined. Practical guidelines introduced by the American Psychiatric Association help clinicians to decide when a given set of symptoms represents a mental disorder, but leave "gray" areas in which arbitrary distinctions are necessary. The predominant biological/medical approach to mental disorders asserts that they *are* or *are analogous to* physical diseases. Freud's psychoanalytic perspective, for example, regards mental disorders as analogous to physical diseases, suggesting that they occur when mental conflict produces more anxiety than a person can effectively cope with. Major alternatives to the biological/medical view include the cognitive-behavioral perspective, which stresses learning and thought patterns, and the sociocultural perspective, which emphasizes the effects of the values, norms, and psychological pressures that prevail in a given culture.

Regardless of their perspective, theorists agree that mental disorders have multiple causes, which can be divided into three categories—predisposing, precipitating, and maintaining. The scientific study of mental disorders has led not only to the categorization of causes but to the categorization of the disorders themselves. *DSM-III* and *DSM-IV*, the standard diagnostic guides prepared by the American Psychiatric Association, divide disorders into different classes according to their objective symptoms. Studies have shown that, for a variety of reasons, males and females tend to be diagnosed differently. The labeling involved in making a diagnosis can affect a person's self-concept, the way others view him or her, and even the person's chances of recovery.

Anxiety disorders have anxiety or fear as their most prominent symptom. They include generalized anxiety disorder, which involves a high degree of relatively unfocused anxiety; phobias, which are intense, irrational fears of specific objects or events; obsessive-compulsive disorder, which involves repetitive

thoughts and actions; panic disorder, in which people have unpredictable attacks of overwhelming terror; and post-traumatic stress disorder, which may strike the survivors of extremely traumatic experiences such as plane crashes or wars.

Mood disorders fall into two general categories—depressive disorders (major depression and dysthymia), in which the problem is downward mood swings, and bipolar disorders, in which mood swings both downward and upward. The best-established biological theory about the cause of depressive disorders implicates underactivity at synapses where the neurotransmitters are monoamines, but conflicting evidence makes this theory controversial. Other perspectives suggest that depression involves learned helplessness and a particular style of attributing negative experiences. Research on bipolar disorder and cyclothymia indicates that it is strongly influenced by genes; however, neither the environmental nor the biological factors that may induce the mood swings have been identified. Another mood disorder, seasonal affective disorder, seems to be more environmentally triggered.

People with somatoform disorders experience some type of bodily ailment that is not due to a physical disease. These disorders are particularly difficult to diagnose because it is not always possible to determine whether symptoms are of mental or physical origin. In conversion disorders, a person loses some bodily function, such as sight or sensation in the hand; somatoform pain disorder involves pain in some part of the body; somatization disorder involves a history of vague medical complaints; and hypochondriasis is characterized by an unwarranted preoccupation with one's physical health.

Behavior and emotions can not only cause physical symptoms with no physical basis; they can also affect the onset or course of a real physical malady. Research has shown that psychological factors can increase the chances of catching a cold and may affect the cardiovascular and immune systems.

Psychoactive substance-use disorders include, as the name indicates, problems of abuse or dependence on drugs. The most common such disorder involves alcohol abuse and/or dependence. Research indicates that there may be more than one type of alcoholism and that heritability for alcoholism is greater for males than for females. Learning mechanisms, beliefs about the positive value of the drug, and cultural pressures in favor of or against drug use play important roles in these disorders.

Dissociative disorders involve an inability to recall some period of one's life. The simplest form of this disorder is psychologically induced amnesia; the most severe form is multiple personality. A person with multiple personality disorder may manifest quite distinct personalities at different times. Research indicates that this disorder is much more common in women than men and represents an attempt to cope with severe childhood abuse.

Schizophrenia is a serious mental disorder characterized by cognitive or perceptual disortions and by a deterioration from a former level of functioning. Symptoms may include delusions, hallucinations, formal thought disturbances, social withdrawal, bizarre behavior, and flattened affect. Schizophrenia is associated with an unusual pattern of activity at synapses where dopamine is the neurotransmitter. A person's predisposition to schizophrenia may be increased by prenatal stress and birth traumas. Sociocultural factors, while they do not affect incidence of the disorder, do appear to affect the chances of recovery.

*LOOK over the table of contents for this chapter in your textbook before you continue with your study.*

*Notice that there are focus questions in the margins of the text for your use in studying the material. The following chart lists which study guide questions relate to which focus questions.*

| Focus Questions | Study Guide Questions |
| --- | --- |
| Basic Concepts and Perspectives | |
| 1–2 | 1–3 |
| 3–4 | 4–7 |
| 5 | 8–10 |
| 6–7 | 11–17 |
| 8 | 18–19 |
| 9 | 20–21 |
| Anxiety Disorders | |
| 10–15 | 1–20 |
| Mood Disorders | |
| 16–20 | 1–13 |
| 21–22 | 14–17 |
| Somatoform Disorders | |
| 23–24 | 1–5 |
| Psychological Factors Affecting Medical Condition | |
| 25–27 | 1–4 |
| Psychoactive Substance-Use Disorders | |
| 28–30 | 1–7 |
| Dissociative Disorders | |
| 31 | 1–5 |
| Schizophrenia | |
| 32–33 | 1–3 |
| 34–36 | 4–10 |

## Basic Concepts and Perspectives (pages 605–616)

*CONSIDER these questions before you go on. They are designed to help you start thinking about this subject, not to test your knowledge.*

What are mental disorders? Are they illnesses with biological causes, learned patterns of maladaptive thought and behavior, or something else altogether?

Is the prevalence of particular mental disorders the same from one culture to another?

Why are men diagnosed with specific mental disorders, and women with others?

How might labeling a person with a mental disorder affect other people's treatment of him or her? Can it affect the judgment of trained clinical observers?

*READ this section of your text lightly. Then go back and read thoroughly, completing the Workout as you proceed.*

Everyone's psychological processes are subject to disturbances of one kind or another in the normal course of living. We may experience a temporary lack of motivation that makes it difficult to keep up with our work or relationships. Anxiety may seem to tie us in knots, keeping us from sleeping, concentrating, or even enjoying our favorite activities. Confusion may overtake us, making clear, orderly thought seem beyond our grasp. But the disturbances that are a normal part of life differ from those that characterize mental disorders in intensity, duration, and frequency and in the extent to which they disrupt the individual's life.

1. Complete the following statements.

   a. A _____ is any characteristic of a person's actions, thoughts, or feelings that could potentially indicate a mental disorder.

   b. A _____ is the entire pattern of symptoms manifested by a given individual.

2. What three criteria must a syndrome satisfy to be classified as a mental disorder, according to the American Psychiatric Association?

   a.

   b.

   c.

3. Is mental disorder a precisely and unambiguously defined concept? Explain.

Various perspectives on mental disorders describe disorders differently and think about their causes in different ways.

4. Answer the following questions about the biological/medical perspective (or medical model), which is the dominant perspective in Europe and North America.

   a. How are the assumptions of this model evident in the language associated with it?

   b. The mental health professionals most likely to accept the medical model are

      _____ ; _____

      are less likely to accept it.

   c. Describe two versions of the medical model and indicate which fits best with the diagnostic manual of the American Psychiatric Association.

5. Answer the following questions about Freud's psychodynamic perspective, also known as psychoanalysis.

   a. How is Freud's perspective related to the medical model?

   b. What causes mental disorders, according to Freud?

6. Answer the following questions about the cognitive-behavioral perspective.

   a. Describe the focus of the two traditions that have today merged into the cognitive-behavioral perspective.

b. How does the language of those who adopt this perspective reflect their viewpoint?

c. From this perspective, what are so-called mental disorders?

According to the sociocultural perspective, mental disorders are products not only of the person and the immediate environment but also of the culture in which the person develops.

7. Are there cultural differences in the prevalence of particular symptoms and syndromes? Explain.

Regardless of their perspective on mental disorders, all theorists acknowledge that disorders have multiple causes. These causes can be divided into three categories.

8. Define each of the following types of causes.

a. predisposing causes

b. precipitating causes

c. maintaining causes

9. Classify each of the following examples as a predisposing, precipitating, or maintaining cause.

_____ a. Jackie has more freedom to behave in socially unacceptable ways because many people think such behavior is due to her disorder and beyond her control.

_____ b. Winona's best friend has committed suicide, which has caused Winona to fall into a deep and long-lasting depression.

_____ c. Because of his bizarre behavior, Jeremy has been treated unkindly by strangers and rejected by friends, which makes his recovery more difficult.

_____ d. Ted has a genetically inherited susceptibility to schizophrenia.

_____ e. From early childhood on, Emma has learned to believe that life is hard and that there is little she can do to affect whatever happens to her.

10. How is the degree of predisposition to a mental disorder related to the amount of stress that will bring on the disorder?

The scientific study of mental disorders demands that we have some system for assigning them to specific categories. Categorization is important for learning about causes, treatments, and outcomes. From the perspective of the medical model, the assignment of labels is called *diagnosis*.

11. The _____ of a diagnostic system is the extent to which different diagnosticians, all trained in the system, reach the same conclusions when independently diagnosing the same individuals.

12. Distinguish between *neuroses* and *psychoses*. What inadequacy in these categories led the American Psychiatric Association to develop the original *DSM*?

13. Specify the overriding goal of the group that developed *DSM-III*. Describe how the creators attempted to reach that goal in *DSM-III* (and *DSM-IV*). Has the goal been achieved? Explain.

14. The _____ of a diagnostic system reflects the extent to which the categories it identifies are clinically meaningful.

15. Can we say with confidence that the diagnostic categories of *DSM-III* (and *DSM-IV*) are valid? Explain. What basic procedure is used in research on the validity of diagnostic categories?

16. How is the validity of *DSM* dependent upon its reliability?

17. How can research lead to enhanced validity for *DSM* categories?

How common are mental disorders? The National Institute of Mental Health has undertaken a large-scale study of the prevalence of mental disorders in the United States. Although males and females are similar in the overall prevalence of disorders, they differ in the specific types of diagnoses they tend to receive.

18. Women are more likely than men to be diagnosed with _____ and _____ disorders, while men are more likely than women to be diagnosed with _____ and other _____ disorders.

Although gender differences in diagnosis may be due to biological factors, they may also result from sociocultural factors.

19. Briefly discuss three sociocultural hypotheses offered to explain these differences. For each, present supporting research evidence.

    a.  differences in tendency to report or suppress psychological distress

    b.  bias in diagnosis

    c.  differences in stressfulness of men's and women's experiences

Labeling has important clinical and scientific uses, but it also has certain drawbacks.

20. Describe some evidence that labels can have harmful effects.

**21.** What partial solution to the problem of labeling has been suggested by the American Psychiatric Association?

## Anxiety Disorders   (pages 617–621)

*CONSIDER these questions before you go on. They are designed to help you start thinking about this subject, not to test your knowledge.*

Anxiety seems to prevail in contemporary Western culture, so where do we draw the line between normal anxiety and anxiety that indicates a disorder?

Do people with irrational fears realize that their fears are irrational?

Are men and women equally likely to be diagnosed with phobias about spiders or snakes? about public speaking or meeting new people?

What is it like to experience a panic attack?

What kinds of obsessions and compulsions do people with this disorder experience? Are they fundamentally different from the obsessions and compulsions that most people experience at times?

Why were Vietnam veterans more likely than veterans of World War II to develop post-traumatic stress disorders?

*READ this section of your text lightly. Then go back and read thoroughly, completing the Workout as you proceed.*

Evolution has equipped us to experience fear, an emotion with adaptive value. But because we are complex, thinking creatures living in cultural environments that present a variety of real and imagined threats, our fear can be triggered in circumstances in which it is not adaptive. In anxiety disorders, fear or anxiety is the most prominent symptom.

**1.** Are the terms *fear* and *anxiety* used interchangeably? Explain.

**2.** In comparison to other disorders, how easy are anxiety disorders to treat and how good are the chances of recovery?

*DSM-IV* recognizes five subclasses of anxiety disorders. In generalized anxiety disorder, the anxiety is attached to a variety of threats, real and imagined, rather than to one specific threat.

**3.** In addition to anxiety itself, what are some other symptoms of the disorder? What is the most common complaint?

**4.** How prevalent is generalized anxiety disorder? Does everyone who experiences generalized anxiety have the disorder? Explain.

**5.** Describe the typical etiology of the disorder.

**6.** What might the sociocultural perspective tell us about the high incidence of generalized anxiety?

A phobia is a type of anxiety disorder in which an intense, irrational fear is clearly associated with a specific category of object or event.

7. Distinguish between simple and social phobias and give examples of each. At what stage of life does each type of phobia tend to originate? Which type of phobia is much more common in one gender than the other?

8. Do people who have phobias fail to realize that their fears are irrational? Explain.

9. We do not really know what causes phobias; however, several hypotheses have been offered. Answer the following questions about these hypotheses.

   a. How have behaviorists generally explained the development of phobias? Why is this explanation problematic?

   b. What is Martin Seligman's position on this issue and what observation does his theory help to explain?

   c. Can phobias take different forms in different cultures? Explain.

Another class of anxiety disorder is obsessive-compulsive disorder.

10. Distinguish between obsessions and compulsions.

a. A(n) _____ is a disturbing thought that intrudes repeatedly on a person's consciousness even though the person recognizes it as irrational.

b. A(n) _____ is a repetitive action usually performed in response to an obsession.

11. Compare and contrast obsessive-compulsive disorder with a phobia.

12. Are the obsessions of people with the disorder similar to those experienced by people who do not have the disorder? Do compulsions always bear a logical relation to the obsessions that trigger them? Explain.

13. Briefly state how each of the following types of theorists view obsessive-compulsive disorder and present relevant evidence where possible.

   a. behavioral theorists

   b. cognitive theorists

   c. biologically oriented theorists

People with panic disorder are subject to feelings of helpless terror that strike unpredictably and without any connection to specific environmental threats.

14. Describe a typical panic attack. Is the individual generally free of anxiety between attacks? Explain. What type of phobia do most panic-attack victims develop?

15. Present evidence suggesting that heredity can predispose individuals to panic disorder.

16. Do environmental events play a role in the onset of the disorder? Explain.

17. How are cognitive factors involved in panic disorder?

Post-traumatic stress disorder differs from other anxiety disorders in that it is clearly connected to one or more traumatic experiences in the affected person's life.

18. Describe the kinds of traumas that most commonly lead to post-traumatic stress disorder.

19. What are the typical symptoms of the disorder? Do they always occur immediately after the traumatic experience? Explain.

20. The rate of post-traumatic stress disorder has been much higher in U.S. veterans of the Vietnam War than in U.S. veterans of World War II. Why might this be so?

*Mood Disorders* (pages 621–627)

*CONSIDER these questions before you go on. They are designed to help you start thinking about this subject, not to test your knowledge.*

Are biological factors important in determining who suffers from depressive disorders and who doesn't?

Can certain patterns of thinking make people more prone to depression?

Why don't people who experience severe depression just pull themselves out of it?

Is there any truth to the popular notion that moodiness and creativity are associated?

*READ this section of your text lightly. Then go back and read thoroughly, completing the Workout as you proceed.*

Some days we seem to experience life through a haze of sadness that affects our view of everything and everyone; at other times, we are full of laughter, warmth, and great expectations, impervious to the frustrations and worries that normally beset us. Moods are a part of normal psychological experience, but if they are too intense or prolonged, as in mood disorders, they can be harmful.

1. Define mania.

2. Identify and briefly describe the two main categories of mood disorders.

   a.

**b.**

3. How is depression related to generalized anxiety?

Depression can powerfully affect a person's feelings, thoughts, and actions.

4. What are the symptoms of depression? When is a diagnosis of a depressive disorder warranted, according to *DSM-IV*?

5. Distinguish between major depression and dysthymia. What is double depression?

6. In terms of overall prevalence, major depression and dysthymia are quite _____ ; the prevalence differs for men and women, with _____ being diagnosed with both more often.

Much biologically oriented research on depression has focused on the role of neurotransmitters called monoamines.

7. What is the basic contention of the monoamine theory of depression? What findings led to its proposal?

8. Why is the validity of the monoamine theory still in question?

Depression may also be related to stressful experiences.

9. What did Andrew Billings and his colleagues find in their interviews of depressed men and women?

10. Explain Martin Seligman's learned helplessness theory of depression and show how it may be compatible with the monoamine theory.

11. What kind of observation provided a starting point for cognitive theories of depression? Illustrate the cognitive perspective by noting Aaron Beck's conclusions regarding depressed clients.

12. Answer the following questions about Lyn Abramson and Martin Seligman's hopelessness theory of depression.

    **a.** What does the theory share with Seligman's earlier theory of learned helplessness? What new point is added in hopelessness theory?

b. Describe the attributional style associated with depression in this theory.

c. Is there evidence to show that this attributional style is *correlated* with depression? that it *causes* depression? Explain.

13. What is the vicious triangle of severe depression? Which therapy is related to which corner of the triangle?

In addition to the unipolar disorders of major depression and dysthymia, *DSM-IV* identifies bipolar disorders (commonly called manic-depression), which involve both upward and downward mood swings.

14. Describe bipolar disorders and distinguish between bipolar disorder and cyclothymia.

15. Answer the following questions about manic episodes.

a. Characterize the manic episodes of bipolar disorders.

b. Cite evidence suggesting that the mild to moderate mania found in cyclothymia is associated with enhanced creativity.

c. What are some negative effects of mania?

16. Comment on the heritability of bipolar disorders.

17. Seasonal affective disorder (SAD) is different from both bipolar disorder and cyclothymia. Describe SAD, its cause and its treatment.

## Somatoform Disorders   (pages 627–629)

*CONSIDER these questions before you go on. They are designed to help you start thinking about this subject, not to test your knowledge.*

How can we tell the difference between bodily ailments with physical causes and those that stem from psychological causes?

Can a person experience a problem as severe as blindness or paralysis for psychological reasons?

*READ this section of your text lightly. Then go back and read thoroughly, completing the Workout as you proceed.*

People with somatoform disorders experience physical ailments—even ailments as extreme as blindness or paralysis—that are not due to physical diseases.

1. Identify the four types of somatoform disorders described in *DSM-IV* by correctly labeling the following descriptions.

_____ a. A person with this disorder has a long history of dramatic complaints about many different medical conditions, most of which are vague and unverifiable, such as dizziness or nausea.

_____ **b.** A person with this disorder reports pain in some part of the body.

_____ **c.** A long-term, unwarranted preoccupation with physical health and a belief that every minor ailment signals the presence of a serious disease characterize this disorder.

_____ **d.** In this disorder, a person temporarily loses some bodily function—such as vision, hearing, or motor functions, in more dramatic cases.

2. Why are somatoform disorders so difficult to diagnose?

3. What is the psychodynamic view of conversion disorder? Illustrate this perspective by describing the case of Baer, a young construction worker, in psychodynamic terms.

4. Describe evidence that conversion disorders can be explicitly related to real environmental threats or traumatic experiences.

5. How are somatoform disorders viewed from the sociocultural perspective? How has this thinking been applied to chronic fatigue syndrome?

## *Psychological Factors Affecting Medical Condition*   (pages 629–632)

*CONSIDER these questions before you go on. They are designed to help you start thinking about this subject, not to test your knowledge.*

Can our minds really affect our vulnerability to physical ailments?

Can we learn to fight disease by changing our pattern of emotional response?

*READ this section of your text lightly. Then go back and read thoroughly, completing the Workout as you proceed.*

*DSM-IV* notes that the mind can influence the onset or progress of a disease that has a physical basis. The psychological factors that affect a person's medical condition are not, strictly speaking, disorders but have been the focus of research because of their potentially important health consequences.

1. What was Friedman and Rosenman's original hypothesis about the relationship between personality and heart disease? Describe their evidence for this hypothesis.

2. Summarize the more recent view of the relationship between Type A behavior and heart disease.

3. Describe some evidence that emotional distress can increase our chances of getting a cold. Explain how this effect could be mediated by the immune system.

4. Is there evidence to suggest that psychological state can affect one's survival of a serious illness such as cancer? Explain.

b. withdrawal effects

c. permanent effects

## Psychoactive Substance-Use Disorders  (pages 632–635)

> CONSIDER these questions before you go on. They are designed to help you start thinking about this subject, not to test your knowledge.

What is the most commonly abused drug?

Do some people have a hereditary predisposition to alcoholism?

How can people's beliefs or expectations make them more vulnerable to drug abuse?

> READ this section of your text lightly. Then go back and read thoroughly, completing the Workout as you proceed.

A psychoactive substance is a drug that can affect the way we feel, think, and behave. Psychoactive substance-use disorders involve the abuse of or dependence on such drugs.

1. Distinguish between *drug abuse* and *drug dependence*. Which term is synonymous with *addiction*?

Psychoactive substances exert their influences on mood, emotion, perception, thought, and behavior by affecting the functioning of the brain.

2. Define each of the following types of drug effects and illustrate them through the effects of alcohol, the most comonly abused drug.

a. intoxicating effects

3. Is alcohol abuse and/or dependence heritable? Explain. Are there gender differences in the heritability of alcoholism?

Behavioral theorists attempt to explain psychoactive substance-use disorders in terms of conditioning.

4. How might operant and classical conditioning each play a part in alcoholism or other drug addictions?

Cognitive theorists focus on the importance of beliefs or expectancies concerning drugs such as alcohol.

5. Describe research evidence that teenagers' beliefs about alcohol can lead to predictions about who will later abuse alcohol.

6. Studies have shown that a change in the way someone uses alcohol may represent a serious step toward alcoholism. Explain that change. On the basis of such findings, M. Lynne Cooper and her colleagues have proposed two predisposing causes of alcoholism. What are they?

Some theorists point out that the beliefs that can make people susceptible to addiction arise in a particular social and cultural context.

7. Present some observations that are consistent with the sociocultural view.

## Dissociative Disorders   (pages 635–637)

> CONSIDER these questions before you go on. They are designed to help you start thinking about this subject, not to test your knowledge.

What kind of person is most likely to develop multiple personalities?
What kind of life experience may cause the disorder to develop?

> READ this section of your text lightly. Then go back and read thoroughly, completing the Workout as you proceed.

Can you imagine losing all memory of your life up to this point and going on to establish a new identity? Can you envision yourself having an additional personality within you that sometimes shows itself in the external world without your knowing anything about it? Dissociation is a psychological process in which a person is unable to recall a period of his or her life, or able to recall it only under special conditions.

1. How might dissociative disorders be related to hypnosis?

*DSM-IV* distinguishes dissociative disorders in terms of their complexity. (Note: One of the most common errors people make regarding mental disorders is to confuse multiple personality disorder with a very different type of disorder, schizophrenia. Because this error is so often perpetuated by the media and in conversation, you may want to take special care to correct it in your own thinking.)

2. Describe the following disorders, listed in order of increasing complexity.

   a.   dissociative amnesia

   b.   dissociative fugue

   c.   multiple personality disorder

3. Briefly comment on the dramatic increase in the number of reported cases of multiple personality disorder.

4. What profile of the individual with multiple personality disorder emerged from the long-term study by Philip Coons and his colleagues?

5. How might repeated abuse during childhood lead to multiple personality disorder? What may account for the fact that only some victims of severe childhood abuse develop multiple personality disorder?

## Schizophrenia   (pages 637–643)

> CONSIDER *these questions before you go on. They are designed to help you start thinking about this subject, not to test your knowledge.*

Are the hallucinations experienced by some people with schizophrenia related to normal mental imagery in people without the disorder?

How might people with schizophrenia differ biologically from people who do not have schizophrenia?

What kinds of environments may tend to be especially difficult for children with a genetic predisposition to schizophrenia?

> READ *this section of your text lightly. Then go back and read thoroughly, completing the Workout as you proceed.*

The term *schizophrenia* comes from the Greek words for "split mind." Schizophrenia involves a split in the mental processes, such that attention, perception, emotion, motivation, and thought become disorganized and fail to work together. Bizarre thoughts and behaviors can result. The disorder is both serious and relatively common, occurring in about 1 percent of people at some time during their lives. Recovery, partial or full, is sometimes possible.

1. Specify the two criteria necessary for a diagnosis of schizophrenia, according to *DSM-IV*.

2. Describe each of the following types of symptoms and identify specific forms that each may take in schizophrenia.

   a. delusions

   b. hallucinations

   c. formal thought disturbances

   d. negative symptoms

Individuals with schizophrenia manifest a wide variety of specific symptoms. Since Eugen Bleuler first gave the disorder its name, theorists have attempted to subclassify schizophrenia into different types.

3. Briefly describe two categorization systems and assess their success.

As with all other mental disorders, the question of causation in schizophrenia has provoked great interest but has not led to definitive answers. Biological causes are one area of active investigation. Recall from Chapter 3 that there is considerable evidence of a strong genetic component in susceptibility to schizophrenia. Other biological factors have also been studied.

4. Explain the dopamine theory of schizophrenia and describe early evidence consistent with it.

5. How and why has the original theory been modified?

6. What other brain abnormalities are sometimes manifested?

7. How might prenatal factors and birth traumas be implicated in schizophrenia?

Regardless of possible biological causes, schizophrenia is manifested and diagnosed primarily as a set of cognitive symptoms.

8. Distinguish between episode indicators and vulnerability indicators.

9. What is some evidence that a deficit in attention may be a predisposing cause of schizophrenia?

Research has provided evidence of cross-cultural consistency in the onset of schizophrenia.

10. What does the concept of expressed emotion refer to? How has it been used to explain cross-cultural differences in recovering from schizophrenia?

> Be sure to READ the Concluding Thoughts at the end of the chapter. Note important points in your Workout. Then consolidate your learning by answering the focus questions in the margins of the text.

> After you have studied the chapter thoroughly, CHECK your understanding with the self-test that follows.

## Self-Test 1

*Multiple-Choice Questions*

1. Which of the following statements is true?
   a. The terms *syndrome* and *symptom* are synonymous.
   b. A syndrome is the same thing as a mental disorder.
   c. A syndrome is the pattern of symptoms a person manifests.
   d. Syndromes are collections of related mental disorders, such as dissociative or anxiety disorders.

2. Research indicates that the susceptibility for schizophrenia involves a strong genetic contribution. Heredity would thus be considered _____ cause of schizophrenia.
   a. a predisposing
   b. a precipitating
   c. a maintaining
   d. both a predisposing and a maintaining

3. Studies show that the diagnostic categories established in *DSM-III* and *DSM-IV* have:
   a. both high reliability and high validity.
   b. low reliability but high validity.
   c. high validity, but the question of reliability is harder to answer.
   d. high reliability, but the question of validity is harder to answer.

4. Labeling people as mentally disordered:
   a. is essential to our ability to study disorders scientifically.

b. can affect their self-esteem as well as the way others treat them.

c. is sufficient to establish the validity of diagnostic categories, provided the scientific community generally agrees with these labels.

d. involves both a. and b.

5. A person with no other mental disorders experiences anxiety that is not attached to any particular threat. The anxiety persists for a prolonged period and disrupts the person's daily functioning. This person appear to be suffering from:

a. a simple phobia.

b. obsessive-compulsive disorder.

c. panic disorder.

d. generalized anxiety disorder.

6. Behaviorists have suggested that phobias are acquired through:

a. classical conditioning, which is consistent with the fact that most people with phobias can recall a specific experience that initiated their intense fear.

b. classical conditioning, which is questioned on the grounds that most people with phobias cannot recall a specific experience that initiated their intense fear.

c. operant conditioning, which is consistent with the fact that most people with phobias can recall a specific experience that initiated their intense fear.

d. operant conditioning, which is questioned on the grounds that most people with phobias cannot recall a specific experience that initiated their intense fear.

7. Feelings of worthlessness and loss of interest and pleasure in life are particularly characteristic of a person with:

a. anxiety.

b. depression.

c. mania.

d. dissociation.

8. Biological explanations of depression have centered on the idea that it involves:

a. reduced activity at synapses where monoamines are the neurotransmitters.

b. overactivity at synapses where monoamines are the neurotransmitters.

c. abnormally small cerebral ventricles.

d. abnormally large cerebral ventricles.

9. The hopelessness of depression combines the _____ and _____ perspectives.

a. sociocultural; behavioral

b. behavioral; cognitive

c. biological; behavioral

d. biological; cognitive

10. A disorder in which the person temporarily loses some bodily function—becoming blind, deaf, or paralyzed, in the most dramatic cases—is:

a. hypochondriasis.

b. hysteria.

c. somatization disorder.

d. conversion disorder.

11. Research suggests that alcohol dependence is:

a. not heritable.

b. more heritable in males than in females.

c. more heritable in females than in males.

d. more heritable in people of European ancestry than in those of Asian or African ancestry.

12. An extensive interview study by Philip Coons and his colleagues suggests that multiple personality:

a. develops as a way of coping with severe and repeated childhood abuse.

b. is not a real disorder but rather a product of the therapist's imagination.

c. is closely related to obsessive-compulsive disorder and shares a common biochemical basis with it.

d. is more common in people who are incapable of being hypnotized.

13. Katrina, who has been diagnosed with schizophrenia, reports that she has been sent from a parallel universe to study the people of Earth. Her statement clearly reflects:

a. a formal thought disturbance.

b. a delusion.

c. a hallucination.

d. flattened affect.

14. Evidence suggests that the hallucinations associated with schizophrenia are:

a. not related to normal mental imagery.

b. experienced as coming from inside the person's own head.

c. much more likely to be visual than auditory.

d. due to the enhancement of creative ability that occurs during active phases of the disorder.

15. Certain deficits in attention may be considered _____ for schizophrenia.

a. episode indicators

b. vulnerability indicators

c. predisposing causes

d. all of the above

*Essay Questions*

16. Describe the symptoms of bipolar disorders and distinguish two forms. Is there any truth to the notion that some people with bipolar disorders experience heightened creativity? Explain.

17. Discuss two different hypotheses concerning the biological causes of schizophrenia.

---

*After you have assessed your understanding on the basis of Self-Test 1 and have tried to strengthen your preparation in any areas of weakness, GO ON to Self-Test 2.*

# Self-Test 2

*Multiple-Choice Questions*

1. Anorexia nervosa is an example of a _____ and supports the _____ perspective.
   a. culture-bound syndrome; cognitive
   b. culture-bound syndrome; sociocultural
   c. somatoform disorder; cognitive
   d. somatoform disorder; sociocultural

2. Which of the following does *not* describe a maintaining cause of a mental disorder?
   a. Norman's anxiety has made him unable to work effectively, which has caused him to lose his job.
   b. Camilla's depression came on as she faced the unexpected demands of caring for her infant son.
   c. Bradley's family and friends openly believe it will be impossible for him to recover from schizophrenia.
   d. Burton's alcohol dependence has won him a great deal of attention and sympathy from his wife.

3. The major goal of the people who developed *DSM-III* and *DSM-IV* was to:
   a. more clearly distinguish neuroses from psychoses.
   b. define disorders in terms of their causes.
   c. increase the reliability of diagnostic categories.
   d. organize diagnostic categories in terms of the amount of anxiety they involve.

4. According to research evidence, gender differences in the prevalence of anxiety and mood disorders may be due to:
   a. the greater tendency of men to express their anxiety and distress.
   b. gender bias in the diagnosis of mental disorders.
   c. the greater likelihood that males in our society will experience the kinds of stress that contribute to these disorders.
   d. all of the above.

5. The type of anxiety disorder known as a simple phobia:
   a. is more common in males than in females.
   b. tends to develop in late abolescence or early adulthood.
   c. usually involves a fear of something that is feared to some extent by people who do not have a phobic disorder.
   d. tends to disappear once an individual recognizes the irrational nature of the fear.

6. The great majority of panic-attack victims develop _____ at some point after their first panic attack.
   a. a fear of the dark
   b. agoraphobia
   c. obsessive-compulsive disorder
   d. mania

7. Post-traumatic stress disorder is an example of a(n) _____ disorder.
   a. dissociative
   c. mood
   b. anxiety
   d. schizophrenia

8. In an extensive survey of people beginning treatment for depression, Andrew Billings and his colleagues found that they had:
   a. experienced more losses, such as divorces or deaths, during the previous year.
   b. fewer sources of prolonged pressure, such as medical problems or work pressures.
   c. sought much more emotional support from friends and relatives.
   d. done all of the above.

9. According to the hopelessness theory of depression, the people most prone to depression are those who attribute their negative experiences to causes that are:
   a. unstable and specific.
   b. stable and global.
   c. unstable and global.
   d. stable and specific.

10. Which of the following is the most severe type of manic-depressive mood disorder?
    a. dysthymia
    c. bipolar disorder
    b. major depression
    d. cyclothymia

11. SAD, seasonal affective disorder, is apparently due to seasonal changes in:
    a. temperature.
    c. sunlight.
    b. social interactions.
    d. precipitation.

12. Which of the following statements is true?
    a. Psychoactive substance-use disorders include drug abuse but not drug dependence.
    b. Psychoactive substance-use disorders include drug dependence but not drug abuse.
    c. Drug abuse and drug dependence are the same thing.
    d. Drug dependence equals drug addiction.

13. Longitudinal research has shown that nondrinking teenagers who believe that alcohol has valued effects—such as making a person more sociable—are:
    a. no more likely than other teens to become alcohol abusers within the next 2 years, a finding consistent with the cognitive perspective.
    b. no more likely than other teens to become alcohol abusers within the next 2 years, a finding that does not fit well with the cognitive perspective.

    c. more likely than other teens to become alcohol abusers within the next 2 years, a finding consistent with the cognitive perspective.
    d. more likely than other teens to become alcohol abusers within the next 2 years, a finding that does not fit well with the cognitive perspective.

14. Multiple personality is the most complex example of:
    a. schizophrenia.
    b. an anxiety disorder.
    c. a dissociative disorder.
    d. a somatoform disorder.

15. According to *DSM-IV*, the two kinds of symptoms necessary for a diagnosis of schizophrenia are:
    a. flattened affect and cognitive or perceptual distortion.
    b. cognitive or perceptual distortion and deterioration from a former level of functioning.
    c. social withdrawal and hallucinations.
    d. formal thought disturbance and delusions.

## Essay Questions

16. Discuss the relationship between mental disorders and normal psychological experiences. What are the American Psychiatric Association's criteria for determining that a particular syndrome represents a mental disorder?

**17.** Describe the sociocultural perspective on mental disorders and present two kinds of evidence that illustrate its value. Be certain to discuss the issue of labeling.

# Answers

## Basic Concepts and Perspectives

1. **a.** symptom, **b.** syndrome

4. **b.** psychiatrists; clinical psychologists

9. **a.** maintaining, **b.** precipitating, **c.** maintaining, **d.** predisposing, **e.** predisposing

11. reliability

14. validity

18. anxiety; mood; alcohol; drug-use

## Anxiety Disorders

10. **a.** obsession, **b.** compulsion

## Mood Disorders

6. common; women

## Somatoform Disorders

1. **a.** somatization disorder, **b.** somatoform pain disorder, **c.** hypochondriasis, **d.** conversion disorder

## Self-Test 1

1. **c.** A syndrome is labeled as a mental disorder by *DSM-IV* standards only if it meets certain criteria. (p. 605)

2. **a.** Although one's genetic endowment remains the same after one has developed a disorder, it is not considered a maintaining cause because the genes are not a *consequence* of the disorder. (p. 609)

3. **d.** (pp. 610–611)

4. **b.** Evidence suggests that labeling can change a person's self-esteem and the judgments of clinically trained observers. Additional evidence comes from the observation that people with schizophrenia in societies where negative reactions and expectations are associated with this label have poorer chances of recovery than those in societies without such negative associations. (p. 616)

5. **d.** (p. 617)

6. **b.** (p. 619)

7. **b.** (pp. 621–622)

8. **a.** (p. 622)

9. **b.** (pp. 623–624)

10. **d.** (p. 627)

11. **b.** (p. 633)

12. **a.** Coons and his associates also found that the disorder was much more common in women than in men. (pp. 636–637)

13. **b.** Katrina is showing evidence of a delusion, which is a false belief maintained despite compelling evidence against it. She would be reporting a hallucination if she said she heard voices telling her to learn more about earth people or to come back to her home universe. (p. 638)

14. **b.** (p. 638)

15. **d.** (p. 642)

16. Bipolar disorders (also called manic-depression) are mood disorders in which the individual has both downward mood swings, called depressive episodes, and upward mood swings, called manic episodes. The depressive and manic episodes vary in duration and the individual may experience relatively normal mood between episodes. Cyclothymia is the less severe form of the disorder and bipolar disorder is the more severe type.

    Depressive episodes involve the same symptoms found in major depression—a lack of interest in life, a reduced ability to experience pleasure, feelings of inadequacy and hopelessness, as well as effects on eating and sleeping. Manic episodes are typically characterized by feelings of confidence, energy, and power. Extreme mania may involve bizarre thoughts and potentially dangerous behaviors, while less severe manias may involve spending sprees, sexual adventures, or other behaviors that the person would not normally engage in and may later regret.

People who experience manic episodes often report feelings of enhanced creativity, and there may actually be some truth to that impression in the case of cyclothymia. Cyclothymia is unusually common in highly creative writers and artists, who appear to do much of their best work during manic phases. People with the more severe bipolar disorder do not appear to enjoy this enhanced creativity, perhaps because the extremity of their mania leads also to disorganized thinking and behavior. (pp. 625–626)

17. The major focus of biological interpretations of the cause of schizophrenia is dopamine, a neurotransmitter in the brain. The dopamine theory of schizophrenia holds that the symptoms of schizophrenia result from overactivity at synapses where dopamine is the neurotransmitter. Antipsychotic drugs, which reduce this activity, are effective in controlling the symptoms of schizophrenia. Drugs that increase activity at synapses involving dopamine can exaggerate existing schizophrenic symptoms or even bring them on.

However, not all research findings are clearly supportive of the dopamine hypothesis. For example, *clozapine*, a highly effective new antipsychotic drug, tends to affect dopamine to a lesser extent than traditional antipsychotics. A modified version of the dopamine hypothesis is that schizophrenia involves an unusual form of dopamine activity, one that might include underactivity in some areas and overactivity in others.

Other biological hypotheses focus on prenatal factors and birth traumas. The hypothesis involving prenatal factors is supported by evidence that, in cases of discordant identical twins, the twin who developed schizophrenia had a less favorable position in the uterus. The hypothesis involving birth traumas is supported by the finding that people with schizophrenia are more likely than others to have undergone a difficult birth, possibly involving oxygen deprivation or other forms of brain trauma. (pp. 640–642)

## Self-Test 2

1. **b.** (p. 608)

2. **b.** The unexpected demands of caring for her baby were a precipitating cause of Camilla's disorder. (p. 609)

3. **c.** To accomplish this end, they attempted to define disorders in terms of objective symptoms that could be reported by the client or observed by the clinician. The reliability of most diagnostic categories in *DSM-III* and *DSM-IV* is reasonably high, provided that the diagnostic criteria are carefully followed. (p. 610)

4. **b.** (pp. 613–614)

5. **c.** This illustrates the fact that many symptoms of mental disorders lie on a continuum with psychological experiences that are considered normal. Fears of such things as spiders, blood, or high places are commonplace, but people who have phobias about such things experience more intense fears that may cause them distress or may interfere with their lives. (p. 618)

6. **b.** (p. 620)

7. **b.** (p. 621)

8. **a.** (p. 623)

9. **b.** (p. 624)

10. **c.** Of the bipolar disorders mentioned, cyclothymia is the milder one. (p. 625)

11. **c.** (p. 626)

12. **d.** (p. 632)

13. **c.** (p. 634)

14. **c.** (p. 635)

15. **b.** (p. 638)

16. The difference between "normal" and "abnormal" is largely arbitrary. This is due in part to the fact that many symptoms associated with mental disorders differ from common psychological experiences not in kind but only in degree. For example, most of us feel unattractive, dejected, or unworthy at times. Such feelings are common in depressive disorders, but are generally more severe, long-lasting, and disruptive to the affected person's life. As another example, the delusions that distinguish schizophrenia from other mental disorders are false beliefs that persist despite compelling evidence to the contrary. Who among us is not to some degree holding on to a few beliefs that are irrational, that run counter to apparent fact? Our fears, erroneous perceptions, moods, and worries are similar in many cases to the symptoms of mental disorders.

The American Psychiatric Association has established certain criteria to help clinicians determine when that arbitrary line between the normal and the abnormal has been crossed. These criteria are: (1) that the syndrome (that is, the person's pattern of symptoms) must involve distress and/or impaired functioning serious enough to warrant professional treatment; (2) that the source of the distress lies within the person, not the environment; and (3) that the disturbance is not due purely to prejudice, poverty, or other social forces that may lead a person to behave contrary to social norms. Even with these guidelines, there is still considerable room for interpretation. We are probably all distressed by our feelings of depression, and we may find it harder than usual to function in our work or relationships, so how do we know when the distress or impaired functioning are serious enough to justify the label of mental disorder? (pp. 605–606)

17. The sociocultural perspective combines insights from various disciplines, including social psychology, sociology, and anthropology. It maintains that we cannot hope to fully understand mental disorders without taking into account the cultural contexts in which people are diagnosed. The culture in which people develop may exert a variety of influences—affecting people's values, their conception of what is normal and expected in society, their experience of certain pressures to act in certain ways or to avoid acting in other ways, even their opinions about what it means to have a mental disorder and whether recovery from that disorder is possible.

Labeling is an issue given considerable attention within this perspective. Sociocultural theorists point out the power of labeling someone as abnormal and as suffering from a given disorder. To label a person as having schizophrenia, for example, is to do more than indicate a diagnostic category for other clinicians to use in treating the individual. Labels can stigmatize. They can make an individual see him- or herself in a negative light, have less hope of recovering, and perhaps make less effort at recovery. They can also affect the way others deal with that person. Even clinicians may fall prey to the stereotypes that are cued by diagnostic labels. In one study, psychotherapists rated a man's level of adjustment more negatively if they believed he was a mental patient than if they believed he was not a mental patient. Other studies show that the chances of recovering from schizophrenia are better in societies that do not label sufferers in ways that stigmatize them and foist negative expectations on them. (pp. 608, 616)

# CHAPTER 18 TREATMENT

*Read the introduction below before you read the chapter in the text.*

For most of human history, people with serious mental disturbances have not received the care they needed; they have often been the victims of other people's ignorance and fear, as well as of their own disorders. Due in large part to nineteenth-century reformers such as Philippe Pinel and Dorothea Dix, as well as modern views on the needs and rights of people with mental disturbances, the treatment of the mentally ill is immensely better, but certainly not ideal. Although some research demonstrates that institutional treatment can be humane and effective, other research shows that the institutional environment can be dehumanizing. A move to deinstitutionalize people and return them to the community has only partially succeeded and has also created new problems.

People with serious mental problems may be treated not only in mental hospitals, but also in general hospitals, nursing homes, and halfway houses. People with less serious problems are more likely to seek help in community mental health centers and in the private offices of mental health professionals. Mental health professionals vary in their training and in the kinds of work they do; they include psychiatrists, clinical psychologists, counseling psychologists, counselors, psychiatric social workers, and psychiatric nurses.

Regardless of where treatment is given or who provides it, clinical assessment is necessary to decide what should be done for the patient or client. Assessment, which includes the initial information gathering required for diagnosis, is an ongoing process, and its goal is understanding the person seeking help in order to create an appropriate plan of therapy. The assessment interview is the most common assessment procedure, but objective questionnaires, psychometric personality tests, projective tests, behavioral monitoring, and neuropsychological assessment are often also used to supplement the interview.

Psychotherapy refers to any formal, systematic, theory-based approach in which a trained therapist uses psychological means to treat people with mental problems or disorders. Because there are so many varieties of psychotherapy, the chapter focuses on the most common forms of individual therapy. In individual therapies, a therapist works with one person at a time rather than a group or a family.

Psychoanalysts and other psychodynamically oriented therapists try to help people with neurotic symptoms to recall emotionally charged memories that have been mentally buried, on the assumption that relief of symptoms will follow. Some major tools of psychoanalysis are free association, dream analysis, and the phenomena of resistance and transference.

Humanistic therapies emphasize the person's need to grow toward his or her potential—in other words, to self-actualize. Therapy is intended to help the person gain control of his or her life by becoming conscious of inner feelings and desires, undistorted by external influences. Carl Rogers's client-centered therapy is the most common humanistic therapy. Rogers contended that the effective therapist shows empathy, positive regard, and genuineness toward the client.

Whereas psychodynamic and humanistic therapies are oriented toward the whole person, cognitive therapy is more problem centered. Cognitive therapists assume that much of the mental distress people suffer is due to maladaptive thinking patterns. For example, a client's depression may result from a tendency to minimize positive experiences or to misattribute negative experiences to personal deficiencies. The cognitive therapist's goal is to help the client replace such thinking patterns with more adaptive ones. Albert Ellis's rational-emotive therapy (RET) and Aaron Beck's cognitive therapy are well-established forms of the cognitive therapeutic approach.

Behavior therapy, rooted in the behaviorist principles of operant and classical conditioning, has close ties to cognitive therapy. In fact, to a considerable degree they have merged to form what is called cognitive-behavior therapy. Behavior therapy has been especially successful in the treatment of simple phobias. Three techniques, all involving exposure to the feared stimulus in order to extinguish the fear, are flooding, counter-conditioning, and systematic desensitization. Less effective and more controversial is aversion treatment to help clients overcome harmful habits. Other behavioral techniques include token economies, contingency contracts, assertiveness and social skills training, and modeling.

Does psychotherapy really work? By combining the results of many experiments, researchers have concluded that: (1) psychotherapy does work; (2) no one kind of psychotherapy is better overall, although some kinds of psychotherapy may work better than others for specific types of problems; and (3) nonspecific factors, such as support and hope, which are not unique to any particular psychotherapeutic approach, are important contributors to the effectiveness of therapy.

Biological treatments for mental problems include drugs, electroconvulsive shock therapy (ECT), and psychosurgery. Drugs, the most common type of biological treatment, are available to treat schizophrenia, depression, bipolar disorder, and anxiety. Some of these drugs present problems in the form of harmful side effects and addiction. ECT is an effective treatment for severe depression; although it can cause some memory loss, a newer form of the technique minimizes this problem. Psychosurgery is the most controversial and least often used of the biological treatments.

*LOOK over the table of contents for this chapter in your textbook before you continue with your study.*

*Notice that there are focus questions in the margins of the text for your use in studying the material. The following chart lists which study guide questions relate to which focus questions.*

| Focus Questions | Study Guide Questions |
|---|---|
| Care as a Social Issue | |
| 1–3 | 1–5 |
| 4 | 6–8 |
| Clinical Assessment | |
| 5–9 | 1–8 |
| Psychotherapies | |
| 10–16 | 1–10 |
| 17–20 | 11–14 |
| 21–23 | 15–17 |
| 24–29 | 18–24 |
| 30–34 | 25–30 |

| Biological Treatments | |
|---|---|
| 35 | 1–4 |
| 36–38 | 5–10 |

# The Integrated Study Workout

*Complete one section at a time.*

## Care as a Social Issue    (pages 647–651)

*CONSIDER these questions before you go on. They are designed to help you start thinking about this subject, not to test your knowledge.*

How were people with mental disorders "treated" in earlier times?

Are mental hospitals today generally doing all that can be done to help those with serious mental disturbances? What kinds of problems persist?

Besides psychiatric hospitals, where can people obtain treatment for mental problems?

What kinds of professionals offer mental health care?

*READ this section of your text lightly. Then go back and read thoroughly, completing the Workout as you proceed.*

The history of Western society's response to people with mental disorders is largely one of ignorance, prejudice, absence of compassion, and even cruelty. Through the Middle Ages and into the seventeenth century, seriously disturbed people were thought to be in league with the devil, and so were tortured and often killed. According to the more secular views of the eighteenth century, the mental problems of disturbed people were due to their own unworthiness and degeneracy. The places in which these people were shut away were scenes of misery and horror. Only in the nineteenth century did significant reforms begin.

1. Briefly describe the work of Philippe Pinel in Europe and Dorothea Dix in the United States.

2. What inspired the movement toward deinstitutionalization that began in the 1950s in the United States? What alternative approach to care was envisioned by supporters of this movement? Was the dream realized? Explain.

5. Describe the approach taken by community intervention programs for the severely disturbed. Does this approach work?

Though some mental hospitals today are genuinely therapeutic environments, problems persist. There is reason to hope, but there are also obstacles to overcome.

3. How did David Rosenhan and his colleagues approach the study of psychiatric hospitals? What conclusions did they reach?

4. Gordon Paul and Robert Lentz compared the effects of different treatment programs for very dysfunctional patients in a state mental hospital system. Describe the treatment programs and indicate their relative success.

   a. standard hospital treatment

   b. milieu therapy

   c. social learning therapy

Not everyone with psychological problems requires treatment in a psychiatric hospital or intensive community intervention programs. In fact, most people have relatively mild problems with anxiety or depression and receive care at other types of treatment facilities.

6. Identify each of the following settings that provide mental health care.

   _____ a. Many older, chronic mental patients who would once have been in a mental hospital live here, but often without benefit of care from mental health personnel.

   _____ b. This facility offers custodial care for patients who require it and brief hospitalization for people experiencing acute psychotic attacks.

   _____ c. This is usually the treatment place of choice for people who can afford it and who do not need hospitalization.

   _____ d. The majority of psychiatric inpatients are treated in this type of facility, which is usually associated with less stigma than a psychiatric hospital and is often well located for visits from family and friends.

   _____ e. This place provides transitional living arrangements for people returning to the community after hospitalization.

   _____ f. This offers free or low-cost services such as psychotherapy or crisis hotlines and may also hold classes, sponsor legislation, or do other work aimed at prevention of mental health problems.

The people who provide mental health treatment vary considerably in the nature and extent of their training and in the kinds of people they tend to treat.

7. List three types of mental health professionals who hold a doctoral degree and indicate those characteristics that differentiate them from one another.

   a.

   b.

   c.

8. List three types of mental health professionals who have bachelor's or master's degrees and indicate those characteristics that differentiate them from one another.

   a.

   b.

   c.

## Clinical Assessment   (pages 651–655)

> CONSIDER these questions before you go on. They are designed to help you start thinking about this subject, not to test your knowledge.

How do clinicians learn enough about a person to choose an appropriate therapeutic approach?

Are projective tests such as the Rorschach valid?

How can a person be tested to determine whether apparent mental problems have physical causes?

> READ this section of your text lightly. Then go back and read thoroughly, completing the Workout as you proceed.

How does a clinician know what a person with a mental health problem really needs? How does he or she know whether the current treatment is working? Clinical assessment is the *ongoing* process through which the mental health professional gathers the information needed to treat a person effectively. Although it generally includes an initial diagnosis, clinical assessment is a much broader enterprise designed to help the person providing treatment understand the person seeking it. Clinicians with different theoretical perspectives often disagree about the kind of information most useful to them in assessment.

1. The most common assessment procedure is the assessment _____, in which the client may talk about _____ , _____ , and personal history. _____ behaviors may also be taken into account.

2. Characterize objective questionnaires and point out some of their advantages.

Psychometric personality tests, designed to measure a wide range of personality characteristics, are objective questionnaires developed through psychometric methods. The one most often used for clinical assessment is the Minnesota Multiphasic Personality Inventory, or MMPI.

3. How was the MMPI developed? Why was the original version often criticized?

4. Briefly describe the new version of the test (MMPI-2). Be sure to mention clinical and content scales, the *L* scale, and the *F* scale.

Projective tests are intended to provide information about the client's unconscious wishes and beliefs.

5. What is the rationale for and the general nature of projective tests?

6. Briefly describe two projective tests and discuss the validity of such assessment techniques.

Behavior therapists are especially likely to use behavioral monitoring but they are not the only clinicians who do.

7. Define behavioral monitoring. Briefly describe an example of the form known as self-monitoring.

In some cases, psychological problems may be symptomatic of brain damage. When a clinician suspects this, neuropsychological assessment may be needed.

8. Name the following neuropsychological assessment techniques.

_____ a. A battery of tests that includes assessment of motor control, perception, and cognition.

_____ b. Pictures of brain sections are produced when the brain is subjected to a strong magnetic field.

_____ c. Multiple brain x-rays are taken from various angles and analyzed by computer.

_____ d. Electrodes attached to the scalp indicate patterns of electrical activity in the brain.

## Psychotherapies (pages 656–678)

*CONSIDER these questions before you go on. They are designed to help you start thinking about this subject, not to test your knowledge.*

How might remembering an emotionally charged experience help to alleviate someone's current psychological symptoms?

What elements of the relationship between a therapist and a client are most important for helping the client?

In what ways might a person's beliefs contribute to psychological problems such as anxiety or depression? How can a therapist help a person change maladaptive patterns of thinking?

How can therapy help someone unlearn a fear—say, a fear of dogs or of driving a car?

Does psychotherapy really work? Are some forms of psychotherapy more effective than others? Are particular therapies better for certain problems?

How important to the success of therapy are such factors as a supportive therapeutic atmosphere or hope?

*READ this section of your text lightly. Then go back and read thoroughly, completing the Workout as you proceed.*

Psychotherapy refers to any formal, theory-based, systematic approach to treating mental problems or disorders through psychological means. It is carried out by a trained therapist working with individuals, couples, families, or groups of unrelated people. Through talking with the client or clients, the therapist attempts to alter ways of feeling, thinking, or acting.

1. Describe psychoanalysis and psychodynamic therapy.

2. Answer the following questions about Joseph Breuer's treatment of Anna O.

a. What were Anna's symptoms? How were they labeled at the time she was treated? How would they be diagnosed now?

b. The technique used by Breuer to make Anna's treatment more efficient was

_____ .

c. Define the term *catharsis* and give an example from Anna's case.

From Anna O.'s case and a few others, Freud began to develop the approach he called *psychoanalysis*.

3. List the ideas that provided the framework for Freud's approach.

a.

b.

c.

4. Discuss Freud's views on the role of early childhood sexual experiences in neuroses. Be sure to distinguish between predisposing and precipitating experiences, giving an example of each.

5. Why did Freud include the word *analysis* in the name he gave to his approach? What was Freud's principal technique for obtaining clues to the unconscious? Briefly describe it.

6. Define the term *resistance* and give an example of how it might be manifested. How is resistance interpreted by the therapist?

7. What is transference and why did Freud consider it an important part of psychoanalysis?

8. How are insight and cure thought to be related in psychoanalysis?

9. Briefly summarize the case of the Rat Man.

Most psychodynamic therapists today practice alternatives to classic Freudian psychoanalysis. They share with Freud's original approach the effort to bring problematic feeling into consciousness, the belief that current troubles result from mental conflict over past experience, and the use of the therapist-client relationship to promote understanding of the client's other relationships.

10. Briefly describe each of the following psychodynamic approaches, indicating those characteristics that most distinguish them.

a. short-term psychodynamic psychotherapies

b. ego-oriented psychodynamic therapies

c. non-Freudian psychodynamic therapies

14. Present two objections that a skeptic might raise regarding what client-centered therapists claim they do (and don't do).

Like psychodynamic therapies, humanistic therapies are designed to help people become conscious of their true feelings and desires, a step considered necessary for self-actualization. Carl Rogers's client-centered therapy is the most common humanistic therapy; in fact, a recent survey of a large sample of psychotherapists indicated that Rogers was the individual who had most influenced them.

11. Why does Rogers call his approach *client-centered* therapy?

Cognitive therapies are based on the notion that people's maladaptive thoughts cause them unnecessary distress, leading to anxiety or depression. These types of therapies attempt to replace maladaptive ways of thinking with more productive ones. Albert Ellis and Aaron Beck are pioneers of this approach.

15. What does it mean to say that cognitive therapy is problem centered? How is the therapist-client relationship characterized? Which therapeutic practice among cognitive therapists is especially consistent with this characterization? (See Figure 18.2 on text page 668.)

12. In Rogers's view, what is the origin of psychological problems?

16. Answer the following questions about Albert Ellis's rational-emotive therapy (RET).

a. What is the basic premise of RET? Illustrate by defining musturbation and awfulizing.

13. In countering the client's maladaptive learning, the Rogerian therapist aims to provide empathy, positive regard, and genuineness. Identify each of the following.

a. _____ reflects the belief that it is impossible to fake empathy and positive regard, that the therapist must really feel them.

b. Explain Ellis's ABC theory of emotions.

b. _____ refers to the therapist's attempt to comprehend what the client is saying or feeling at any given moment from the client's point of view rather than as an outside observer.

c. _____ implies a belief on the therapist's part that the client is worthy and capable even when the client may not feel or act that way.

c. Do irrational beliefs disappear once they are seen to be irrational? Explain.

17. Answer the following questions about Aaron Beck's cognitive therapy.

    a. Beck's observations of the depressed clients he worked with led him to develop his approach. Describe these observations.

    b. Beck's cognitive therapy was designed to treat _____ ; it was later expanded to include clients with _____ disorders.

    c. How does Beck's therapeutic style differ from Ellis's?

Underlying behavior therapy are the behaviorist principles of classical and operant conditioning. Although traditional behaviorists would have ignored such mental phenomena as worrying or obsessive thinking, modern behavior therapy has become allied with cognitive therapy in an approach called cognitive-behavior therapy.

18. List several characteristics that behavior and cognitive therapies have always had in common.

Behavior therapy is especially effective in treating simple phobias. Flooding, counter-conditioning, and systematic desensitization—classed together as exposure treatments—are the primary methods for dealing with phobias.

19. Explain how a behaviorist would interpret a phobia in terms of classical conditioning. Why would extinction be an important phenomenon from the point of view of a behavior therapist?

In exposure treatments, the patient experiences the feared stimulus in a safe context.

20. Describe the following forms of exposure treatment.

    a. flooding

    b. counter-conditioning

    c. systematic desensitization

21. Comment on the effectiveness of exposure treatments. What element of these techniques is now thought to account for their effectiveness? How might psychoanalytic treatments for fear-related conditions be reinterpreted in light of this idea?

Behavior therapy is also used to treat maladaptive habits such as smoking, addictive drinking, and compulsive gambling.

22. Explain how maladaptive habits can be interpreted in terms of operant conditioning. What is the basic obstacle to eliminating bad habits, according to a behaviorist analysis?

23. Answer the following questions about aversion treatment.

   a. Describe the technique and provide an example.

   b. Why has aversion treatment always been controversial?

   c. What problem with the technique is illustrated by the use of the drug *antabuse* to treat alcohol addiction?

A number of other techniques are used by behavior therapists to handle a range of problems.

24. Identify each of the following techniques.

   a. _____ involves direct means to teach the client to be more assertive, effective, and comfortable in social interactions.

   b. _____ is a formal, usually written agreement in which one party promises to provide specific services or rewards if the other party behaves in a specified way.

   c. _____ is an exchange system in which patients earn tokens for performing specific desired activities and trade the tokens for objects or privileges they want.

   d. _____ involves teaching someone to do something, such as dealing with an angry spouse, by having them watch someone else do it.

In order to evaluate the effectiveness of psychotherapy, we must carry out controlled experiments.

25. Why are case studies not sufficient evidence of the value of psychotherapy?

26. List the general conclusions that have been drawn from hundreds of experiments evaluating psychotherapy.

   a.

   b.

   c.

27. The Philadelphia experiment assessed the effectiveness of two forms of psychotherapy for psychiatric outpatients suffering primarily from anxiety disorders. Describe the study and its results. (See Figure 18.5 on text page 675.)

**28.** What method did Mary Lee Smith and her colleagues use to evaluate the effectiveness of different types of psychotherapies? What did they find with regard to the *average* improvement produced by different psychotherapies? Did they find that some therapies are better than others for particular problems? Explain. (See Table 18.2 on text page 676.)

**29.** Answer the following questions about nonspecific factors in psychotherapy.

   **a.** Explain what is meant by the term *nonspecific factors*.

   **b.** Describe the factor called *support* and cite research evidence demonstrating the importance of this factor.

   **c.** Describe the factor called *hope*. What evidence suggests that hope contributes to the effectiveness of psychotherapy? Why is it difficult to determine the extent to which hope contributes to the improvement observed in psychotherapy?

**30.** What does eclectic mean in relation to psychotherapy? Why are therapists becoming more eclectic?

## *Biological Treatments*   (pages 678–682)

> CONSIDER these questions before you go on. They are designed to help you start thinking about this subject, not to test your knowledge.

Can drugs calm anxiety, lift someone out of depression, stop hallucinations, or relieve formal thought disturbances?

What kinds of harmful side effects are caused by drugs used to treat mental disorders?

In what circumstances are people treated with electroconvulsive shock therapy? Is it safe? Is it painful? Does it work?

Can surgery be used effectively to treat some mental disorders?

> READ this section of your text lightly. Then go back and read thoroughly, completing the Workout as you proceed.

Contemporary biological approaches to mental disorders fall primarily into three categories—drugs, electroconvulsive shock therapy, and psychosurgery. Drugs are the most commonly used biological treatment.

**1.** Answer the following questions about antipsychotic drugs.

   **a.** Comment on the positive effects of antipsychotic drugs such as chlorpromazine and other phenothiazines. (See Figure 18.7 on text page 679.)

   **b.** Do these drugs effectively treat the negative symptoms of schizophrenia? What does this imply for the patient's quality of life?

   **c.** Comment on the drug clozapine.

d. Define tardive dyskinesia. List some other unpleasant or potentially harmful side effects of antipsychotic drugs.

e. A controversial issue in the use of antipsychotic drugs is that in some patients they might reduce the chances of full recovery from schizophrenia. Explain.

2. Answer the following questions about antidepressant drugs.

a. Today's most commonly used antidepressant drugs belong to the chemical class called

_____ .

b. How are these drugs thought to work?

c. Cite evidence suggesting that these drugs help people suffering from depression.

d. Comment on the side effects of antidepressant drugs.

3. Briefly discuss the use of lithium in the treatment of bipolar disorder.

4. What drugs are most commonly prescribed to treat anxiety? How do these drugs produce their tranquilizing effects? What are some risks of taking these drugs?

Public perceptions of electroconvulsive shock therapy (ECT) often involve images of brutality, even horror, inflicted under the guise of treatment. Such images, not unlike the scenes in a number of movies, are no longer consistent with reality. ECT as it is used today is both painless and safe.

5. Describe what happens in ECT and compare unilateral and bilateral ECT.

6. What disorder is most effectively treated by ECT? Support your answer.

7. How might ECT produce its antidepressant effect?

8. To what extent does bilateral ECT affect memory? Does unilateral ECT reduce or increase such memory effects?

Psychosurgery, still a controversial approach, is the least common of the biological treatments for mental disorders. It involves surgically cutting or producing lesions in parts of the brain in order to alleviate symptoms.

9. Describe the operation called *prefrontal lobotomy*. For which types of disorders was it used? Why did this treatment, which was once held in high regard, become virtually obsolete?

10. Describe the newer psychosurgical procedures, such as the cingulotomy, that involve electrodes. What are these procedures useful for? Are they safe?

---

*Be sure to READ the Concluding Thoughts at the end of the chapter. Note important points in your Workout. Then consolidate your learning by answering the focus questions in the margins of the text.*

---

*After you have studied the chapter thoroughly, CHECK your understanding with the self-test that follows.*

---

## Self-Test 1

*Multiple-Choice Questions*

1. Nineteenth-century reformers such as Philippe Pinel in Europe and Dorothea Dix in the United States sought to:
   a. release people from mental institutions so that they could be returned to the community.
   b. build institutions to provide humane care for those with mental disorders.
   c. replace psychotherapy with the biological treatments that they considered more effective.
   d. promote scientific research to determine the most effective forms of psychotherapy.

2. In a study of patients in a state hospital system, Gordon Paul and Robert Lentz found that the most effective treatment was:
   a. the standard hospital treatment, which involved both structured routine and drug therapy.

   b. milieu therapy, which involved increased staff-patient interaction, less dependence on drugs, and heightened respect for patients.
   c. social learning therapy, which involved most of the elements of milieu therapy plus specific training in social skills.
   d. rational-emotive therapy, which involved teaching patients to recognize and alter their irrational thought patterns.

3. Which of the following mental health professionals has a medical degree?
   a. counseling psychologists
   b. clinical psychologists
   c. psychiatrists
   d. both clinical psychologists and psychiatrists

4. The MMPI, which is useful for chinical assessment, is classified as a:
   a. psychometric personality test.
   b. method of neuropsychological assessment.
   c. form of behavioral monitoring.
   d. projective test.

5. A psychodynamic therapist would most likely be characterized as a(n):
   a. teacher showing a student how to think in new ways.
   b. archaeologist piecing together clues about the past.
   c. gardner helping plants to grow in their own way.
   d. pastor providing an atmosphere of warmth and concern.

6. Margaret keeps "forgetting" to go to her therapy sessions; when she does go, she refuses to talk about certain issues. Her behavior is characterized as _____ , an important concept in _____ therapy.
   a. transference; psychoanalytic
   b. resistance; psychoanalytic
   c. transference; humanistic
   d. resistance; humanistic

7. The Rat Man, one of Freud's patients, had an unconscious oedipal conflict between love and hatred for his father, and a conflict over whether to marry a particular woman. Which of these conflicts represented a precipitating cause of the Rat Man's disorder?
   a. the conflict over whether or not to marry
   b. the conflict over his feelings toward his father
   c. both conflicts
   d. neither conflict

8. Albert Ellis's rational-emotive therapy focuses most directly on the replacement of:
   a. maladaptive thought patterns with more effective ones.
   b. feelings of guilt with feelings of self-acceptance.
   c. rational, thought-based responses with emotional, feeling-based responses.
   d. fear-induced muscle tension with muscle relaxation.

9. Beck's cognitive therapy is most specifically designed to treat:
   a. fears and maladaptive habits such as smoking or gambling.
   b. conversion disorders.
   c. depression and anxiety disorders.
   d. schizophrenia and mood disorders.

10. Antabuse is a drug that reacts with alcohol shortly after alcohol consumption to produce nausea and headaches. Its use illustrates the limitations of _____ in helping people with long-term addictions.
    a. counter-conditioning    c. antidepressants
    b. flooding                d. aversion treatment

11. Don and Rosemary, a couple with marital problems, have agreed that he will leave the office by 6:00 every workday if she will refrain from complaining about his ambition. This couple has elected to use a behavioral technique known as:
    a. social skills training.
    b. modeling.
    c. a contingency contract.
    d. a token economy.

12. Schizophrenia is often treated with a class of drugs known as:
    a. henzodiazopines.    c. tranquilizers.
    b. phenothiazines.     d. tricyclics.

13. Lithium has proven to be an effective treatment for:
    a. schizophrenia.       c. major depression.
    b. generalized anxiety. d. bipolar disorder.

14. Electroconvulsive shock therapy (ECT) is used as an effective treatment for _____ and is now often applied only to the brain's right hemisphere to minimize the _____ problems that may result.
    a. schizophrenia; motor
    b. schizophrenia; memory
    c. severe depression; motor
    d. severe depression; memory

15. Prefrontal lobotomies, used to treat people with severe cases of schizophrenia and other mental disorders:
    a. have been a common and effective treatment since the 1930s for those who do not respond to drug treatment.
    b. are no longer performed, in part because they permanently damaged the patients' ability to make and follow plans.
    c. are a new, more refined form of psychosurgery that is nevertheless rarely used.
    d. have not been performed since the 1970s because they were shown to have no real effect on the patients' symptoms.

## Essay Questions

16. Why is Carl Rogers's client-centered therapy named as it is? From the perspective of this therapeutic approach, describe the causes of mental problems, the aims of therapy, and two critical elements that must be manifested by the therapist.

**17.** What are exposure treatments used for? Explain the principles of learning on which they are based and illustrate by describing one type of exposure treatment. How might the phenomenon of catharsis in psychoanalysis be interpreted in such behavioral terms?

---

*After you have assessed your understanding on the basis of Self-Test 1 and have tried to strengthen your preparation in any areas of weakness, GO ON to Self-Test 2.*

# Self-Test 2

*Multiple-Choice Questions*

**1.** In the United States, from the 1950s to the 1970s, reform was aimed at deinstitutionalizing mental patients and returning them to the community. This movement:
   **a.** failed to achieve either goal.
   **b.** succeeded in achieving both goals.
   **c.** succeeded in deinstitutionalizing many patients but largely failed to reintegrate them into the community.
   **d.** succeeded in deinstitutionalizing only a small percentage of patients but successfully reintegrated them into the community.

**2.** In the 1970s, David Rosenhan and his colleagues carried out a study of mental hospitals by:
   **a.** surveying recently released patients; they found that patient-staff interaction in the hospitals was frequent and generally compassionate.
   **b.** surveying recently released patients; they found that patient-staff interaction in the hospitals was infrequent and often dehumanizing.
   **c.** posing as patients themselves; they found that patient-staff interaction in the hospitals was frequent and generally compassionate.
   **d.** posing as patients themselves; they found that patient-staff interaction in the hospitals was infrequent and often dehumanizing.

**3.** The general term for the process of gathering and compiling information about a patient for the purpose of developing a plan of treatment is:
   **a.** client-centered therapy.
   **b.** clinical assessment.
   **c.** evaluation research.
   **d.** behavioral monitoring.

**4.** Joseph Breuer found that Anna O.'s conscious recall of previously forgotten, emotionally charged memories:
   **a.** resulted in the relief of symptoms associated with the memories.
   **b.** was responsible for the original development of her symptoms.
   **c.** worsened the symptoms associated with the memories.
   **d.** produced no noticeable change in her condition.

**5.** The person seeking help figures out what is wrong, makes plans for improvement, and decides when improvement has taken place, in _____ therapy.
   **a.** psychoanalytic    **c.** rational-emotive
   **b.** client-centered    **d.** behavior

**6.** Carl Rogers believed that the therapist should reflect back the ideas and feelings that the client expresses as a way of achieving and demonstrating:
   **a.** genuineness.    **c.** positive regard.
   **b.** transference.    **d.** empathy.

**7.** Humanistic therapy resembles psychodynamic therapy in that it:
   **a.** is problem centered.
   **b.** focuses on inner feelings and wishes.
   **c.** casts the therapist as the expert on the client's problems.
   **d.** treats self-actualization as a central concept in therapy.

**8.** According to Albert Ellis's ABC theory of emotions, the therapist should help the client to directly alter _____ in order to change _____.
   **a.** activating events (*A*); beliefs (*B*)
   **b.** beliefs (*B*); activating events (*A*)

c. emotional consequences (C); beliefs (B)

d. beliefs (B); emotional consequences (C)

9. Aaron Beck observed that depressed persons tend to _____, a pattern of thinking similar to what Albert Ellis labeled _____.

a. minimize positive experiences; awfulizing

b. maximize negative experiences; awfulizing

c. misattribute negative experiences to their own deficiencies; musturbation

d. see their lives as the product of an unalterable fate; musturbation

10. The type of therapist most likely to employ homework assignments as a means of helping clients is a _____ therapist.

a. psychodynamic    c. cognitive

b. client-centered    d. biologically oriented

11. Agnes is being treated for fear of flying by learning to relax physically while imagining increasingly fearful scenes related to flying. Her therapist is using a technique called:

a. modeling.

b. systematic desensitization.

c. flooding.

d. aversion treatment.

12. Acceptance, empathy, encouragement, and guidance are aspects of an important nonspecific factor in therapy called:

a. support.        c. hope.

b. warmth.        d. eclecticism.

13. Antipsychotic drugs, such as chlorpromazine, are thought to work by:

a. increasing dopamine activity in the brain.

b. decreasing dopamine activity in the brain.

c. increasing dopamine concentrations in the bloodstream.

d. decreasing dopamine concentrations on the bloodstream.

14. Tardive dyskinesia, a serious and often irreversible motor disturbance, occurs in many patients who receive long-term treatment with:

a. antidepressant drugs.

b. antipsychotic drugs.

c. lithium.

d. tranquilizers.

15. The least often used form of biological treatment for mental disorders is:

a. drug therapy.

b. electroconvulsive shock therapy.

c. psychosurgery.

d. exposure therapy.

*Essay Questions*

16. Explain the roots of mental problems from the Freudian perspective. What, then, is the job of the psychoanalytic therapist and what are some means available for carrying out that job?

17. Why is it necessary to perform experiments in order to determine whether therapy is effective? What has analysis of such studies generally shown? Are different therapies equally effective or ineffective? Explain.

# Answers

## Care as a Social Issue

6. **a.** nursing home, **b.** mental hospital, **c.** private office, **d.** general hospital, **e.** halfway house, **f.** community mental health center

## Clinical Assessment

1. interview; immediate symptoms; home and work environment; nonverbal

8. **a.** Halstead-Reitan battery

   **b.** magnetic resonance imaging (MRI)

   **c.** CAT scan

   **d.** electroencephalogram (EEG)

## Psychotherapies

2. **b.** hypnosis

3. **a.** genuineness, **b.** empathy, **c.** positive regard

17. **b.** depression; anxiety

24. **a.** assertiveness and social skills training

    **b.** contingency contract

    **c.** token economy

    **d.** modeling

## Biological Treatments

2. **a.** tricyclics

## Self-Test 1

1. **b.** Although such asylums were built, they did not receive sufficient amounts of continuing financial support and so reverted to the conditions that had originally horrified reformers. (pp. 647–648)

2. **c.** (pp. 649–650)

3. **c.** (p. 651)

4. **a.** (p. 653)

5. **b.** The therapist described in a. sounds most like a cognitive therapist, while that described in c. sounds like a humanistic therapist. The description in d. is nonspecific. (p. 656)

6. **b.** (pp. 658–659)

7. **a.** The Rat Man resolved this conflict (linked to the predisposing cause described in b.) by developing neurotic symptoms, which made it impossible for him to continue his studies and begin a career, and thus impossible for him to marry. (p. 660)

8. **a.** By altering beliefs, one can also alter emotions, according to cognitive therapists such as Ellis. (pp. 665–666)

9. **c.** (p. 667)

10. **d.** Treatment with antabuse does not tend to produce a conditioned aversion to alcohol. When they are no longer taking antabuse, most alcoholics resume drinking. (p. 673)

11. **c.** (p. 673)

12. **b.** (p. 678)

13. **d.** (p. 680)

14. **d.** (pp. 681–682)

15. **b.** (p. 682)

16. Carl Rogers used the term *client-centered therapy* because it focuses on what the *client* knows and what the *client* can do rather than on the therapist's knowledge and abilities. The job of directing therapy, choosing which path to take, deciding how to handle particular issues, assessing progress, and so on, is in the hands of the client. This therapeutic approach is especially consistent with humanistic psychology's respect for the capability and growth potential that lies within each person.

    Rogers believed that mental problems stem from people's denial or distortion of the desires and feelings that lie within them. The denial and distortion are thought to result when people learn from parents or other authorities in their lives, such as teachers, that they cannot trust their own feelings or decisions. When this happens, people look outward, to be told by others what to feel or how to behave; but they cannot be satisfied in this fashion and may thus feel resentful, rebellious, or "not real" inside. Therapy is intended to help clients become aware of and accept their own feelings and desires and to learn to trust their ability to make decisions. Letting the client take the lead in directing therapy is fully consistent with this goal and powerfully communicates the message that what is inside the client can be trusted.

    Rogers believed that empathy and genuineness were two important elements that the therapist must provide in order to create a climate conducive to the client's learning and growth process. Empathy is the therapist's attempt to understand the client's thoughts and feelings from the client's own viewpoint. Genuineness refers to the reality of the feelings and attitudes that the therapist expresses toward the client, such as empathy; if they are faked, the client will detect this fact and therapy will not succeed. (Positive regard—the therapist's belief that the client is worthy and capable—is another element you could have discussed here.) (pp. 662–664)

17. Exposure treatments are used by behavior therapists to treat phobias. From the behavioral perspective, fears are considered to be learned responses. A stimulus that can elicit an unconditioned fear response may be paired with another stimulus, which thereby becomes a conditioned stimulus capable of eliciting a conditioned fear response. Of course, what can be learned can also be unlearned, according to the behaviorist. If the conditioned stimulus is repeatedly presented without the unconditioned stimulus, extinction will occur. For example, if an intersection with a four-way stop sign was paired with the frightening and painful experience of a car crash in a person's experience, that person might come to fear such intersections. On the other hand, if the person is repeatedly exposed to such intersections without further harm, then the fear should be unlearned. Systematic desensitization is a type of exposure treatment in which a person relaxes while imagining increasingly frightening forms of the feared stimulus. Through the repeated exposure, even though the exposure is only imagined, the fear is extinguished, or unlearned. The phenomenon of catharsis in psychoanalysis may actually reflect such unlearning—that is, a person with a troubling, fear-provoking memory, such as the Rat Man, may unlearn the fear by repeatedly facing the memory in the safe context of therapy. (pp. 669–671)

## Self-Test 2

1. c. (p. 648)
2. d. (pp. 648–649)
3. b. (p. 651)
4. a. This connection between the uncovering of repressed, emotionally charged memories and symptom relief is fundamental to psychodynamic therapies. (pp. 657–658)
5. b. (p. 662)
6. d. (p. 663)
7. b. (p. 662)
8. d. (p. 666)

9. b. (pp. 666, 667)
10. c. (p. 665)
11. b. Alternative c., the other exposure treatment listed, does not involve a gradual increase in the fear level of the stimulus or an imagined presentation of the stimulus. Neither of the other treatments is used for phobias. (p. 671)
12. a. (p. 676)
13. b. (pp. 678–679)
14. b. (p. 679)
15. c. (p. 682)
16. Freud believed that mental problems, in the form of neuroses, develop because of an interaction between two types of experiences: (a) predisposing experiences, which take place in early childhood and involve sexual desires and conflicts; and (b) precipitating experiences, which take place later in life and more immediately bring on the neurotic symptoms. The person's emotions and conflicts are expressed in the form of neurotic symptoms because they are unacceptable and are thus kept from conscious awareness by a variety of means. The psychoanalyst's job is to help the individual become aware of the conflict-laden material buried in the unconscious. According to the theory, when the person faces and deals with such information consciously, neurotic symptoms will go away. The psychoanalyst must essentially prospect for and piece together clues about the nature of the underlying memories and conflicts to figure out how the memories and feelings of childhood are meaningfully related to present circumstances and symptoms.

   Two means of gaining such clues are dream analysis and free association, in which an individual talks freely about whatever comes to mind. The assumption is that what appear to be illogical and unrelated ideas actually reflect symbolically the unconscious memories and wishes that are at the heart of the problem. Another means is to analyze transference, ways in which the patient relates to the therapist as a symbolic substitute for a significant person in his or her life. The therapist can also gain information by analyzing signs of resistance, which could include canceling appointments, silence, or efforts to redirect the discussion. (pp. 658–660)

17. Life is full of ups and downs and it is generally at the low points rather than the high points that people enter therapy. Therefore, the fact that a person feels better and functions more effectively following therapy is not a clear indication that

psychotherapy was responsible for the improvement. After all, the person might have improved anyway, perhaps because of changing social circumstances, or an alteration in body chemistry, or any number of other factors. Only with the control possible through experiments can we tell whether therapy produces some improvement over and above what would have been expected otherwise.

In general, analysis of such studies has shown that psychotherapy is effective overall and that no one form of therapy emerges as clearly superior to others. However, some studies indicate that specific types of problems may be more effectively handled with certain types of therapy. For example, fear may be especially well treated through behavioral or cognitive means, while problems of self-esteem may be most successfully treated through humanistic therapies. (pp. 674–676)

# STATISTICAL APPENDIX

*Read the introduction below before you read the Appendix in the text.*

This appendix supplements the coverage of statistics in Chapter 2. Psychologists use statistical procedures to help them analyze and understand the data they collect. Simple techniques allow us to organize a set of scores and to describe important characteristics of that set of scores. Scores are often organized into a frequency distribution, which shows the number of times scores in particular intervals occurred. For example, a frequency distribution could tell us how many people in a sample earn between $15,000 and $20,000; how many earn between $20,000 and $25,000; and so on.

When a frequency distribution is depicted as a graph, the shape of the curve formed by the scores is important. Normal curves, or approximations to normal curves, are bell-shaped curves that are common in psychology. Measures of central tendency represent the center of the distribution, indicating a typical score in that distribution. The mean and median are two measures of central tendency that are based on different definitions of the "center" of a distribution. Measures of variability express the degree to which scores tend to vary from the central tendency. Variance and standard deviation are common measures of variability.

Sometimes we wish to compare scores. In order to do so, we need a language for sensibly describing relationships among scores. A score's percentile rank indicates the percentage of scores in a distribution that fall at or below the score of interest. Thus, if a person earned a score of 64 on a test and that score is at the 88th percentile, then 88 percent of the scores are at 64 or below. Standardized scores, such as z scores, provide another way of converting scores into a form that can be used for purposes of comparison.

Psychologists often ask how two variables are related. How is IQ related to success in college? How are scores on a test of artistic creativity related to later success as an artist? How is age related to performance on a memory test? As explained in Chapter 2, a correlation coefficient indicates the strength and direction of such relationships. This appendix illustrates the computation of a product-moment correlation coefficient for a small set of data.

The final section of the appendix does *not* supplement Chapter 2; rather, it supplements the material on psychophysical scaling in Chapter 8. This section is not dealt with in this guide.

*LOOK over the table of contents for this chapter in your textbook before you continue with your study.*

## The Integrated Study Workout

*CONSIDER these questions before you go on. They are designed to help you start thinking about this subject, not to test your knowledge.*

How can we meaningfully describe and summarize a set of scores?

If people are given two tests—one on ability to speak French and the other on ability to comprehend it—how can their standing as speakers be compared with their standing as comprehenders?

What does it mean to say someone is at the 45th percentile on a particular measure?

How can we determine the degree of relationship between two variables, such as IQ and GPA?

*READ the Appendix lightly. Then go back and read thoroughly, completing the Workout as you proceed.*

Statistics are an important tool for psychologists, helping them to make sense of the data they collect. Descriptive statistics are useful for learning about the shape, central tendency, and variability of distributions of measurements.

1. What is a frequency distribution? Describe how it is constructed. (See Table A.1 on text page A-1 and Table A.2 on text page A-2.)

2. Why is a graphical representation of a frequency distribution helpful? (See Figure A.1 on text page A-2.)

The shape of a distribution can be described in a number of ways. (See the four panels shown in Figure A.2 on text page A-3.)

3. Describe the shape of a normal distribution, or normal curve, and produce a rough sketch of one.

4. Why are normal distributions important in psychology? In general, when might we expect a distribution to approximate a normal curve?

5. Define the term *mode* and then distinguish between bimodal and unimodal distributions. Into which of these categories does a normal curve fall? Sketch a bimodal distribution.

6. Describe positively and negatively skewed distributions. Sketch an example of each type of distribution.

A measure of central tendency summarizes a set of scores in terms of a single number. That single number represents the center of the distribution. However, the "center" can be defined in more than one way.

7. Define the following two measures of central tendency.

   a. median

   b. mean

8. Compute the median and mean for the following set of scores: 3 5 6 9 12.

   a. median _____

   b. mean _____

9. Where will the mean be relative to the median in each of the following kinds of distributions?

   a. normal distribution

   _____

   b. positively skewed distribution

   _____

   c. negatively skewed distribution

   _____

10. Which measure of central tendency—the mean or the median—is preferable? Explain.

Variability is another characteristic of a distribution of scores. As with measures of central tendency, there is more than one measure of variability.

11. Explain the concept of variability. Sketch two distributions that have the same mean but different amounts of variability. (See Figure A.3 on text page A-4.)

**12.** What is the range of a set of scores and why is it inadequate as a measure of variability?

**13.** Two measures of variability that take into account all the scores in a distribution are _____ and _____ .
The measure of variability that is expressed in the original units of measurement rather than in squared units is the _____ .

It is often informative to compare a given score with other scores. For example, we may want to know how a given score stands relative to the other scores in the same distribution. Or we might want to compare score *A*'s standing within its distribution to score *B*'s standing within its distribution. In order to make such comparisons, we must convert scores into a form that permits us to speak of relationships among scores.

**14.** Define a percentile rank. Look at Table A.1 on text page A-1 and indicate the percentile rank of the score 61.

**15.** A _____ is one that is expressed in terms of the number of standard deviations that the original score is from the mean of original scores.

**16.** Answer the following questions about z scores.

    **a.** How is a score converted to the type of standardized score called a z score?

    **b.** In a distribution with a mean of 50 and a standard deviation of 10, the z score of the score 65 is _____ .

    **c.** If a z score is positive, the original score is _____ (above/below/equal to) the mean.

    **d.** The percentage of scores that lies at or below a z score of +2 is _____ .
The percentage of scores at or above a z score of +1 is _____ . (See Figure A.4 on text page A-7.)

Statistical techniques also permit us to describe the relationship between two variables—such as the relationship between age and income, between IQ and creativity, between hours of weekly television viewing and grade point average. A correlation coefficient summarizes in one number the strength of the relationship (how related the two variables are) and the direction of the relationship (whether high scores on one variable tend to go with low scores or high scores on the other variable).

**17.** Which aspect of the correlation coefficient indicates the strength of the relationship? Which indicates the direction of the relationship?

**18.** Look at the scatter plot below and indicate whether there appears to be a negative or a positive relationship between variables *X* and *Y*. Is the correlation perfect? Support your answer. (See Figure A.5 on text page A-8, along with the corresponding discussion.)

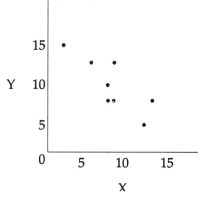

19. In "25 words or less," explain how a correlation coefficient is calculated. In other words, explain where this number comes from.

---

*After you have studied the Appendix thoroughly, CHECK your understanding with the self-test that follows.*

---

# Self-Test

*Multiple-Choice Questions*

1. A normal curve is:
   a. unimodal and asymmetrical.
   b. unimodal and symmetrical.
   c. bimodal and asymmetrical.
   d. bimodal and symmetrical.

2. The scores on a particular test range from 30 to 100. Most scores center around 85, but a number are lower. The frequency of these low scores gradually declines as we approach the lowest score of 30. This distribution sounds as if it is:
   a. positively skewed.
   b. negatively skewed.
   c. normal.
   d. bimodal.

3. In which of the following cases are the mean and median of a distribution necessarily identical?
   a. bimodal distribution
   b. positively skewed distribution
   c. negatively skewed distribution
   d. normal distribution

4. If a distribution is skewed, is one measure of central tendency generally preferred to another?
   a. yes, the median
   b. yes, the mean
   c. yes, the mode
   d. no

5. Which of the following measures of variability take(s) into account all the scores in a distribution?
   a. only the range
   b. the range and the variance

c. the variance and the standard deviation
d. only the variance

6. Liz says she scored at the 57th percentile on a test of eye-hand coordination. This means that:
   a. Liz's measured score, out of 100, was 57.
   b. 57 percent of the people tested earned the same score Liz did.
   c. Liz has 57 percent as much coordination as the most coordinated person tested.
   d. 57 percent of the people tested had a measured score equal to or lower than Liz's.

7. If Carmela scores a 70 on a test with a mean of 60 and a standard deviation of 10, her z score is:
   a. +1.00.     c. +10.00.
   b. −1.00.     d. −10.00.

8. Which of the following statements is true?
   a. If a distribution of scores is normal, one can convert from a percentile rank to a z score, but not vice versa.
   b. If a distribution of scores is normal, one can convert from a z score to a percentile rank, but not vice versa.
   c. If a distribution of scores is normal, one can convert from a percentile rank to a z score, and vice versa.
   d. There is no way to convert between percentile ranks and z scores regardless of the shape of the distribution.

9. The best way to express the direction and degree of relationship between verbal SAT scores and interest in reading is a:
   a. correlation coefficient.
   b. percentile rank.
   c. psychophysical scale.
   d. measure of central tendency.

10. The correspondence between variable $X$ and variable $Y$ is illustrated below.

| $X$: | 1 | 2 | 3 | 4 | 5 | 6 |
|------|---|---|---|----|----|----|
| $Y$: | 4 | 5 | 7 | 10 | 14 | 19 |

Is the relationship between $X$ and $Y$ linear?
   a. yes
   b. no, because each value of $Y$ differs from the corresponding value of $X$
   c. no, because the increase in $Y$ that corresponds to a unit of increase in $X$ varies
   d. It's not possible to say from the information given.

# Answers

*The Integrated Study Workout*

8. **a.** 6, **b.** 7

9. **a.** identical to it, **b.** above it, **c.** below it

13. variance and standard deviation; standard deviation

14. 75th percentile ($\frac{15}{20} = 0.75$))

15. standardized score

16. **b.** +1.5 [$(65 - 50)/10 = \frac{15}{10}$], **c.** above, **d.** 97.72%; 84.13%

18. The scatter plot suggests a negative correlation, which is not perfect because the points do not lie on a straight line.

*Self-Test*

1. **b.** (p. A-2)

2. **b.** On the $x$ axis, negative scores lie toward the left and positive scores toward the right. You can remember that a negatively skewed distribution is one whose tail "points toward" the negative end of the axis; a positively skewed distribution is one whose tail "points toward" the positive end. (p. A-3)

3. **d.** They could be identical in a bimodal distribution, but they are not necessarily so. (p. A-3)

4. **a.** (p. A-4)

5. **c.** (pp. A-4–A-5)

6. **d.** (p. A-5)

7. **a.** $(70 - 60)/10 = 1$ (p. A-6)

8. **c.** (p. A-7)

9. **a.** (p. A-7)

10. **c.** (p. A-9)